Boys over Flowers
Hana Yori Dango
Vol. #14
Shôjo Edition

**Story and Art by
Yoko Kamio**

**English Adaptation by
Gerard Jones**

Translation/JN Productions
Touch-up Art & Lettering/Stephen Dutro
Cover & Interior Design/Yuki Ameda
Editor/Ian Robertson

Managing Editor/Annette Roman
Director of Production/Noboru Watanabe
Vice President of Publishing/Alvin Lu
Sr. Director of Acquisitions/Rika Inouye
Vice President of Sales & Marketing/Liza Coppola
Publisher/Hyoe Narita

HANA-YORI DANGO © 1992 by Yoko Kamio
All rights reserved. First published in Japan in 1992 by
SHUEISHA Inc., Tokyo. English translation rights in the
United States of America and Canada arranged by
SHUEISHA Inc. The stories, characters and incidents
mentioned in this publication are entirely fictional.

No portion of this book may be reproduced or transmitted
in any form or by any means without written permission
from the copyright holders.

Printed in Canada.

Published by VIZ Media, LLC
P.O. Box 77010
San Francisco, CA 94107

10 9 8 7 6 5 4 3 2 1
First printing, September 2005

PARENTAL ADVISORY
BOYS OVER FLOWERS is rated T for Teen
and is recommended for ages 13 and up.
May contain sexual themes.

www.viz.com

store.viz.com

Story thus far

Tsukushi and her friend Yuki have headed to Canada on a snow-boarding vacation for their first time abroad, but Tsukushi quickly finds out that those nasty Eitoku girls have invited themselves—not to mention Tsukasa—along! The Eitoku girls send Tsukushi out on a wild goose chase to find Yuki in below freezing temperatures. Tsukasa comes to her rescue and actually saves her life! The two of them "warm up" in a nearby cabin while they wait for the blizzard to die down. When they return no one is pleased with the Eitoku girls' deadly game and a few different revenge plots are tossed around. Sakurako has some particularly twisted and sick ideas on what to do to them, but in the end something much gentler is decided on. They decide to scare the hell out of them, but what happens next ends up scaring everyone. Shizuka has returned.

BOYS over FLOWERS

Hana Yori Dango

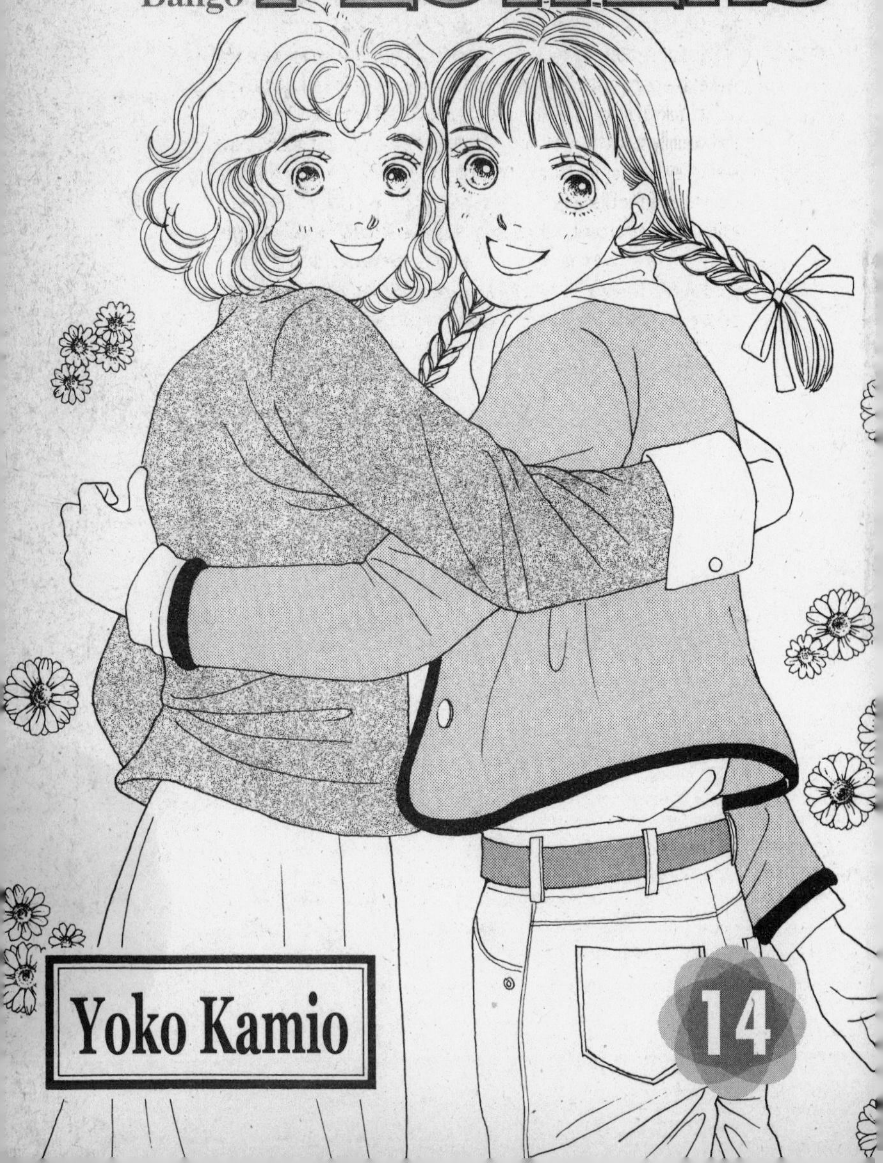

Yoko Kamio

14

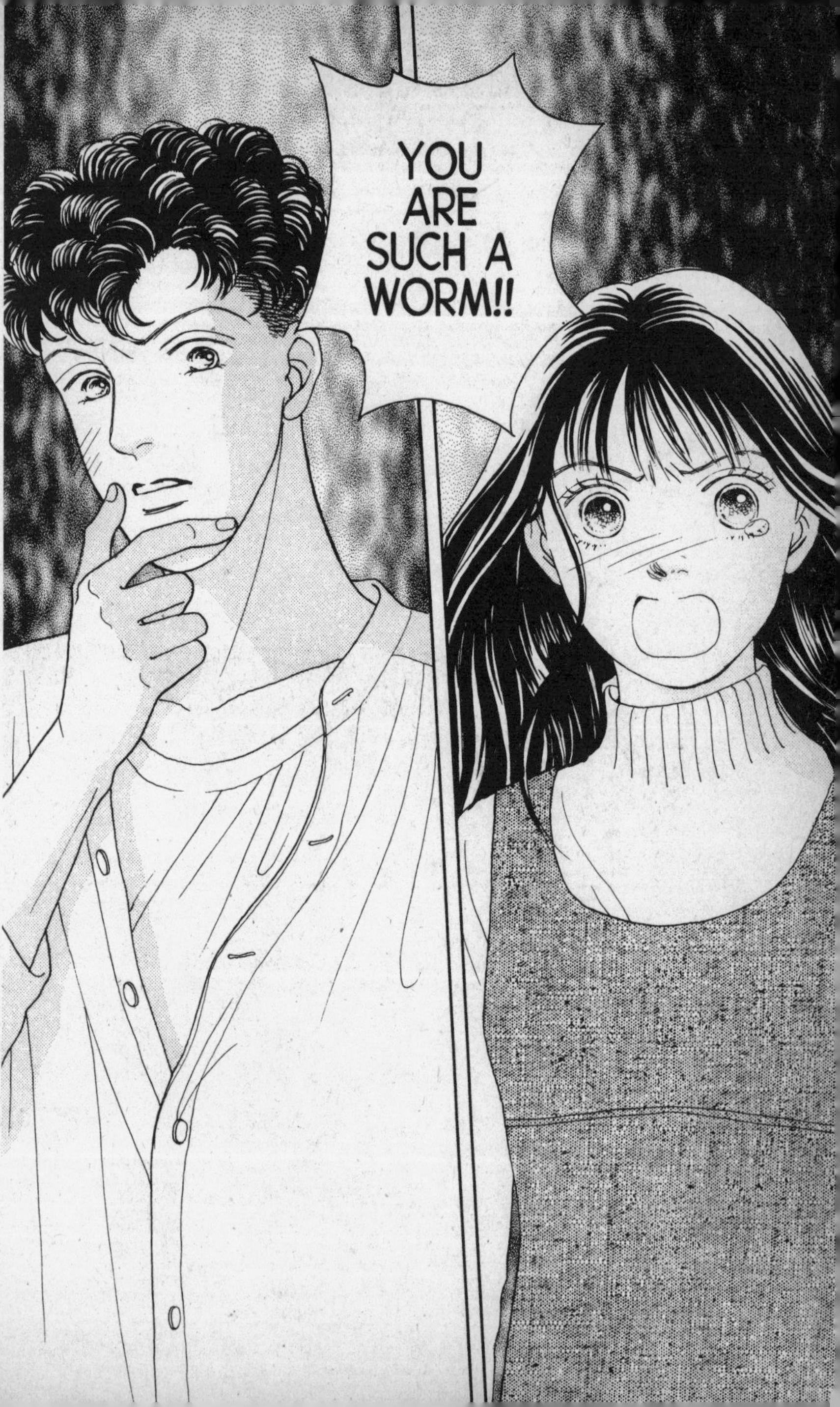
YOU ARE SUCH A WORM!!

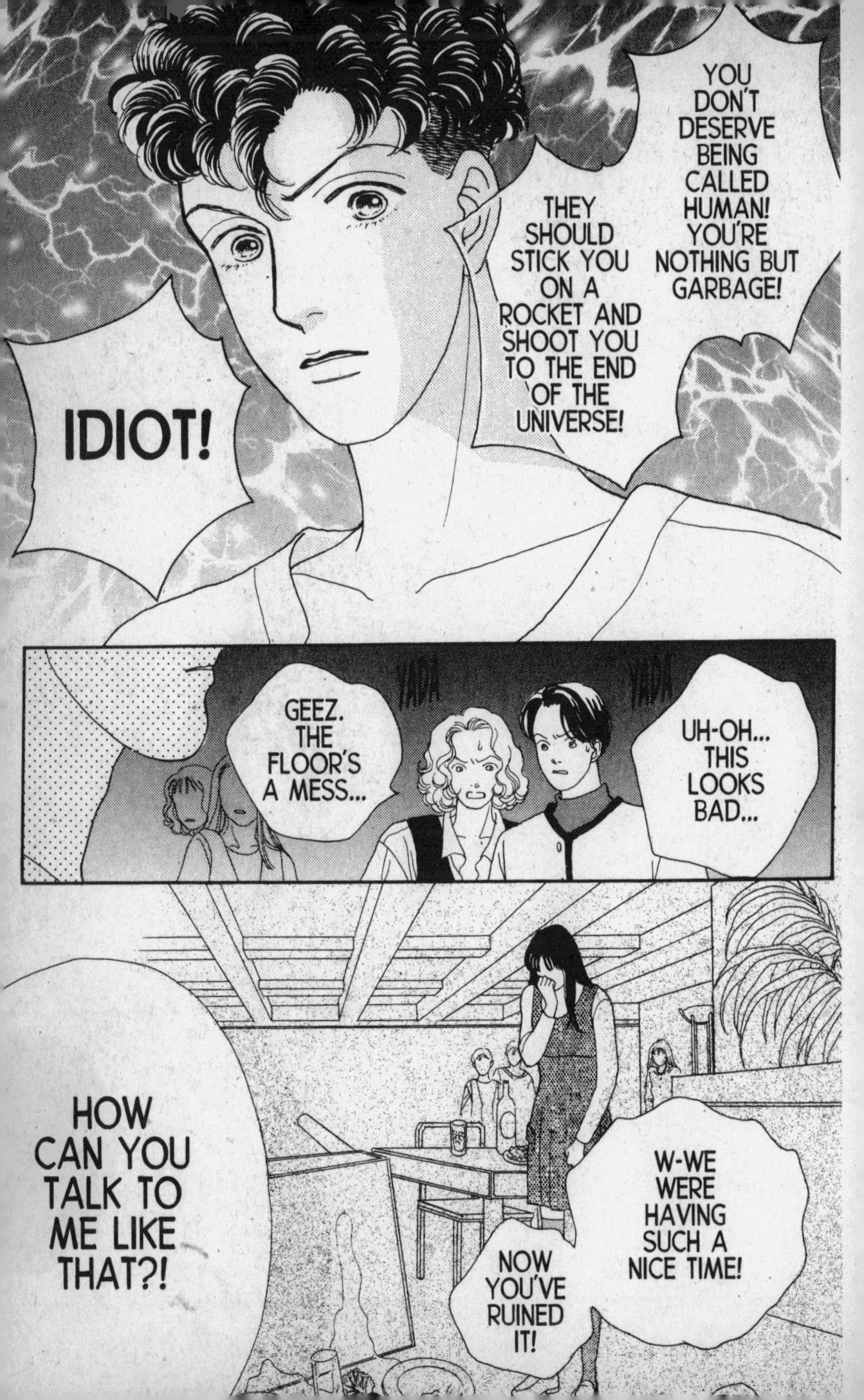
YOU DON'T DESERVE BEING CALLED HUMAN! YOU'RE NOTHING BUT GARBAGE!
THEY SHOULD STICK YOU ON A ROCKET AND SHOOT YOU TO THE END OF THE UNIVERSE!
IDIOT!
UH-OH... THIS LOOKS BAD...
YADA
YADA
GEEZ. THE FLOOR'S A MESS...
W-WE WERE HAVING SUCH A NICE TIME!
NOW YOU'VE RUINED IT!
HOW CAN YOU TALK TO ME LIKE THAT?!

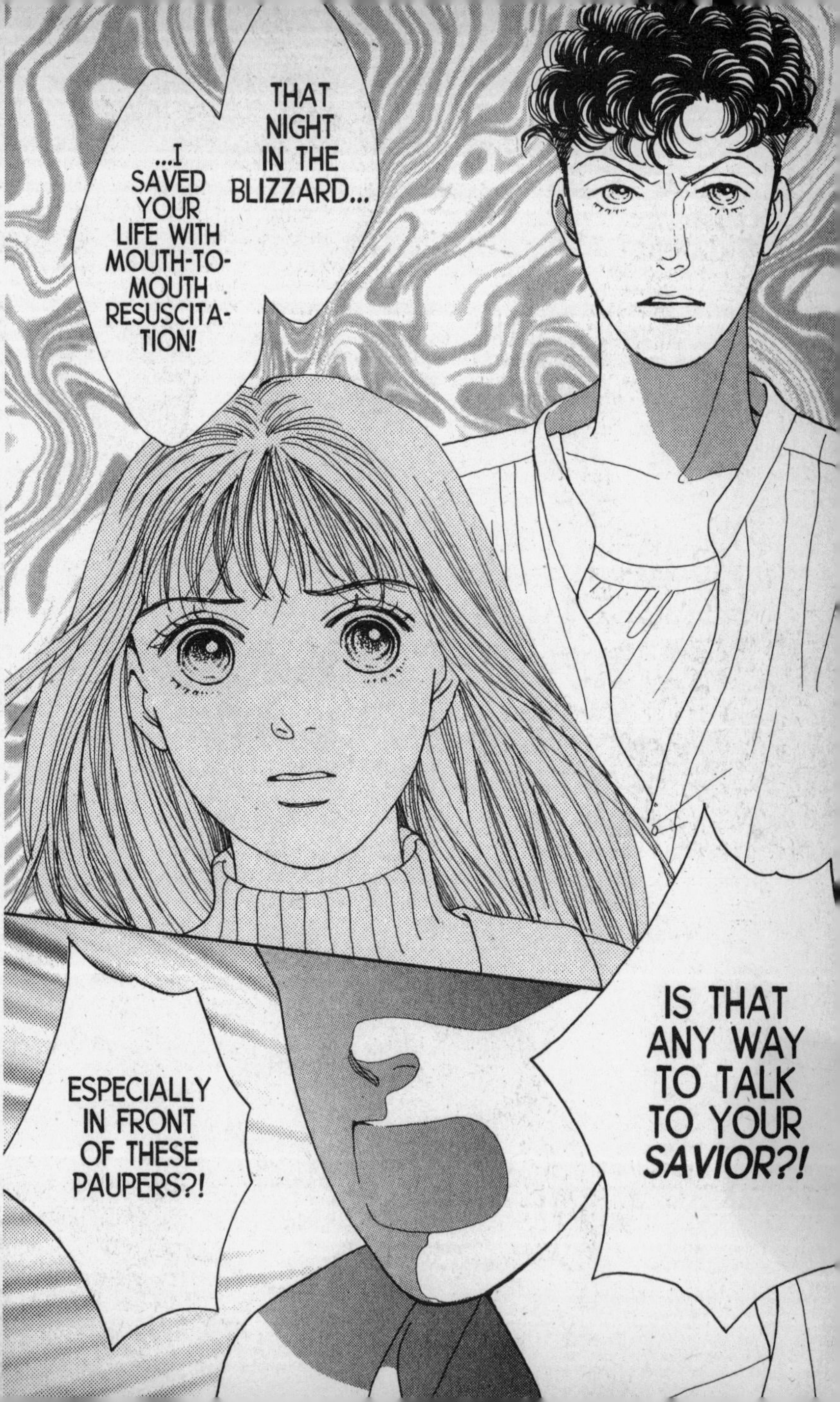
THAT NIGHT IN THE BLIZZARD...
...I SAVED YOUR LIFE WITH MOUTH-TO-MOUTH RESUSCITATION!
IS THAT ANY WAY TO TALK TO YOUR *SAVIOR?!*
ESPECIALLY IN FRONT OF THESE PAUPERS?!

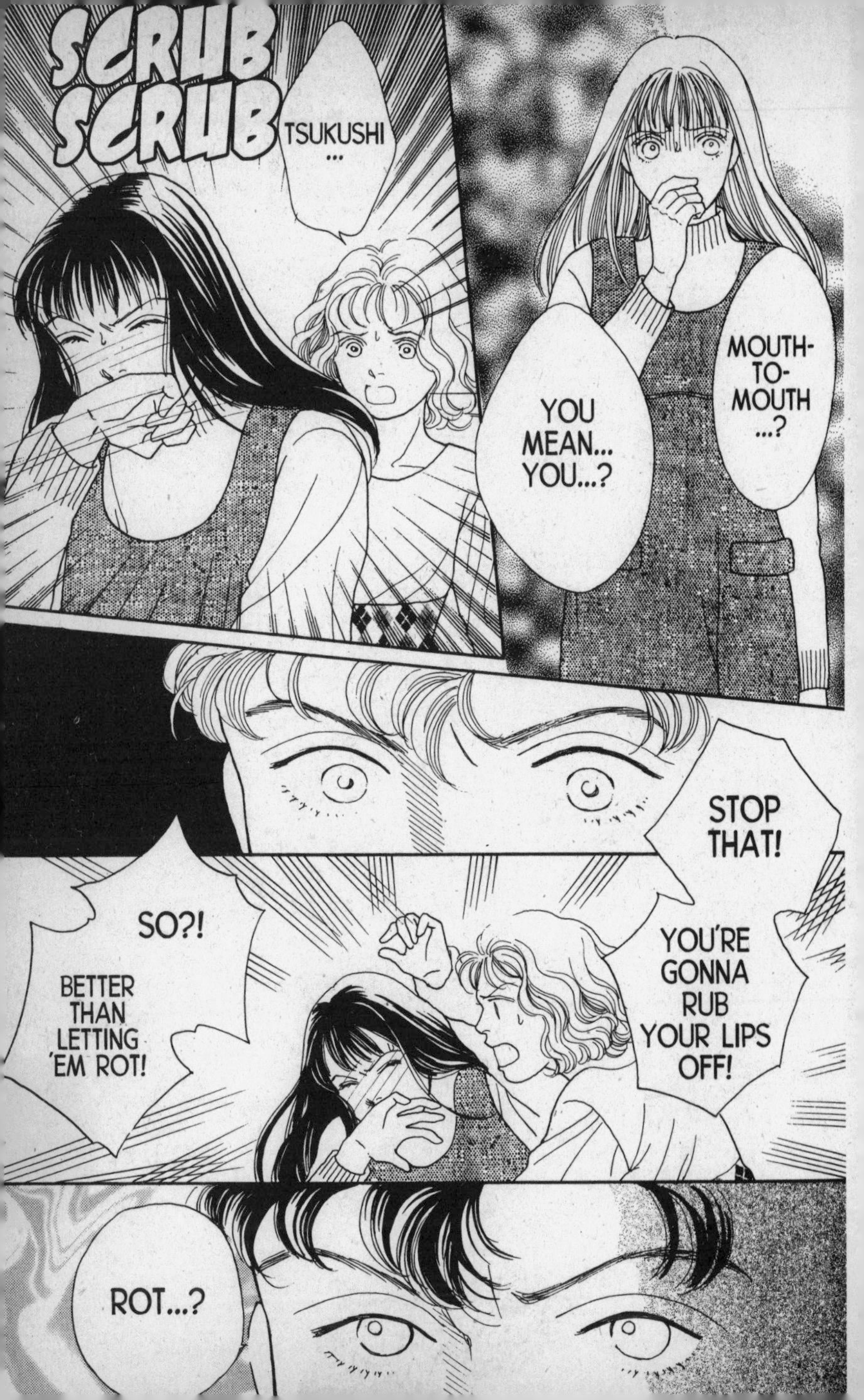
MOUTH-TO-MOUTH ...?
YOU MEAN... YOU...?
TSUKUSHI ...
SCRUB SCRUB
STOP THAT!
YOU'RE GONNA RUB YOUR LIPS OFF!
SO?!
BETTER THAN LETTING 'EM ROT!
ROT...?

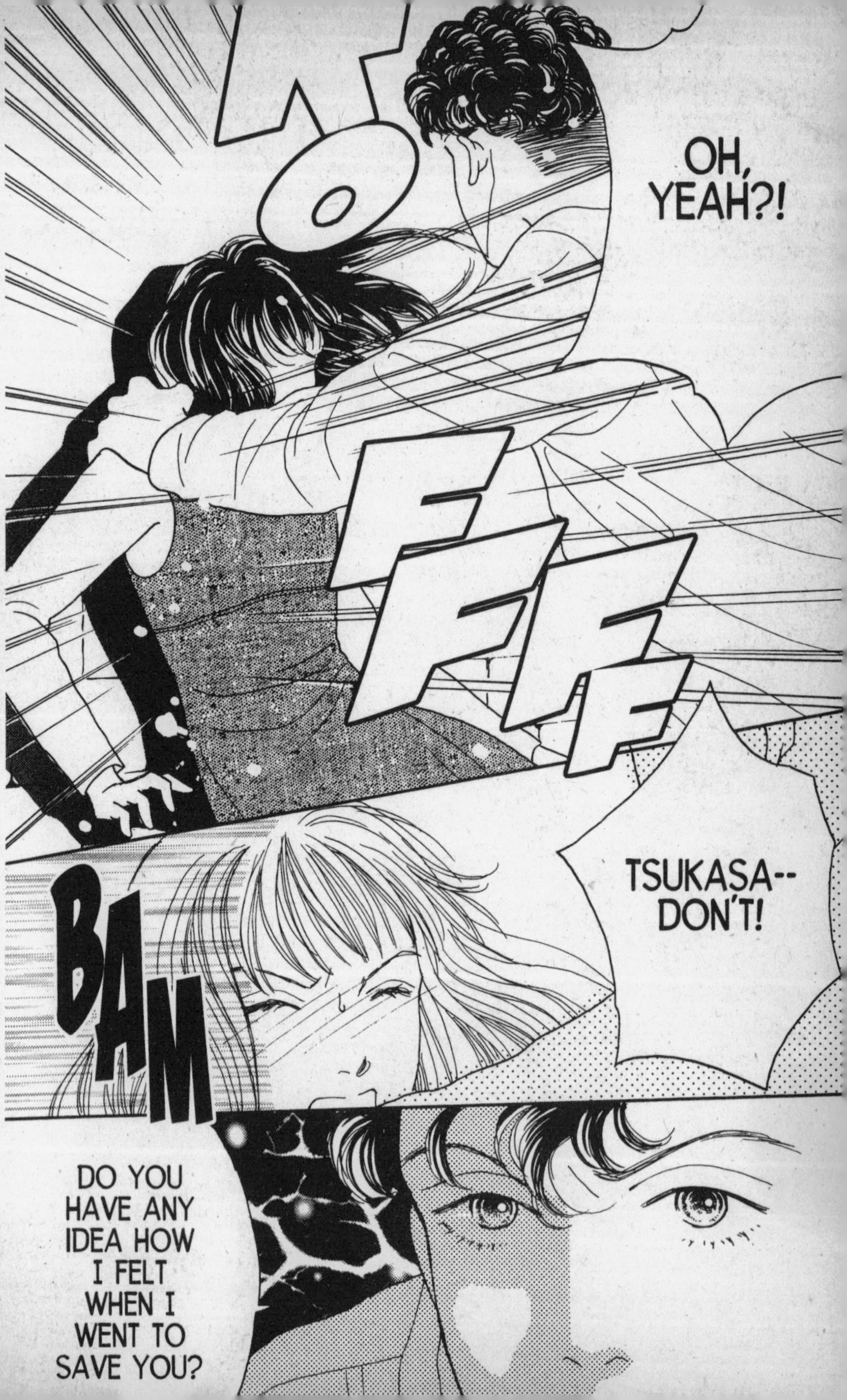
OH, YEAH?!
FFFF
TSUKASA-- DON'T!
BAM
DO YOU HAVE ANY IDEA HOW I FELT WHEN I WENT TO SAVE YOU?

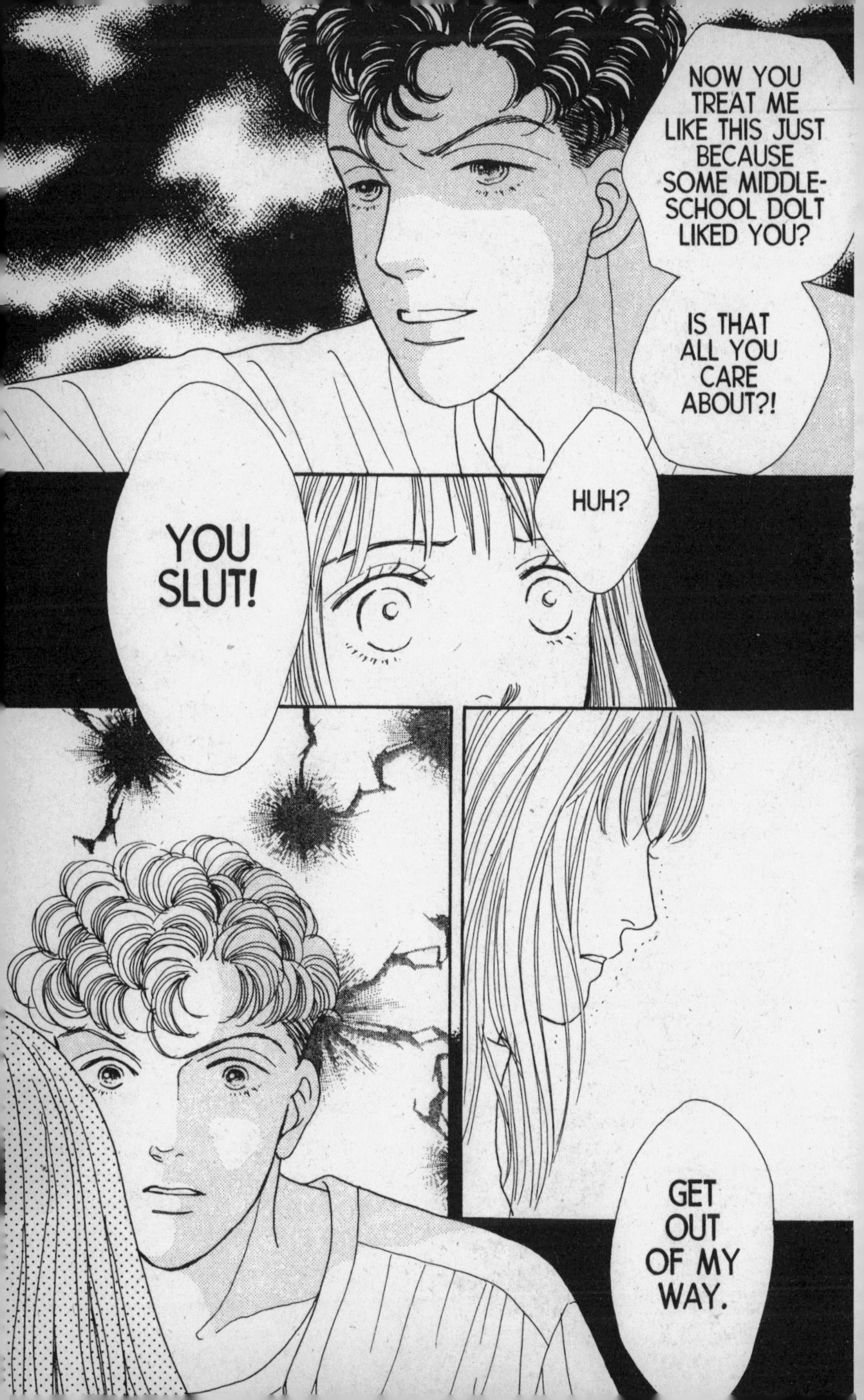
NOW YOU TREAT ME LIKE THIS JUST BECAUSE SOME MIDDLE-SCHOOL DOLT LIKED YOU?
IS THAT ALL YOU CARE ABOUT?!
HUH?
YOU SLUT!
GET OUT OF MY WAY.

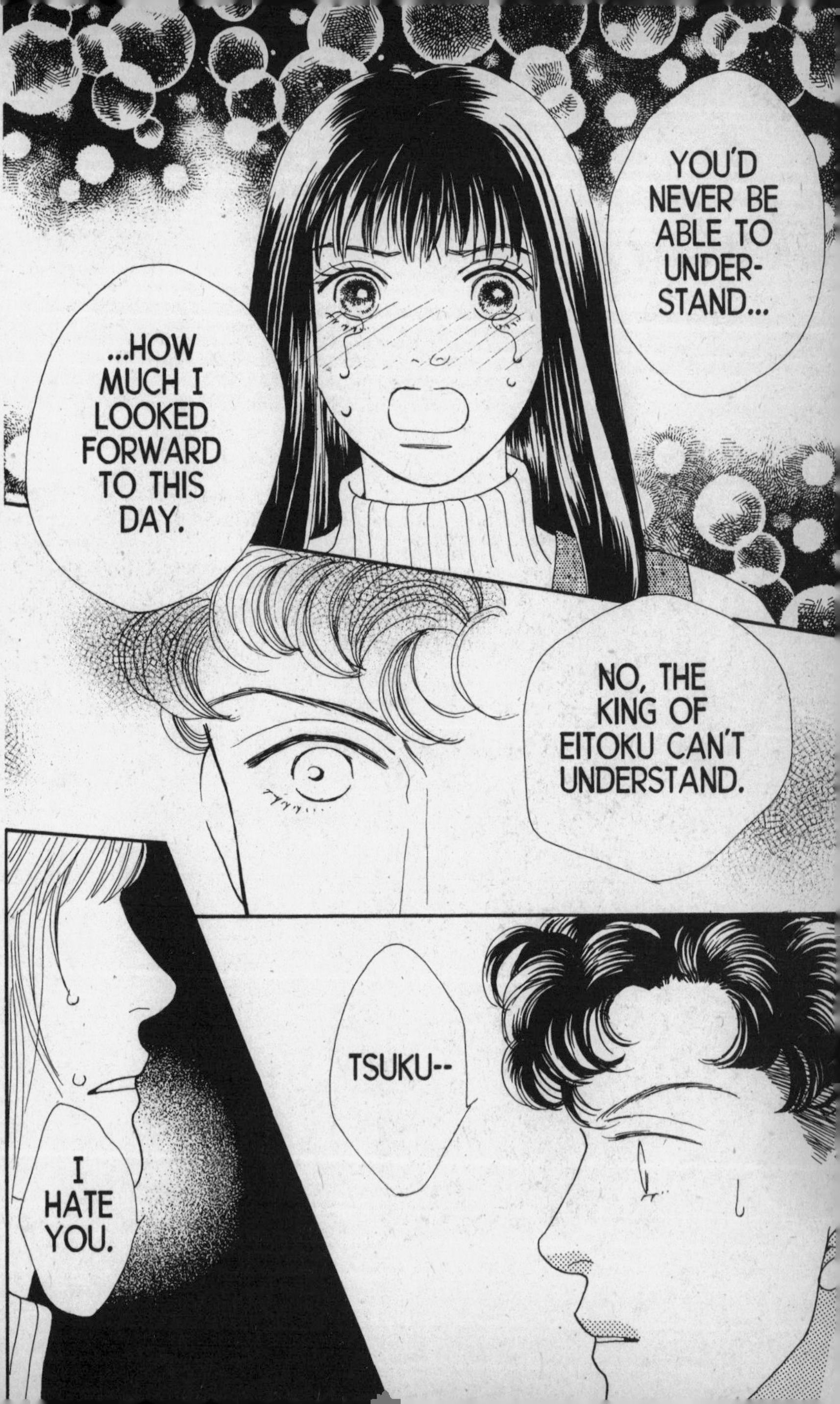
YOU'D NEVER BE ABLE TO UNDER-STAND...
...HOW MUCH I LOOKED FORWARD TO THIS DAY.
NO, THE KING OF EITOKU CAN'T UNDERSTAND.
TSUKU--
I HATE YOU.

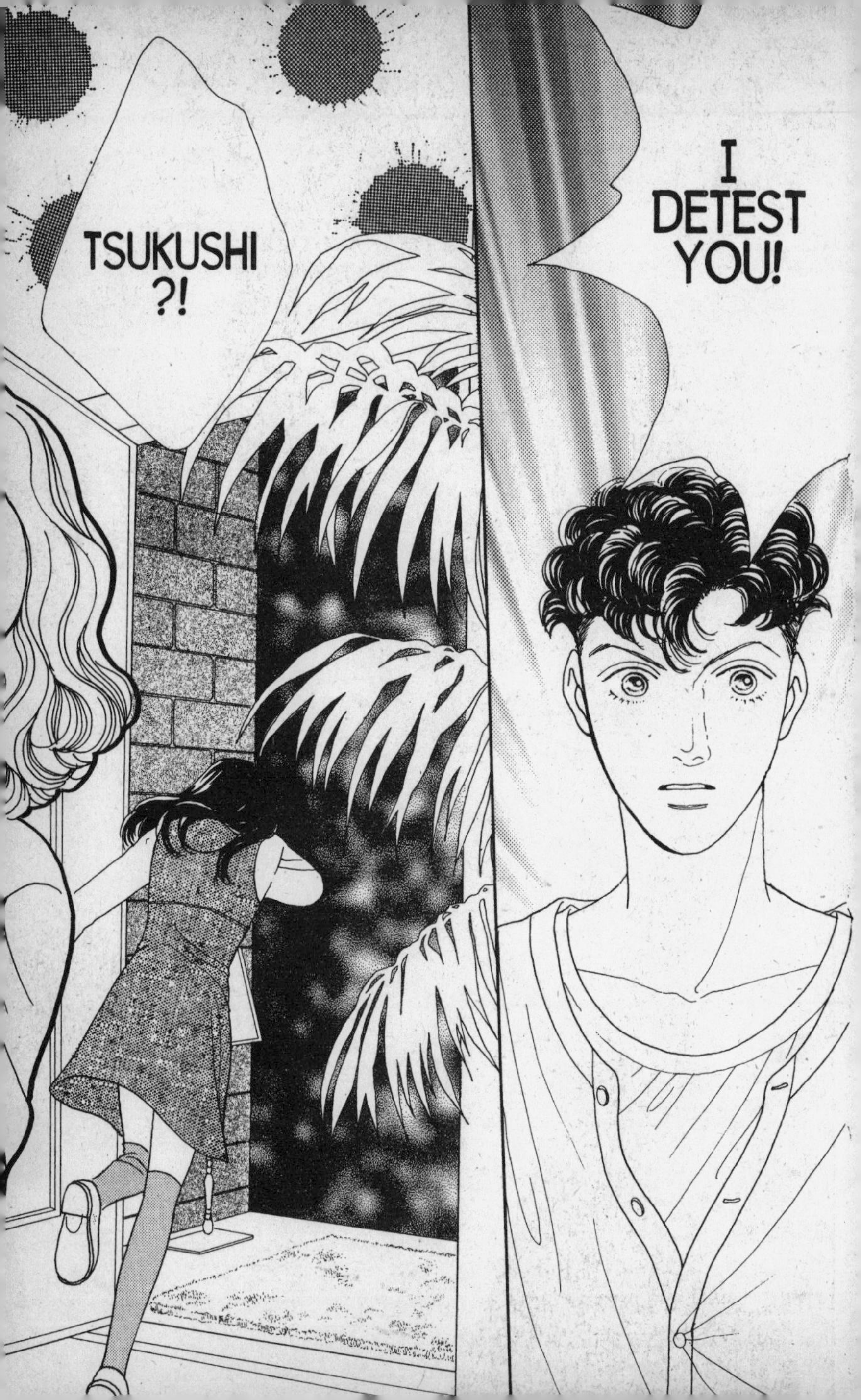
I DETEST YOU!
TSUKUSHI ?!

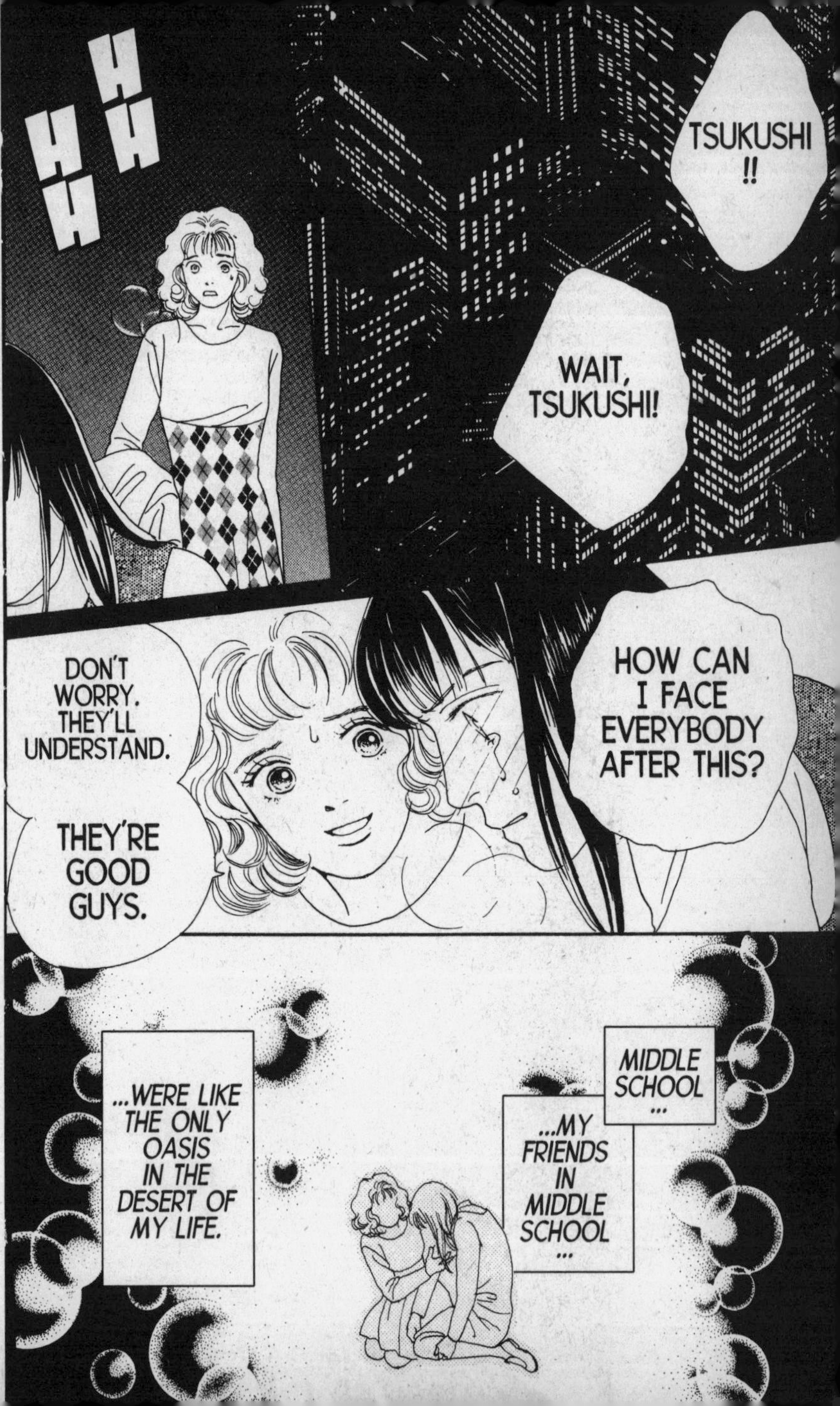
TSUKUSHI !!
WAIT, TSUKUSHI!
HUHHH
HOW CAN I FACE EVERYBODY AFTER THIS?
DON'T WORRY. THEY'LL UNDERSTAND.
THEY'RE GOOD GUYS.
MIDDLE SCHOOL ...
...MY FRIENDS IN MIDDLE SCHOOL ...
...WERE LIKE THE ONLY OASIS IN THE DESERT OF MY LIFE.

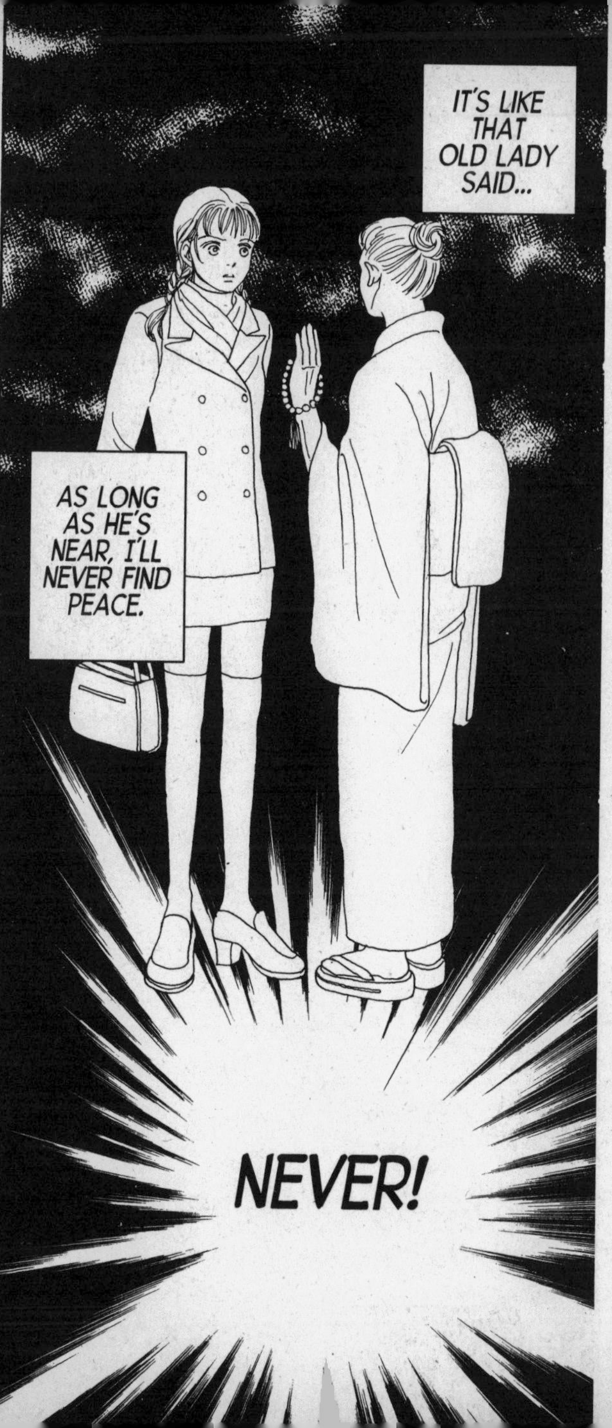
IT'S LIKE THAT OLD LADY SAID...
AS LONG AS HE'S NEAR, I'LL NEVER FIND PEACE.
NEVER!

HELLO!!

It's been a while. Volume 14 already!

I moved again recently.

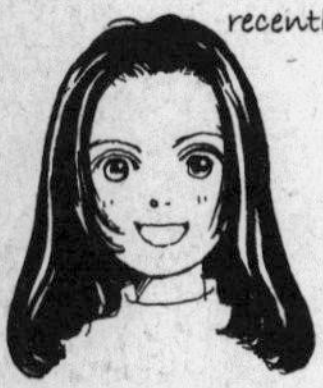

How are you? I took a trip to Italy in June.

You can read all about it on pages 28 and 190!

I hope you enjoy this volume!

Lately, it's been so hot, I'm all wrung out.

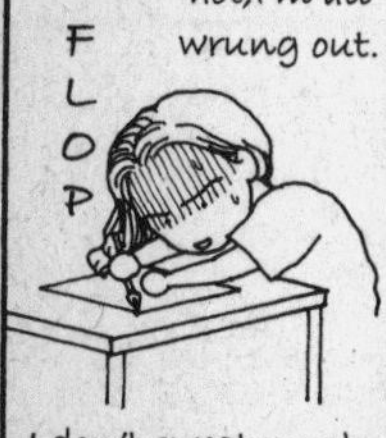
FLOP

I don't sweat much, so my body really feels the heat. Summers are hell.

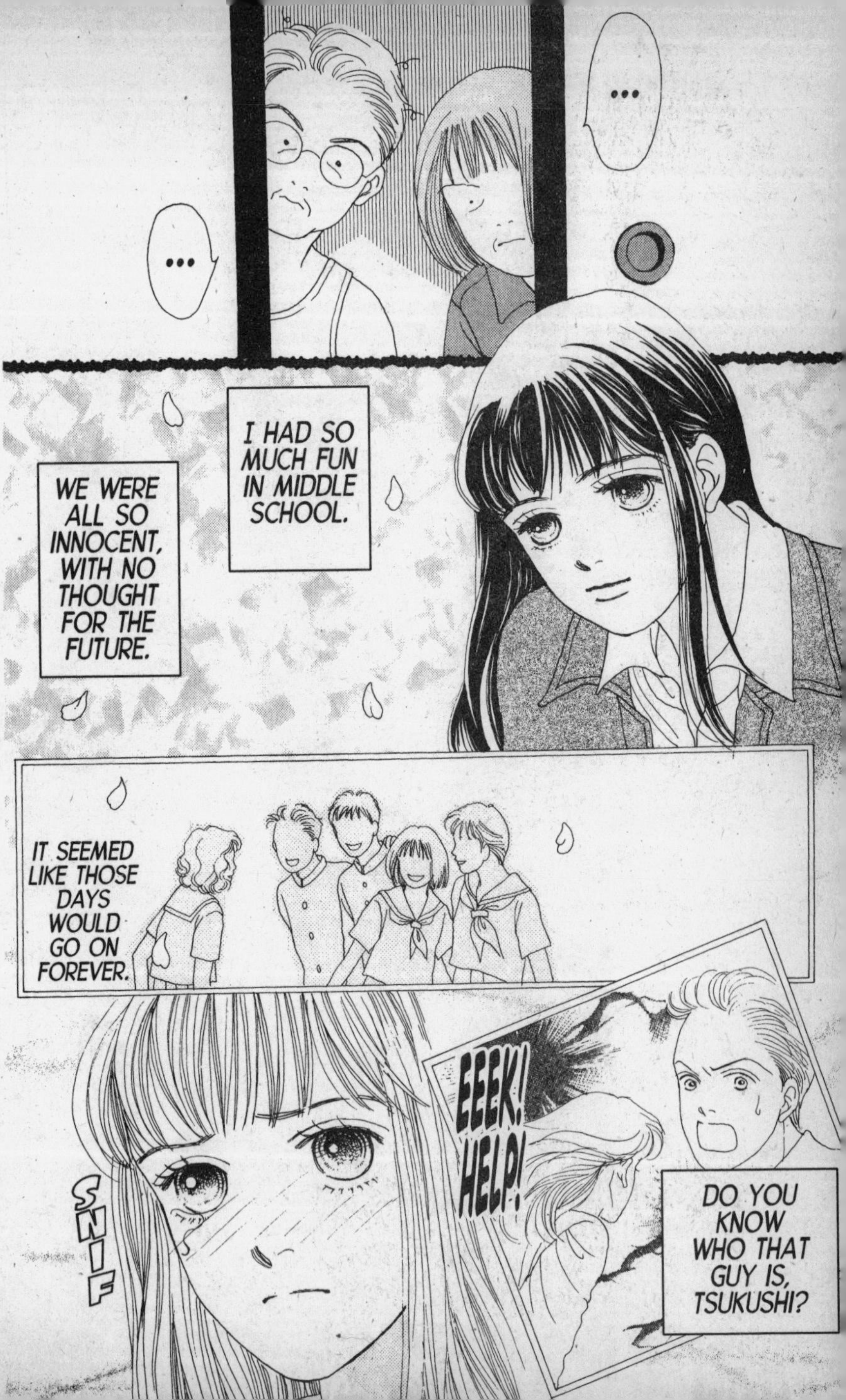
...
...
I HAD SO MUCH FUN IN MIDDLE SCHOOL.
WE WERE ALL SO INNOCENT, WITH NO THOUGHT FOR THE FUTURE.
IT SEEMED LIKE THOSE DAYS WOULD GO ON FOREVER.
EEEK! HELP!
DO YOU KNOW WHO THAT GUY IS, TSUKUSHI?
SNIF

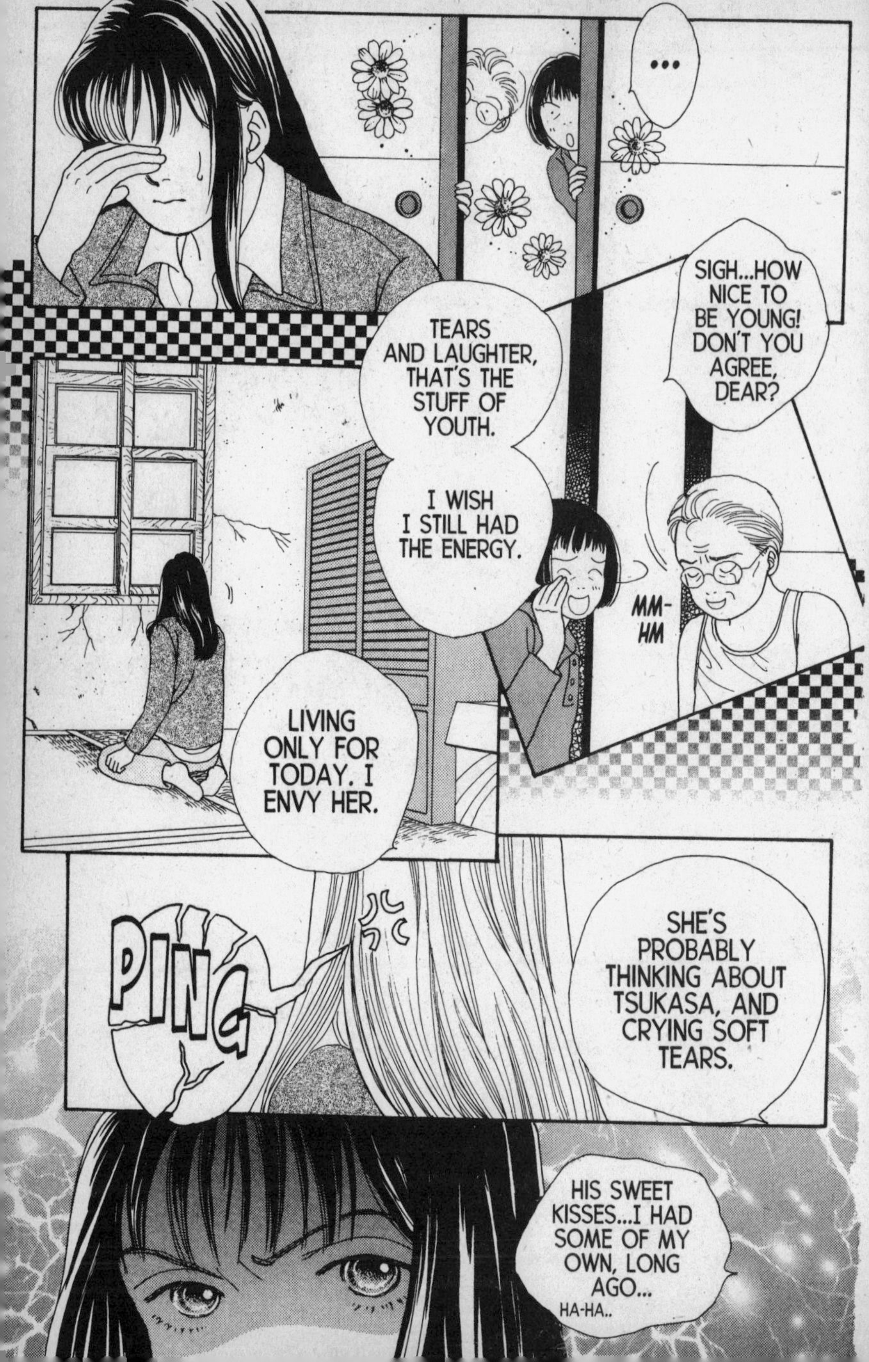
...
SIGH...HOW NICE TO BE YOUNG! DON'T YOU AGREE, DEAR?
MM-HM
TEARS AND LAUGHTER, THAT'S THE STUFF OF YOUTH.
I WISH I STILL HAD THE ENERGY.
LIVING ONLY FOR TODAY. I ENVY HER.
SHE'S PROBABLY THINKING ABOUT TSUKASA, AND CRYING SOFT TEARS.
PING
HIS SWEET KISSES...I HAD SOME OF MY OWN, LONG AGO...
HA-HA..

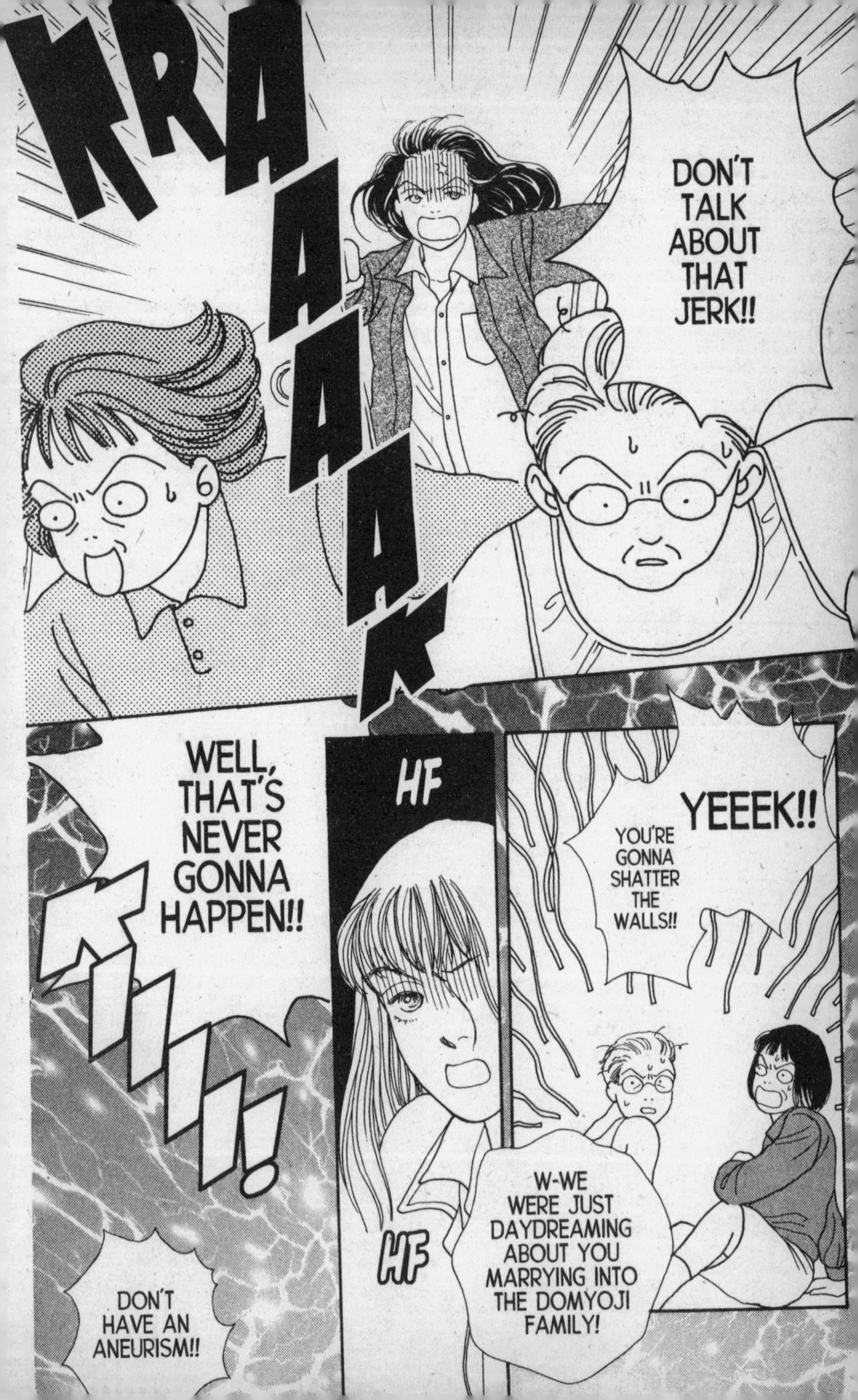
DON'T TALK ABOUT THAT JERK!!
KRAAAAAK
YEEEK!!
YOU'RE GONNA SHATTER THE WALLS!!
W-WE WERE JUST DAYDREAMING ABOUT YOU MARRYING INTO THE DOMYOJI FAMILY!
HF
HF
WELL, THAT'S NEVER GONNA HAPPEN!!
KIIII!!
DON'T HAVE AN ANEURISM!!

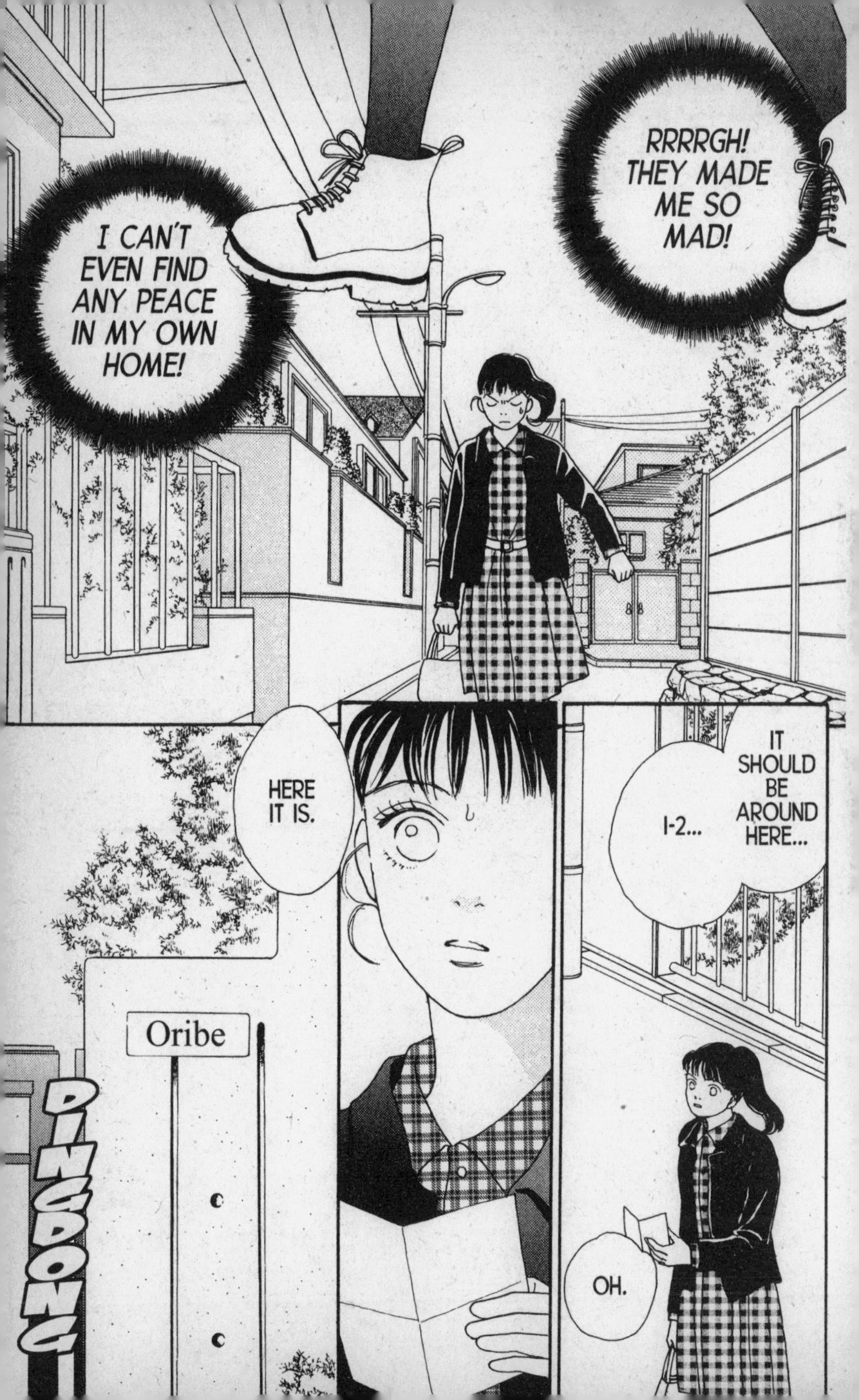
RRRRGH! THEY MADE ME SO MAD!
I CAN'T EVEN FIND ANY PEACE IN MY OWN HOME!
IT SHOULD BE AROUND HERE...
1-2...
OH.
HERE IT IS.
Oribe
DINGDONG

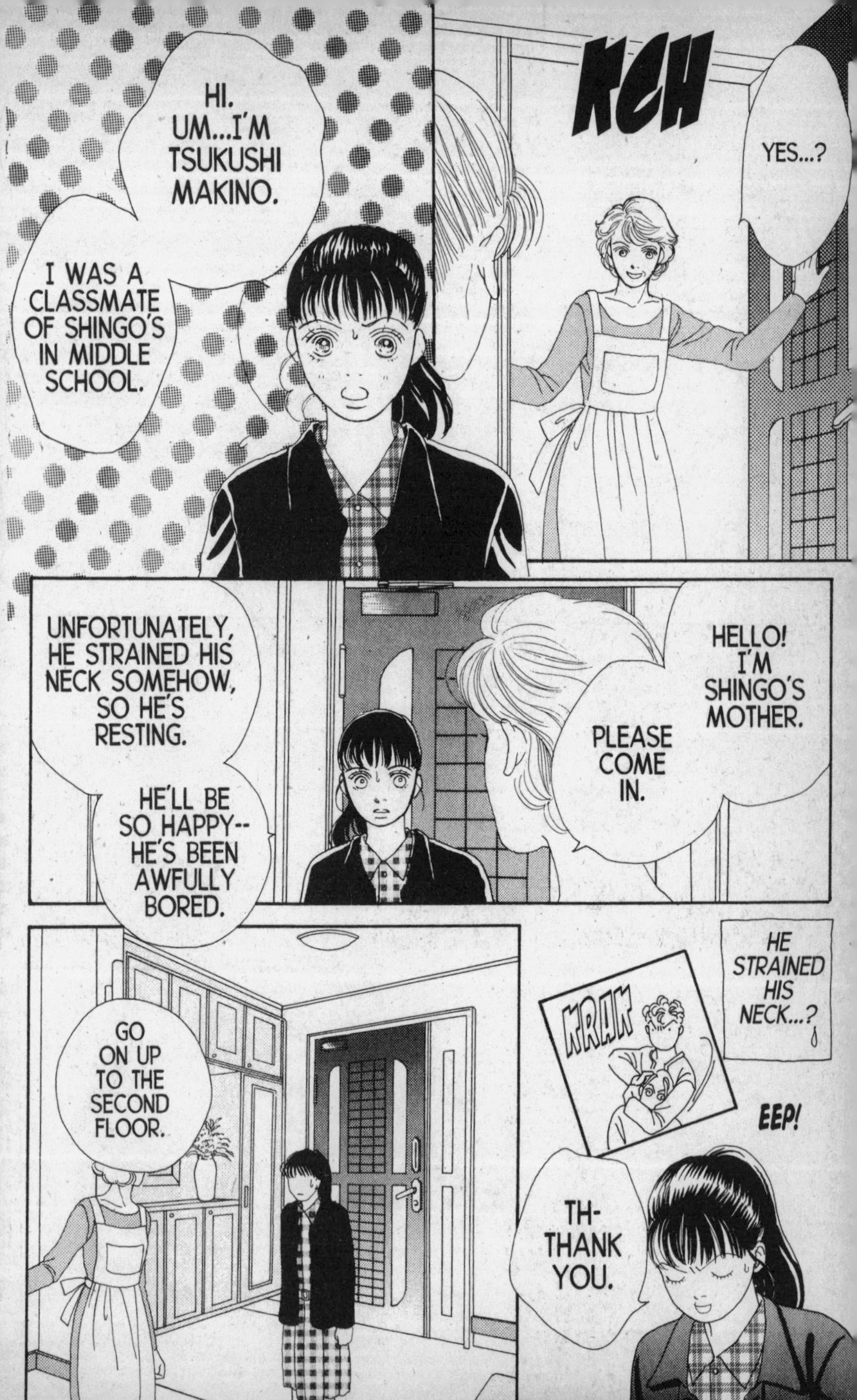
KCH
YES...?
HI. UM...I'M TSUKUSHI MAKINO.
I WAS A CLASSMATE OF SHINGO'S IN MIDDLE SCHOOL.
HELLO! I'M SHINGO'S MOTHER.
PLEASE COME IN.
UNFORTUNATELY, HE STRAINED HIS NECK SOMEHOW, SO HE'S RESTING.
HE'LL BE SO HAPPY-- HE'S BEEN AWFULLY BORED.
HE STRAINED HIS NECK...?
KRAK
EEP!
TH- THANK YOU.
GO ON UP TO THE SECOND FLOOR.

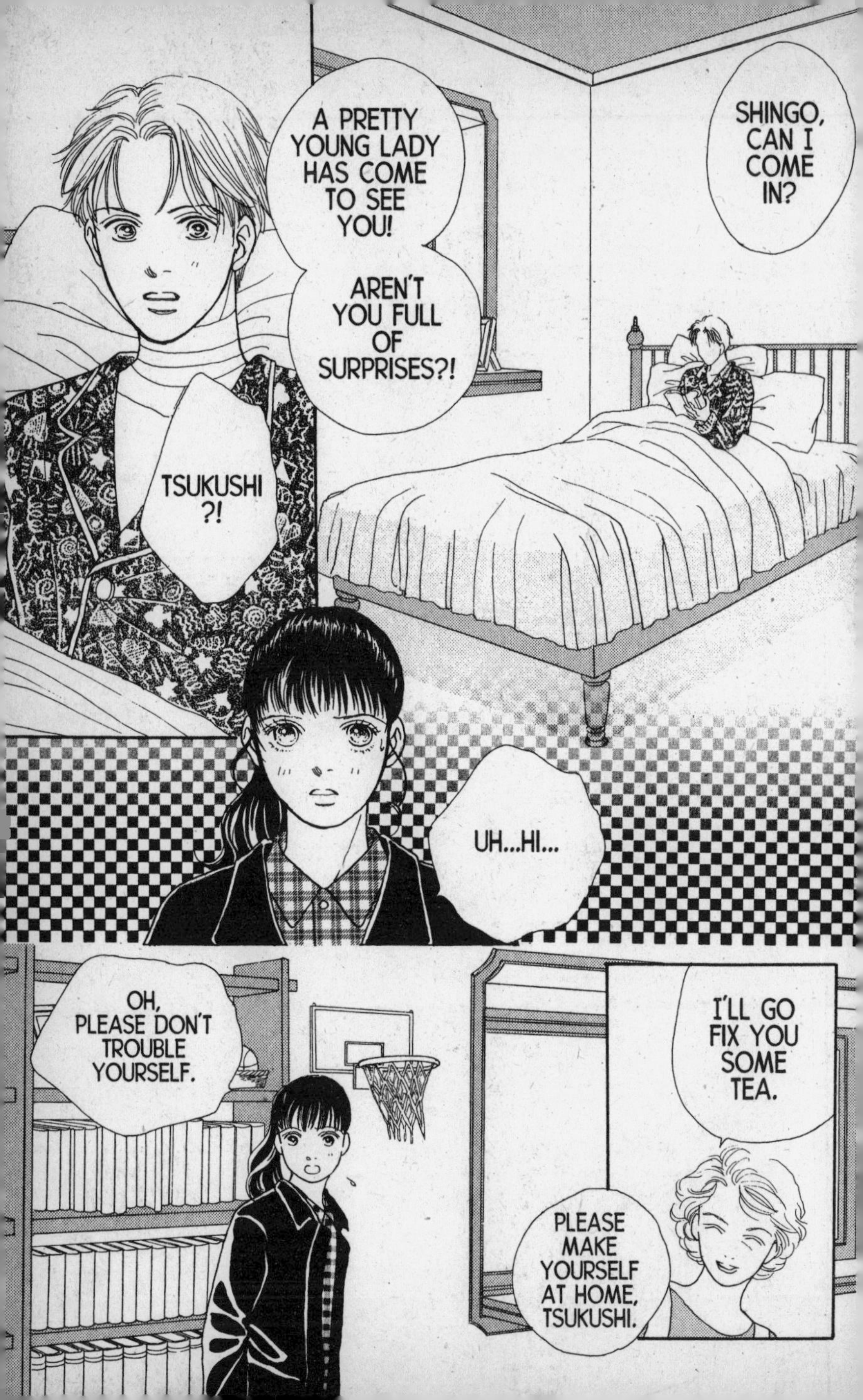
SHINGO, CAN I COME IN?
A PRETTY YOUNG LADY HAS COME TO SEE YOU!
AREN'T YOU FULL OF SURPRISES?!
TSUKUSHI ?!
UH...HI...
I'LL GO FIX YOU SOME TEA.
PLEASE MAKE YOURSELF AT HOME, TSUKUSHI.
OH, PLEASE DON'T TROUBLE YOURSELF.

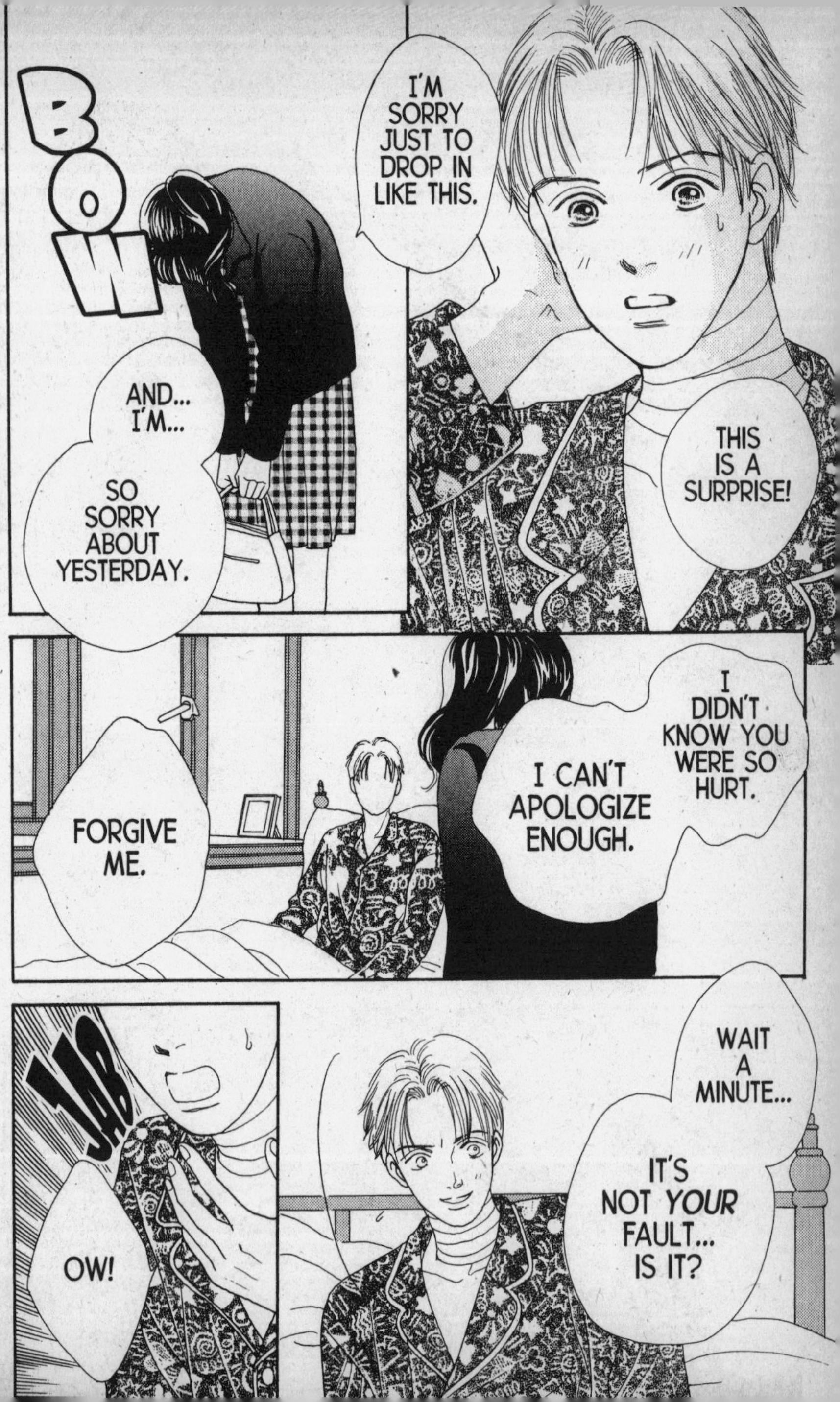
I'M SORRY JUST TO DROP IN LIKE THIS.
THIS IS A SURPRISE!
BOW
AND... I'M...
SO SORRY ABOUT YESTERDAY.
I DIDN'T KNOW YOU WERE SO HURT.
I CAN'T APOLOGIZE ENOUGH.
FORGIVE ME.
WAIT A MINUTE...
IT'S NOT *YOUR* FAULT... IS IT?
JAB
OW!

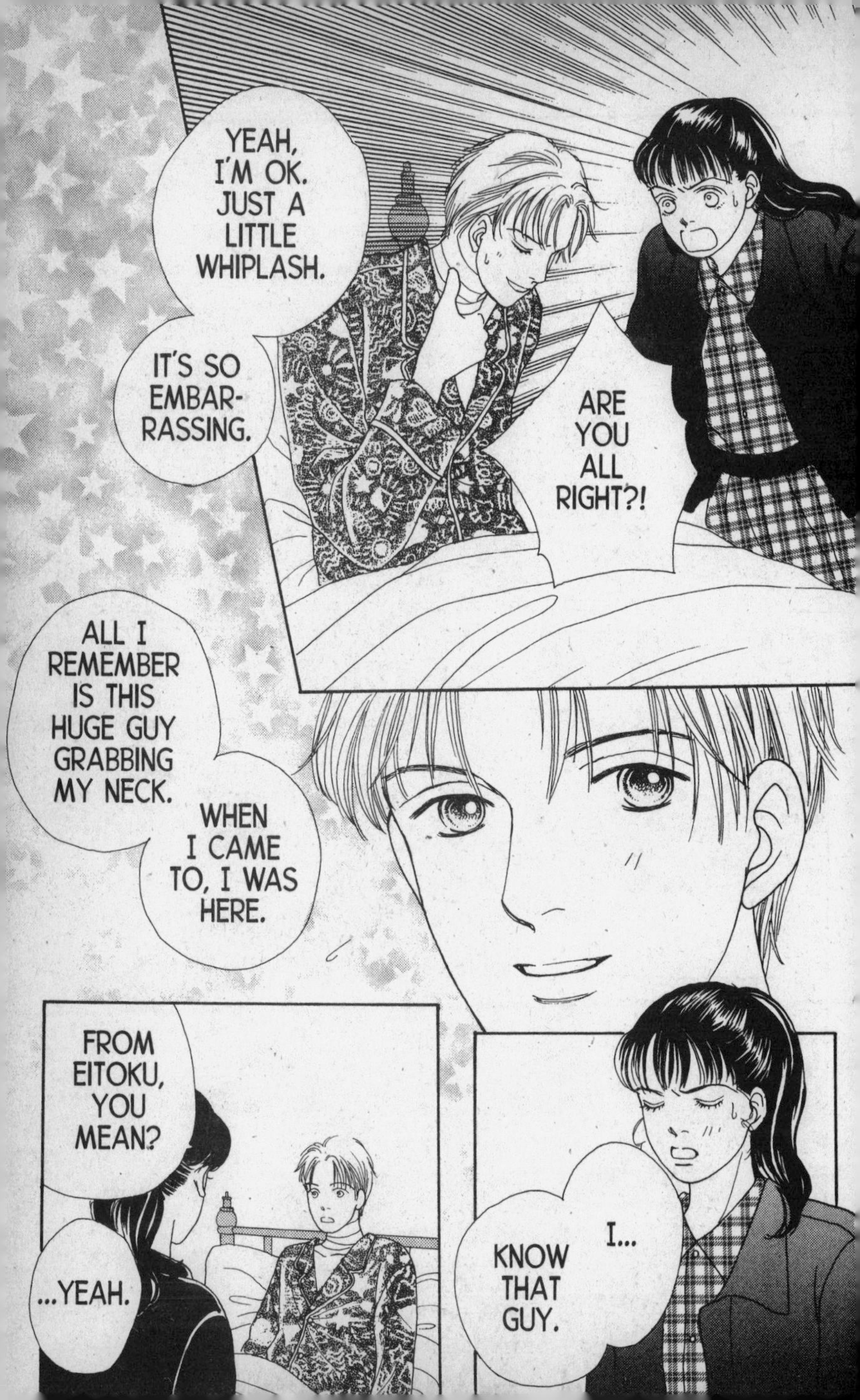
ARE YOU ALL RIGHT?!
YEAH, I'M OK. JUST A LITTLE WHIPLASH.
IT'S SO EMBARRASSING.
ALL I REMEMBER IS THIS HUGE GUY GRABBING MY NECK.
WHEN I CAME TO, I WAS HERE.
I...
KNOW THAT GUY.
FROM EITOKU, YOU MEAN?
...YEAH.

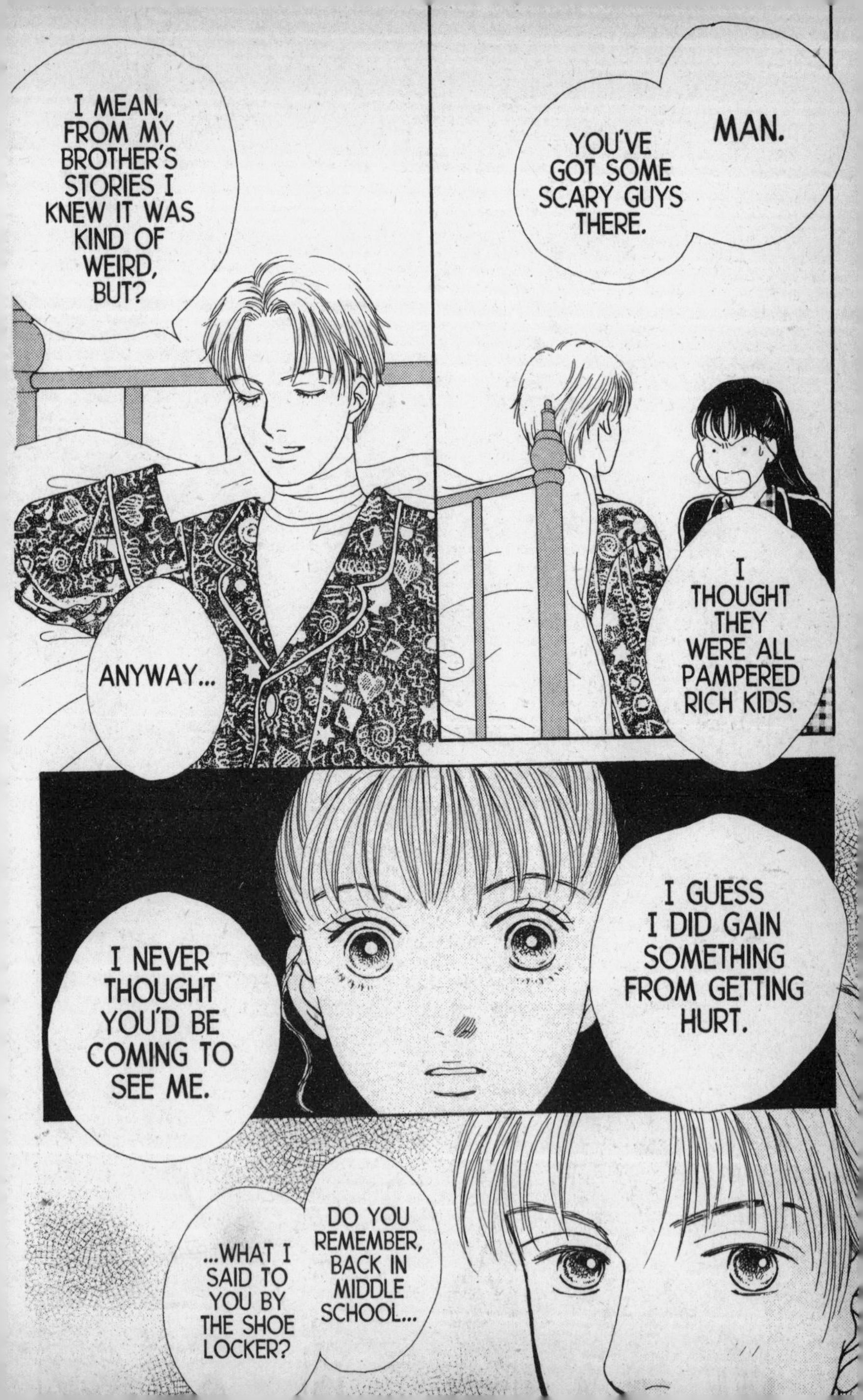
MAN.
YOU'VE GOT SOME SCARY GUYS THERE.
I THOUGHT THEY WERE ALL PAMPERED RICH KIDS.
I MEAN, FROM MY BROTHER'S STORIES I KNEW IT WAS KIND OF WEIRD, BUT?
ANYWAY...
I GUESS I DID GAIN SOMETHING FROM GETTING HURT.
I NEVER THOUGHT YOU'D BE COMING TO SEE ME.
DO YOU REMEMBER, BACK IN MIDDLE SCHOOL...
...WHAT I SAID TO YOU BY THE SHOE LOCKER?

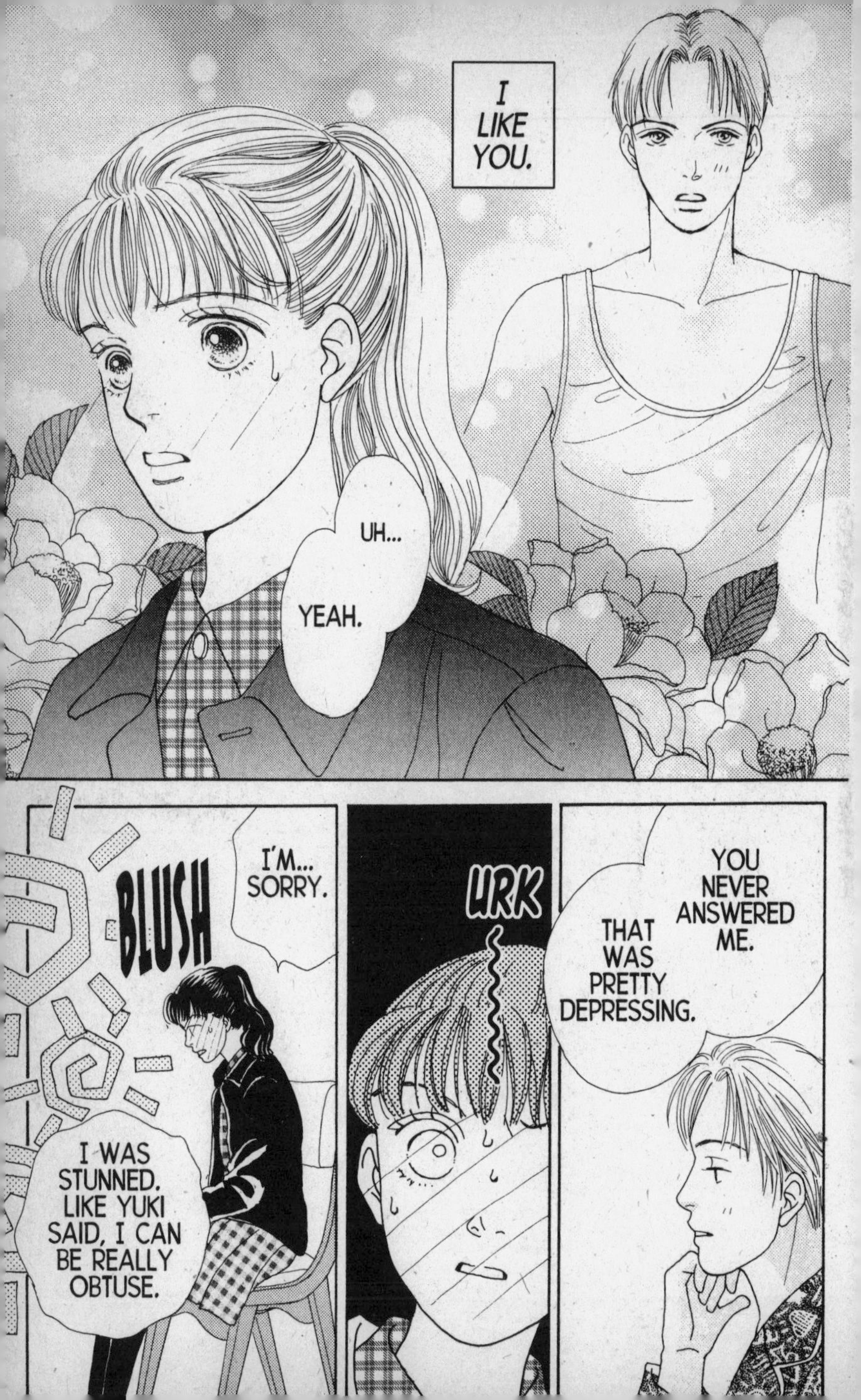
I LIKE YOU.
UH... YEAH.
YOU NEVER ANSWERED ME.
THAT WAS PRETTY DEPRESSING.
URK
I'M... SORRY.
BLUSH
I WAS STUNNED. LIKE YUKI SAID, I CAN BE REALLY OBTUSE.

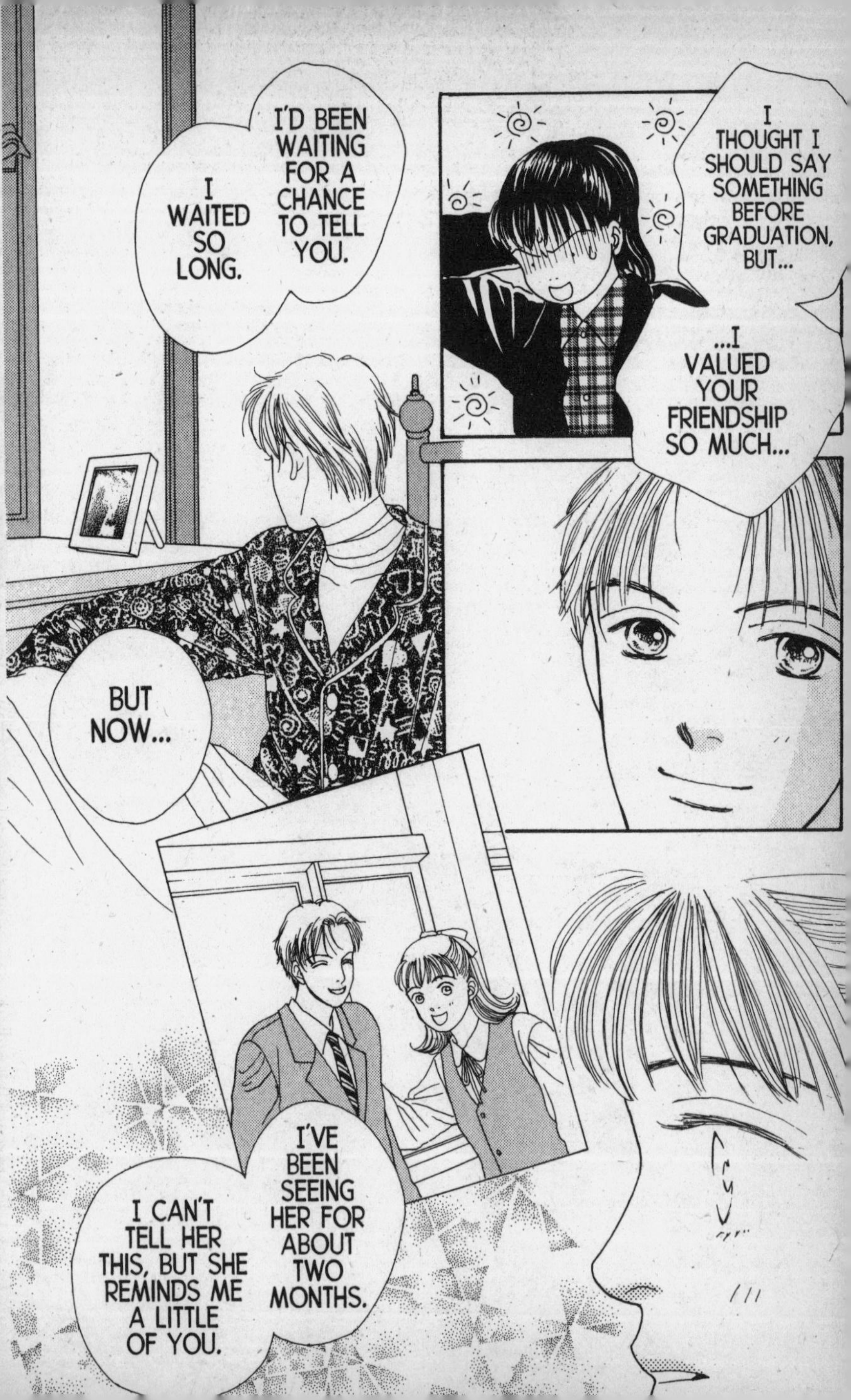
I THOUGHT I SHOULD SAY SOMETHING BEFORE GRADUATION, BUT...
...I VALUED YOUR FRIENDSHIP SO MUCH...
I'D BEEN WAITING FOR A CHANCE TO TELL YOU.
I WAITED SO LONG.
BUT NOW...
I'VE BEEN SEEING HER FOR ABOUT TWO MONTHS.
I CAN'T TELL HER THIS, BUT SHE REMINDS ME A LITTLE OF YOU.

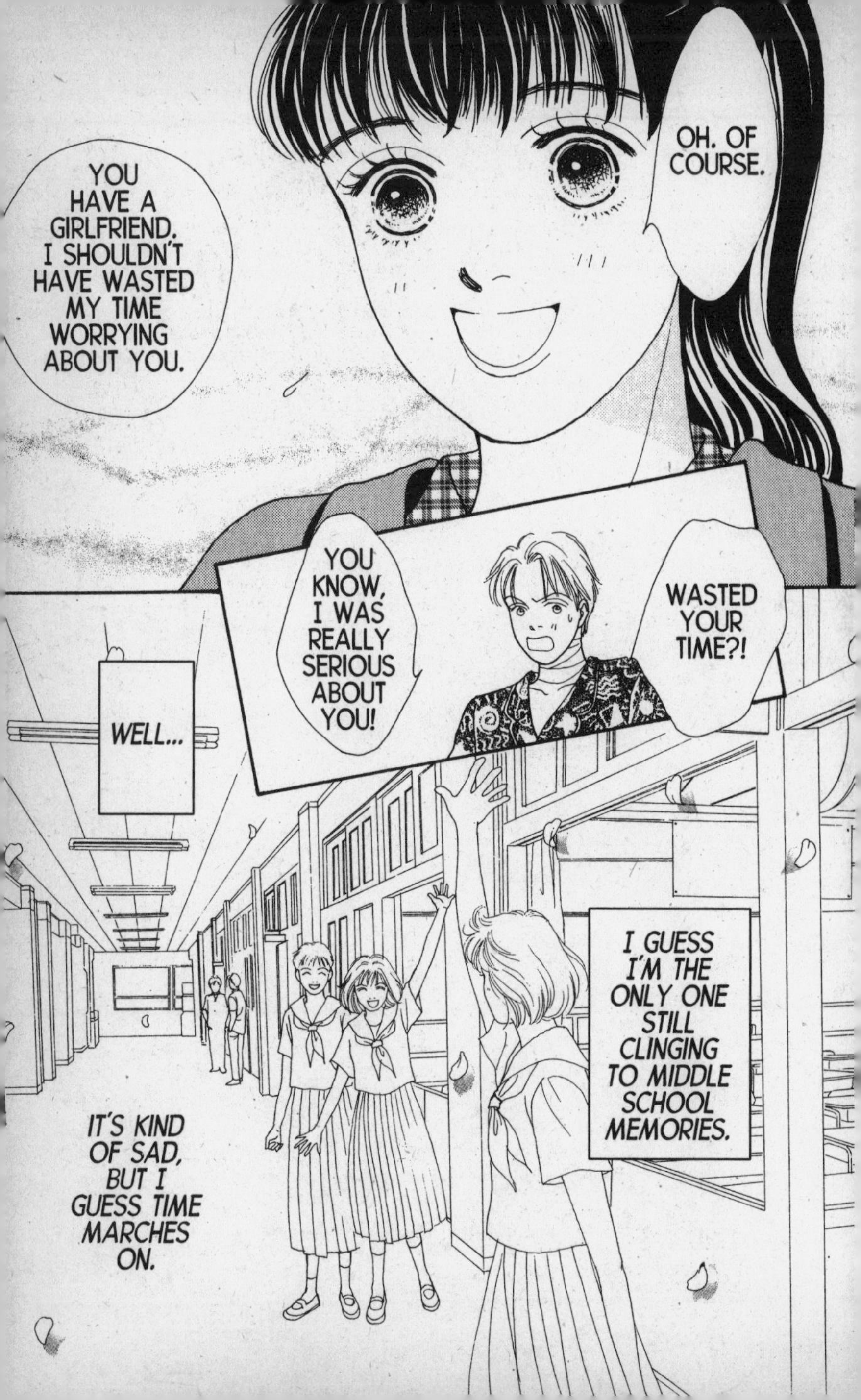
OH. OF COURSE.
YOU HAVE A GIRLFRIEND. I SHOULDN'T HAVE WASTED MY TIME WORRYING ABOUT YOU.
WASTED YOUR TIME?!
YOU KNOW, I WAS REALLY SERIOUS ABOUT YOU!
WELL...
I GUESS I'M THE ONLY ONE STILL CLINGING TO MIDDLE SCHOOL MEMORIES.
IT'S KIND OF SAD, BUT I GUESS TIME MARCHES ON.

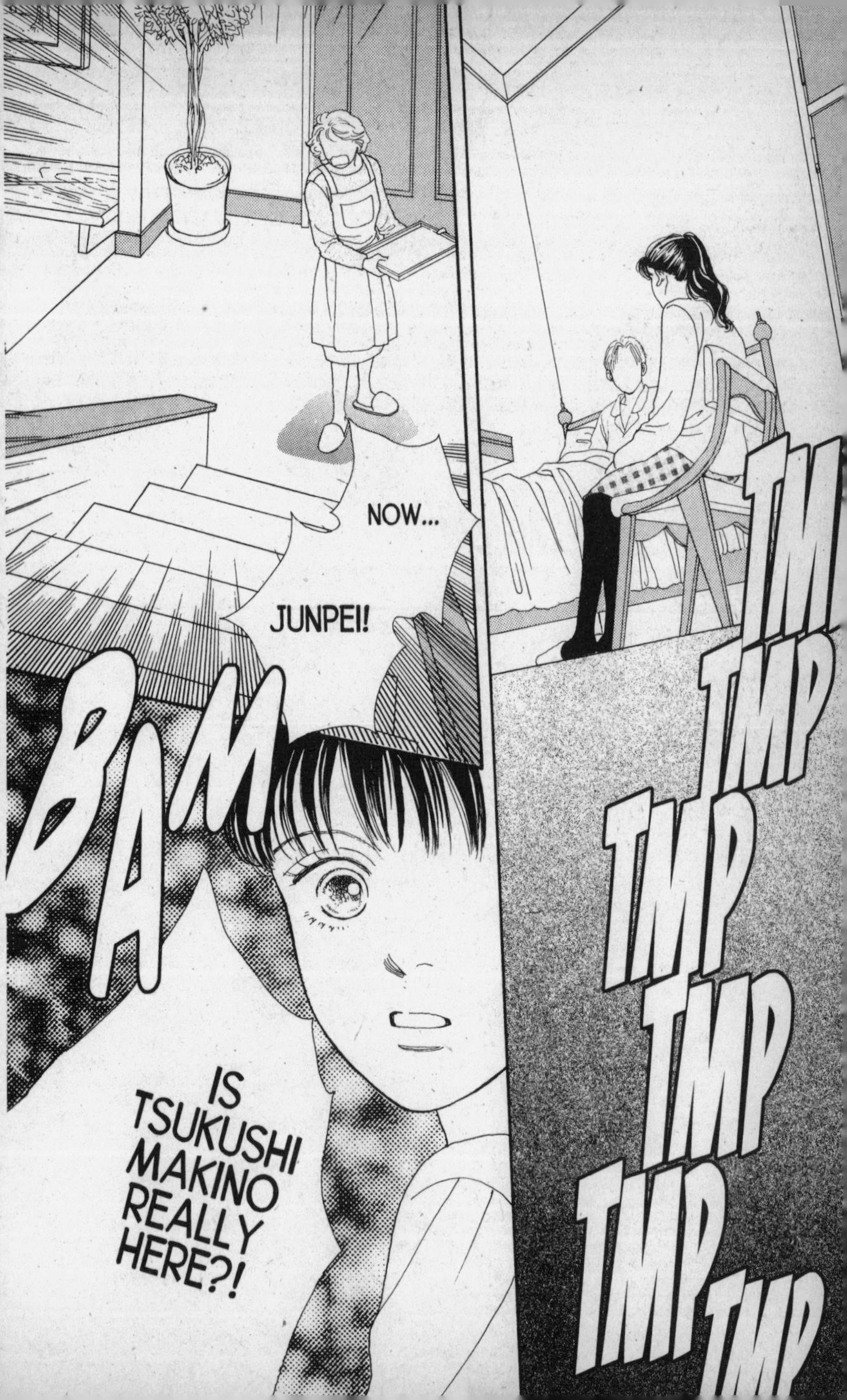
TM TMP
TMP TMP
TMP TMP TMP
NOW... JUNPEI!
BAM
IS TSUKUSHI MAKINO REALLY HERE?!

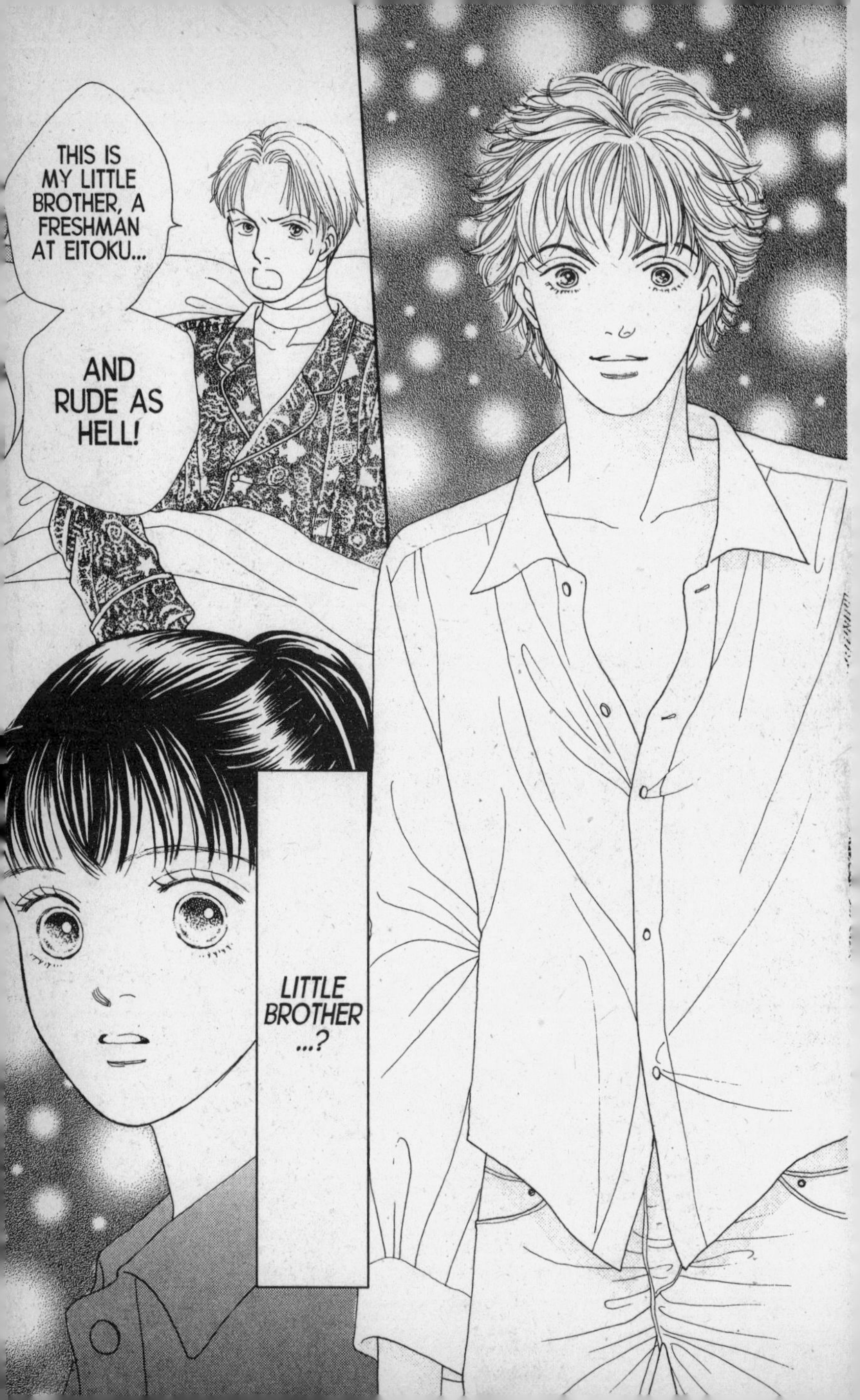
THIS IS MY LITTLE BROTHER, A FRESHMAN AT EITOKU...
AND RUDE AS HELL!
LITTLE BROTHER ...?

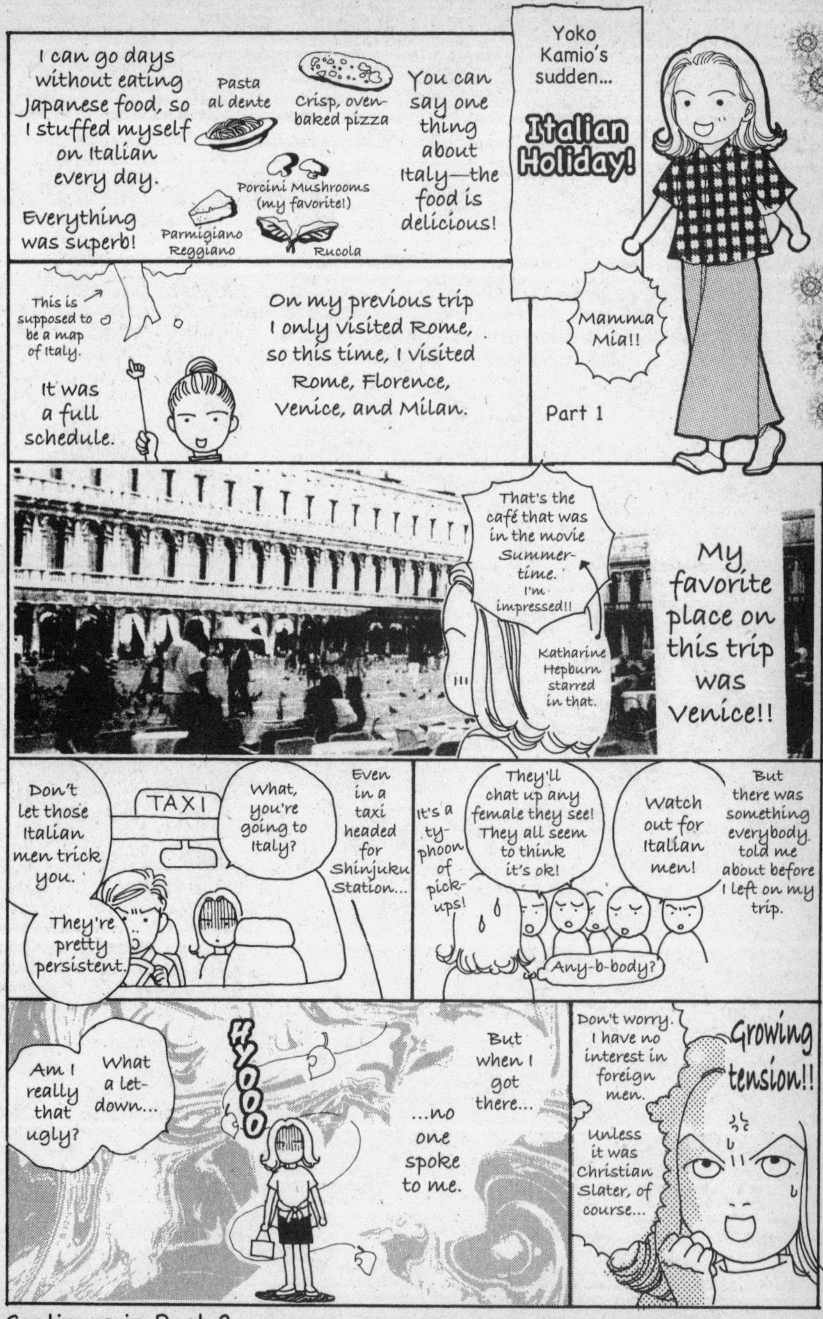
Yoko Kamio's sudden...
Italian Holiday!
Mamma Mia!!
Part 1
You can say one thing about Italy—the food is delicious!
Crisp, oven-baked pizza
Pasta al dente
Porcini Mushrooms (my favorite!)
Rucola
Parmigiano Reggiano
I can go days without eating Japanese food, so I stuffed myself on Italian every day.
Everything was superb!
On my previous trip I only visited Rome, so this time, I visited Rome, Florence, Venice, and Milan.
This is supposed to be a map of Italy.
It was a full schedule.
My favorite place on this trip was Venice!!
That's the café that was in the movie Summertime. I'm impressed!!
Katharine Hepburn starred in that.
But there was something everybody told me about before I left on my trip.
Watch out for Italian men!
They'll chat up any female they see! They all seem to think it's ok!
It's a typhoon of pick-ups!
Any-b-body?
Even in a taxi headed for Shinjuku Station...
What, you're going to Italy?
TAXI
Don't let those Italian men trick you.
They're pretty persistent.
Growing tension!!
Don't worry. I have no interest in foreign men.
Unless it was Christian Slater, of course...
But when I got there...
...no one spoke to me.
HYOOO
What a let-down...
Am I really that ugly?

Continues in Part 2.

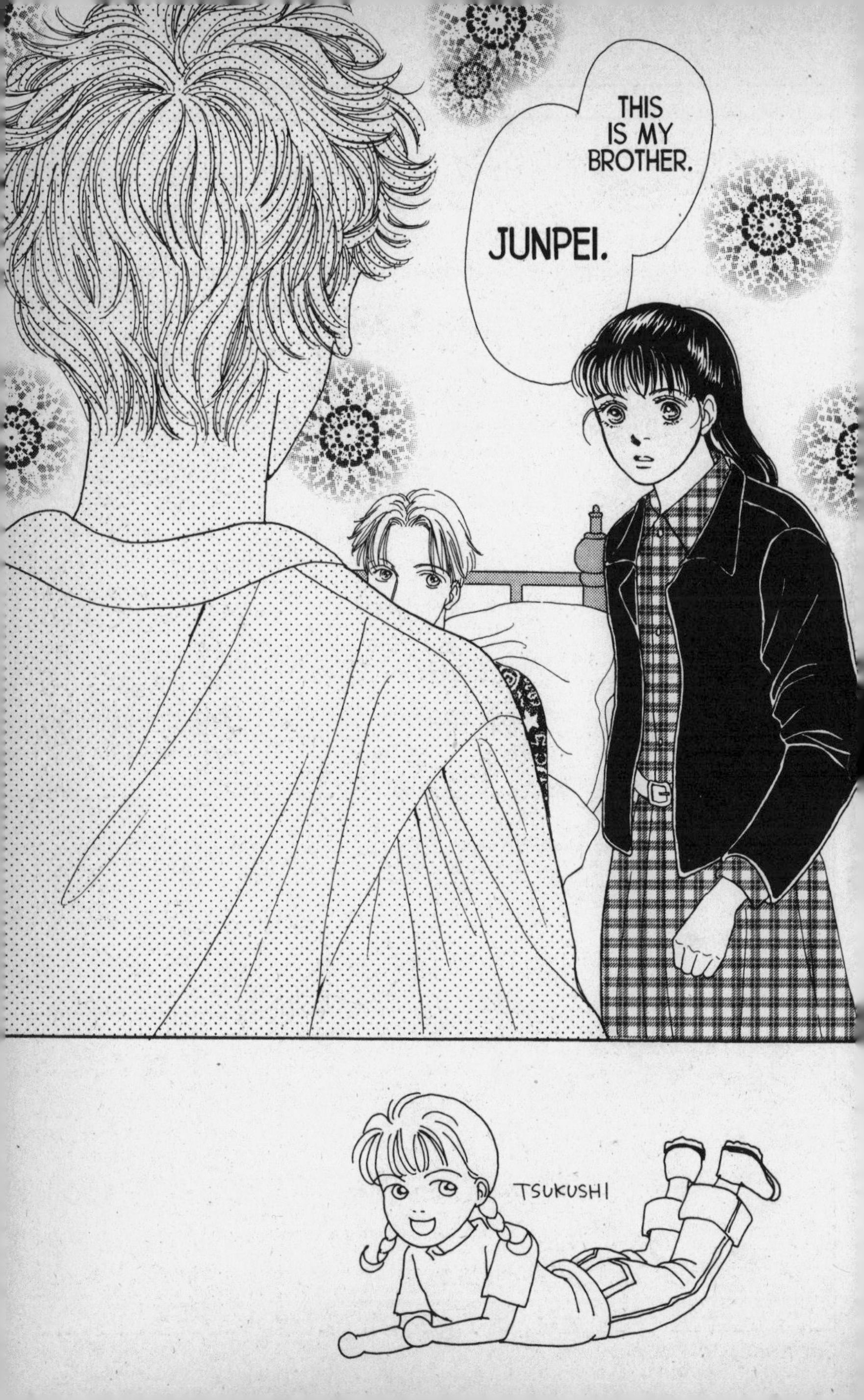
THIS IS MY BROTHER.
JUNPEI.
TSUKUSHI

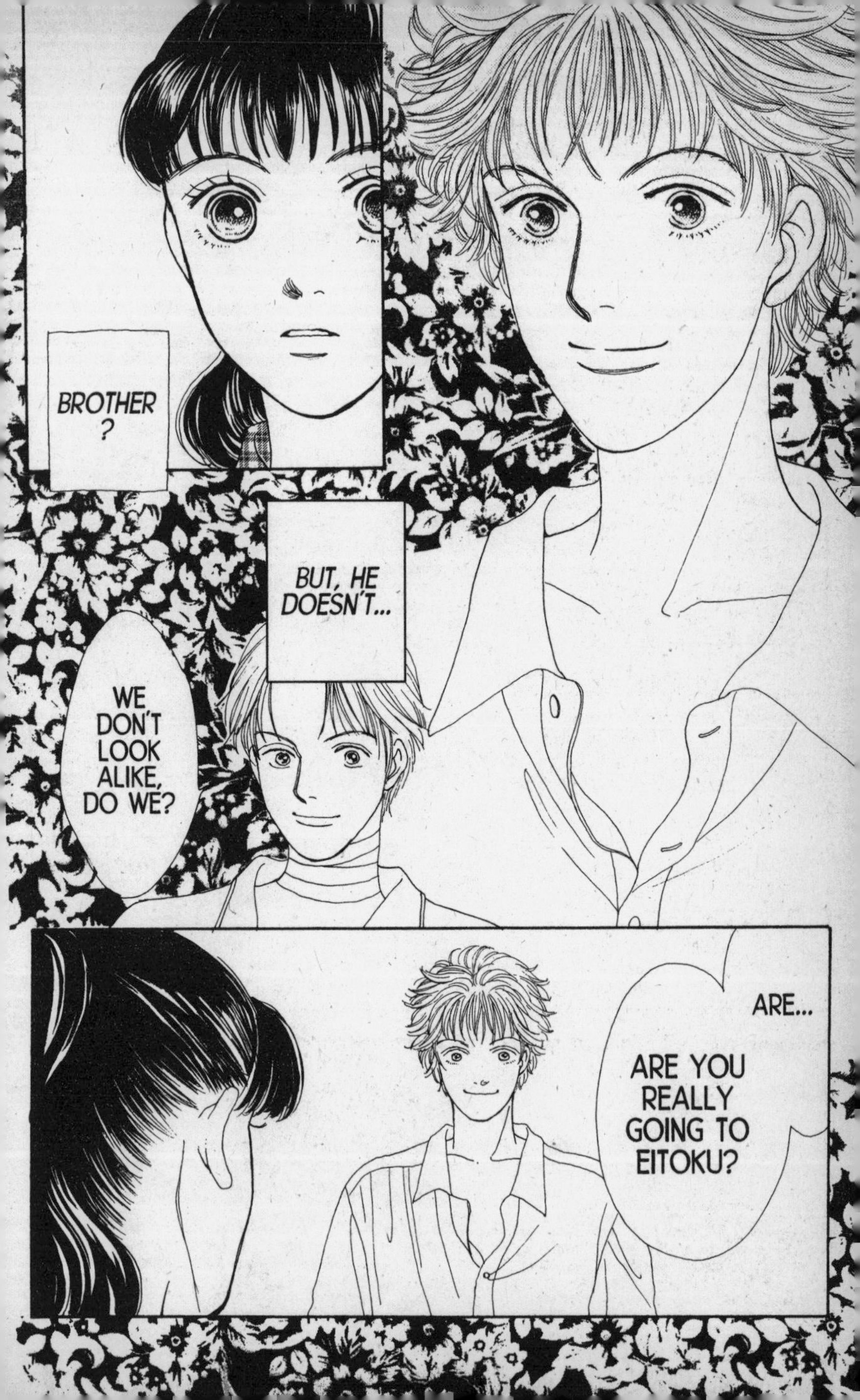
BROTHER ?
BUT, HE DOESN'T...
WE DON'T LOOK ALIKE, DO WE?
ARE...
ARE YOU REALLY GOING TO EITOKU?

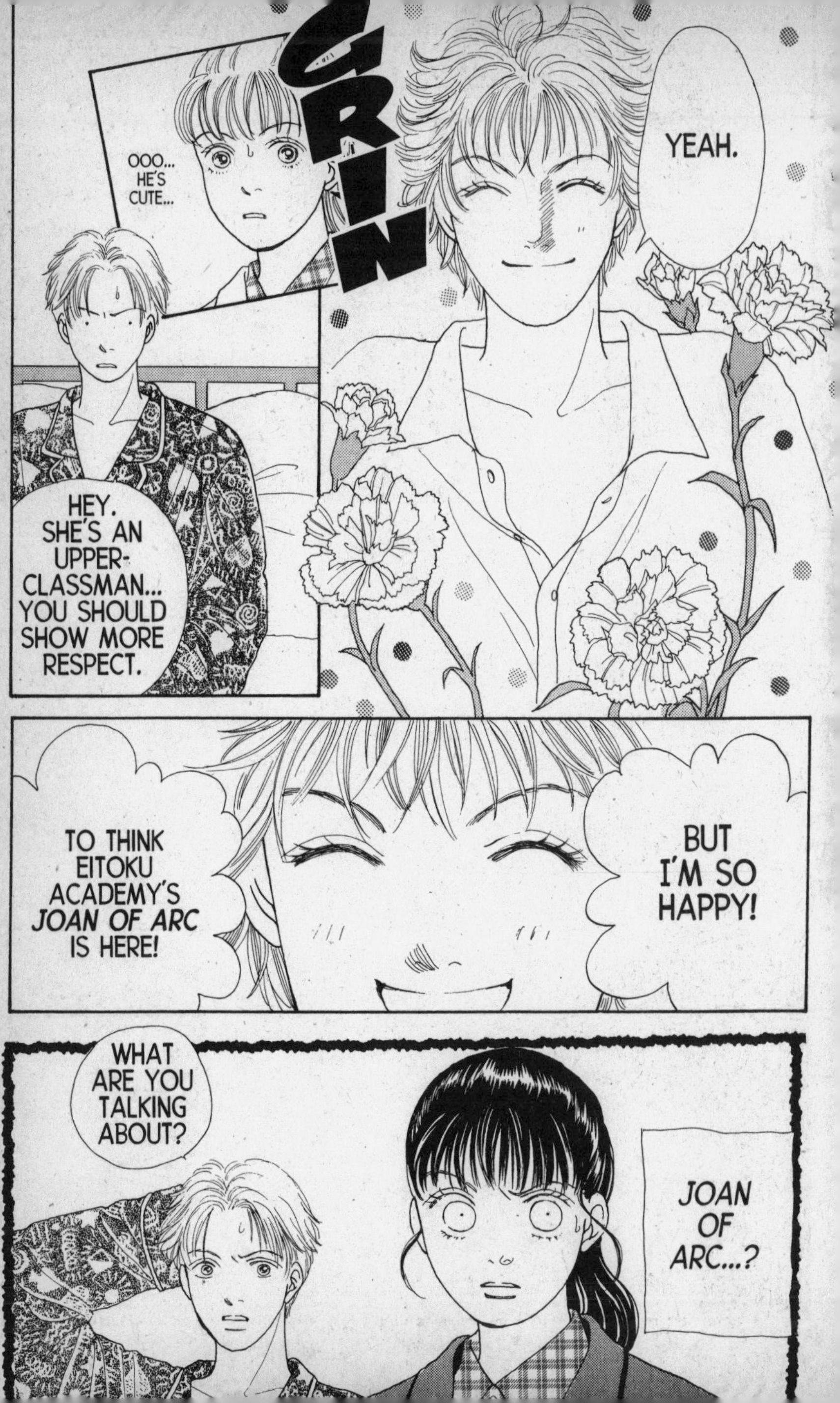
GRIN
YEAH.
OOO... HE'S CUTE...
HEY. SHE'S AN UPPER-CLASSMAN... YOU SHOULD SHOW MORE RESPECT.
BUT I'M SO HAPPY!
TO THINK EITOKU ACADEMY'S *JOAN OF ARC* IS HERE!
JOAN OF ARC...?
WHAT ARE YOU TALKING ABOUT?

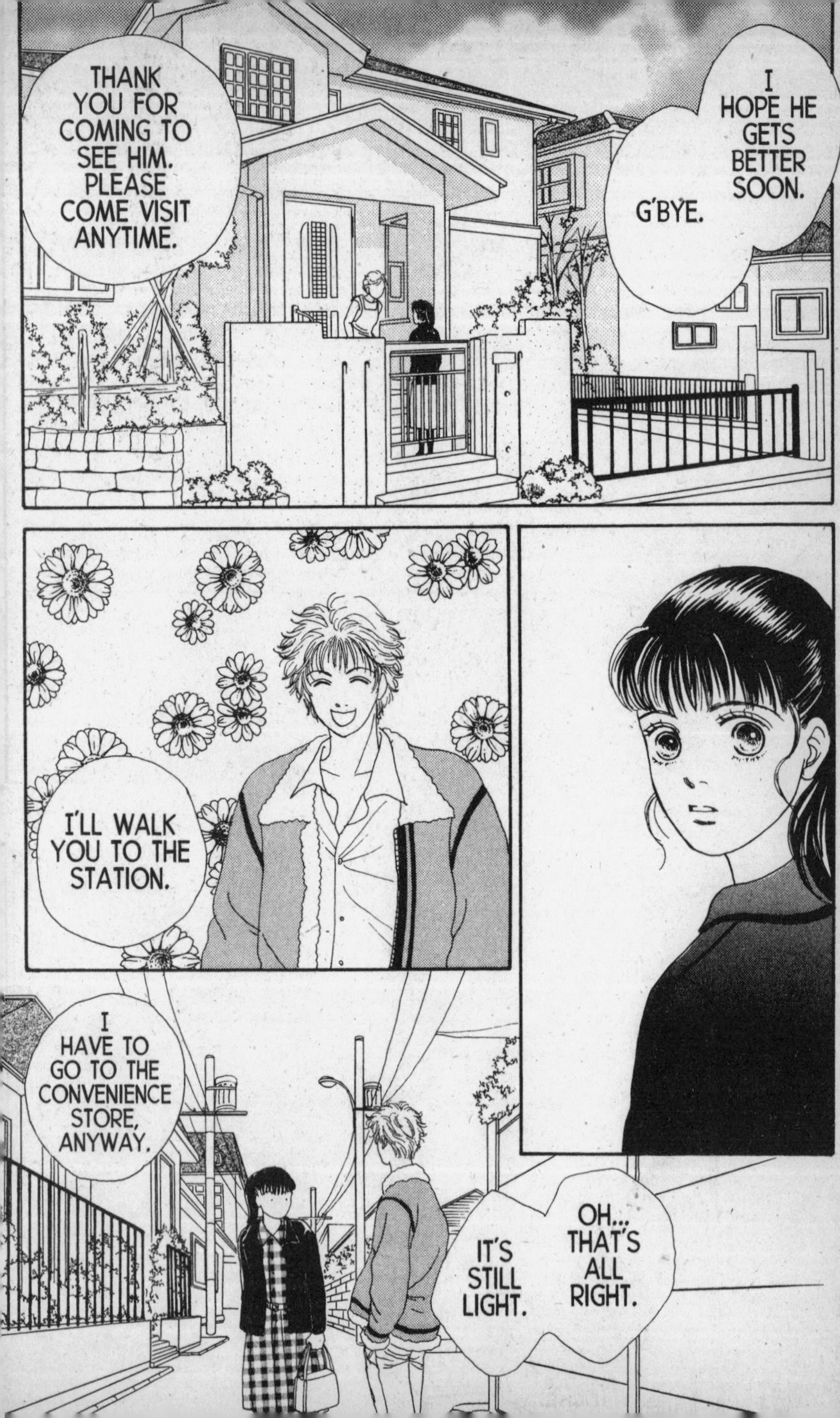
I HOPE HE GETS BETTER SOON.
G'BYE.
THANK YOU FOR COMING TO SEE HIM. PLEASE COME VISIT ANYTIME.
I'LL WALK YOU TO THE STATION.
OH... THAT'S ALL RIGHT.
IT'S STILL LIGHT.
I HAVE TO GO TO THE CONVENIENCE STORE, ANYWAY.

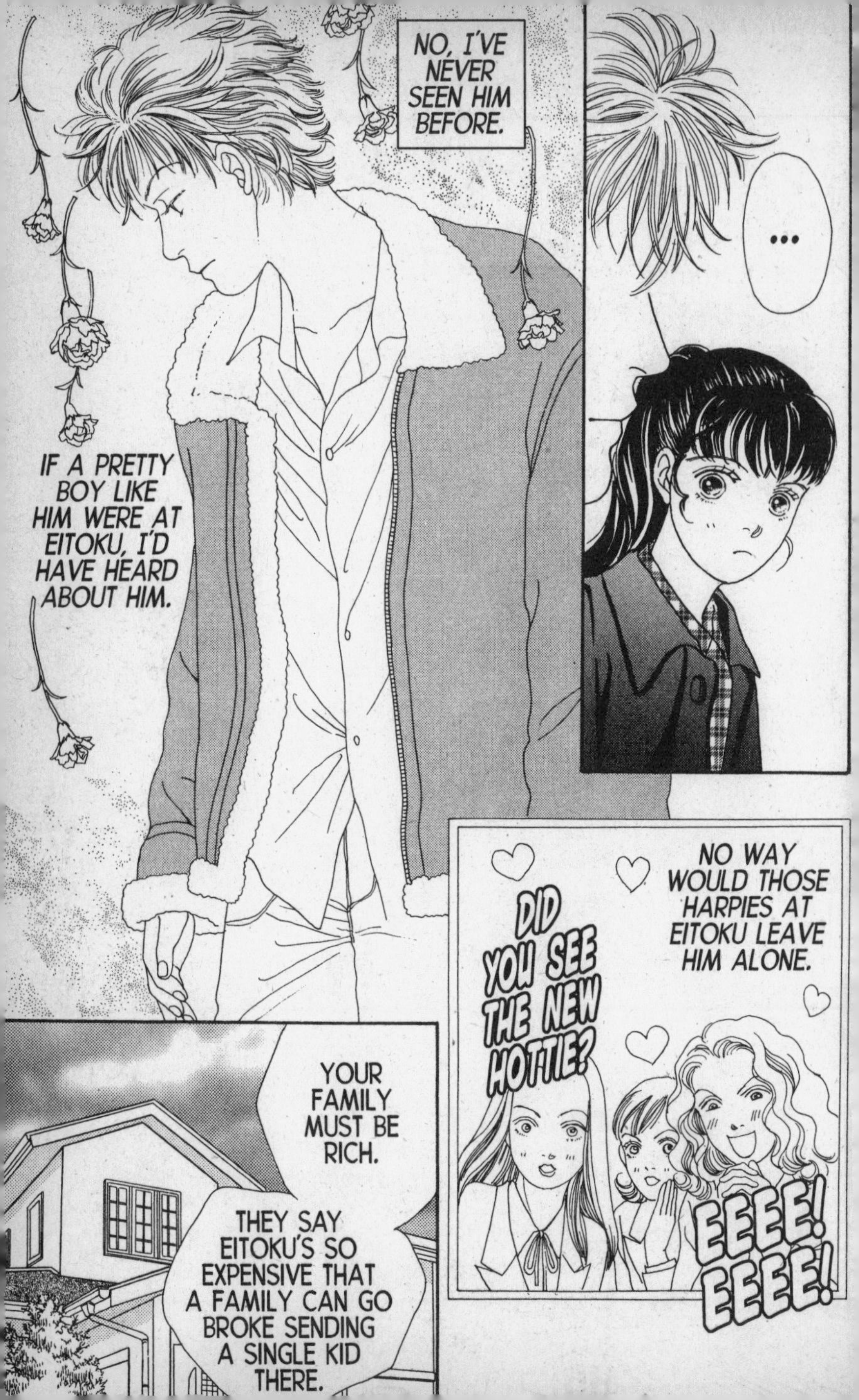
...
NO, I'VE NEVER SEEN HIM BEFORE.
IF A PRETTY BOY LIKE HIM WERE AT EITOKU, I'D HAVE HEARD ABOUT HIM.
NO WAY WOULD THOSE HARPIES AT EITOKU LEAVE HIM ALONE.
DID YOU SEE THE NEW HOTTIE?
EEEE! EEEE!
YOUR FAMILY MUST BE RICH.
THEY SAY EITOKU'S SO EXPENSIVE THAT A FAMILY CAN GO BROKE SENDING A SINGLE KID THERE.

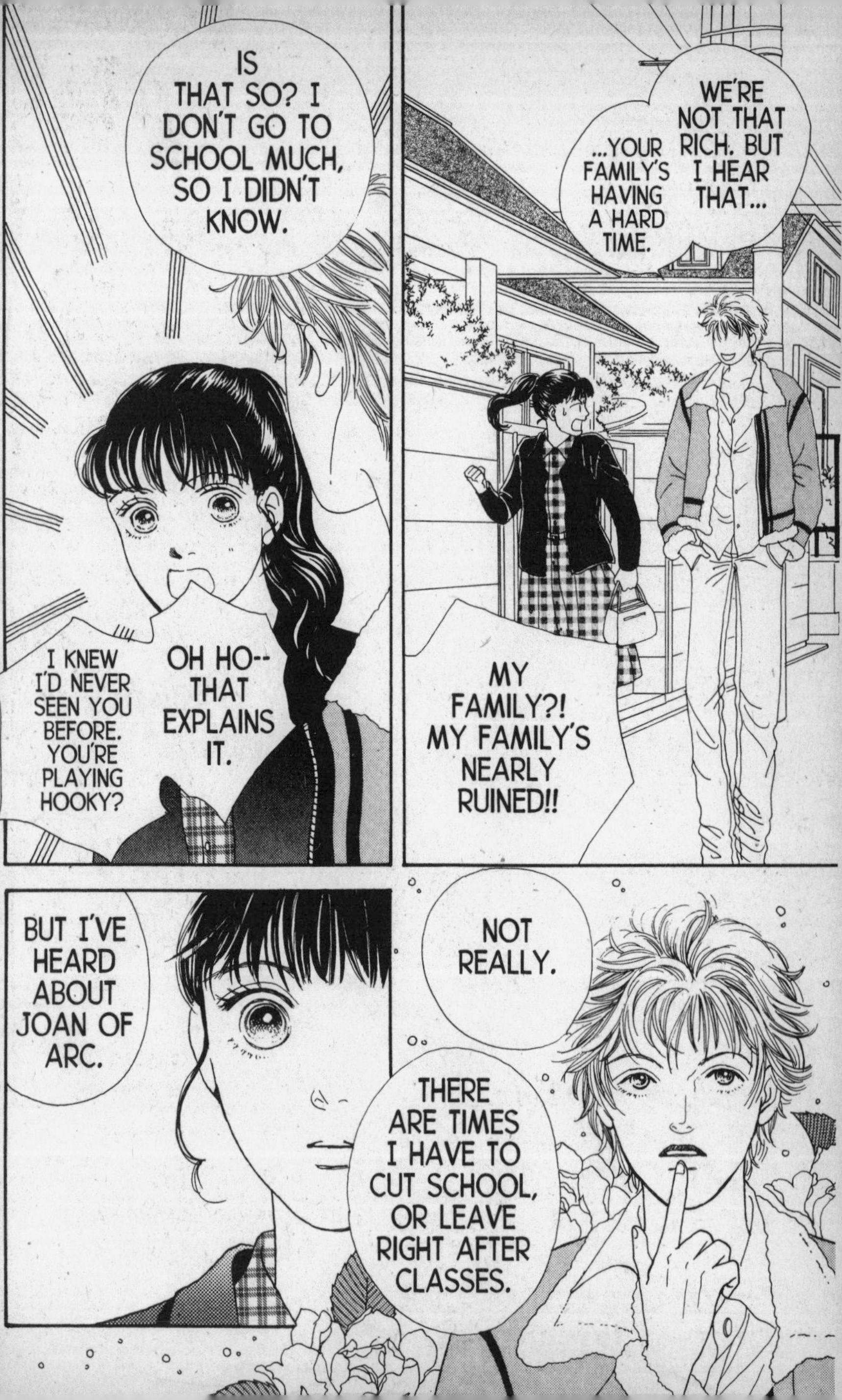
WE'RE NOT THAT RICH. BUT I HEAR THAT...
...YOUR FAMILY'S HAVING A HARD TIME.
MY FAMILY?! MY FAMILY'S NEARLY RUINED!!
IS THAT SO? I DON'T GO TO SCHOOL MUCH, SO I DIDN'T KNOW.
OH HO-- THAT EXPLAINS IT.
I KNEW I'D NEVER SEEN YOU BEFORE. YOU'RE PLAYING HOOKY?
NOT REALLY.
THERE ARE TIMES I HAVE TO CUT SCHOOL, OR LEAVE RIGHT AFTER CLASSES.
BUT I'VE HEARD ABOUT JOAN OF ARC.

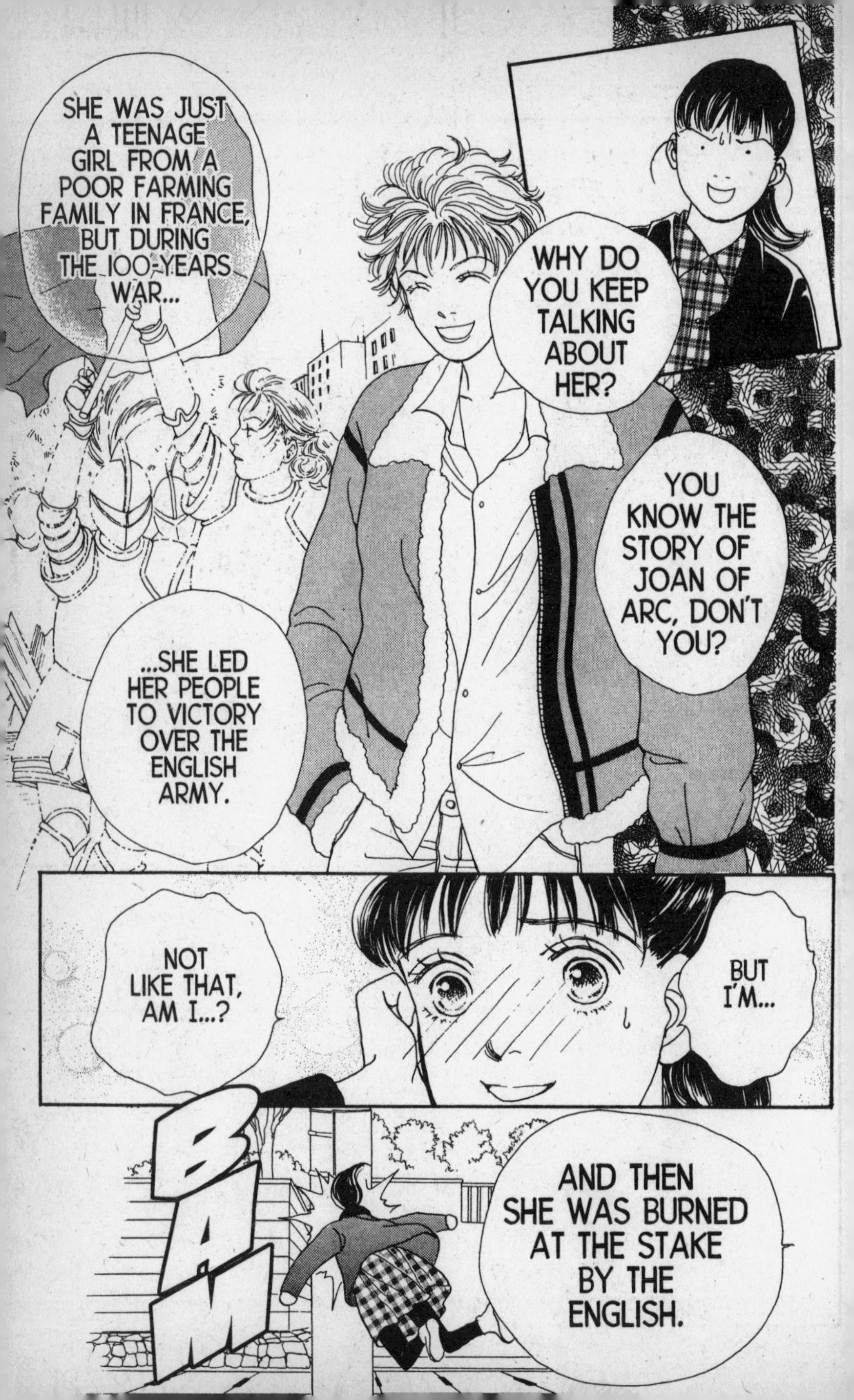
WHY DO YOU KEEP TALKING ABOUT HER?
YOU KNOW THE STORY OF JOAN OF ARC, DON'T YOU?
SHE WAS JUST A TEENAGE GIRL FROM A POOR FARMING FAMILY IN FRANCE, BUT DURING THE 100-YEARS WAR...
...SHE LED HER PEOPLE TO VICTORY OVER THE ENGLISH ARMY.
BUT I'M...
NOT LIKE THAT, AM I...?
AND THEN SHE WAS BURNED AT THE STAKE BY THE ENGLISH.
BAM

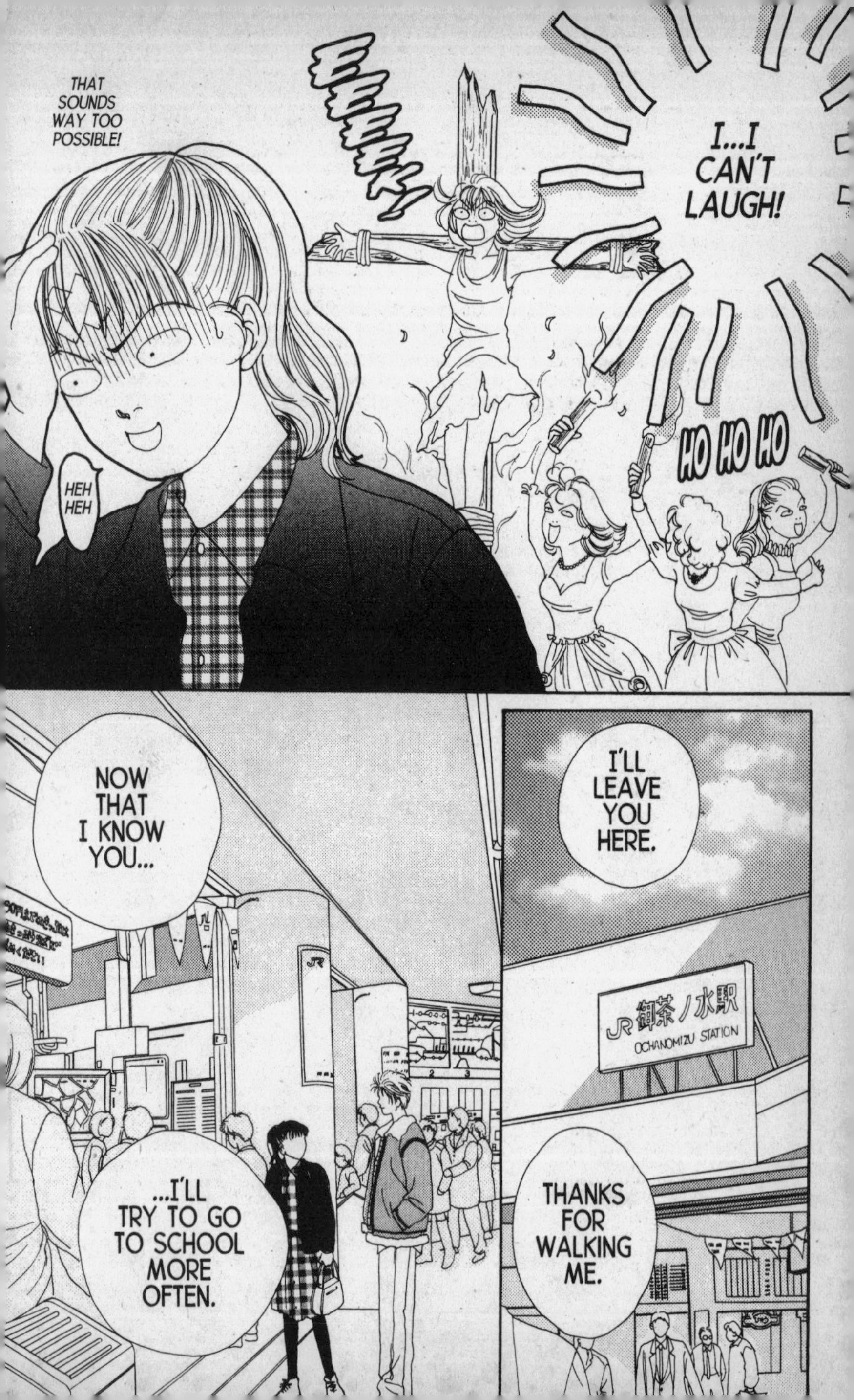
I...I CAN'T LAUGH!
EEEEK!
HO HO HO
THAT SOUNDS WAY TOO POSSIBLE!
HEH HEH
I'LL LEAVE YOU HERE.
JR 御茶ノ水駅
OCHANOMIZU STATION
THANKS FOR WALKING ME.
NOW THAT I KNOW YOU...
...I'LL TRY TO GO TO SCHOOL MORE OFTEN.

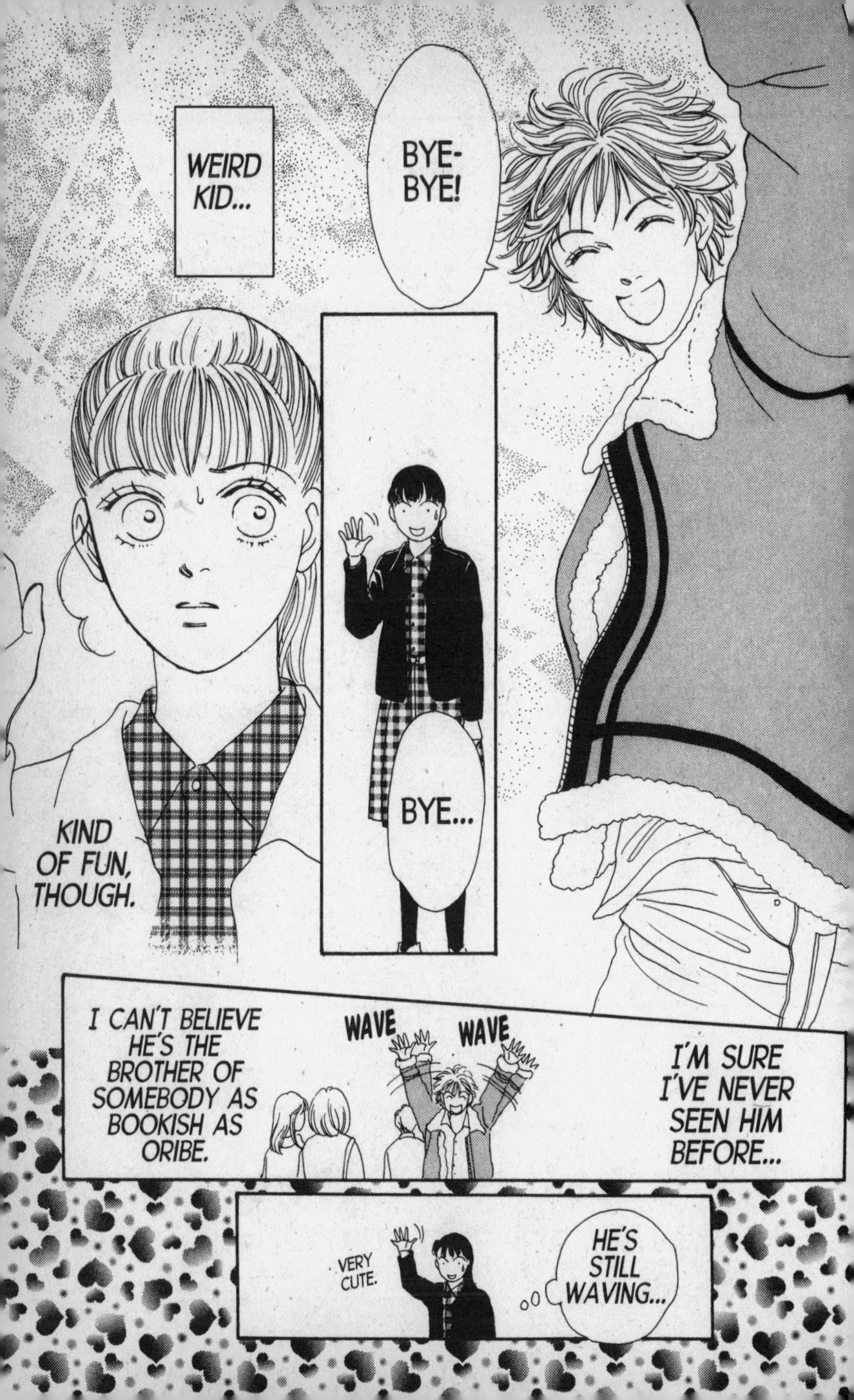
BYE-BYE!
WEIRD KID...
BYE...
KIND OF FUN, THOUGH.
I'M SURE I'VE NEVER SEEN HIM BEFORE...
WAVE
WAVE
I CAN'T BELIEVE HE'S THE BROTHER OF SOMEBODY AS BOOKISH AS ORIBE.
HE'S STILL WAVING...
VERY CUTE.

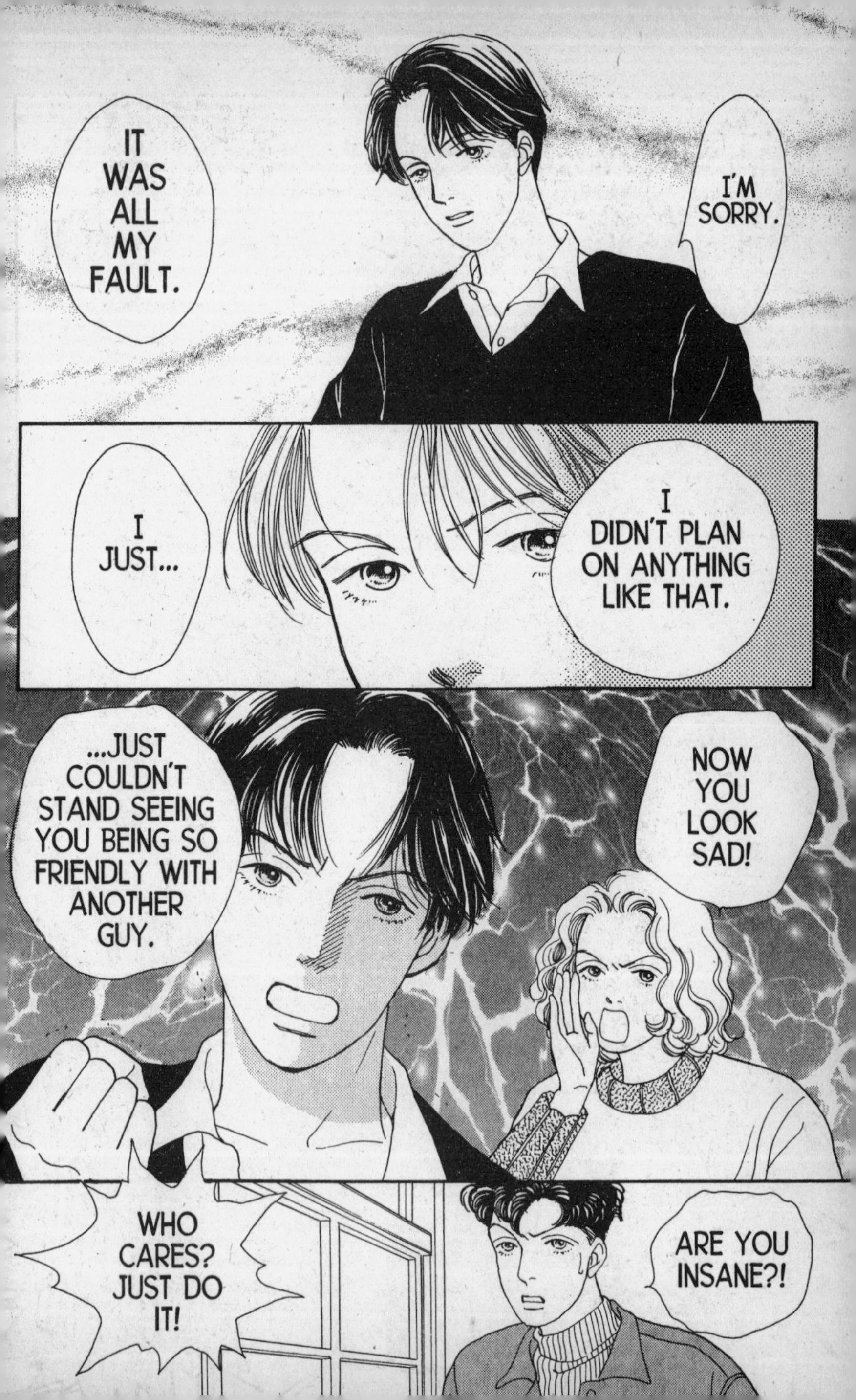
I'M SORRY.
IT WAS ALL MY FAULT.
I DIDN'T PLAN ON ANYTHING LIKE THAT.
I JUST...
NOW YOU LOOK SAD!
...JUST COULDN'T STAND SEEING YOU BEING SO FRIENDLY WITH ANOTHER GUY.
ARE YOU INSANE?!
WHO CARES? JUST DO IT!

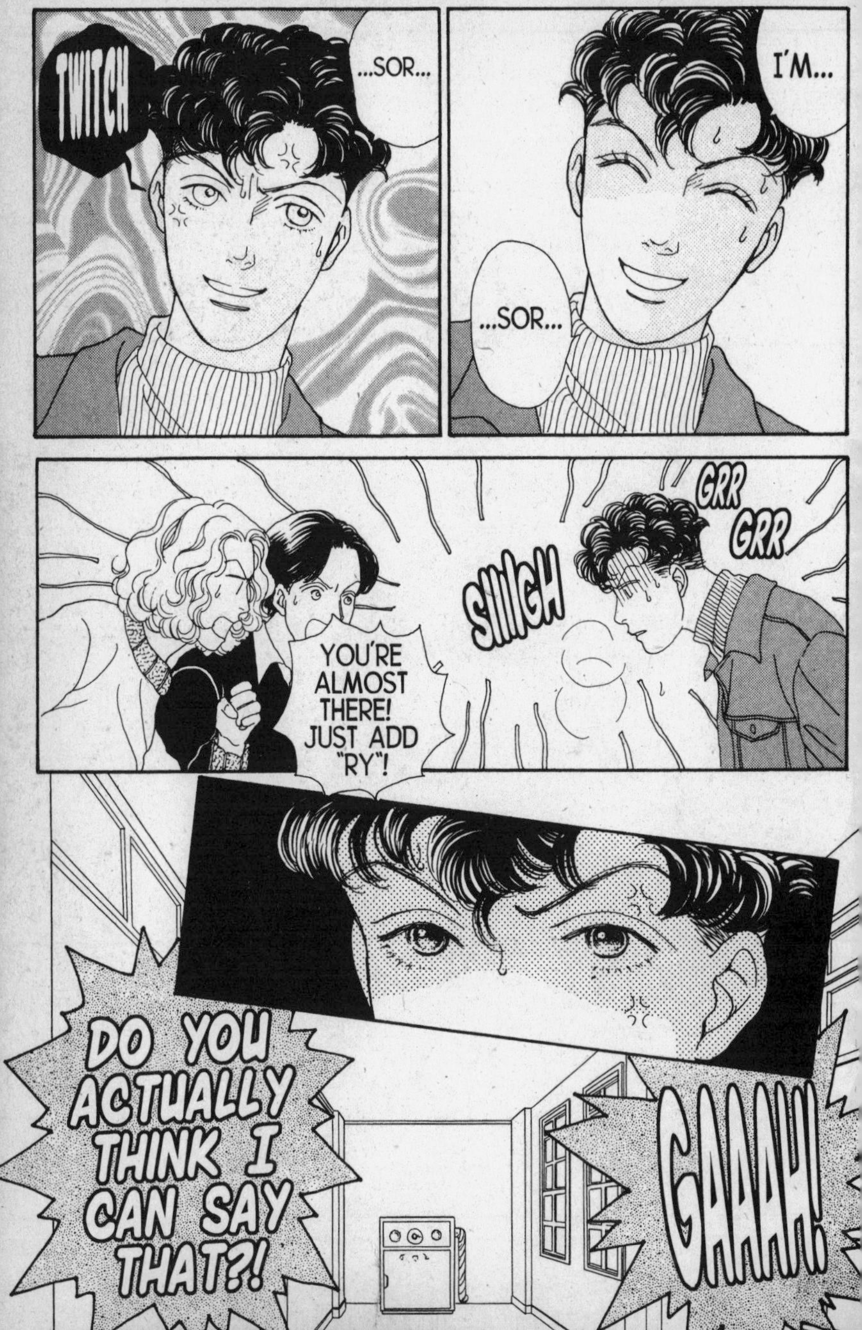
I'M...
...SOR...
TWITCH
...SOR...
GRR
GRR
SIIIGH
YOU'RE ALMOST THERE! JUST ADD "RY"!
GAAAH!
DO YOU ACTUALLY THINK I CAN SAY THAT?!

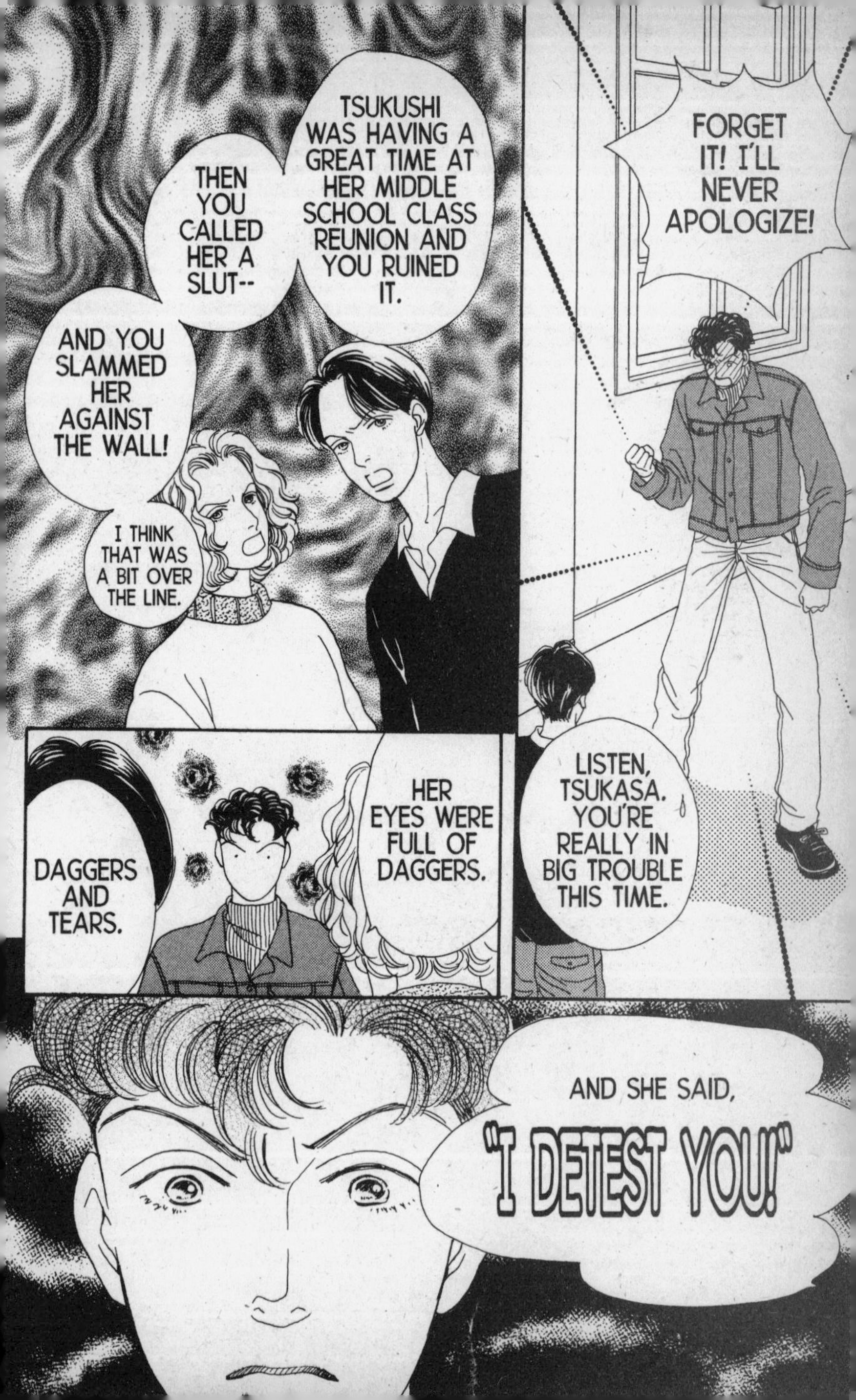
FORGET IT! I'LL NEVER APOLOGIZE!
LISTEN, TSUKASA. YOU'RE REALLY IN BIG TROUBLE THIS TIME.
TSUKUSHI WAS HAVING A GREAT TIME AT HER MIDDLE SCHOOL CLASS REUNION AND YOU RUINED IT.
THEN YOU CALLED HER A SLUT--
AND YOU SLAMMED HER AGAINST THE WALL!
I THINK THAT WAS A BIT OVER THE LINE.
HER EYES WERE FULL OF DAGGERS.
DAGGERS AND TEARS.
AND SHE SAID,
"I DETEST YOU!"

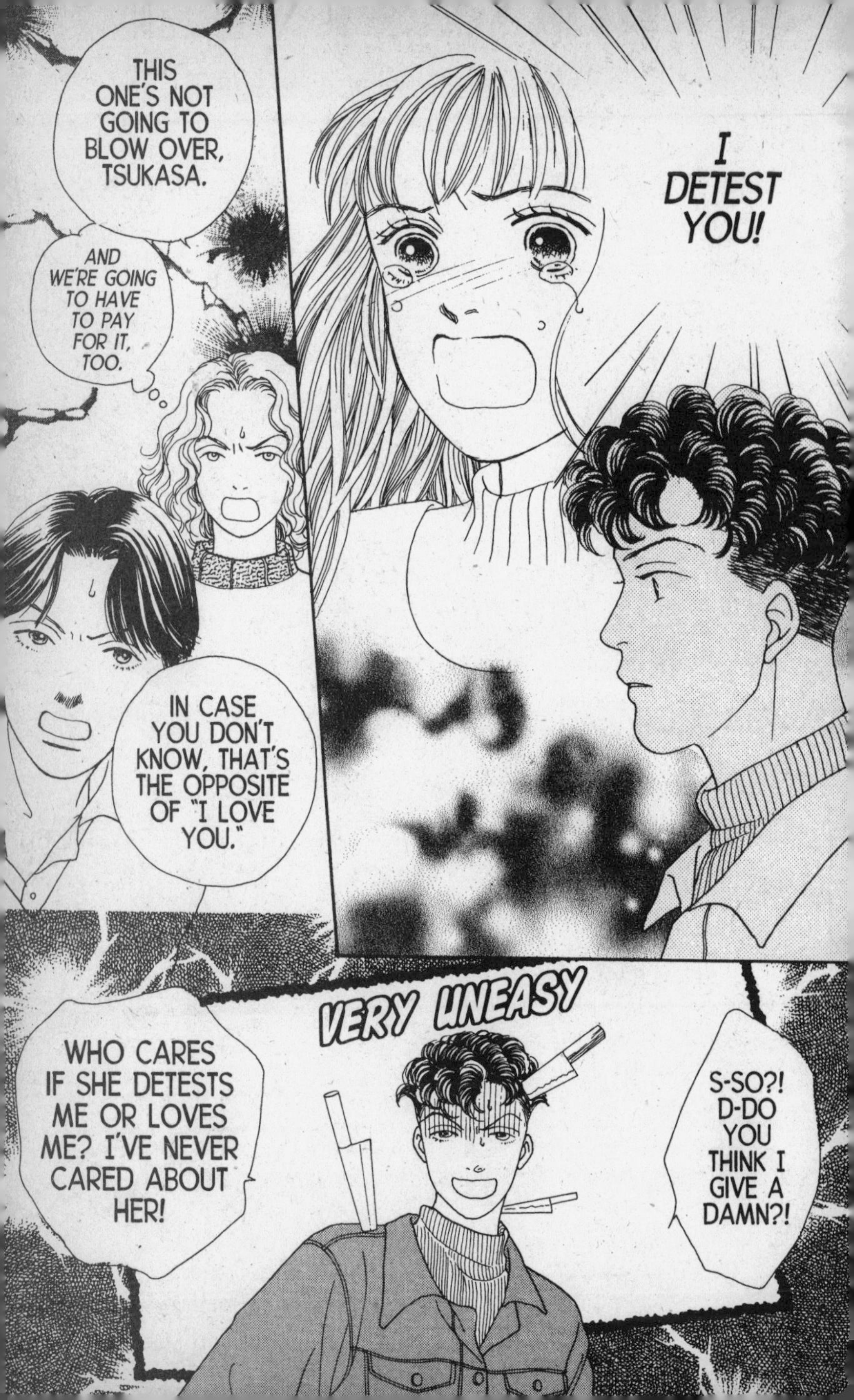
I DETEST YOU!
THIS ONE'S NOT GOING TO BLOW OVER, TSUKASA.
AND WE'RE GOING TO HAVE TO PAY FOR IT, TOO.
IN CASE YOU DON'T KNOW, THAT'S THE OPPOSITE OF "I LOVE YOU."
VERY UNEASY
S-SO?! D-DO YOU THINK I GIVE A DAMN?!
WHO CARES IF SHE DETESTS ME OR LOVES ME? I'VE NEVER CARED ABOUT HER!

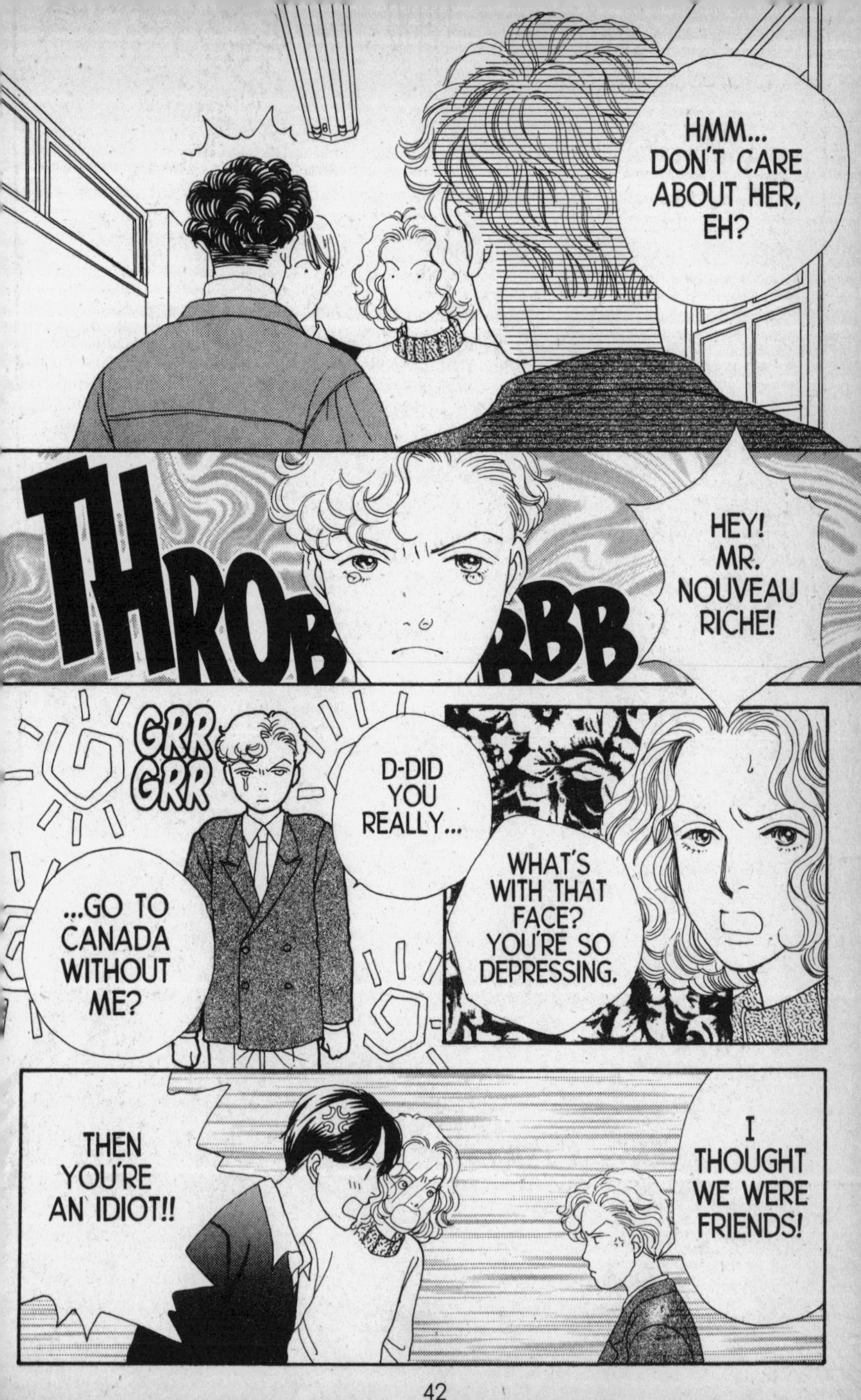
HMM... DON'T CARE ABOUT HER, EH?
HEY! MR. NOUVEAU RICHE!
THROBBBB
WHAT'S WITH THAT FACE? YOU'RE SO DEPRESSING.
D-DID YOU REALLY...
GRR GRR
...GO TO CANADA WITHOUT ME?
I THOUGHT WE WERE FRIENDS!
THEN YOU'RE AN IDIOT!!

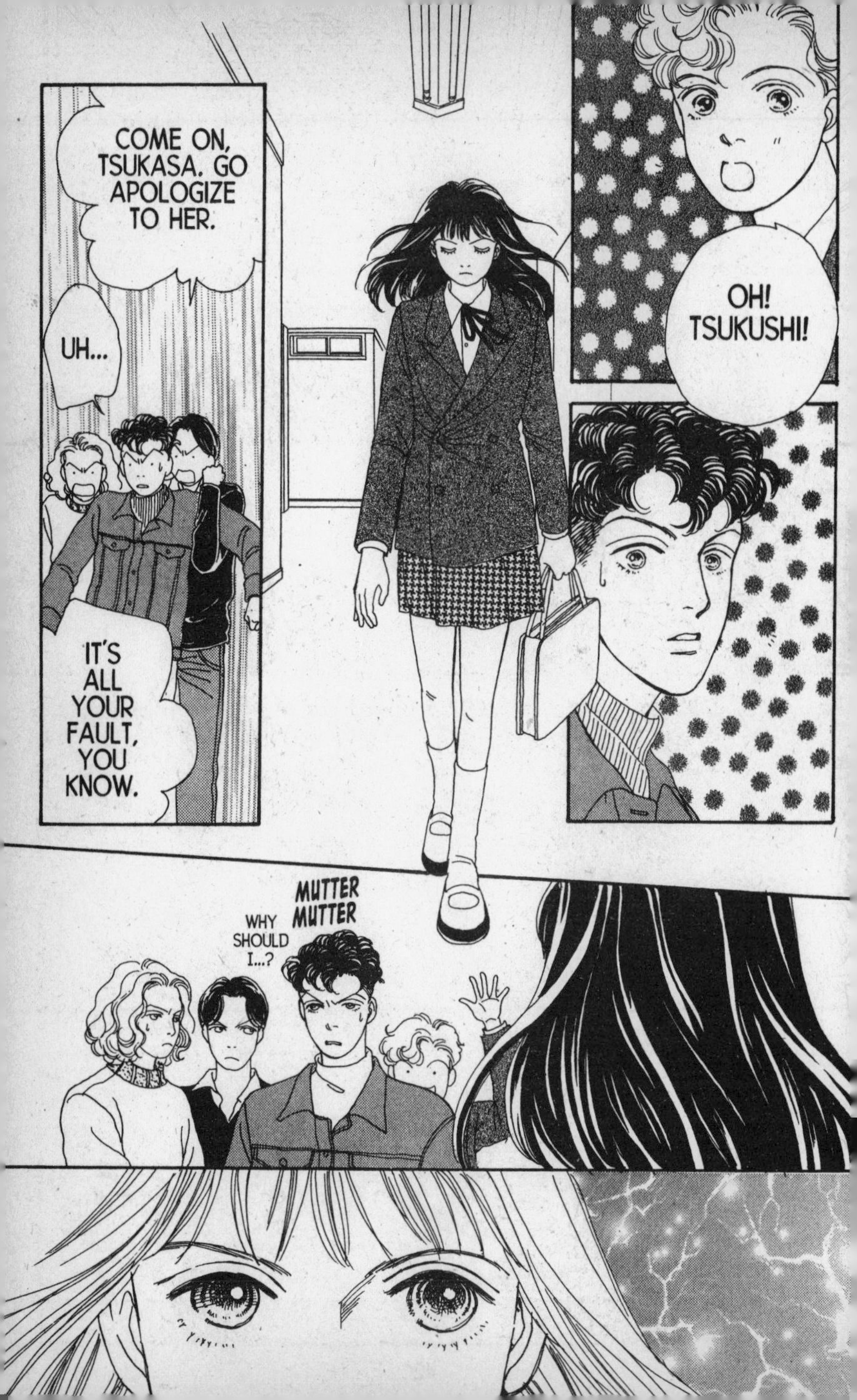
OH! TSUKUSHI!
COME ON, TSUKASA. GO APOLOGIZE TO HER.
UH...
IT'S ALL YOUR FAULT, YOU KNOW.
MUTTER MUTTER
WHY SHOULD I...?

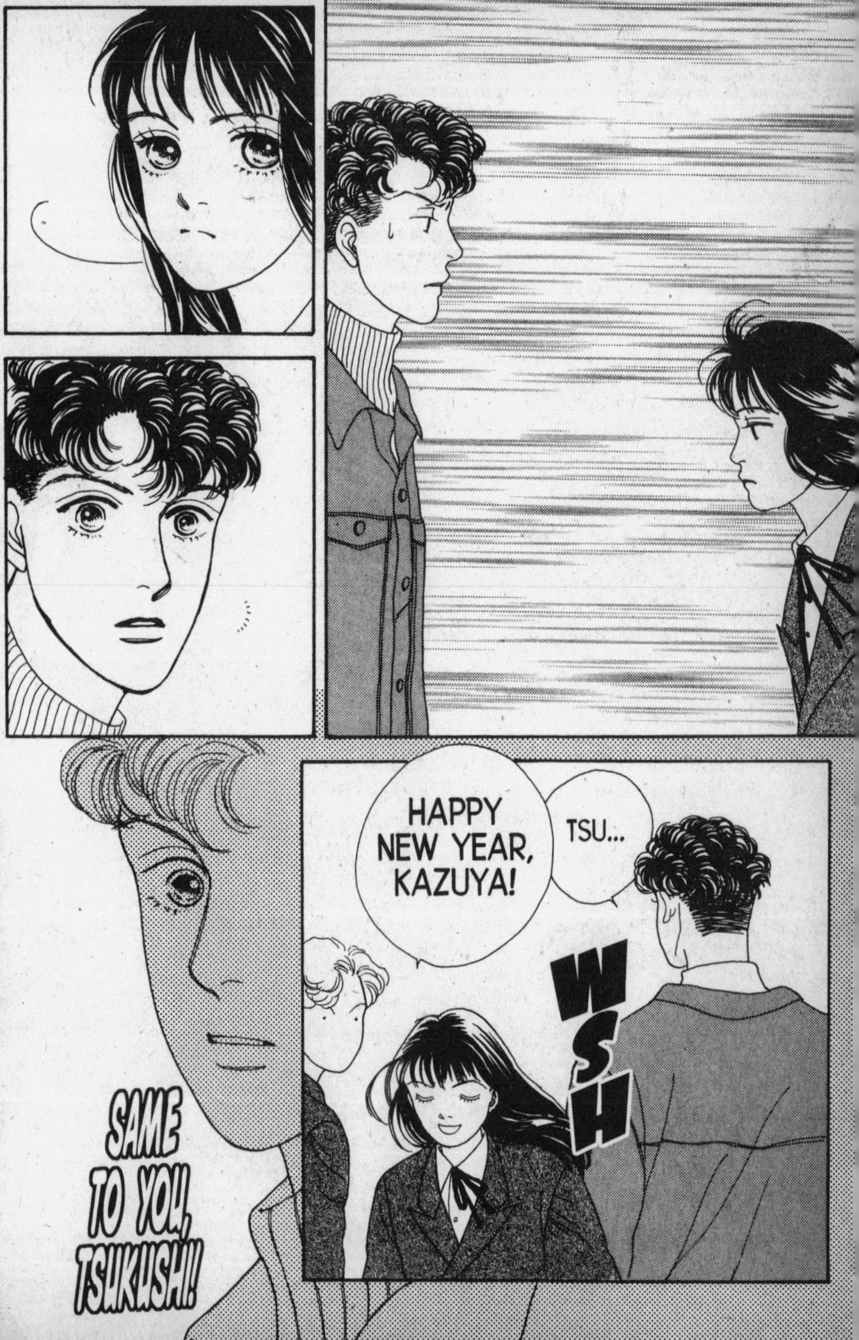
TSU...
HAPPY NEW YEAR, KAZUYA!
WSH
SAME TO YOU, TSUKUSHI!!

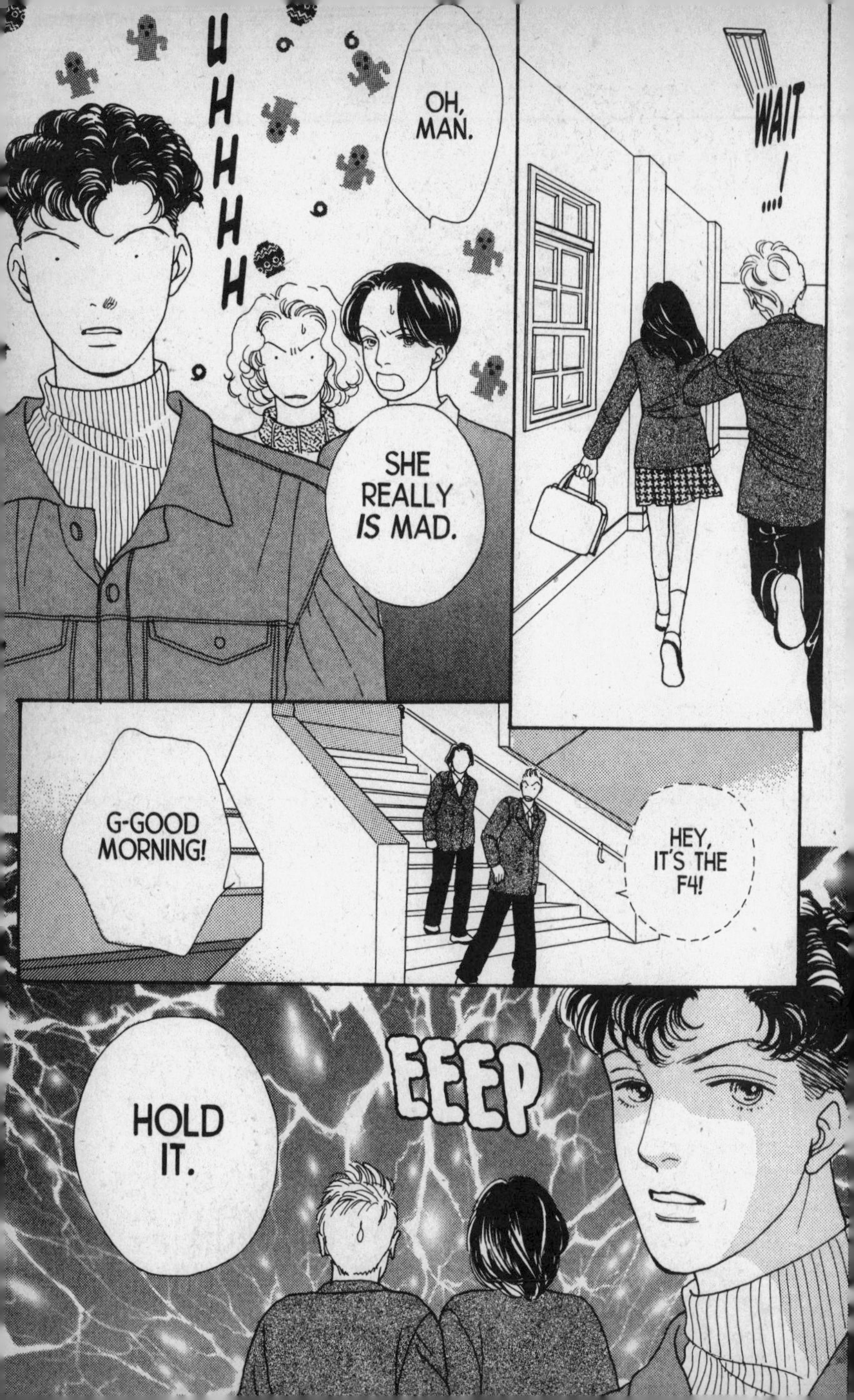
WAIT ...!
OH, MAN.
UHHHH
SHE REALLY *IS* MAD.
HEY, IT'S THE F4!
G-GOOD MORNING!
EEEP
HOLD IT.

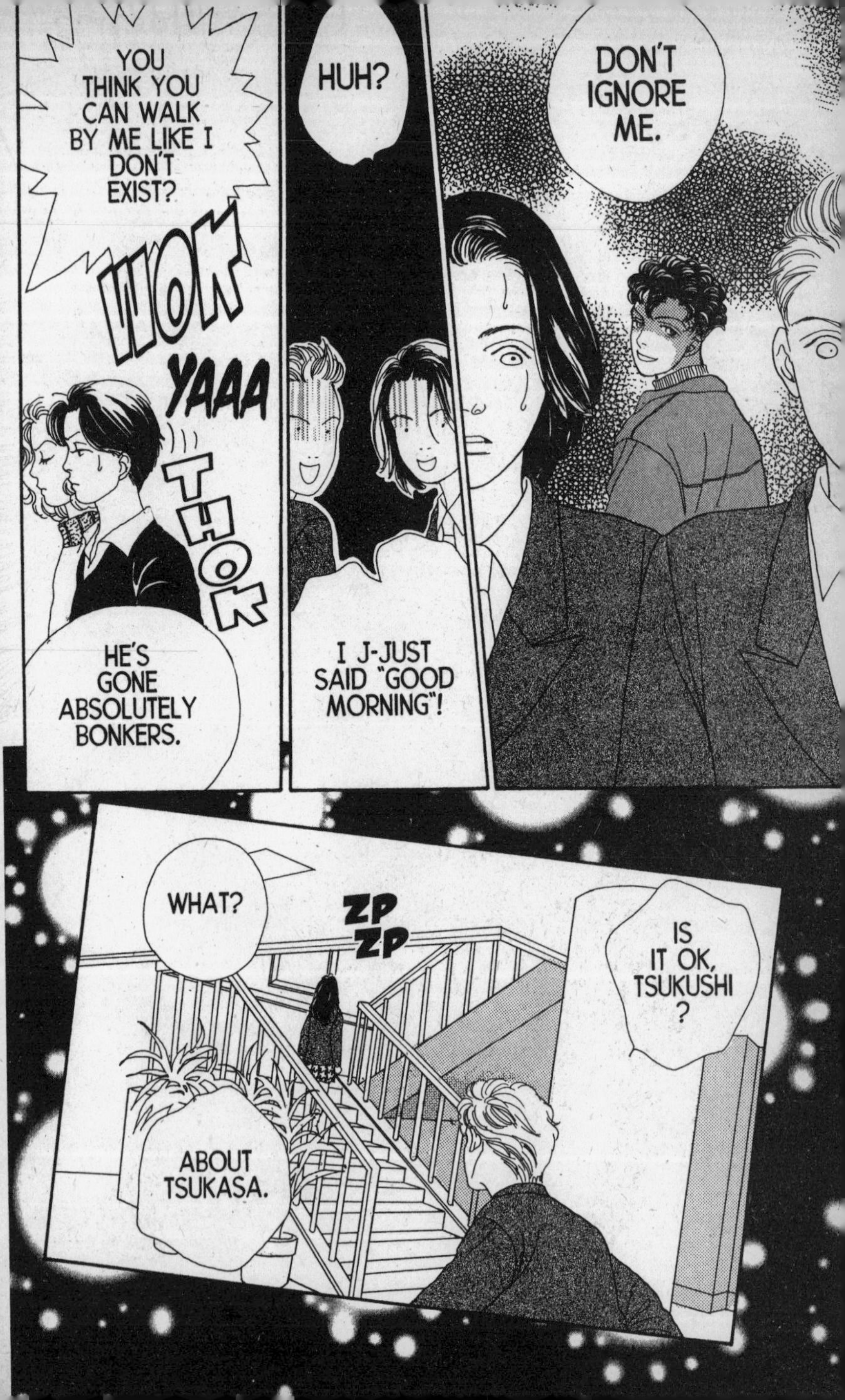
DON'T IGNORE ME.
HUH?
I J-JUST SAID "GOOD MORNING"!
YOU THINK YOU CAN WALK BY ME LIKE I DON'T EXIST?
WHOK
YAAA
THOK
HE'S GONE ABSOLUTELY BONKERS.
IS IT OK, TSUKUSHI?
WHAT?
ZP ZP
ABOUT TSUKASA.

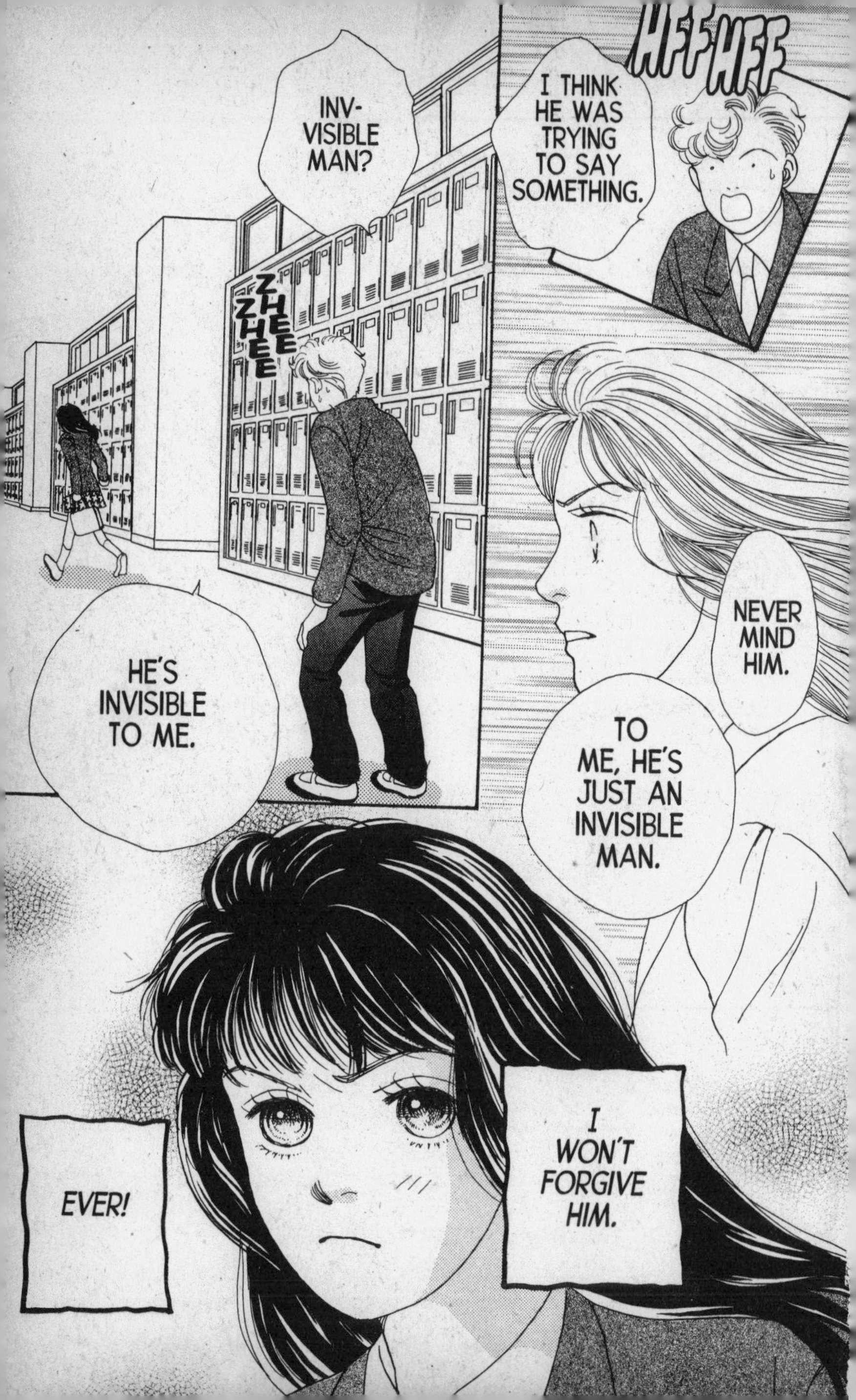
HFF HFF
I THINK HE WAS TRYING TO SAY SOMETHING.
NEVER MIND HIM.
TO ME, HE'S JUST AN INVISIBLE MAN.
INV-VISIBLE MAN?
ZHEE ZHEEE
HE'S INVISIBLE TO ME.
I WON'T FORGIVE HIM.
EVER!

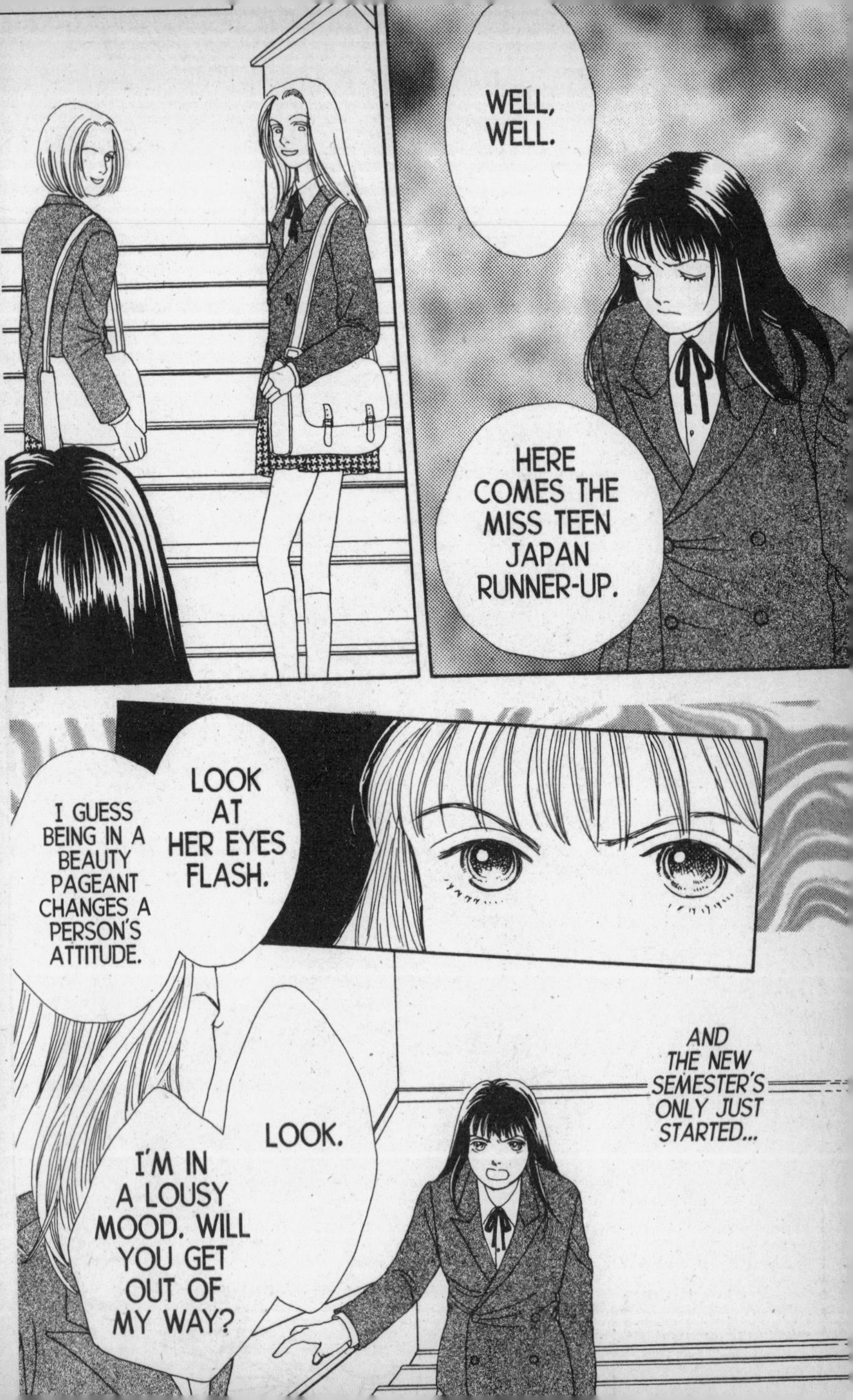
WELL, WELL.
HERE COMES THE MISS TEEN JAPAN RUNNER-UP.
LOOK AT HER EYES FLASH.
I GUESS BEING IN A BEAUTY PAGEANT CHANGES A PERSON'S ATTITUDE.
AND THE NEW SEMESTER'S ONLY JUST STARTED...
LOOK.
I'M IN A LOUSY MOOD. WILL YOU GET OUT OF MY WAY?

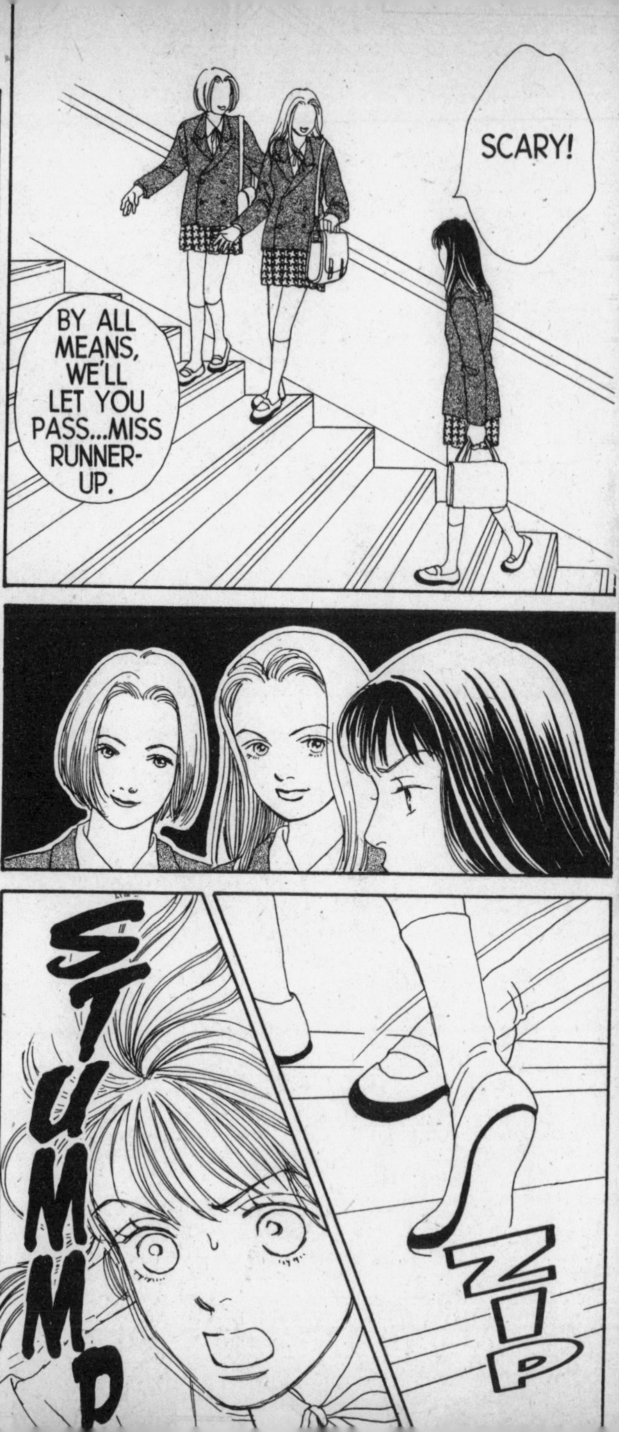
SCARY!
BY ALL MEANS, WE'LL LET YOU PASS...MISS RUNNER-UP.
ZIP
STUMMP

Animation

They're animating this next? Should they really be doing that?

To my teacher, Takeuchi... Thank you for everything!

First a CD book, next a novel, then a movie...

I felt so honored by all that...and now they're animating this series! I've gotten so many letters from you, asking when the series would be turned into an anime...

That'll never happen.

Well, that's what I thought. But it happened! I owe it all to your support. It'll be a little different from the actual "Boys over Flowers" manga series, but I hope you like it!!

I look forward to it every week, even though it's on so early...

I wake up to an alarm.

JIRI JIRI JIRI JIRI

VSH

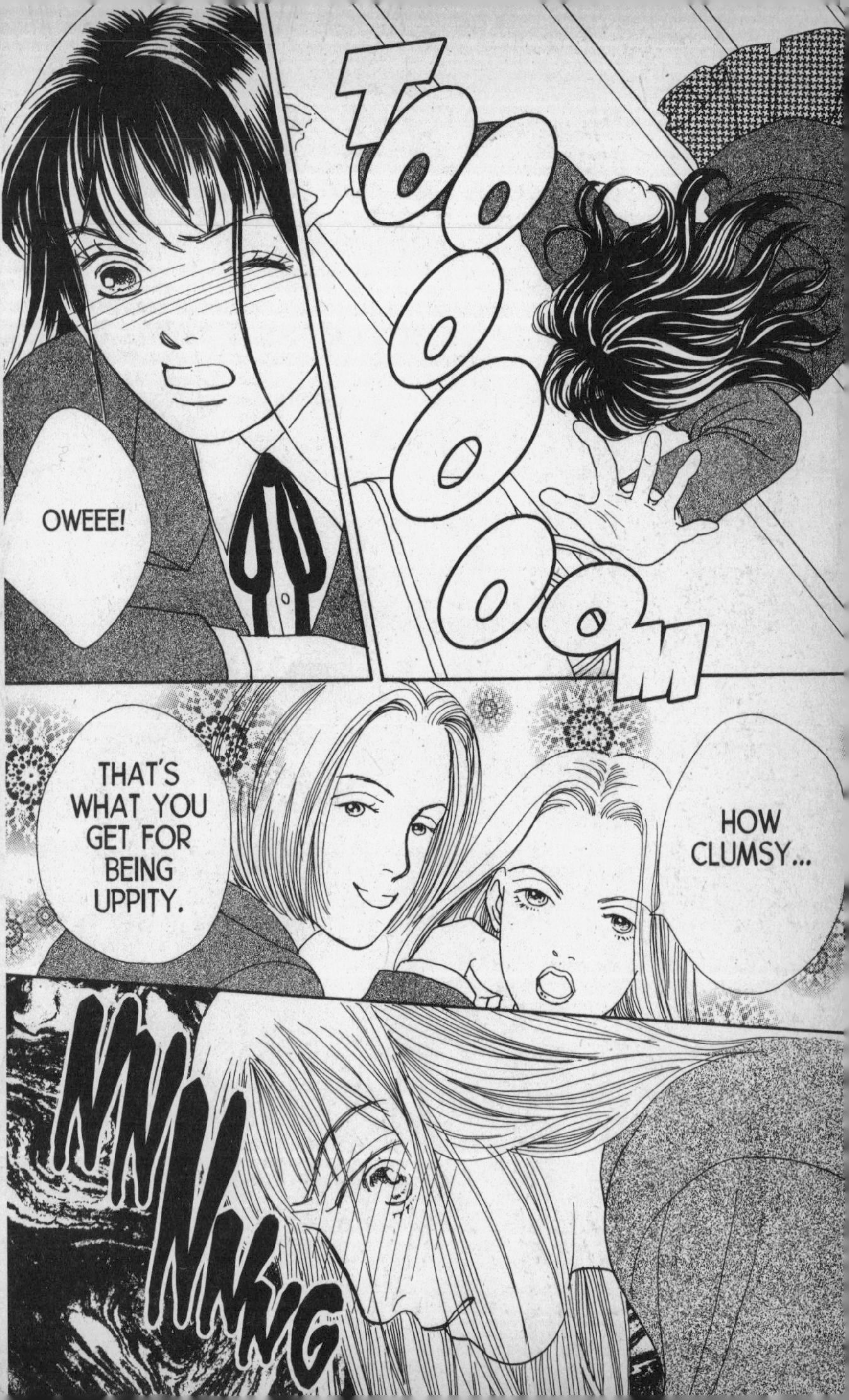
TOOOOOOOM
OWEEE!
HOW CLUMSY...
THAT'S WHAT YOU GET FOR BEING UPPITY.
MNNNNG

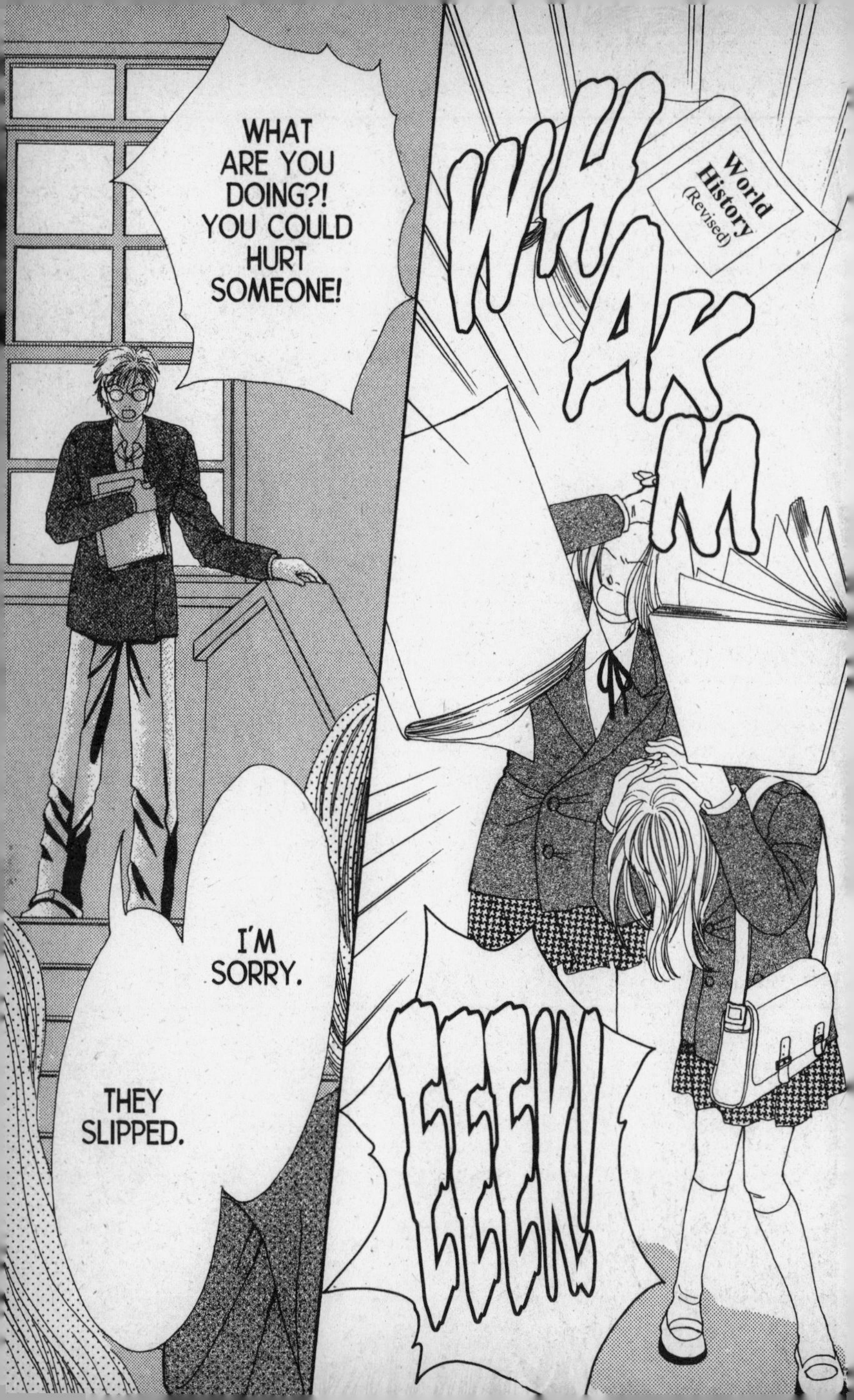
WHAM
World History (Revised)
EEEK!
WHAT ARE YOU DOING?! YOU COULD HURT SOMEONE!
I'M SORRY.
THEY SLIPPED.

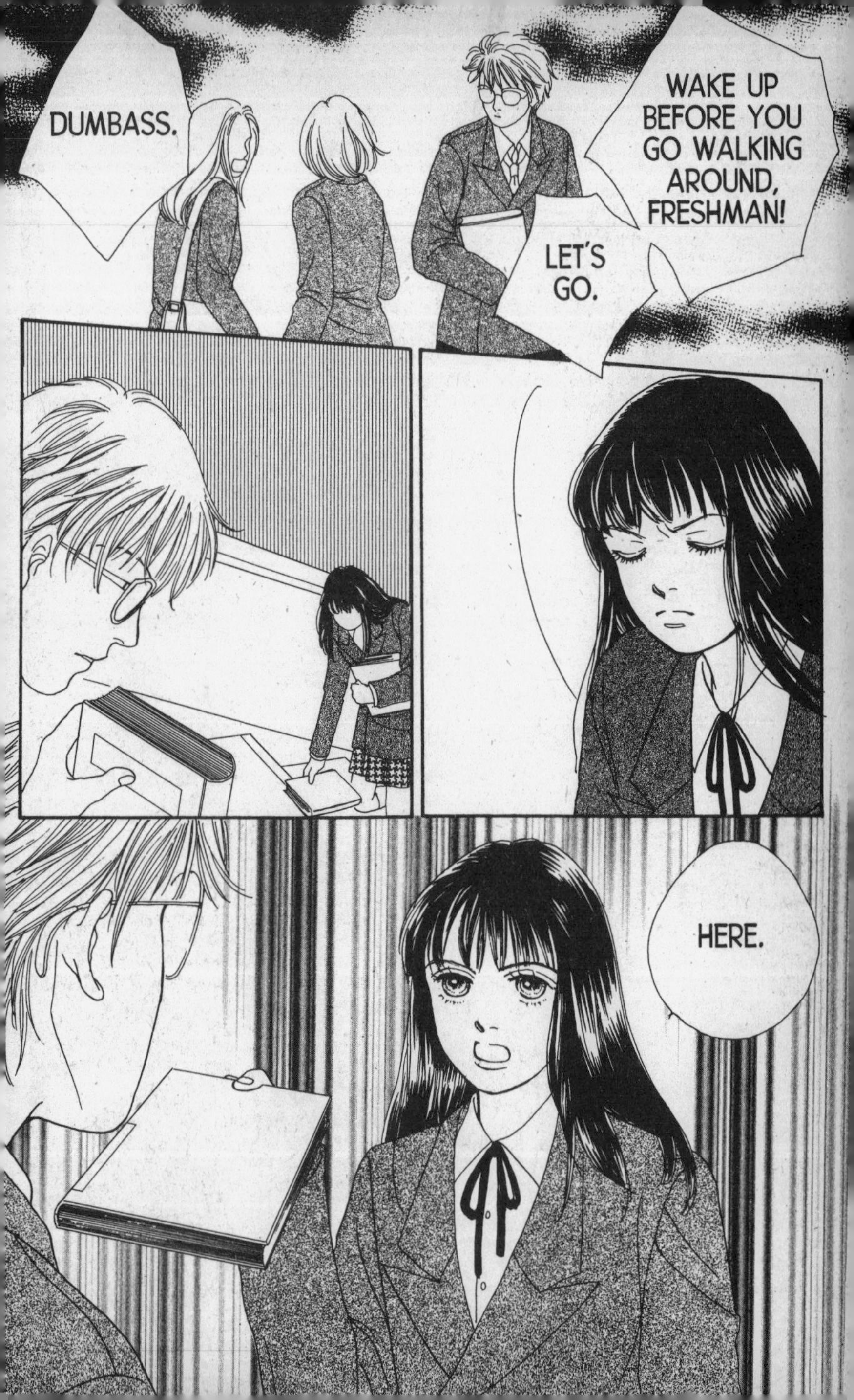
WAKE UP BEFORE YOU GO WALKING AROUND, FRESHMAN!
LET'S GO.
DUMBASS.
HERE.

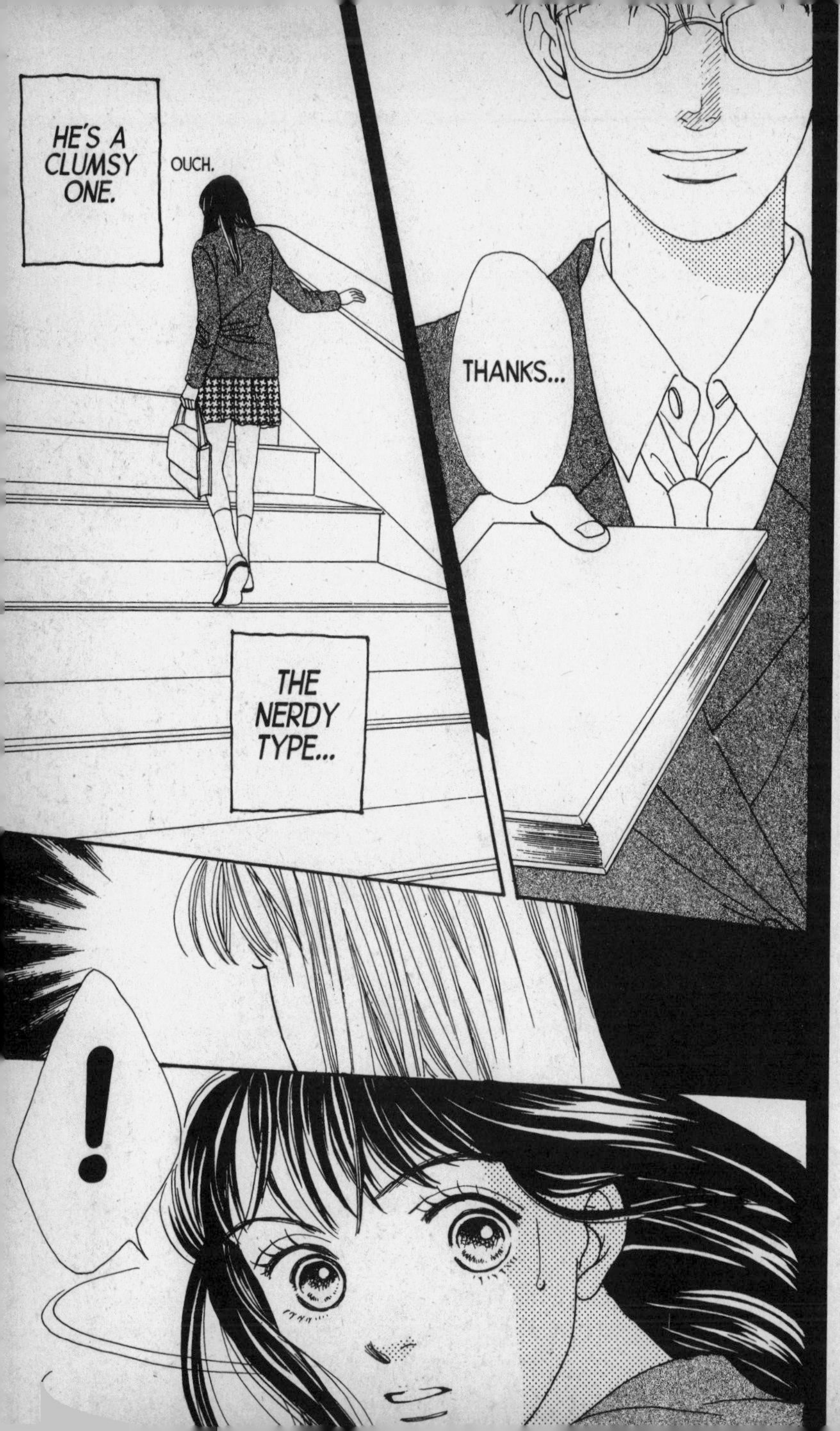
THANKS...
OUCH.
HE'S A CLUMSY ONE.
THE NERDY TYPE...
!

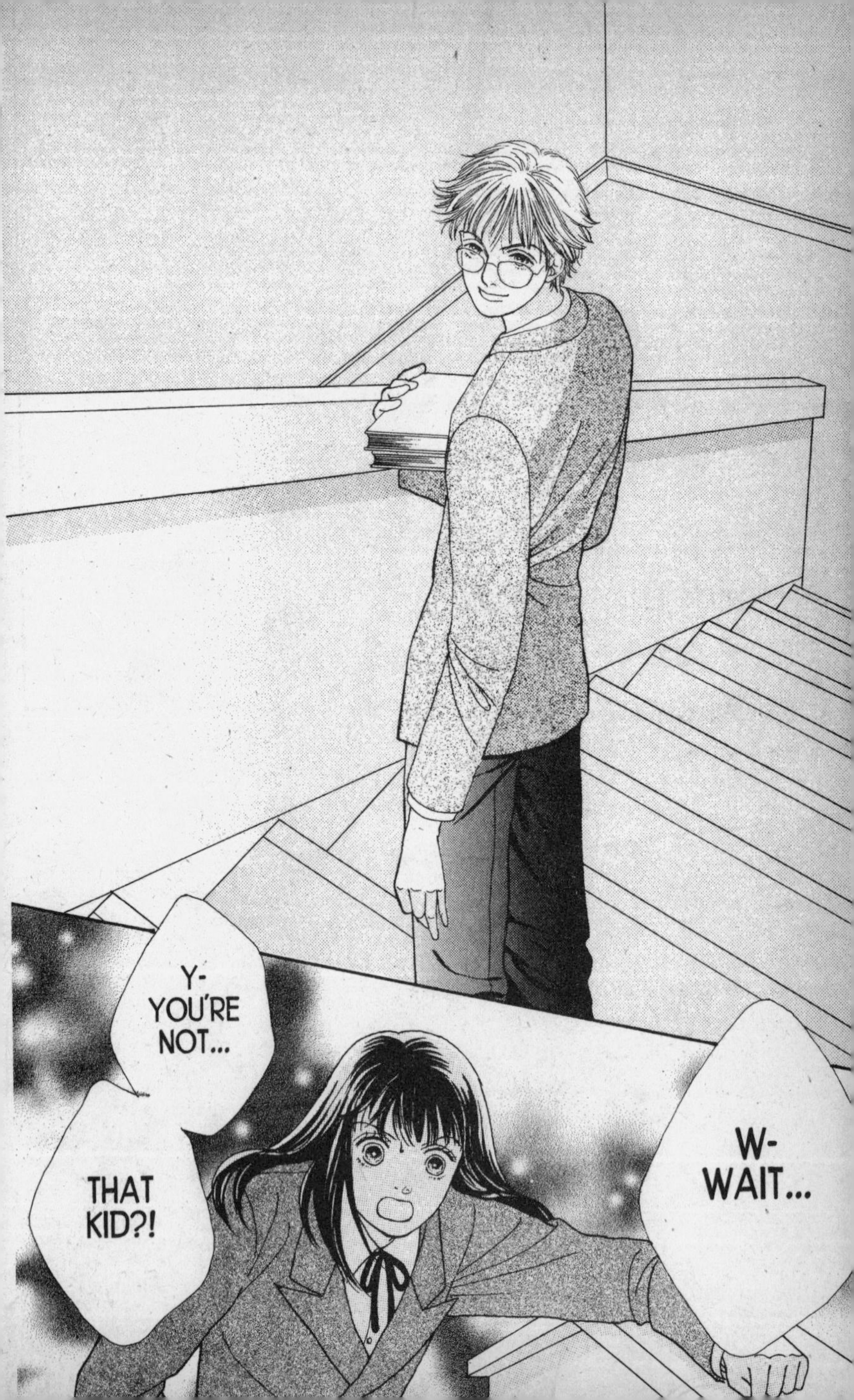
W- WAIT...
Y- YOU'RE NOT...
THAT KID?!

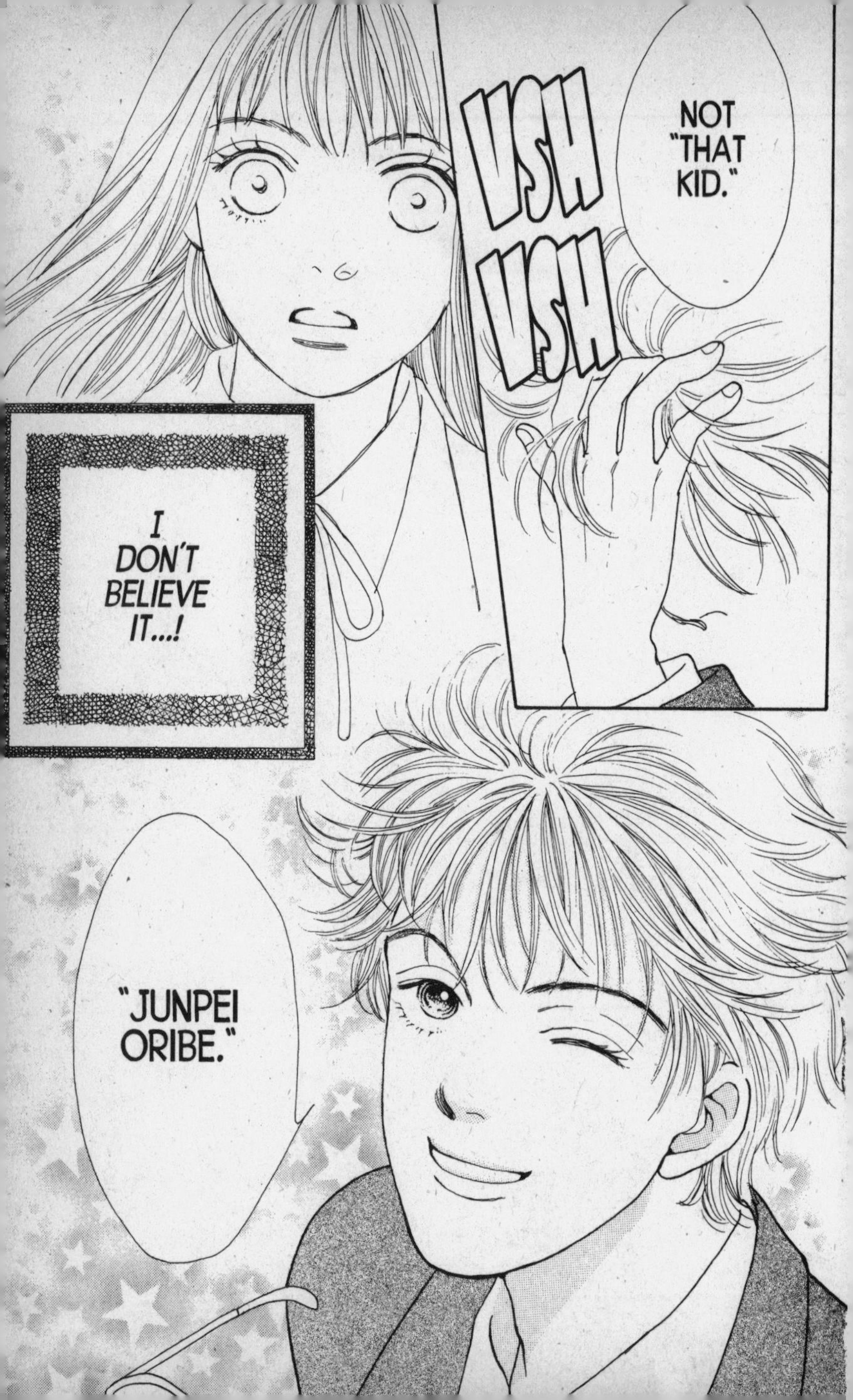
NOT "THAT KID."
VSH VSH
I DON'T BELIEVE IT...!
"JUNPEI ORIBE."

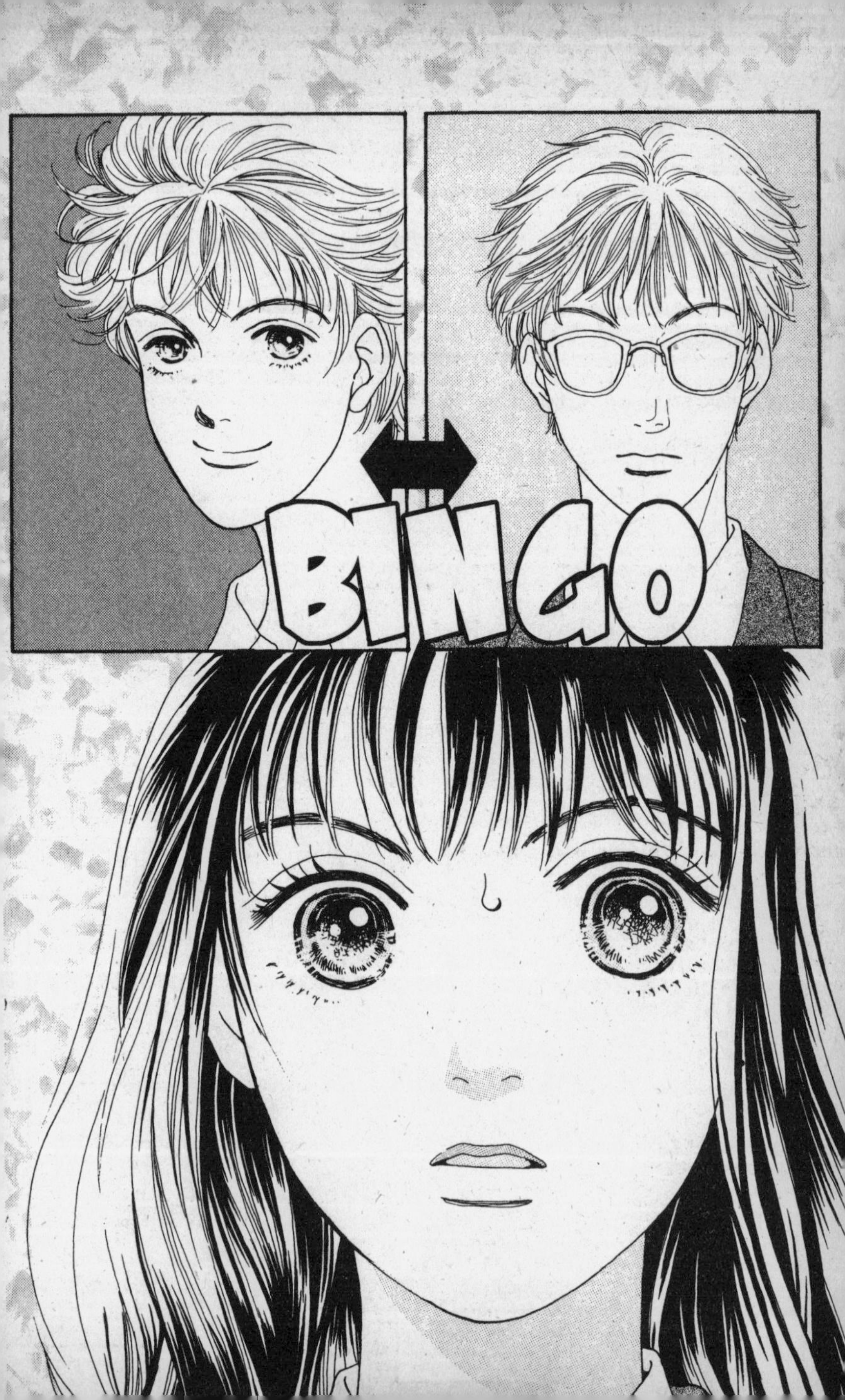
BINGO

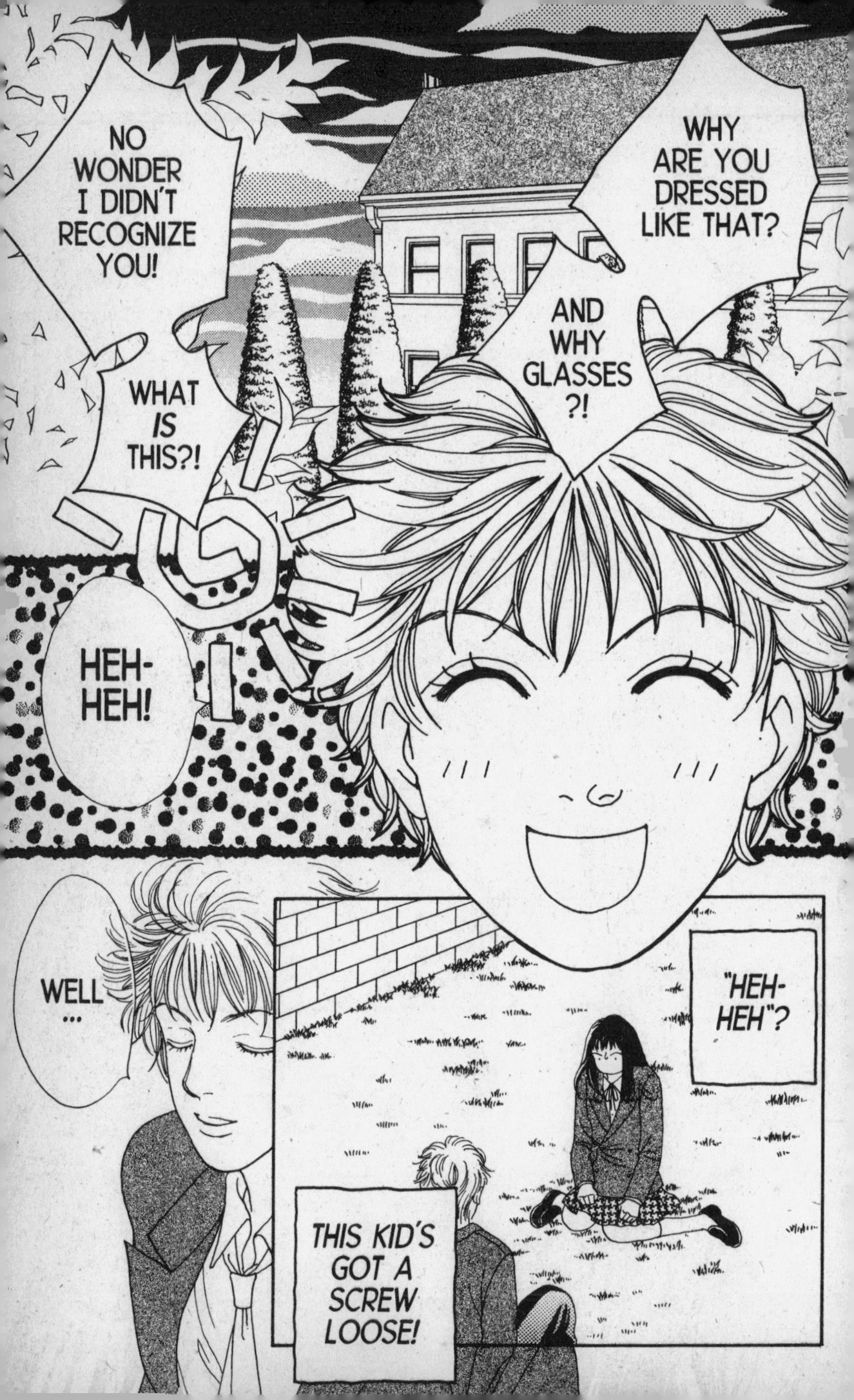
WHY ARE YOU DRESSED LIKE THAT?
AND WHY GLASSES ?!
NO WONDER I DIDN'T RECOGNIZE YOU!
WHAT *IS* THIS?!
HEH-HEH!
"HEH-HEH"?
THIS KID'S GOT A SCREW LOOSE!
WELL ...

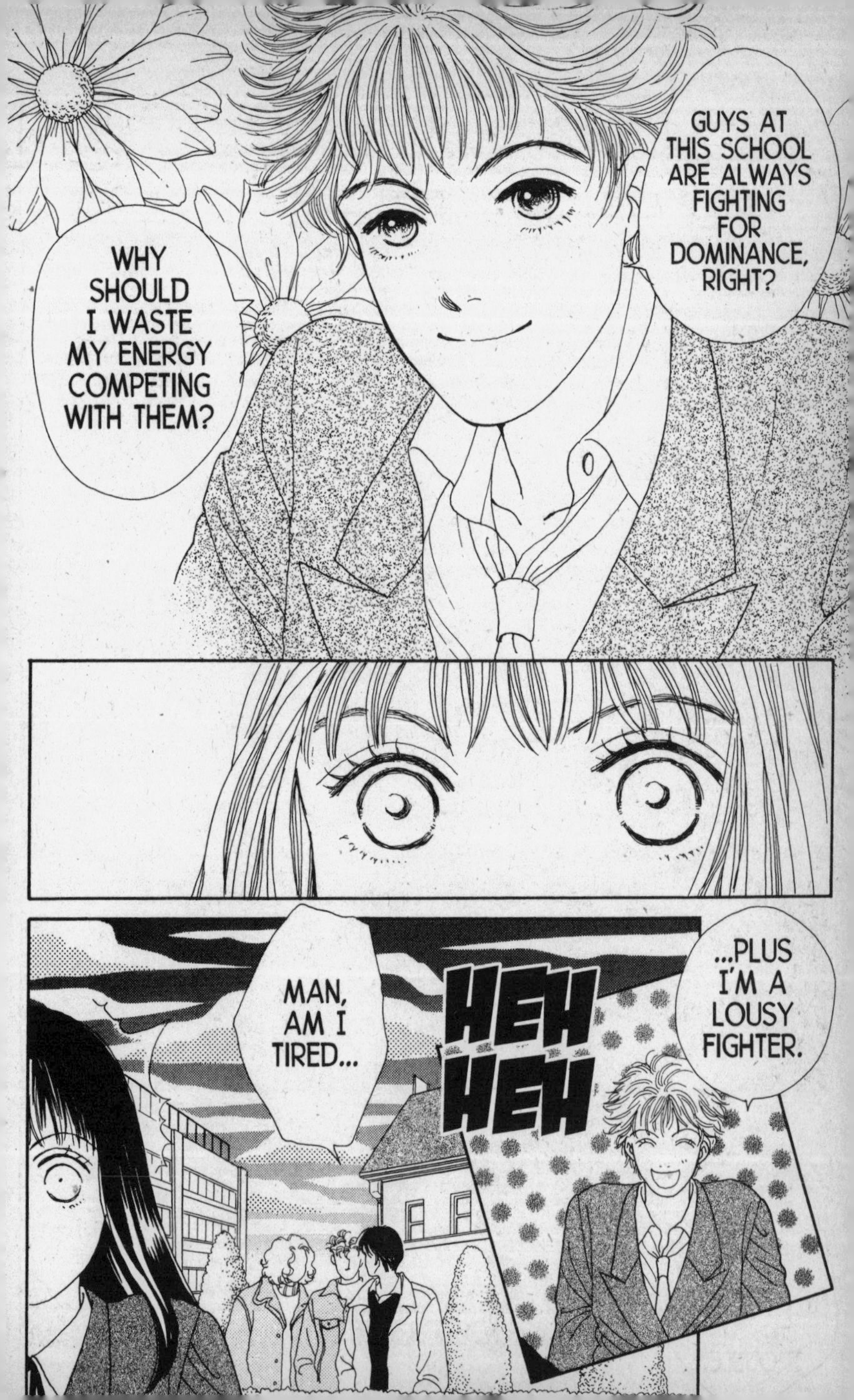
GUYS AT THIS SCHOOL ARE ALWAYS FIGHTING FOR DOMINANCE, RIGHT?
WHY SHOULD I WASTE MY ENERGY COMPETING WITH THEM?
...PLUS I'M A LOUSY FIGHTER.
HEH HEH
MAN, AM I TIRED...

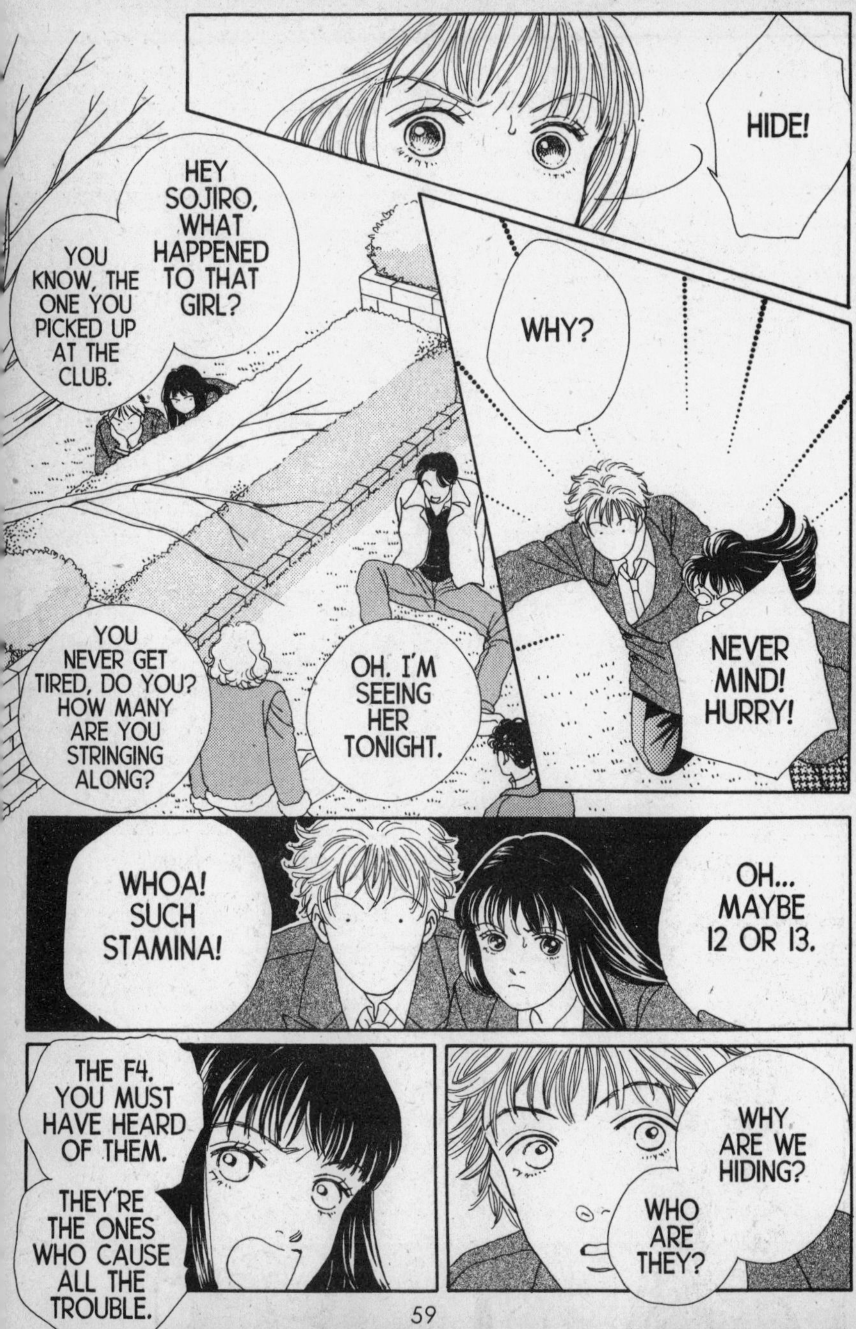
HIDE!
WHY?
NEVER MIND! HURRY!
HEY SOJIRO, WHAT HAPPENED TO THAT GIRL?
YOU KNOW, THE ONE YOU PICKED UP AT THE CLUB.
OH. I'M SEEING HER TONIGHT.
YOU NEVER GET TIRED, DO YOU? HOW MANY ARE YOU STRINGING ALONG?
OH... MAYBE 12 OR 13.
WHOA! SUCH STAMINA!
WHY ARE WE HIDING?
WHO ARE THEY?
THE F4. YOU MUST HAVE HEARD OF THEM.
THEY'RE THE ONES WHO CAUSE ALL THE TROUBLE.

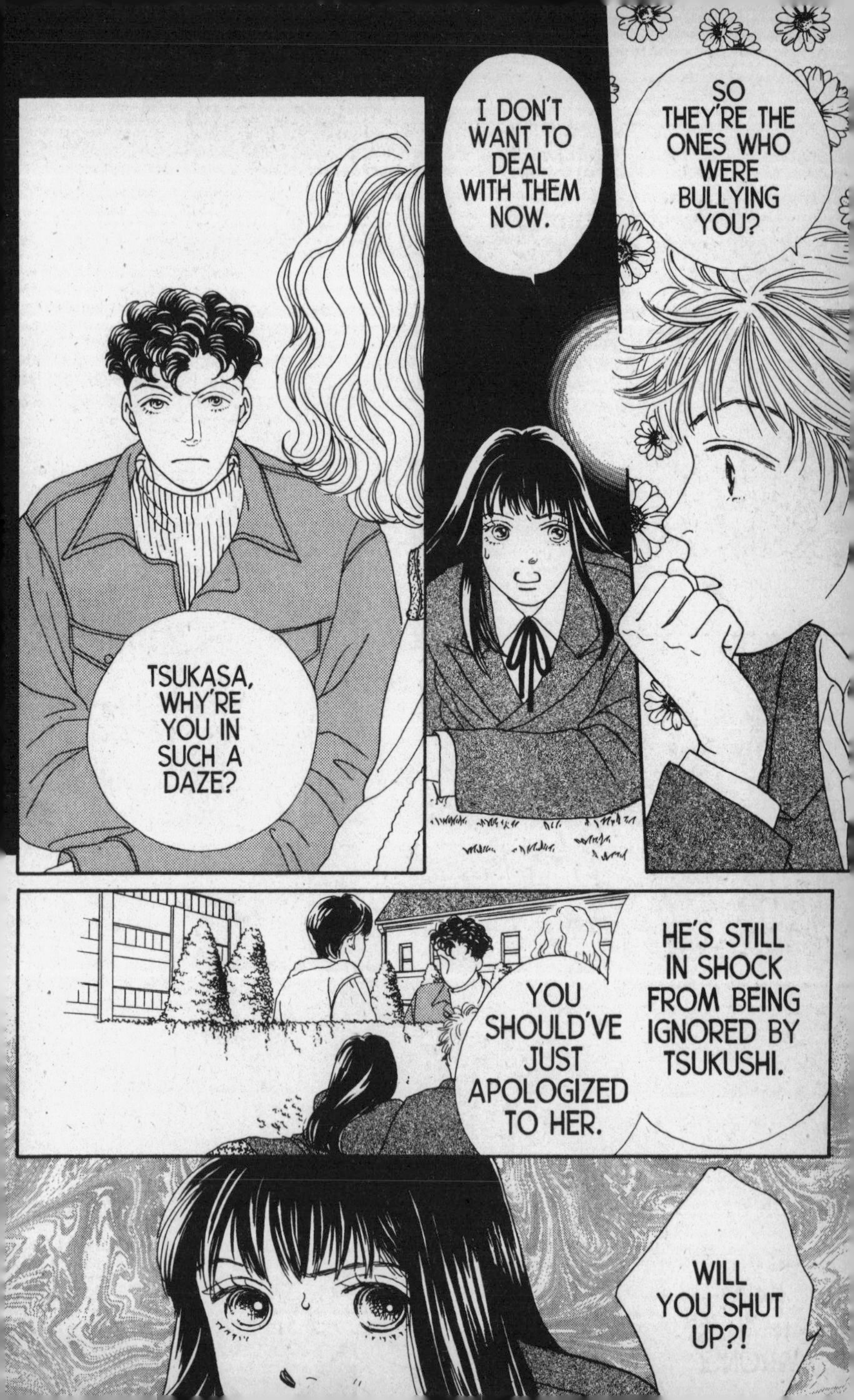
SO THEY'RE THE ONES WHO WERE BULLYING YOU?
I DON'T WANT TO DEAL WITH THEM NOW.
TSUKASA, WHY'RE YOU IN SUCH A DAZE?
HE'S STILL IN SHOCK FROM BEING IGNORED BY TSUKUSHI.
YOU SHOULD'VE JUST APOLOGIZED TO HER.
WILL YOU SHUT UP?!

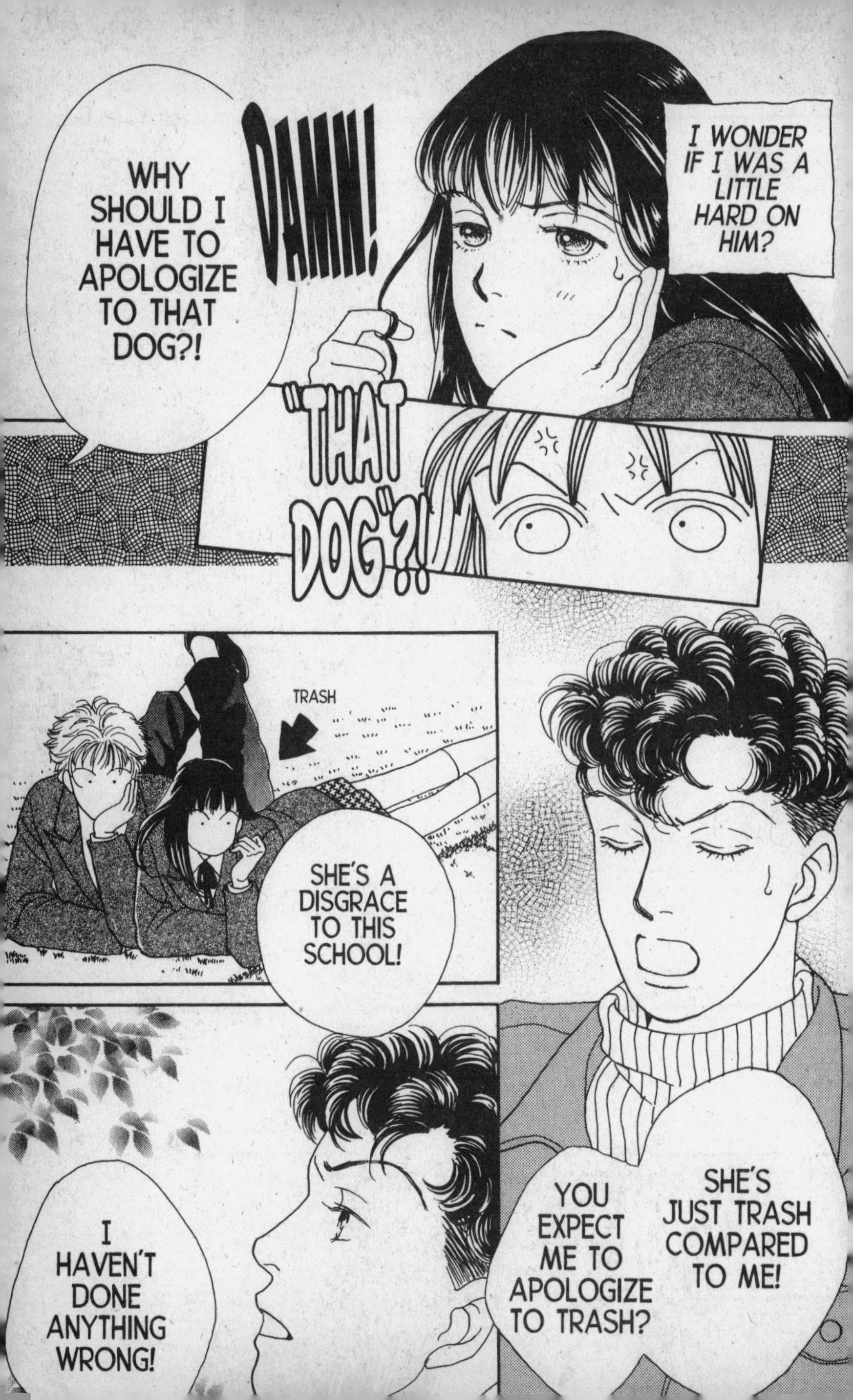
I WONDER IF I WAS A LITTLE HARD ON HIM?
DAMN!
WHY SHOULD I HAVE TO APOLOGIZE TO THAT DOG?!
"THAT DOG"?!
SHE'S A DISGRACE TO THIS SCHOOL!
SHE'S JUST TRASH COMPARED TO ME!
YOU EXPECT ME TO APOLOGIZE TO TRASH?
TRASH
I HAVEN'T DONE ANYTHING WRONG!

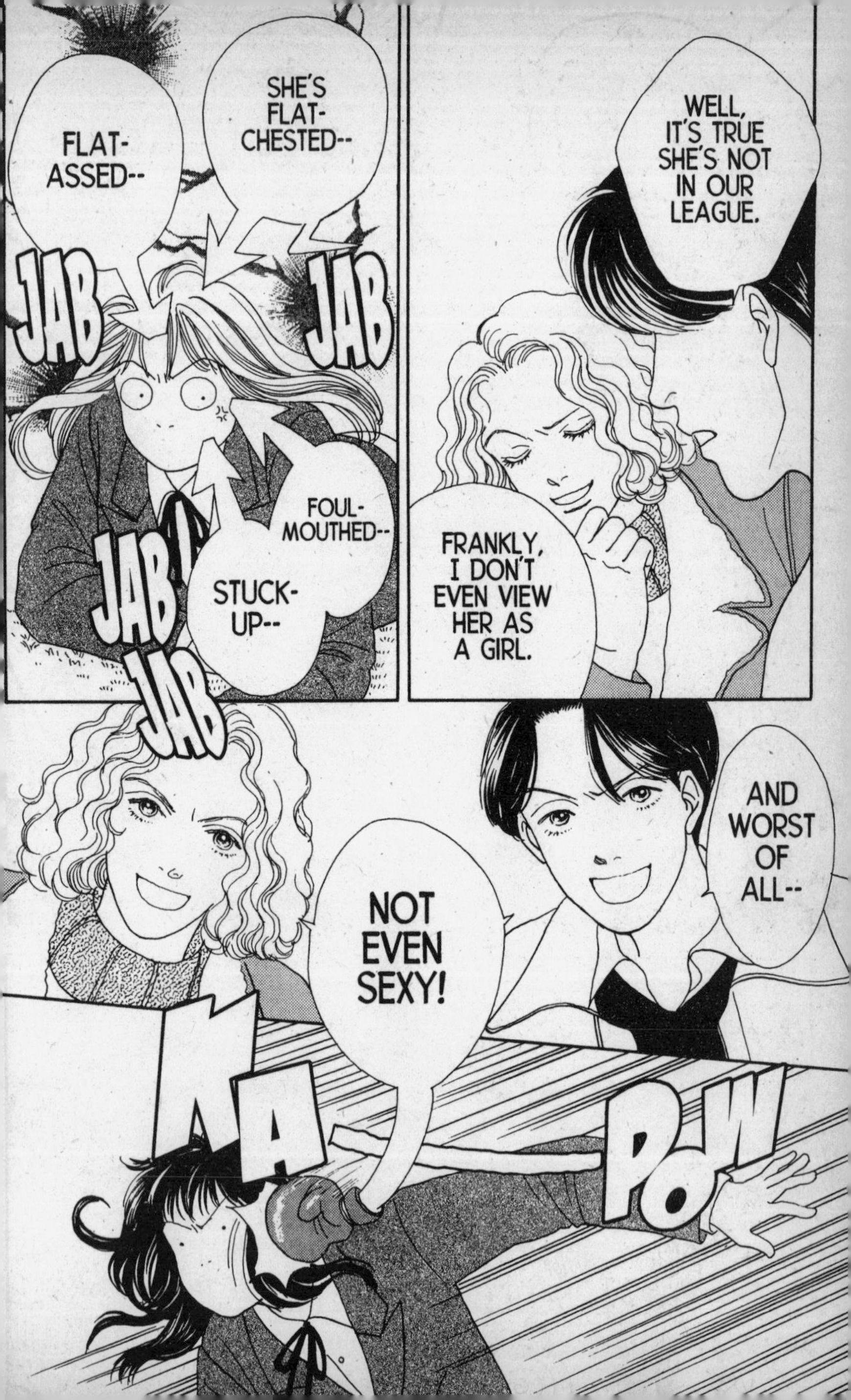
WELL, IT'S TRUE SHE'S NOT IN OUR LEAGUE.
FRANKLY, I DON'T EVEN VIEW HER AS A GIRL.
SHE'S FLAT-CHESTED--
FLAT-ASSED--
JAB
JAB
FOUL-MOUTHED--
STUCK-UP--
JAB
JAB
AND WORST OF ALL--
NOT EVEN SEXY!
WA-POW

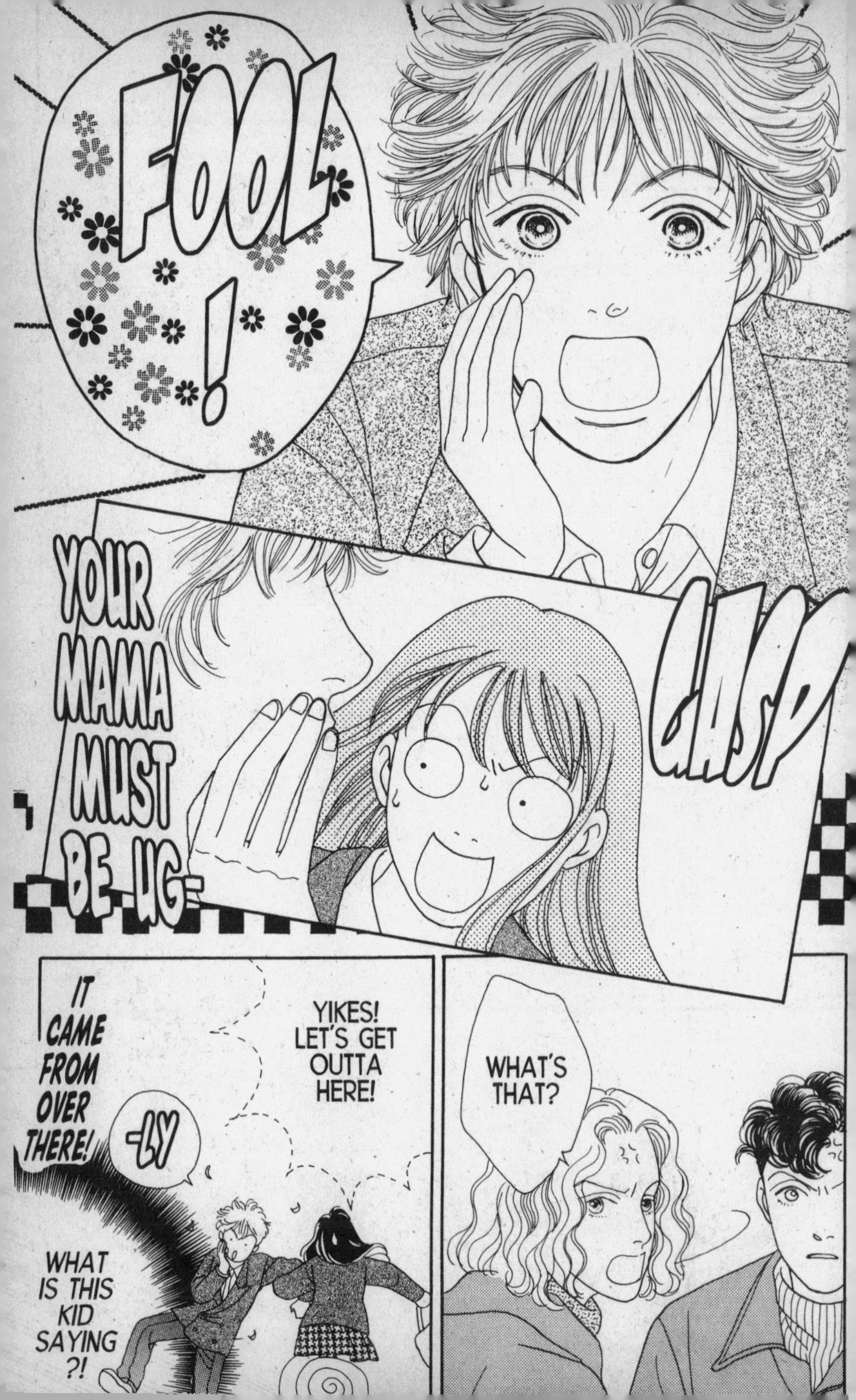
FOOL!
GASP
YOUR MAMA MUST BE UG-
WHAT'S THAT?
YIKES! LET'S GET OUTTA HERE!
IT CAME FROM OVER THERE!
-LY
WHAT IS THIS KID SAYING?!

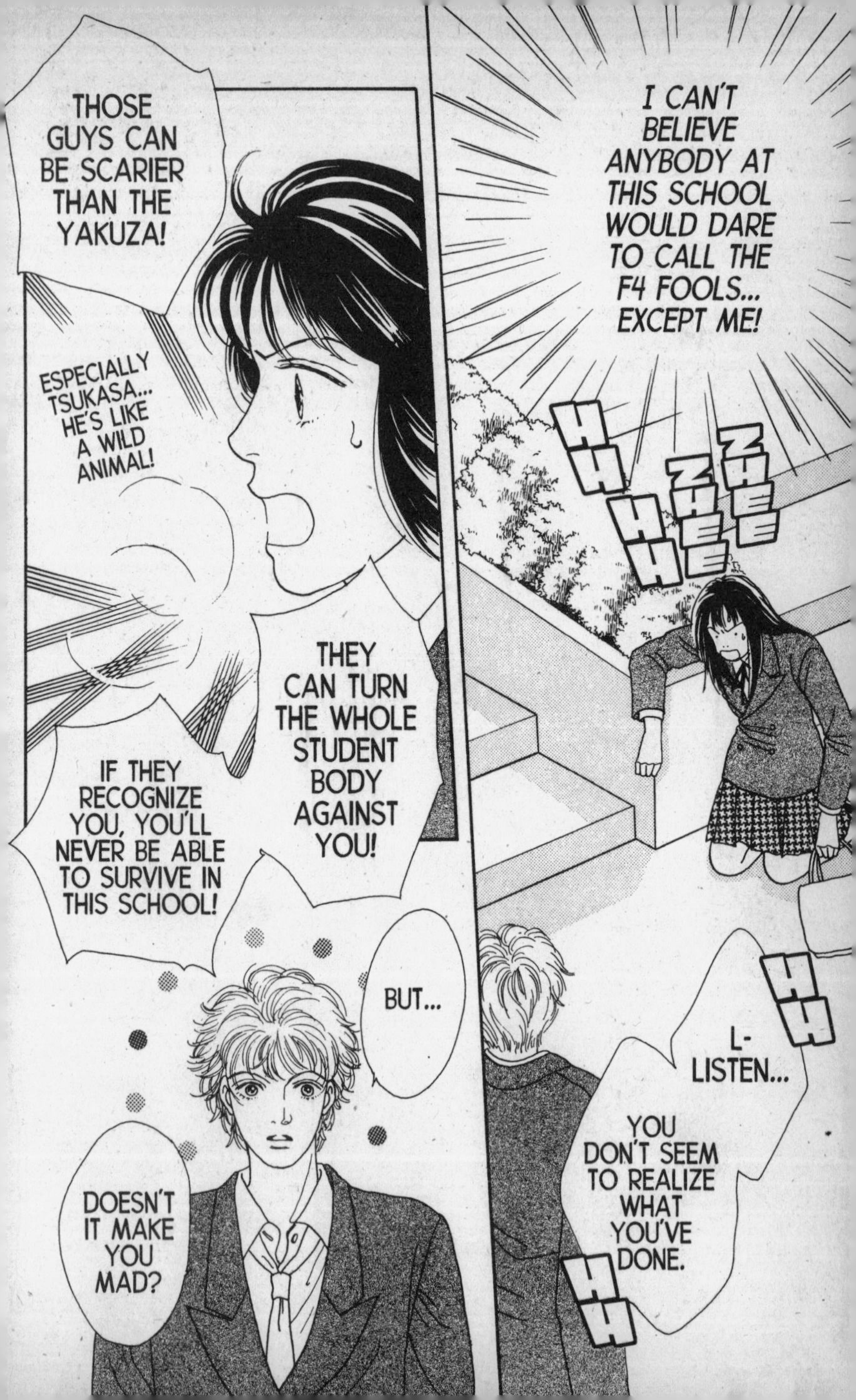
I CAN'T BELIEVE ANYBODY AT THIS SCHOOL WOULD DARE TO CALL THE F4 FOOLS... EXCEPT ME!
HH
HHH
ZHEEE
ZHEE
HH
L- LISTEN...
YOU DON'T SEEM TO REALIZE WHAT YOU'VE DONE.
HH
THOSE GUYS CAN BE SCARIER THAN THE YAKUZA!
ESPECIALLY TSUKASA... HE'S LIKE A WILD ANIMAL!
THEY CAN TURN THE WHOLE STUDENT BODY AGAINST YOU!
IF THEY RECOGNIZE YOU, YOU'LL NEVER BE ABLE TO SURVIVE IN THIS SCHOOL!
BUT...
DOESN'T IT MAKE YOU MAD?

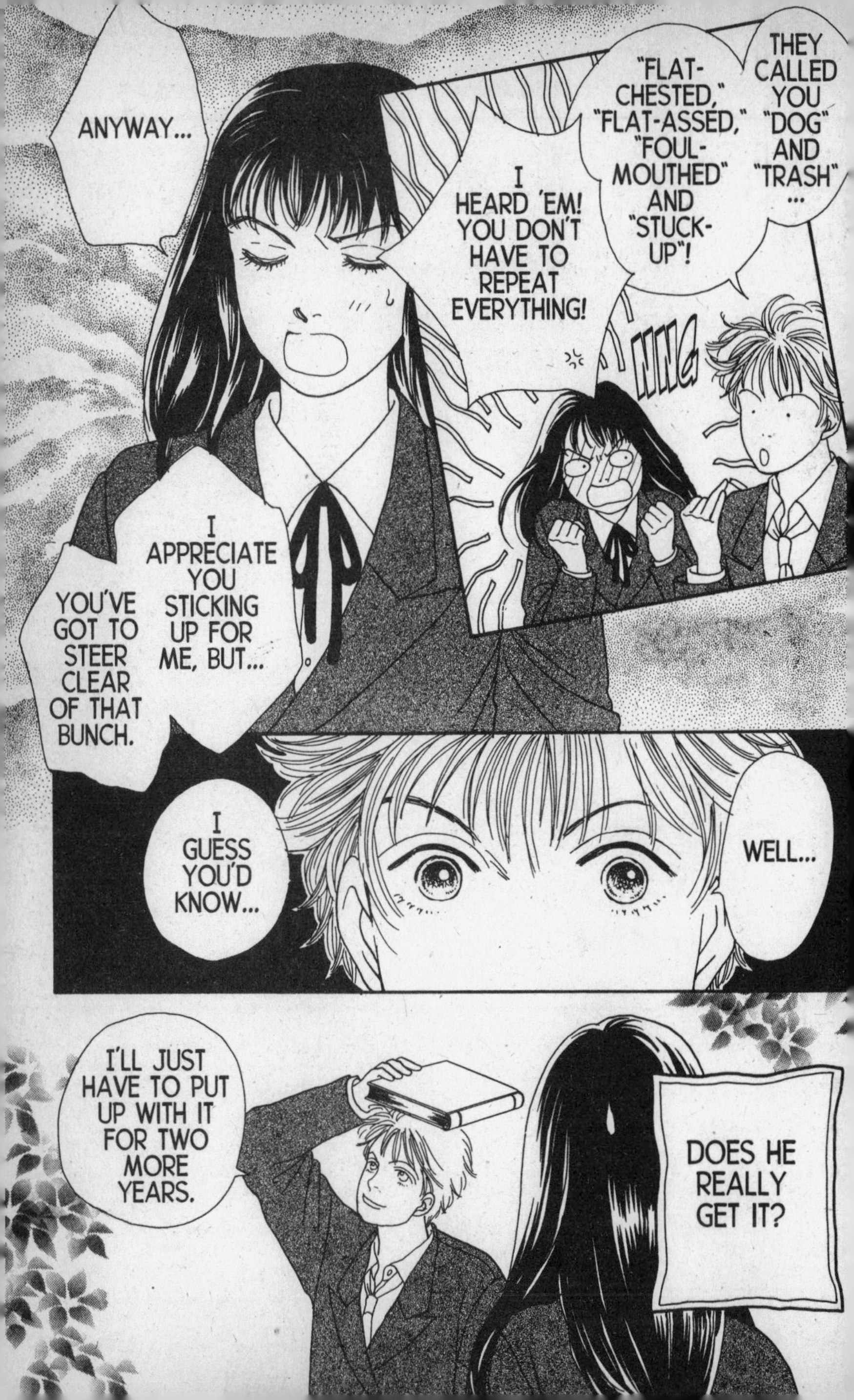
THEY CALLED YOU "DOG" AND "TRASH"...
"FLAT-CHESTED," "FLAT-ASSED," "FOUL-MOUTHED" AND "STUCK-UP"!
I HEARD 'EM! YOU DON'T HAVE TO REPEAT EVERYTHING!
NNG
ANYWAY...
I APPRECIATE YOU STICKING UP FOR ME, BUT...
YOU'VE GOT TO STEER CLEAR OF THAT BUNCH.
WELL...
I GUESS YOU'D KNOW...
DOES HE REALLY GET IT?
I'LL JUST HAVE TO PUT UP WITH IT FOR TWO MORE YEARS.

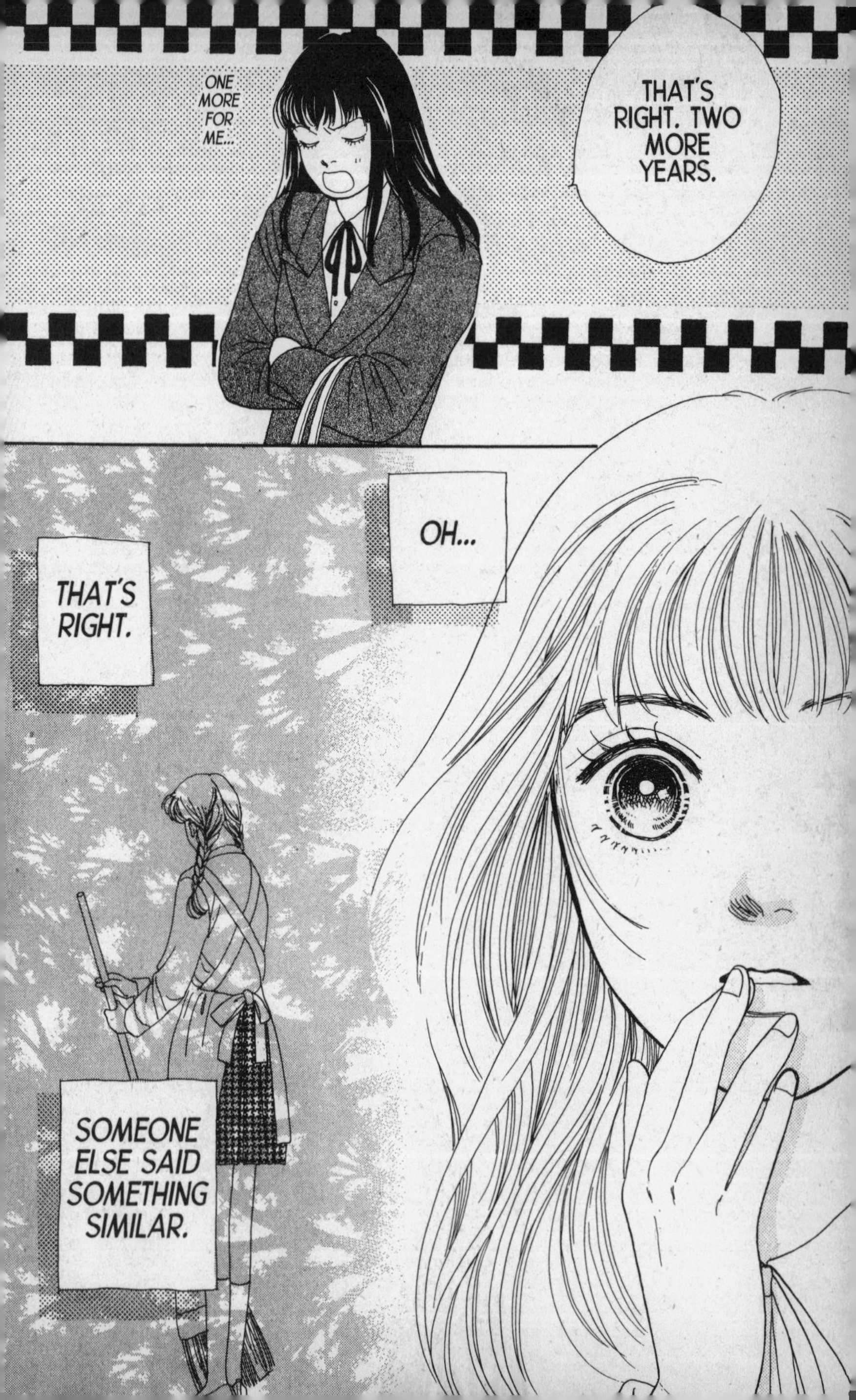
THAT'S RIGHT. TWO MORE YEARS.
ONE MORE FOR ME...
OH...
THAT'S RIGHT.
SOMEONE ELSE SAID SOMETHING SIMILAR.

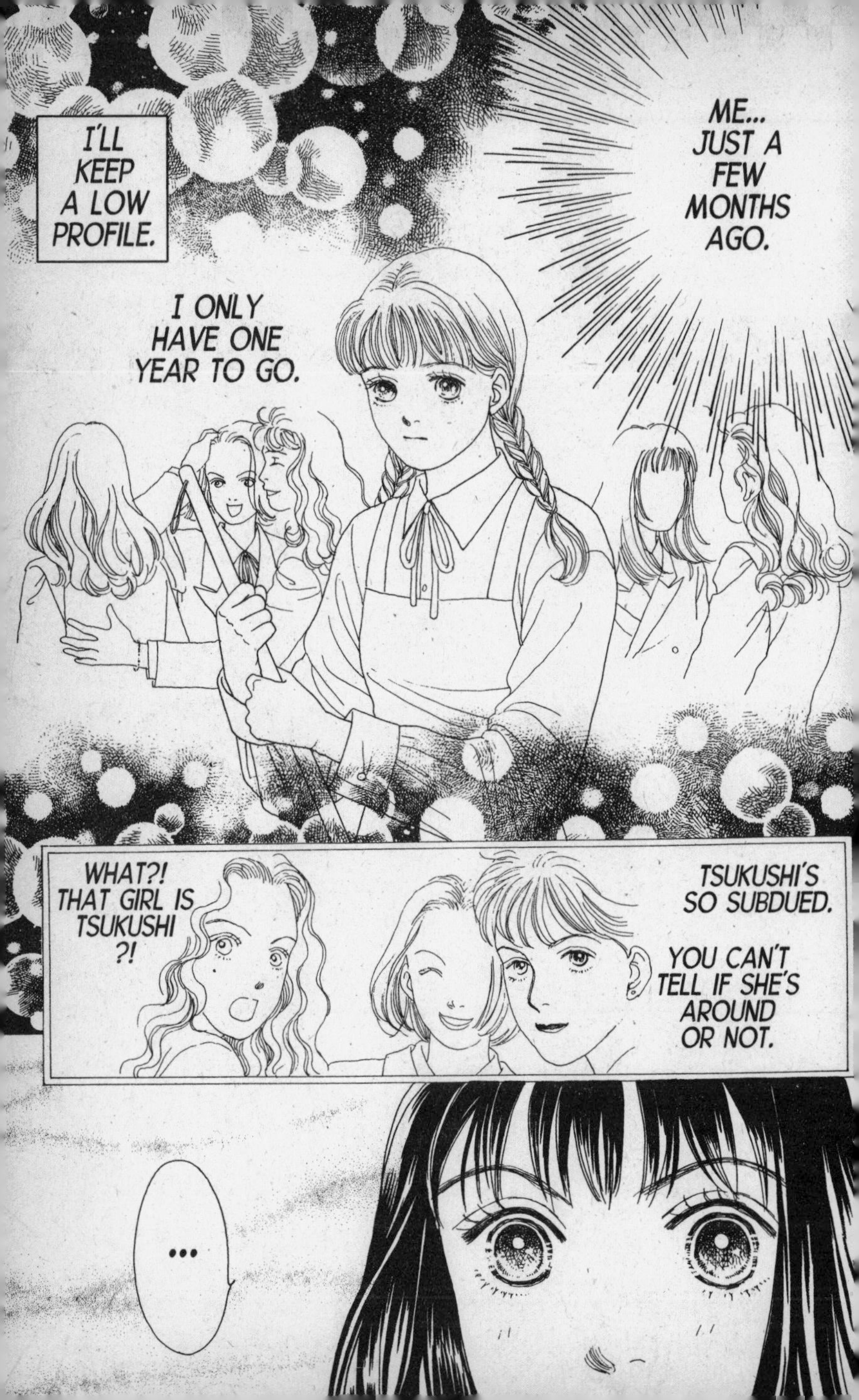
ME... JUST A FEW MONTHS AGO.
I'LL KEEP A LOW PROFILE.
I ONLY HAVE ONE YEAR TO GO.
TSUKUSHI'S SO SUBDUED.
YOU CAN'T TELL IF SHE'S AROUND OR NOT.
WHAT?! THAT GIRL IS TSUKUSHI ?!
...

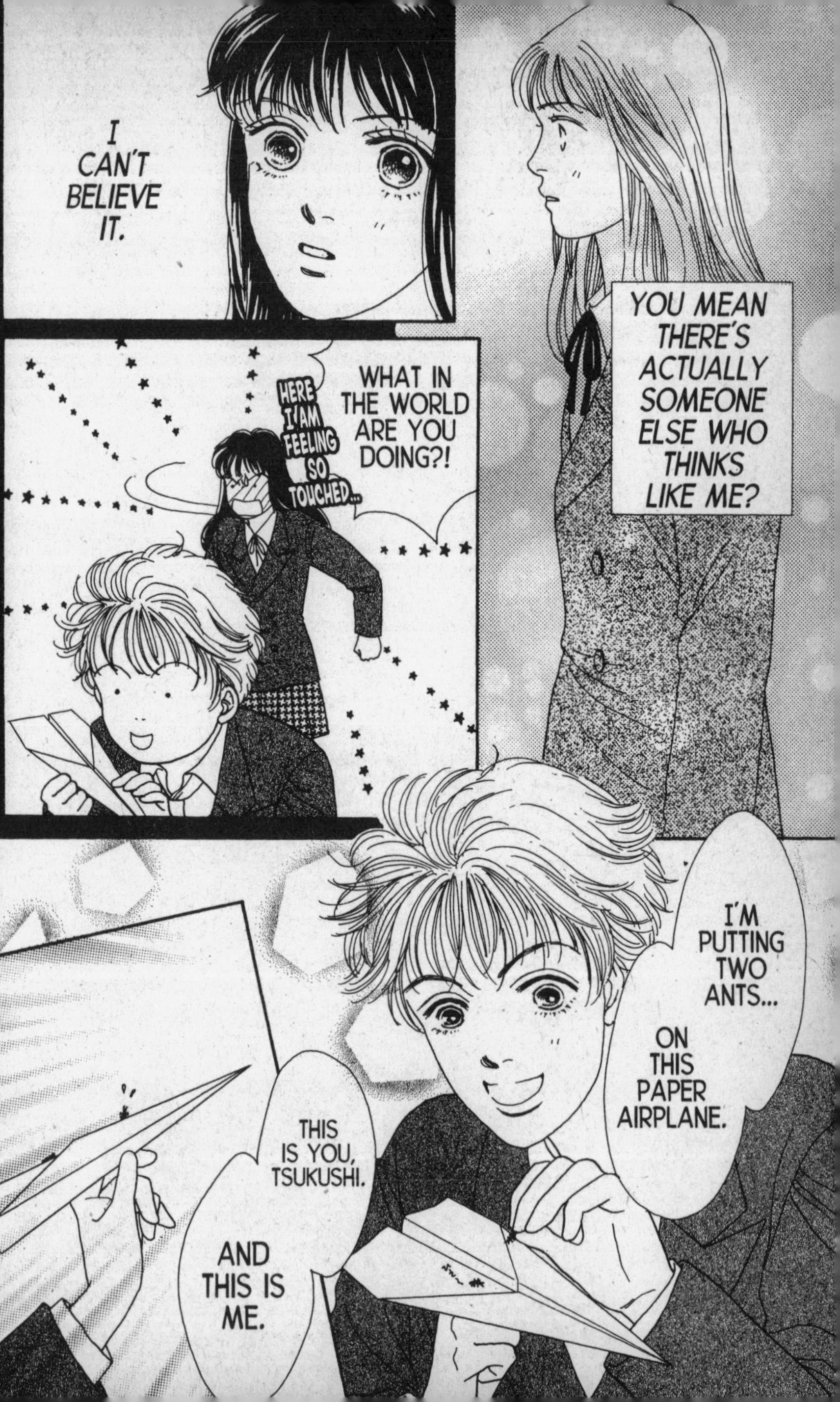
YOU MEAN THERE'S ACTUALLY SOMEONE ELSE WHO THINKS LIKE ME?
I CAN'T BELIEVE IT.
WHAT IN THE WORLD ARE YOU DOING?!
HERE I AM FEELING SO TOUCHED...
I'M PUTTING TWO ANTS...
ON THIS PAPER AIRPLANE.
THIS IS YOU, TSUKUSHI.
AND THIS IS ME.

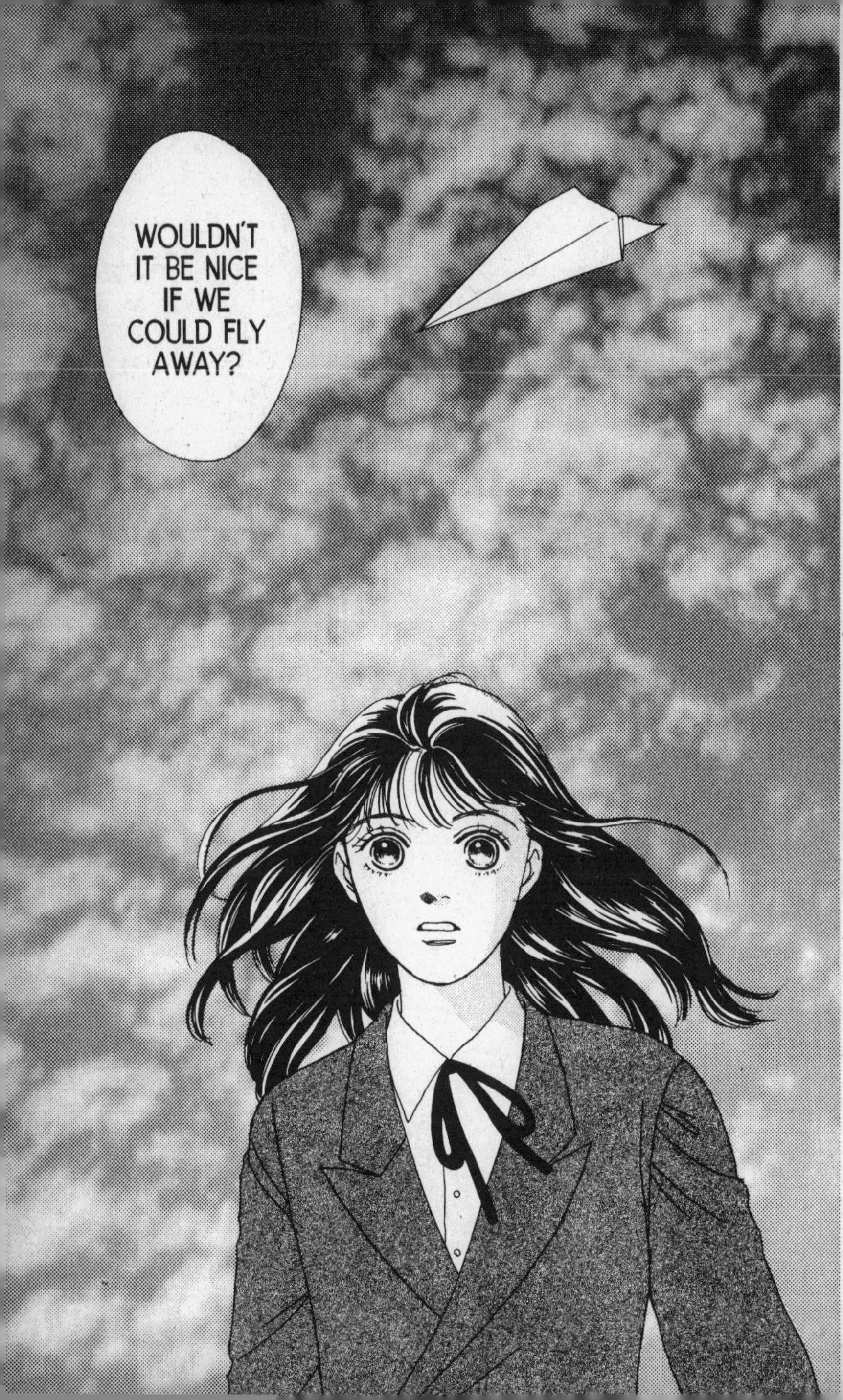
WOULDN'T IT BE NICE IF WE COULD FLY AWAY?

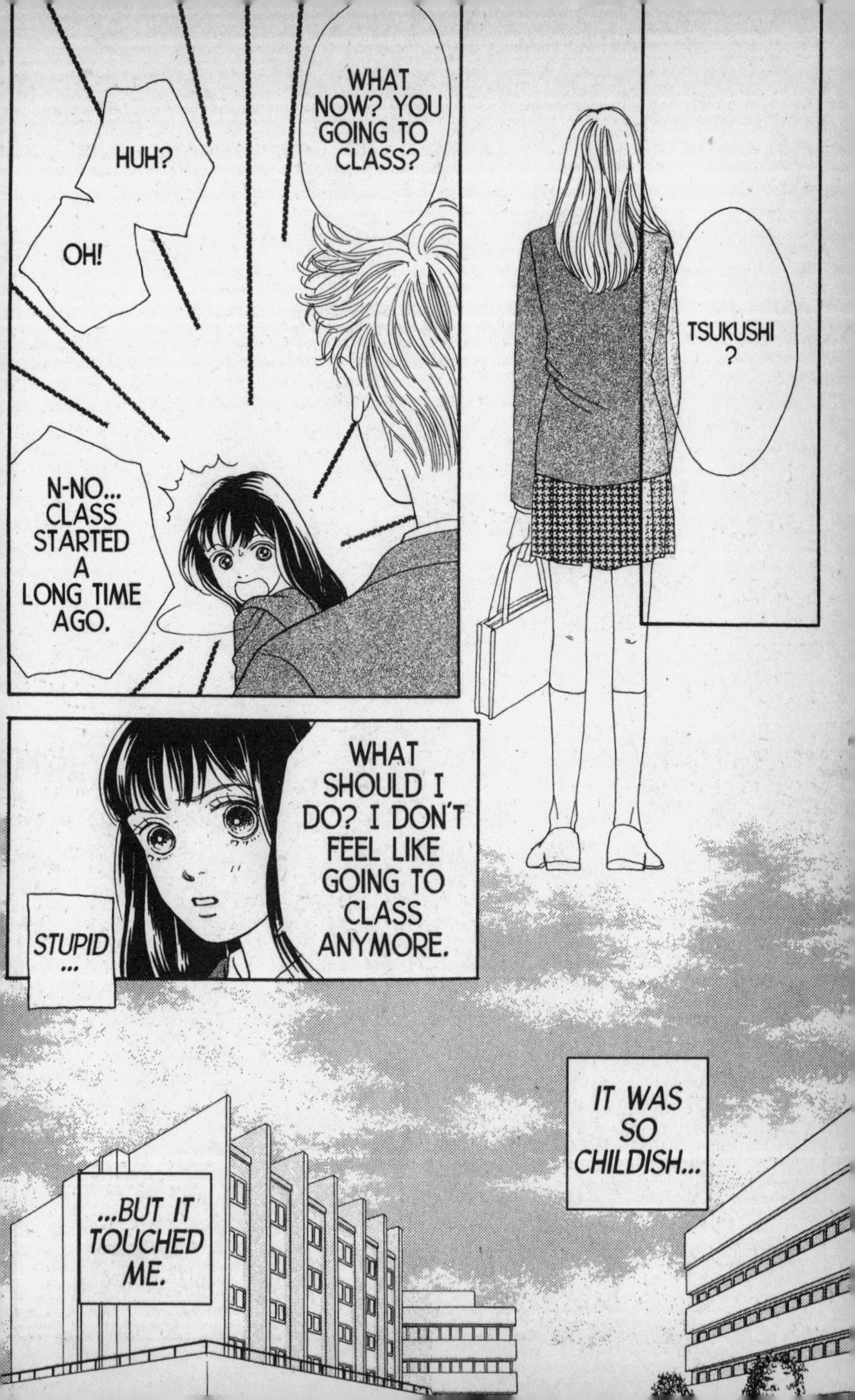
TSUKUSHI ?
WHAT NOW? YOU GOING TO CLASS?
HUH?
OH!
N-NO... CLASS STARTED A LONG TIME AGO.
WHAT SHOULD I DO? I DON'T FEEL LIKE GOING TO CLASS ANYMORE.
STUPID ...
IT WAS SO CHILDISH...
...BUT IT TOUCHED ME.

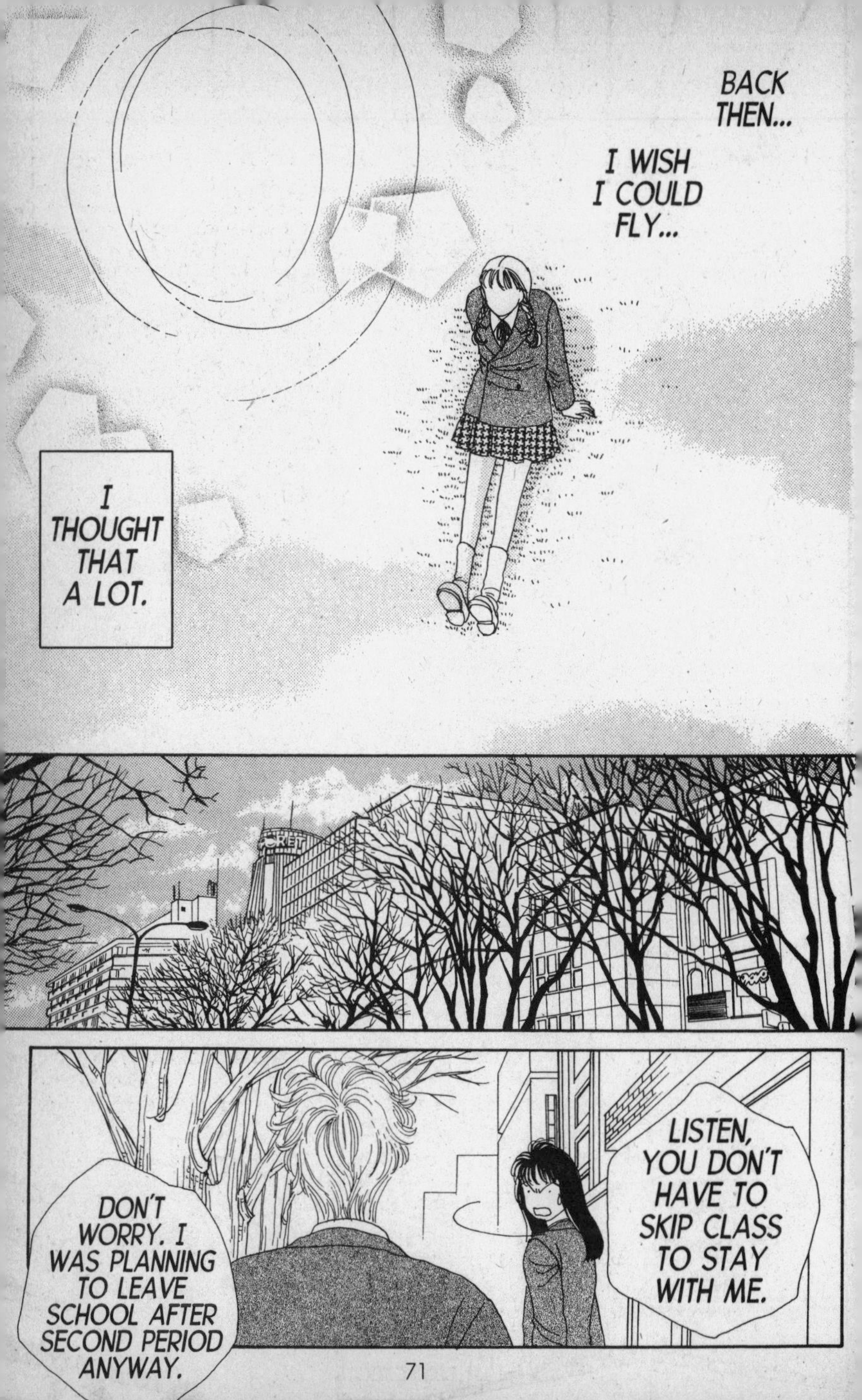
BACK THEN...
I WISH I COULD FLY...
I THOUGHT THAT A LOT.
LISTEN, YOU DON'T HAVE TO SKIP CLASS TO STAY WITH ME.
DON'T WORRY. I WAS PLANNING TO LEAVE SCHOOL AFTER SECOND PERIOD ANYWAY.

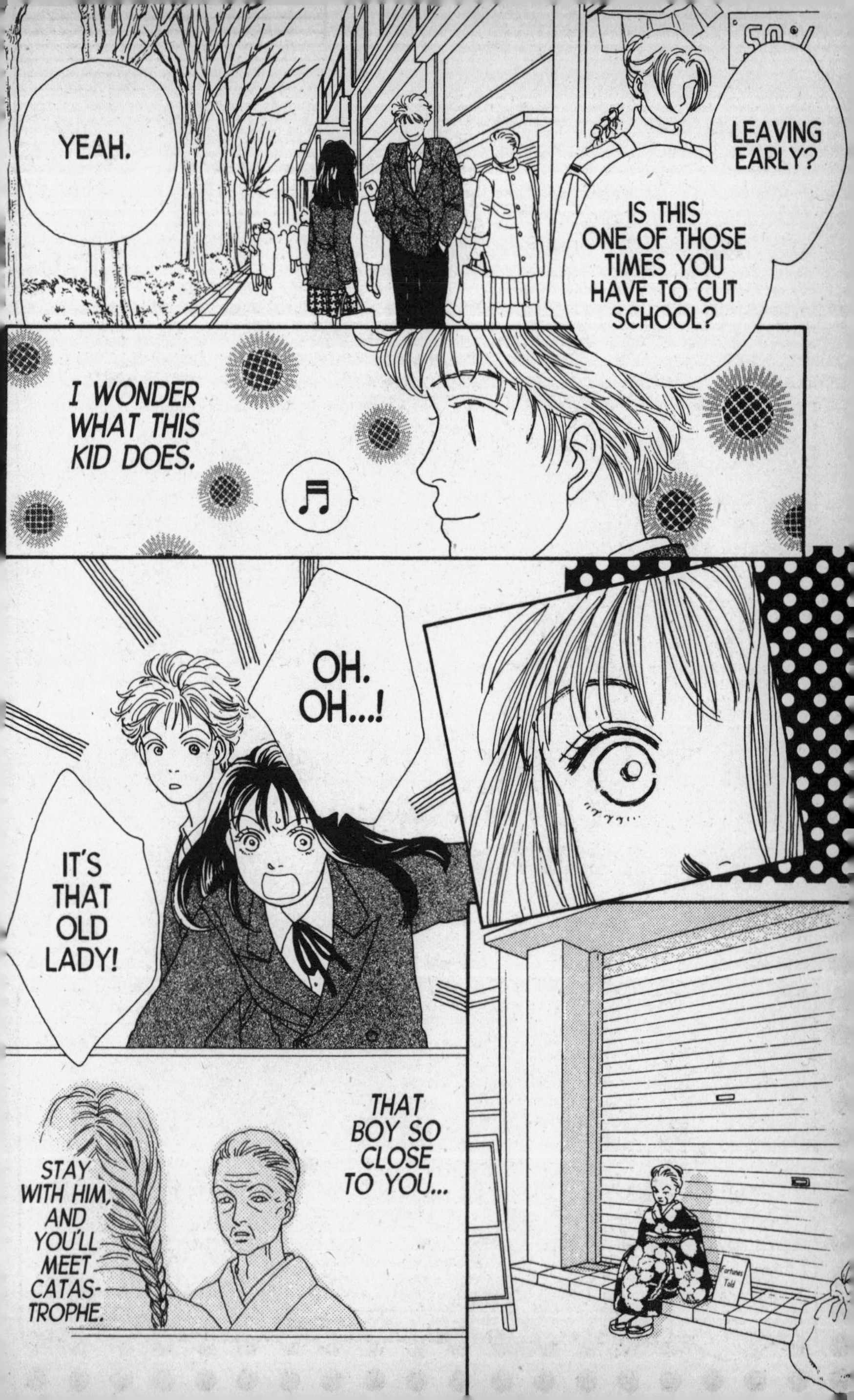
LEAVING EARLY?
IS THIS ONE OF THOSE TIMES YOU HAVE TO CUT SCHOOL?
YEAH.
I WONDER WHAT THIS KID DOES.
♬
OH. OH...!
IT'S THAT OLD LADY!
Fortunes Told
THAT BOY SO CLOSE TO YOU...
STAY WITH HIM, AND YOU'LL MEET CATASTROPHE.

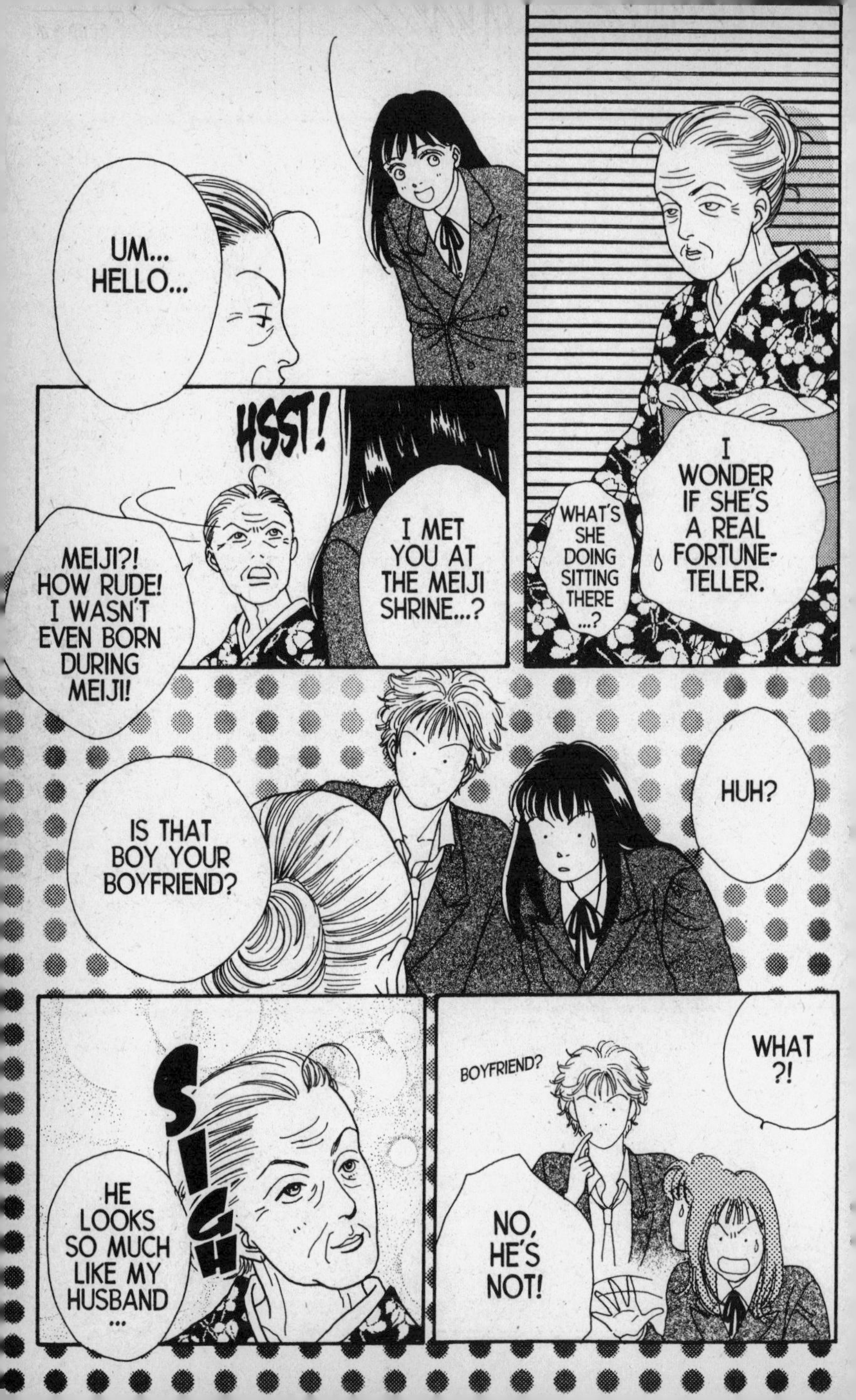
I WONDER IF SHE'S A REAL FORTUNE-TELLER.
WHAT'S SHE DOING SITTING THERE ...?
UM... HELLO...
I MET YOU AT THE MEIJI SHRINE...?
HSST!
MEIJI?! HOW RUDE! I WASN'T EVEN BORN DURING MEIJI!
HUH?
IS THAT BOY YOUR BOYFRIEND?
WHAT ?!
BOYFRIEND?
NO, HE'S NOT!
SIGH
HE LOOKS SO MUCH LIKE MY HUSBAND ...

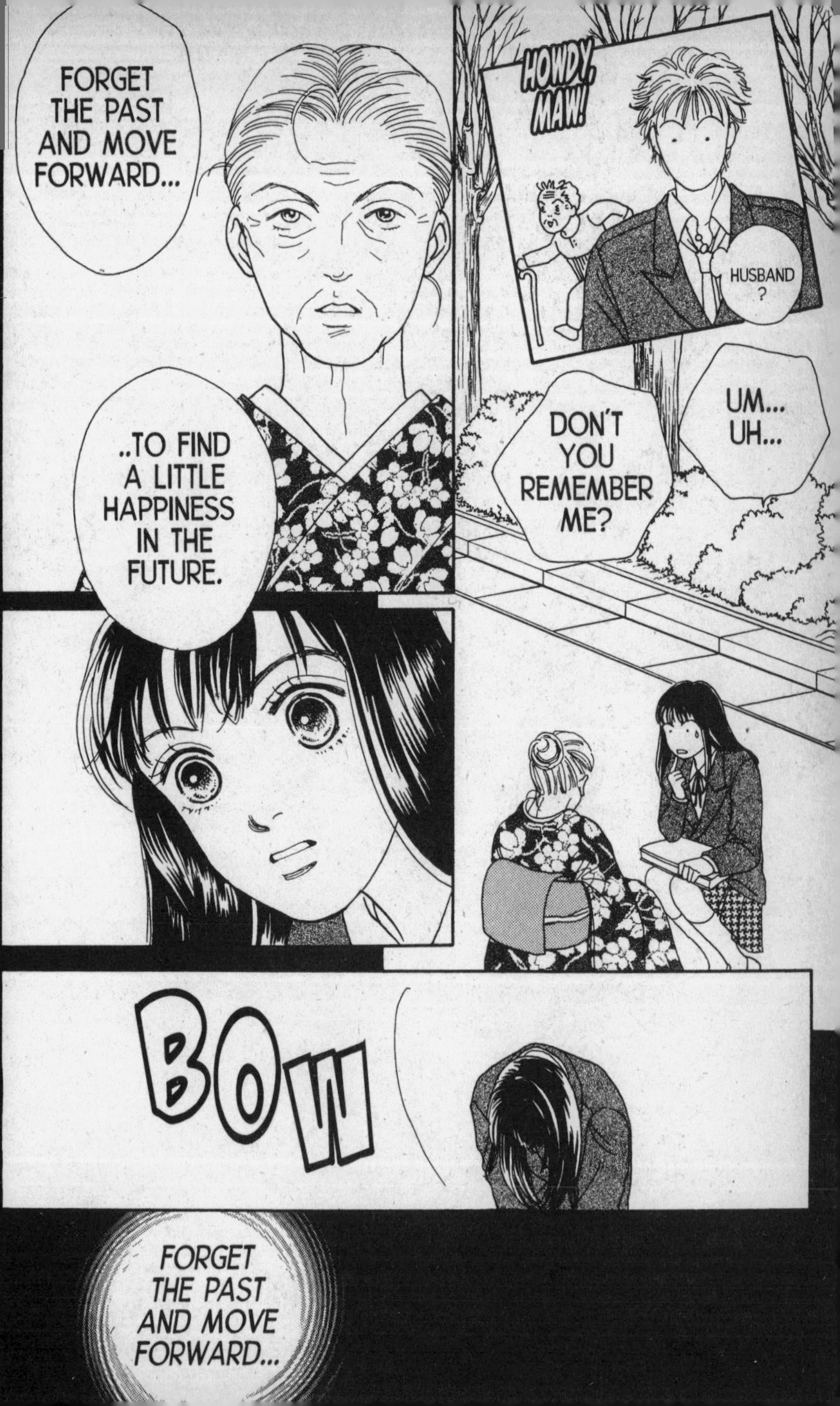
HOWDY, MAW!
HUSBAND ?
UM... UH...
DON'T YOU REMEMBER ME?
FORGET THE PAST AND MOVE FORWARD...
..TO FIND A LITTLE HAPPINESS IN THE FUTURE.
BOW
FORGET THE PAST AND MOVE FORWARD...

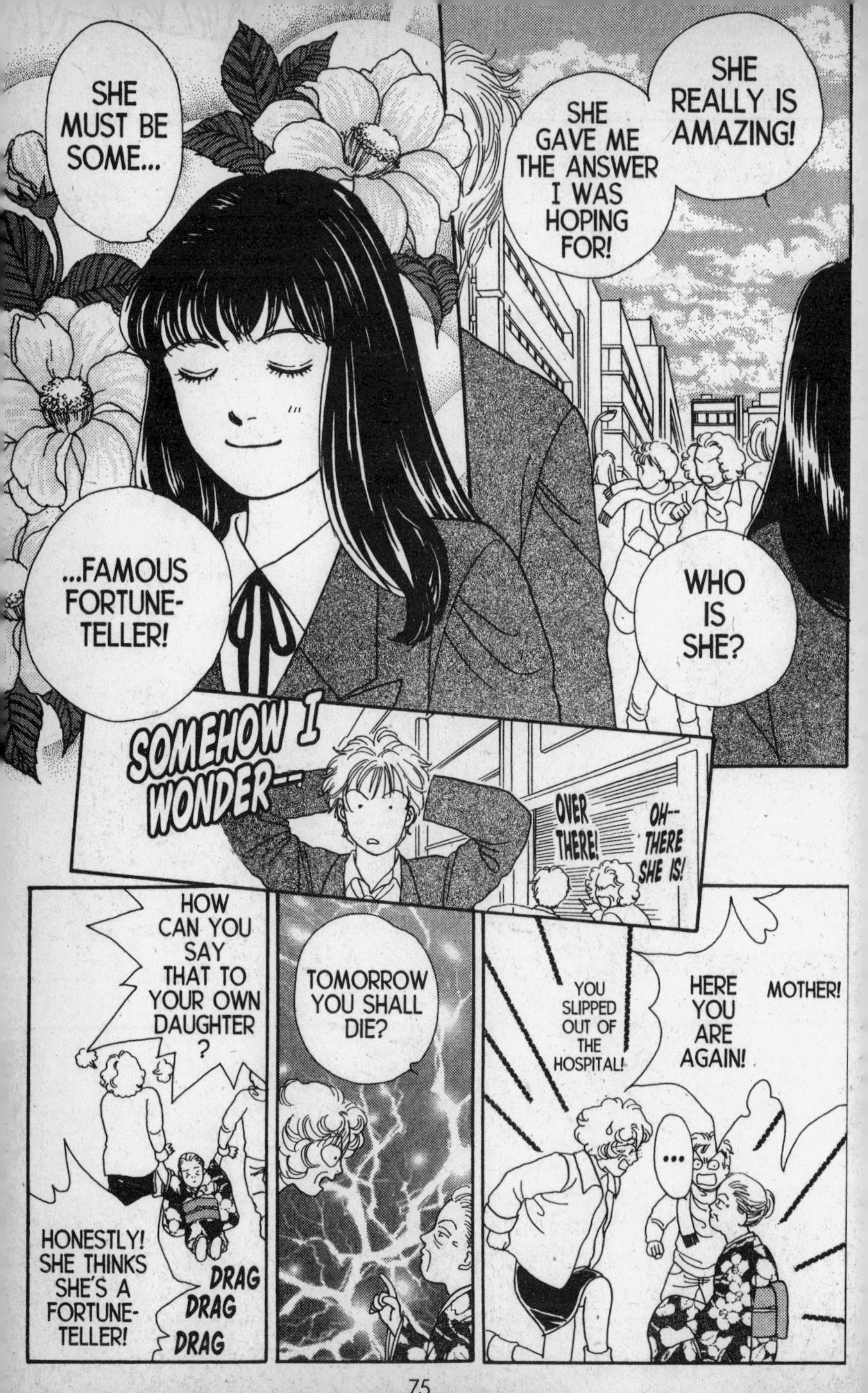
SHE REALLY IS AMAZING!
SHE GAVE ME THE ANSWER I WAS HOPING FOR!
WHO IS SHE?
SHE MUST BE SOME...
...FAMOUS FORTUNE-TELLER!
OH-- THERE SHE IS!
OVER THERE!
SOMEHOW I WONDER--
MOTHER!
HERE YOU ARE AGAIN!
YOU SLIPPED OUT OF THE HOSPITAL!
...
TOMORROW YOU SHALL DIE?
HOW CAN YOU SAY THAT TO YOUR OWN DAUGHTER?
HONESTLY! SHE THINKS SHE'S A FORTUNE-TELLER!
DRAG
DRAG
DRAG

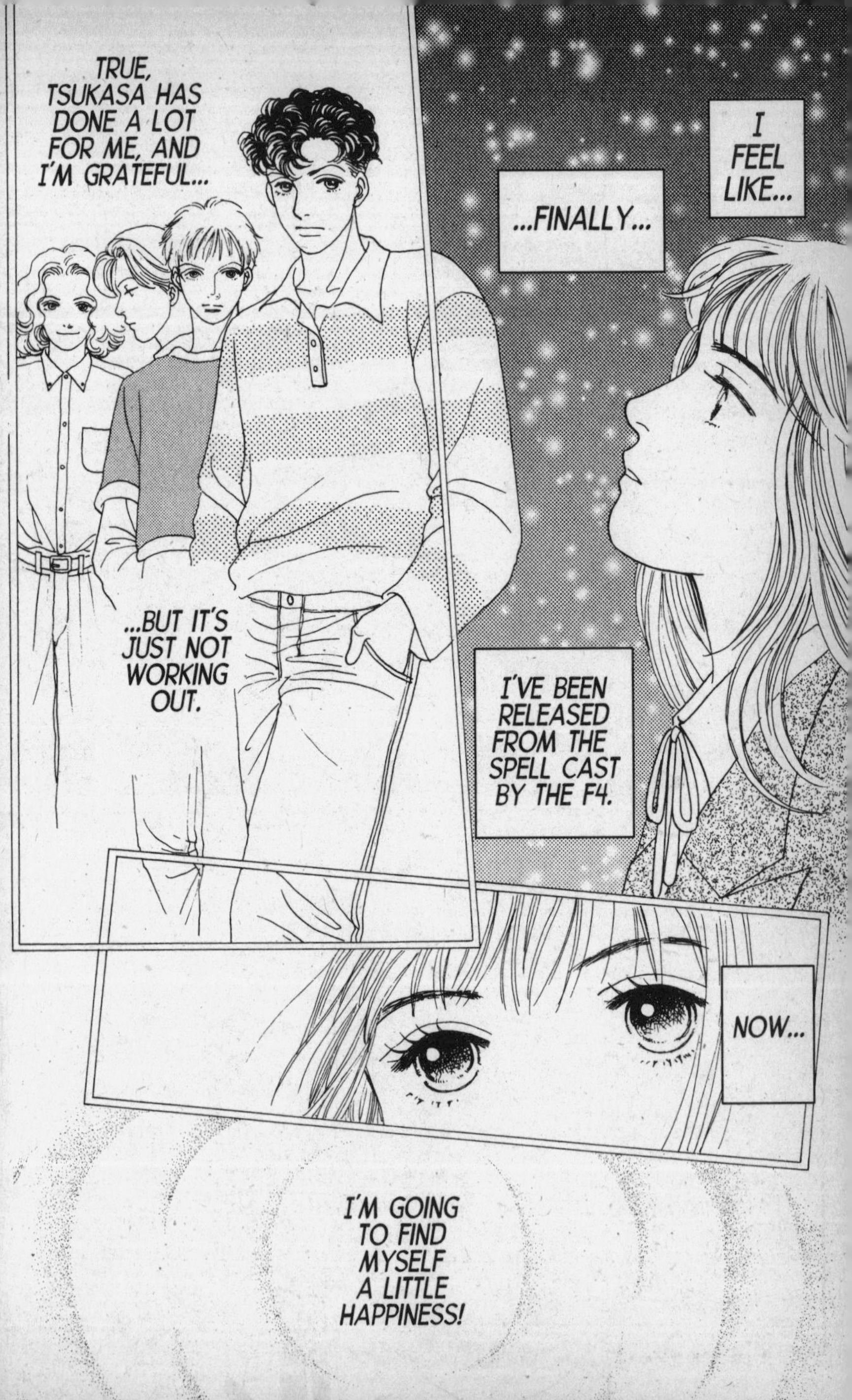
I FEEL LIKE...
...FINALLY...
I'VE BEEN RELEASED FROM THE SPELL CAST BY THE F4.
TRUE, TSUKASA HAS DONE A LOT FOR ME, AND I'M GRATEFUL...
...BUT IT'S JUST NOT WORKING OUT.
NOW...
I'M GOING TO FIND MYSELF A LITTLE HAPPINESS!

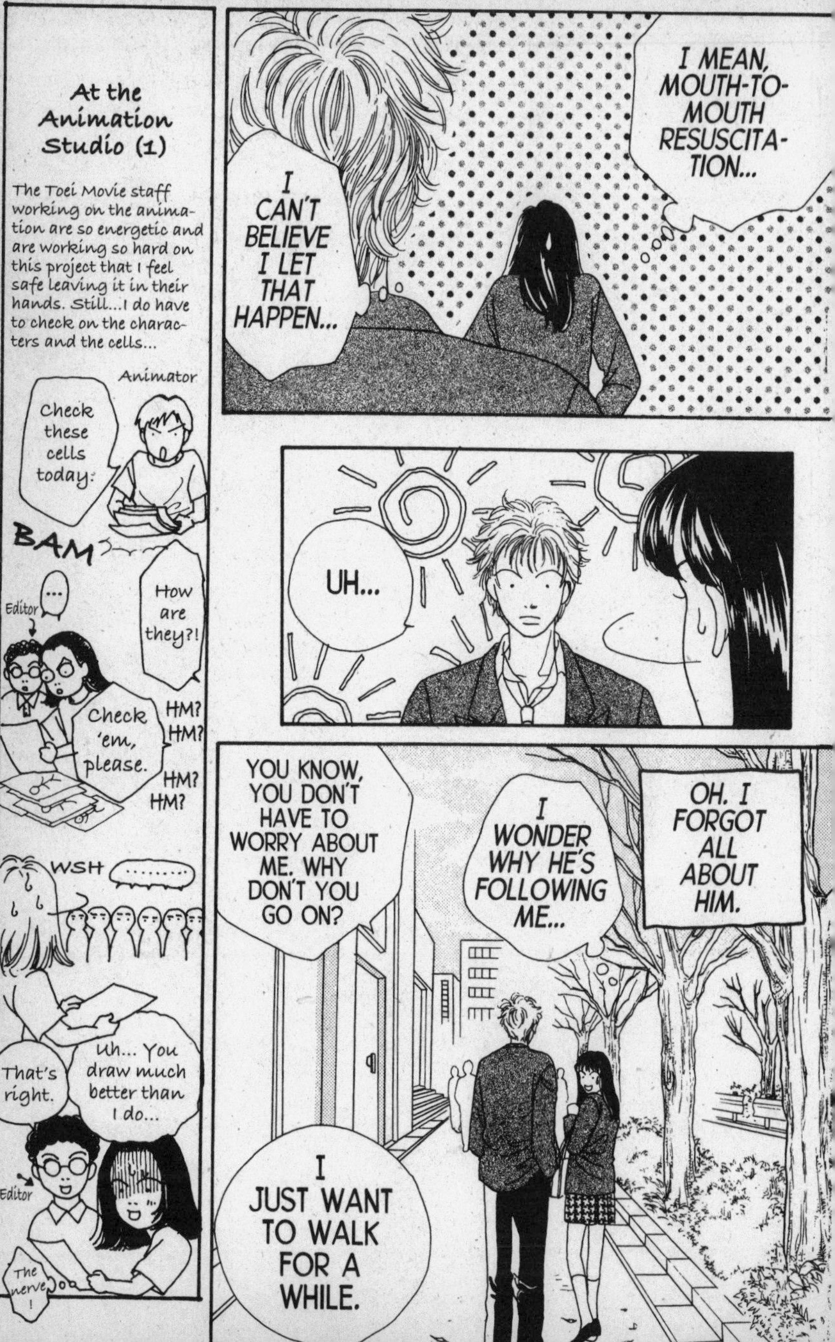
I MEAN, MOUTH-TO-MOUTH RESUSCITATION...
I CAN'T BELIEVE I LET THAT HAPPEN...
UH...
OH. I FORGOT ALL ABOUT HIM.
I WONDER WHY HE'S FOLLOWING ME...
YOU KNOW, YOU DON'T HAVE TO WORRY ABOUT ME. WHY DON'T YOU GO ON?
I JUST WANT TO WALK FOR A WHILE.
At the Animation Studio (1)
The Toei Movie staff working on the animation are so energetic and are working so hard on this project that I feel safe leaving it in their hands. Still...I do have to check on the characters and the cells...
Animator
Check these cells today.
BAM
How are they?!
...
Editor
Check 'em, please.
HM? HM?
HM? HM?
WSH
....
Uh... You draw much better than I do...
That's right.
Editor
The nerve!

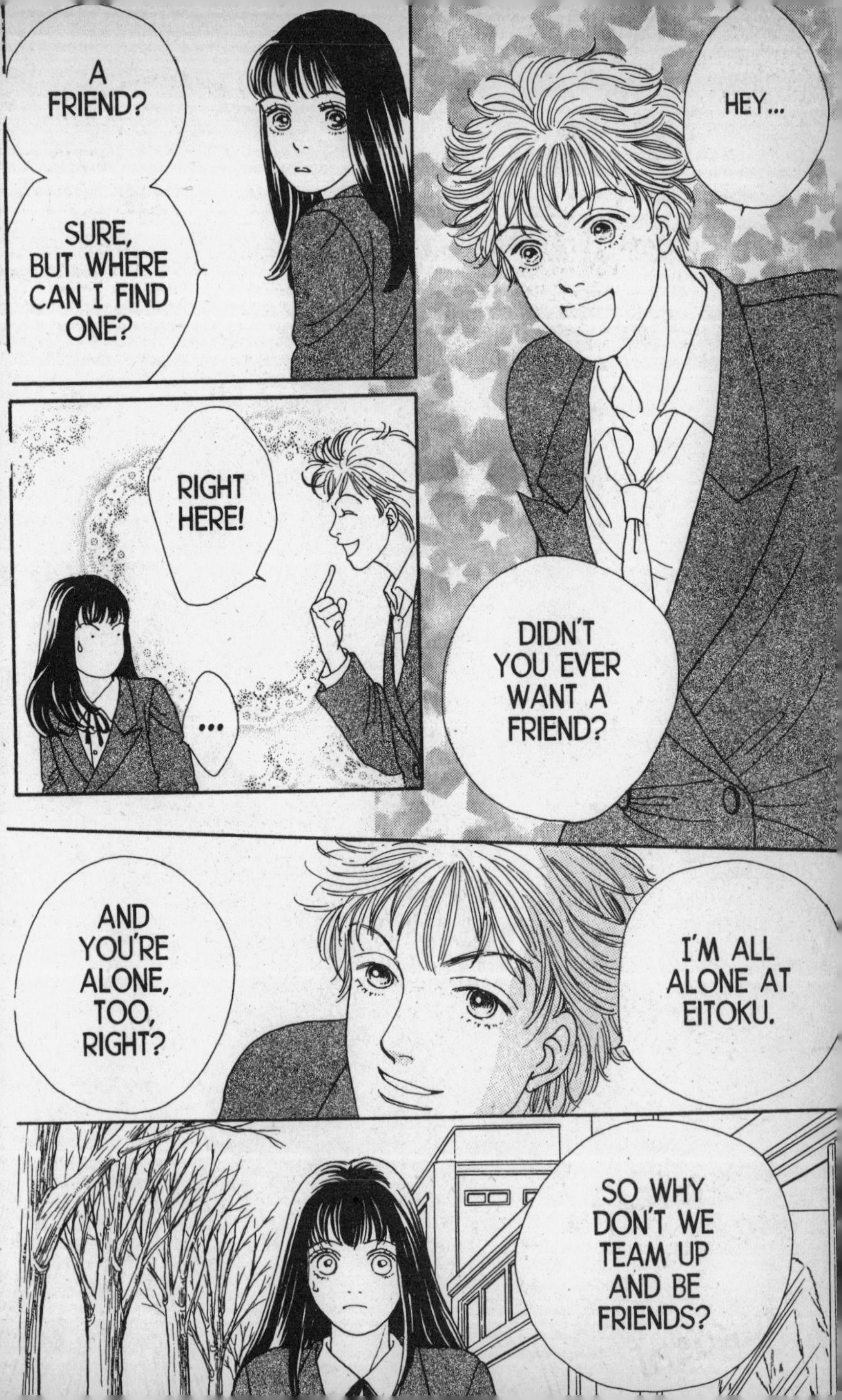
HEY...
DIDN'T YOU EVER WANT A FRIEND?
A FRIEND?
SURE, BUT WHERE CAN I FIND ONE?
RIGHT HERE!
...
I'M ALL ALONE AT EITOKU.
AND YOU'RE ALONE, TOO, RIGHT?
SO WHY DON'T WE TEAM UP AND BE FRIENDS?

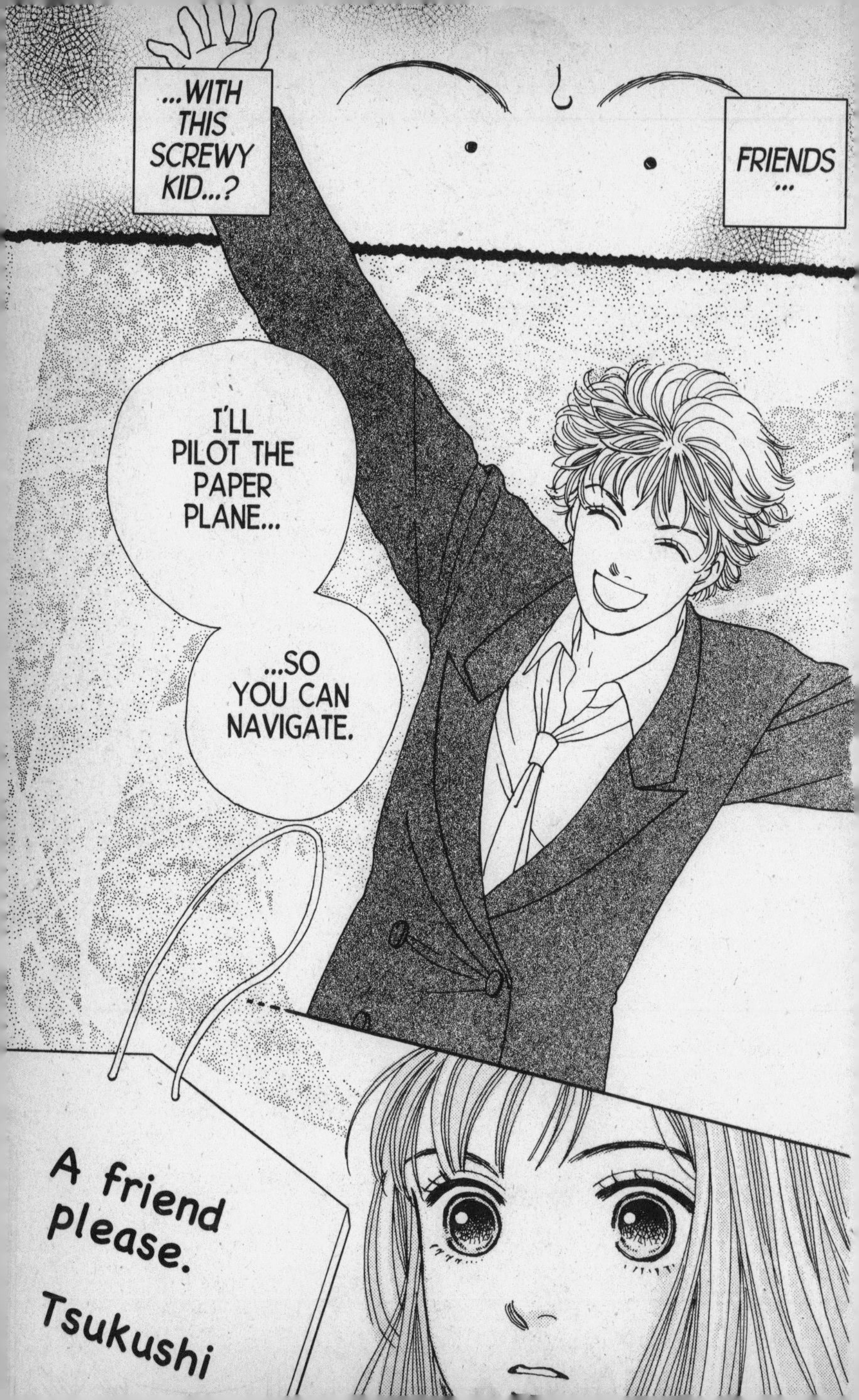
FRIENDS...
...WITH THIS SCREWY KID...?
I'LL PILOT THE PAPER PLANE...
...SO YOU CAN NAVIGATE.
A friend please.
Tsukushi

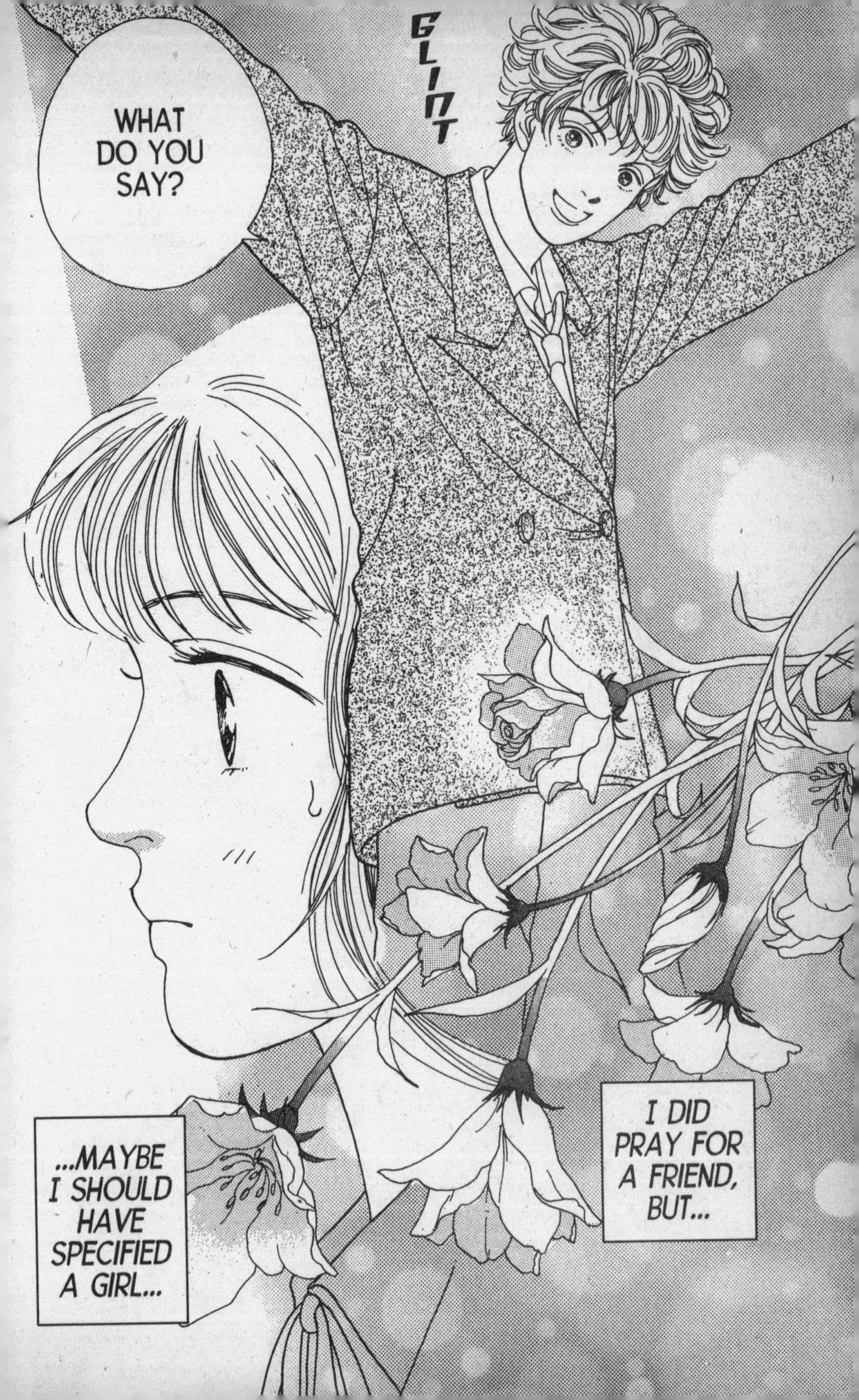
GLINT
WHAT DO YOU SAY?
I DID PRAY FOR A FRIEND, BUT...
...MAYBE I SHOULD HAVE SPECIFIED A GIRL...

BUT THE REASON I FOUND MYSELF NODDING...

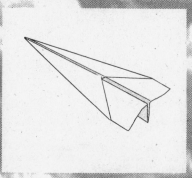

...IS THAT I THOUGHT IT WOULDN'T BE SO BAD TO BE ON THAT PAPER PLANE...

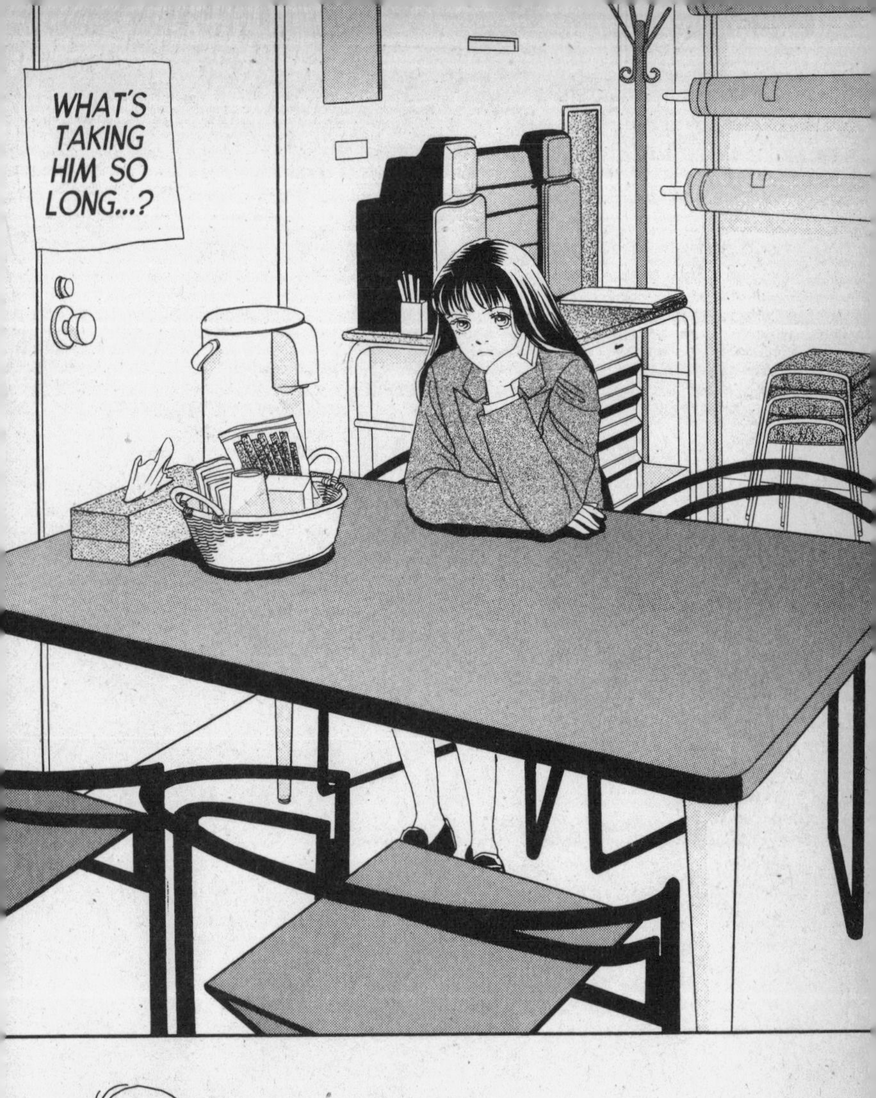
WHAT'S TAKING HIM SO LONG...?

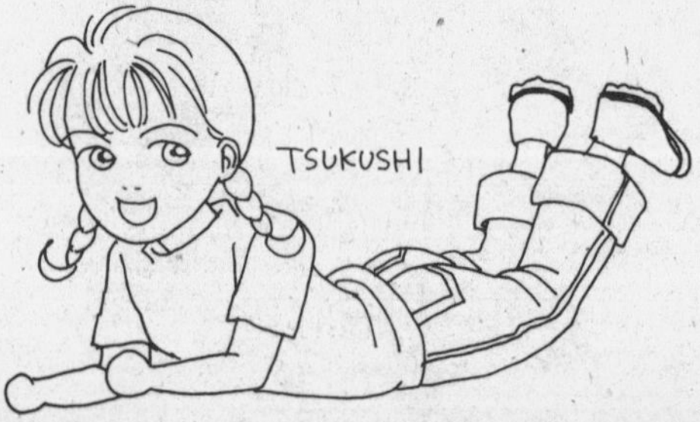
TSUKUSHI

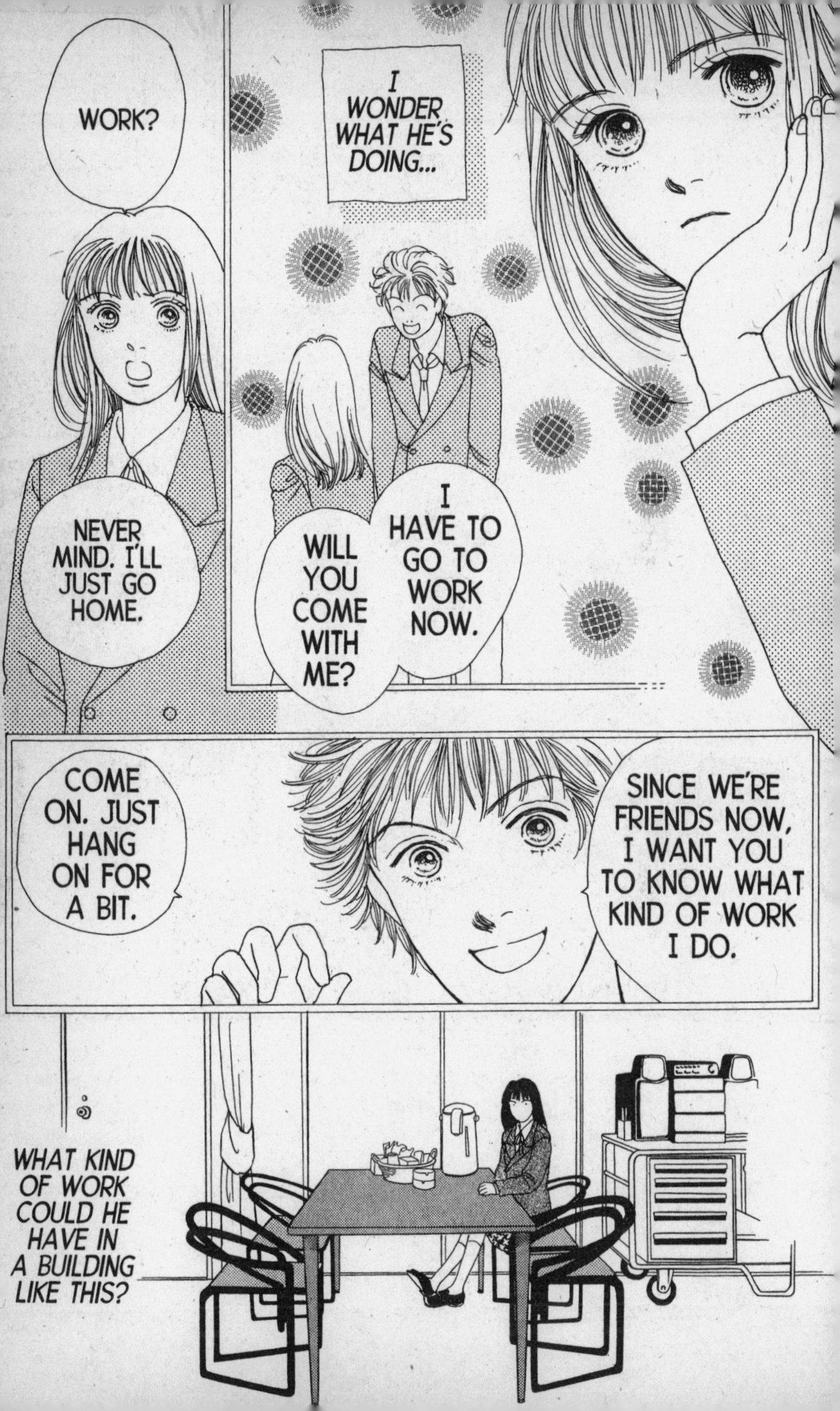
I WONDER WHAT HE'S DOING...
I HAVE TO GO TO WORK NOW.
WILL YOU COME WITH ME?
WORK?
NEVER MIND. I'LL JUST GO HOME.
SINCE WE'RE FRIENDS NOW, I WANT YOU TO KNOW WHAT KIND OF WORK I DO.
COME ON. JUST HANG ON FOR A BIT.
WHAT KIND OF WORK COULD HE HAVE IN A BUILDING LIKE THIS?

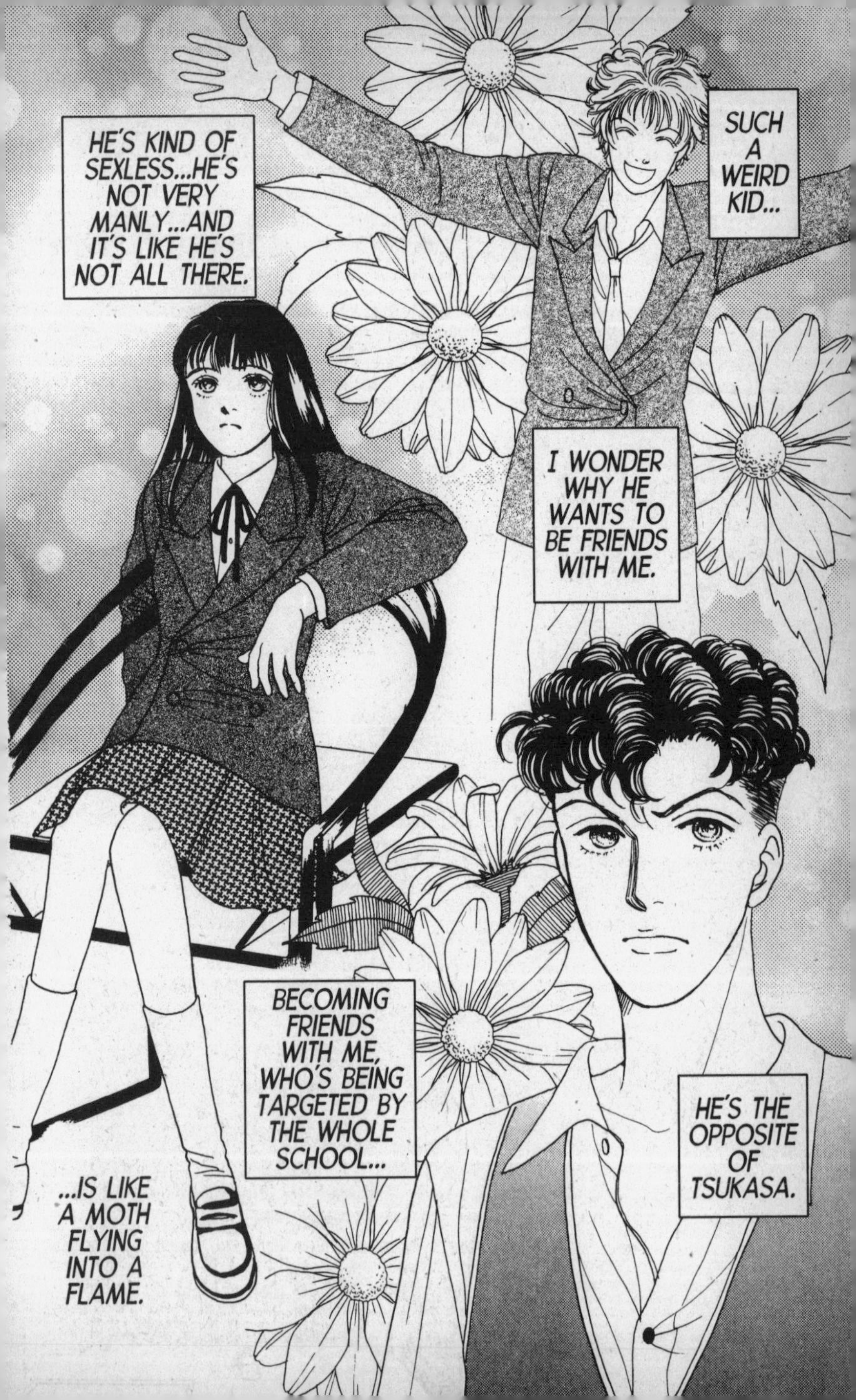
SUCH A WEIRD KID...
HE'S KIND OF SEXLESS...HE'S NOT VERY MANLY...AND IT'S LIKE HE'S NOT ALL THERE.
I WONDER WHY HE WANTS TO BE FRIENDS WITH ME.
HE'S THE OPPOSITE OF TSUKASA.
BECOMING FRIENDS WITH ME, WHO'S BEING TARGETED BY THE WHOLE SCHOOL...
...IS LIKE A MOTH FLYING INTO A FLAME.

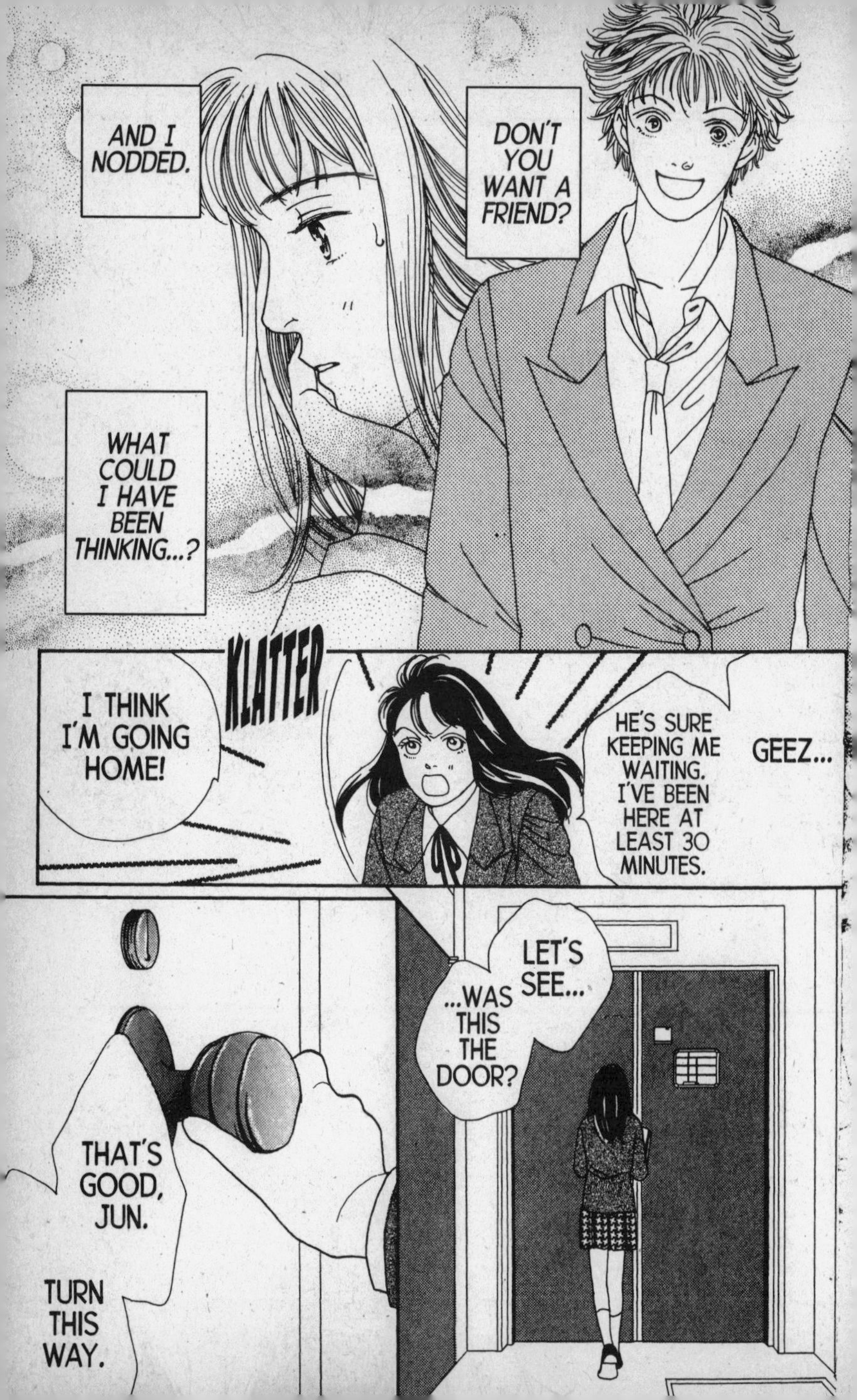
DON'T YOU WANT A FRIEND?
AND I NODDED.
WHAT COULD I HAVE BEEN THINKING...?
GEEZ...
HE'S SURE KEEPING ME WAITING. I'VE BEEN HERE AT LEAST 30 MINUTES.
KLATTER
I THINK I'M GOING HOME!
LET'S SEE...
...WAS THIS THE DOOR?
THAT'S GOOD, JUN.
TURN THIS WAY.

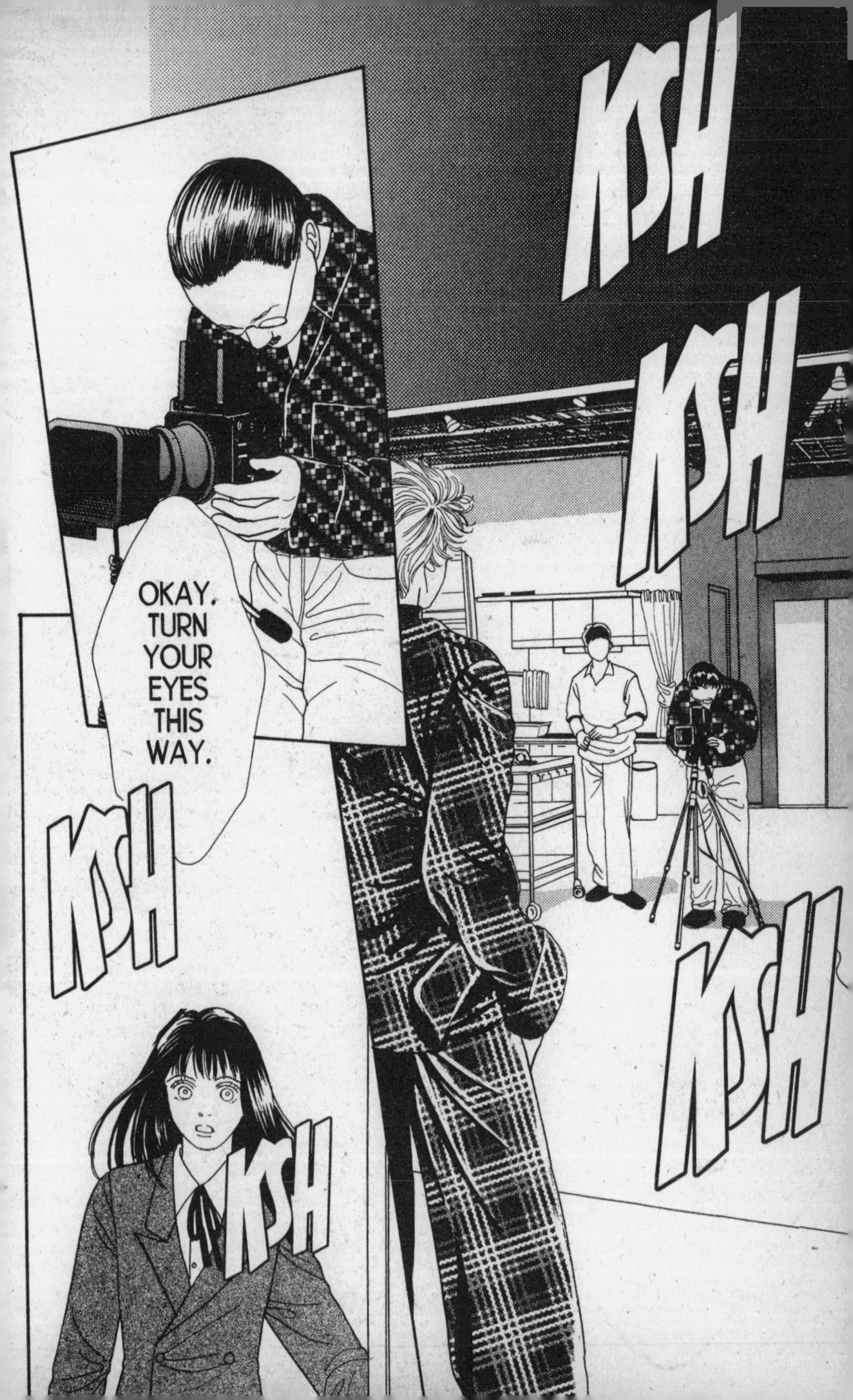
KSH
KSH
OKAY. TURN YOUR EYES THIS WAY.
KSH
KSH
KSH

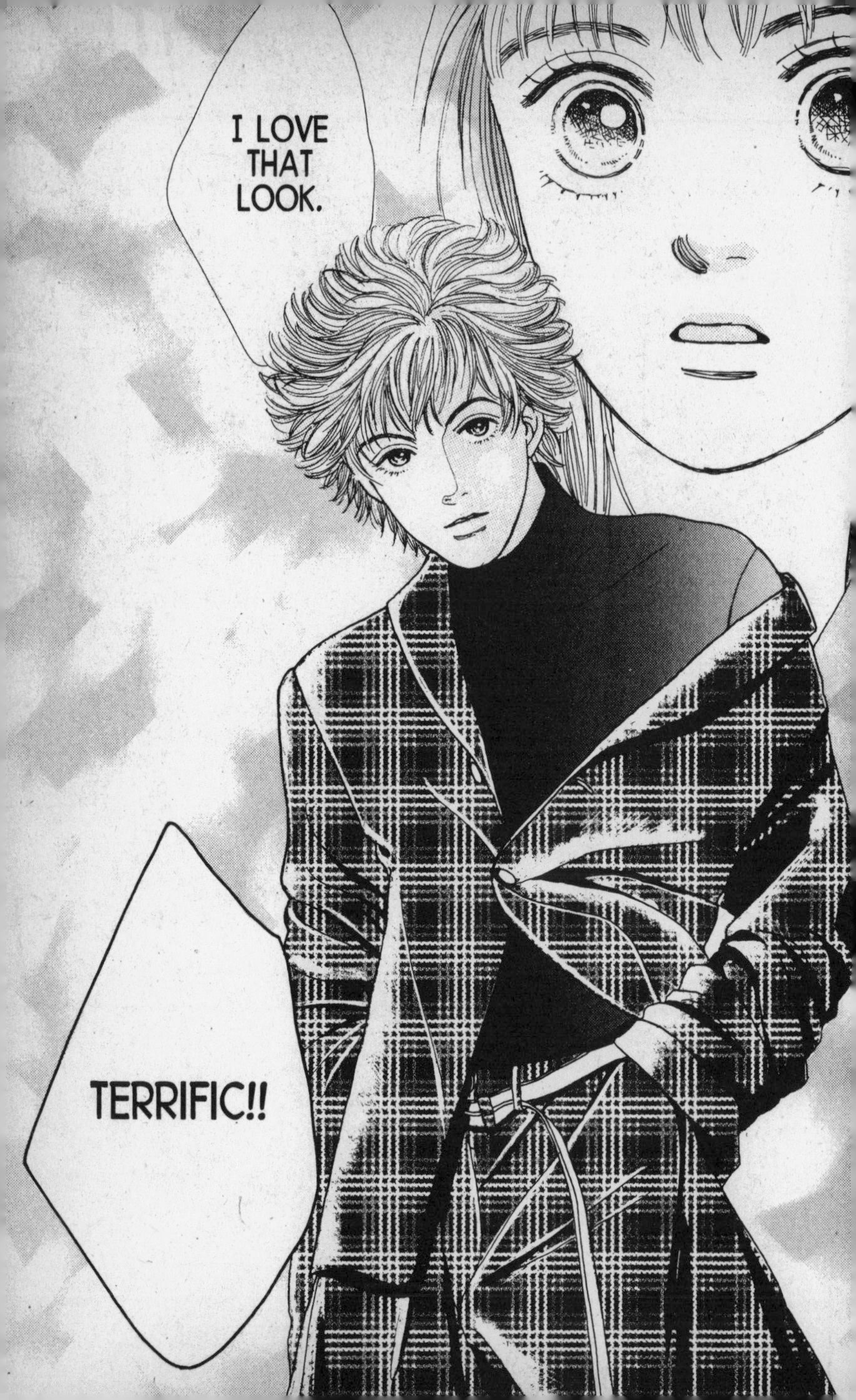
I LOVE THAT LOOK.
TERRIFIC!!

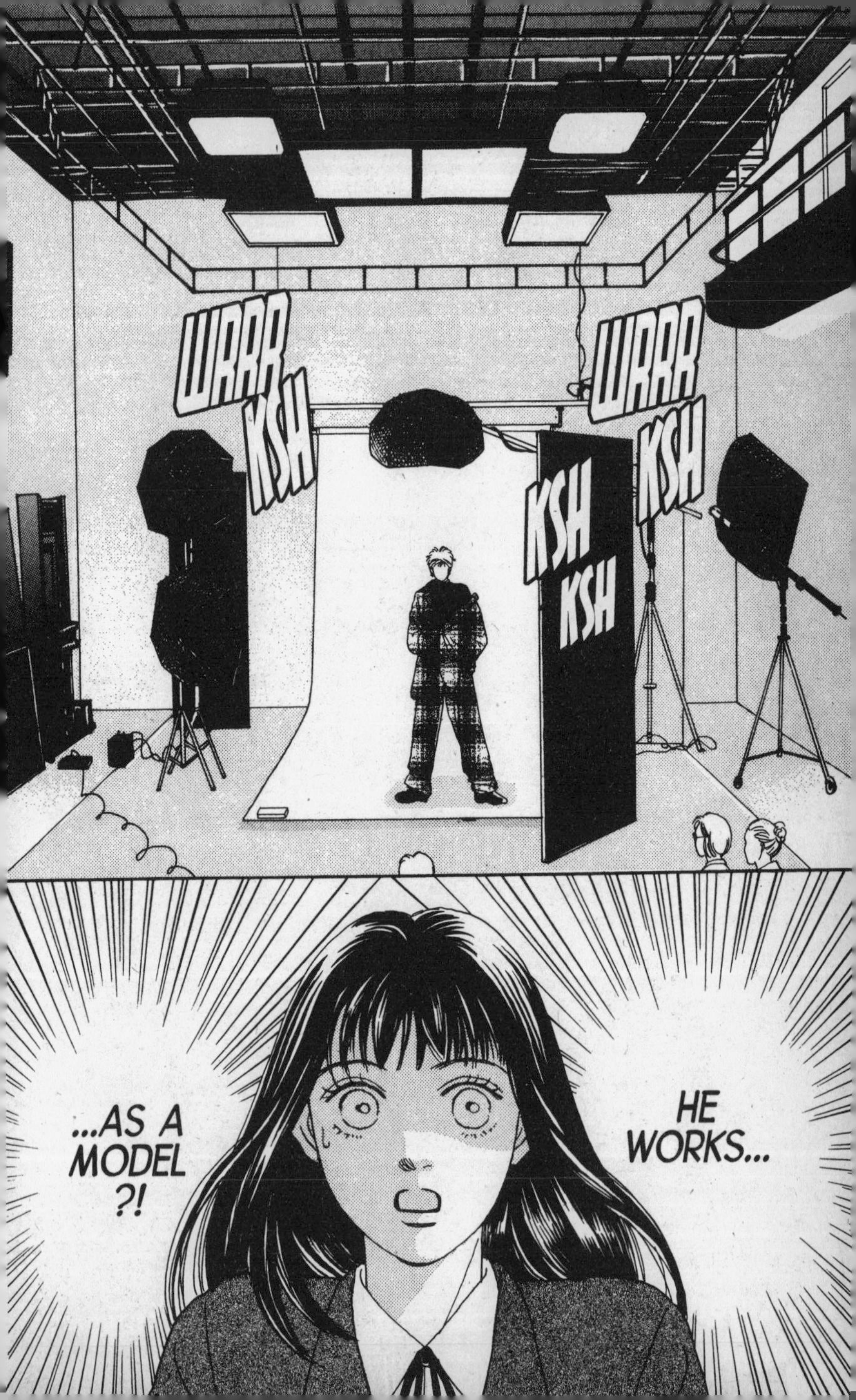
WRRR
KSH
KSH
KSH
KSH
WRRR
KSH
HE WORKS...
...AS A MODEL ?!

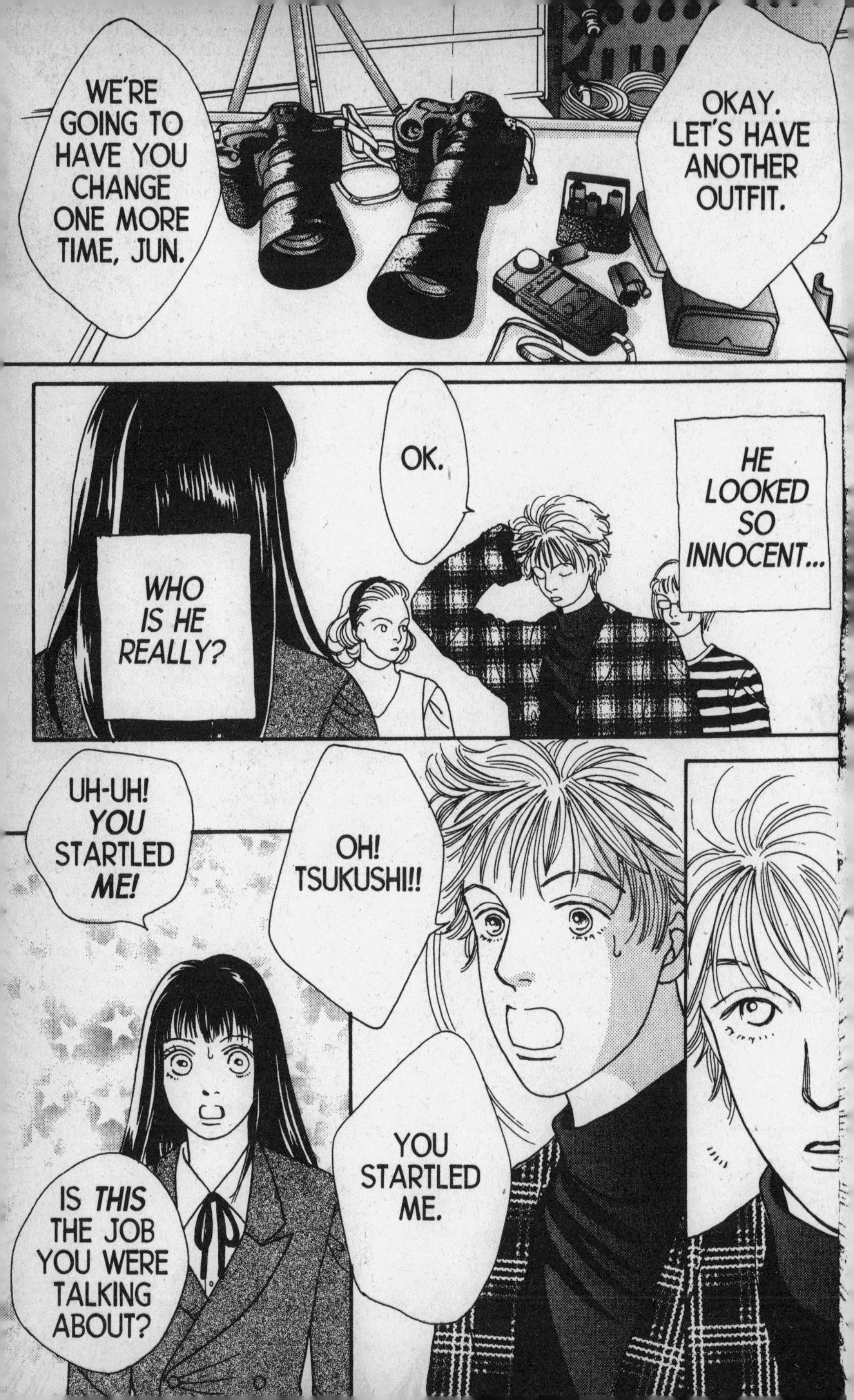
OKAY. LET'S HAVE ANOTHER OUTFIT.
WE'RE GOING TO HAVE YOU CHANGE ONE MORE TIME, JUN.
HE LOOKED SO INNOCENT...
OK.
WHO IS HE REALLY?
OH! TSUKUSHI!!
UH-UH! YOU STARTLED ME!
YOU STARTLED ME.
IS THIS THE JOB YOU WERE TALKING ABOUT?

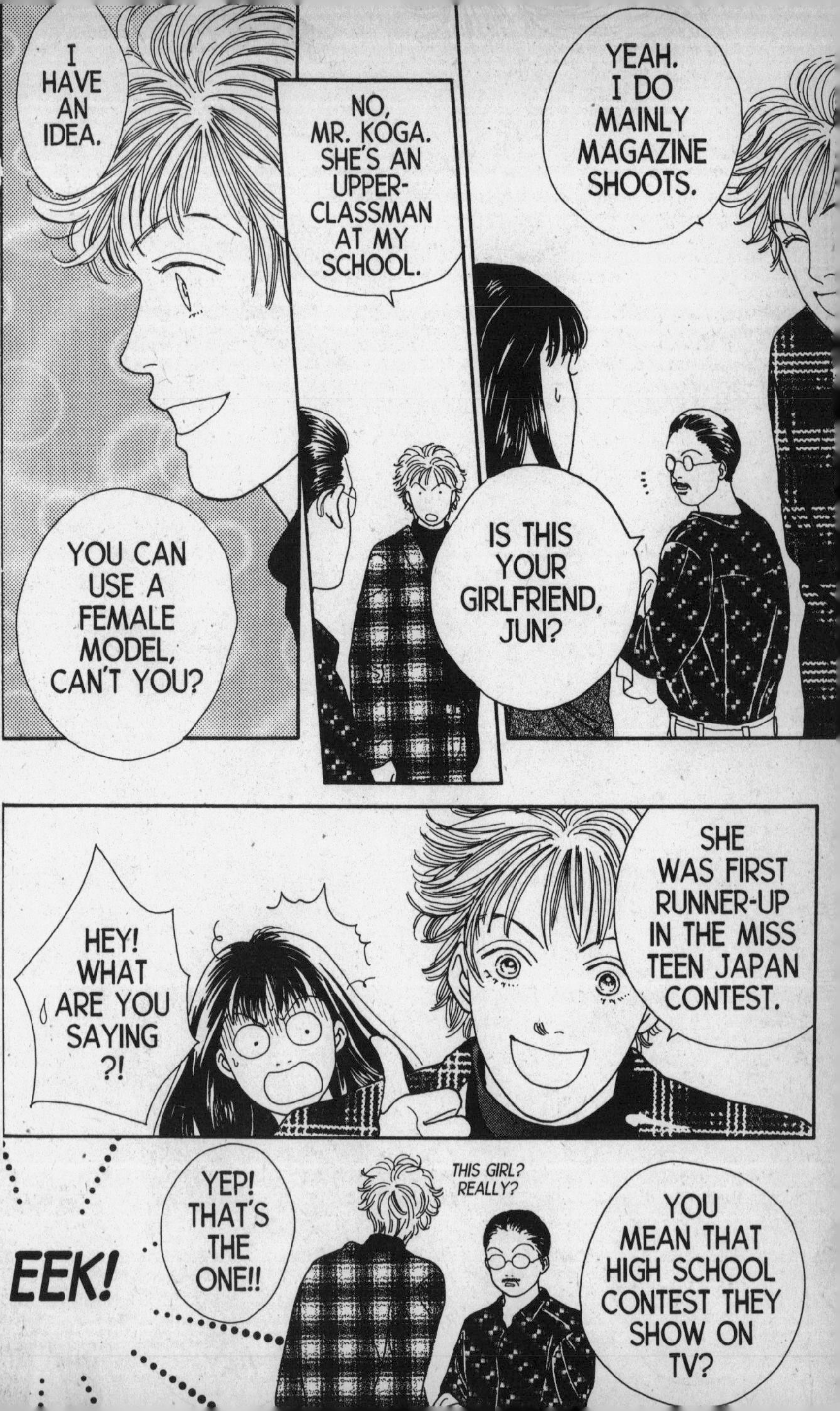
YEAH. I DO MAINLY MAGAZINE SHOOTS.
IS THIS YOUR GIRLFRIEND, JUN?
NO, MR. KOGA. SHE'S AN UPPER-CLASSMAN AT MY SCHOOL.
I HAVE AN IDEA.
YOU CAN USE A FEMALE MODEL, CAN'T YOU?
SHE WAS FIRST RUNNER-UP IN THE MISS TEEN JAPAN CONTEST.
HEY! WHAT ARE YOU SAYING ?!
YOU MEAN THAT HIGH SCHOOL CONTEST THEY SHOW ON TV?
THIS GIRL? REALLY?
YEP! THAT'S THE ONE!!
EEK!

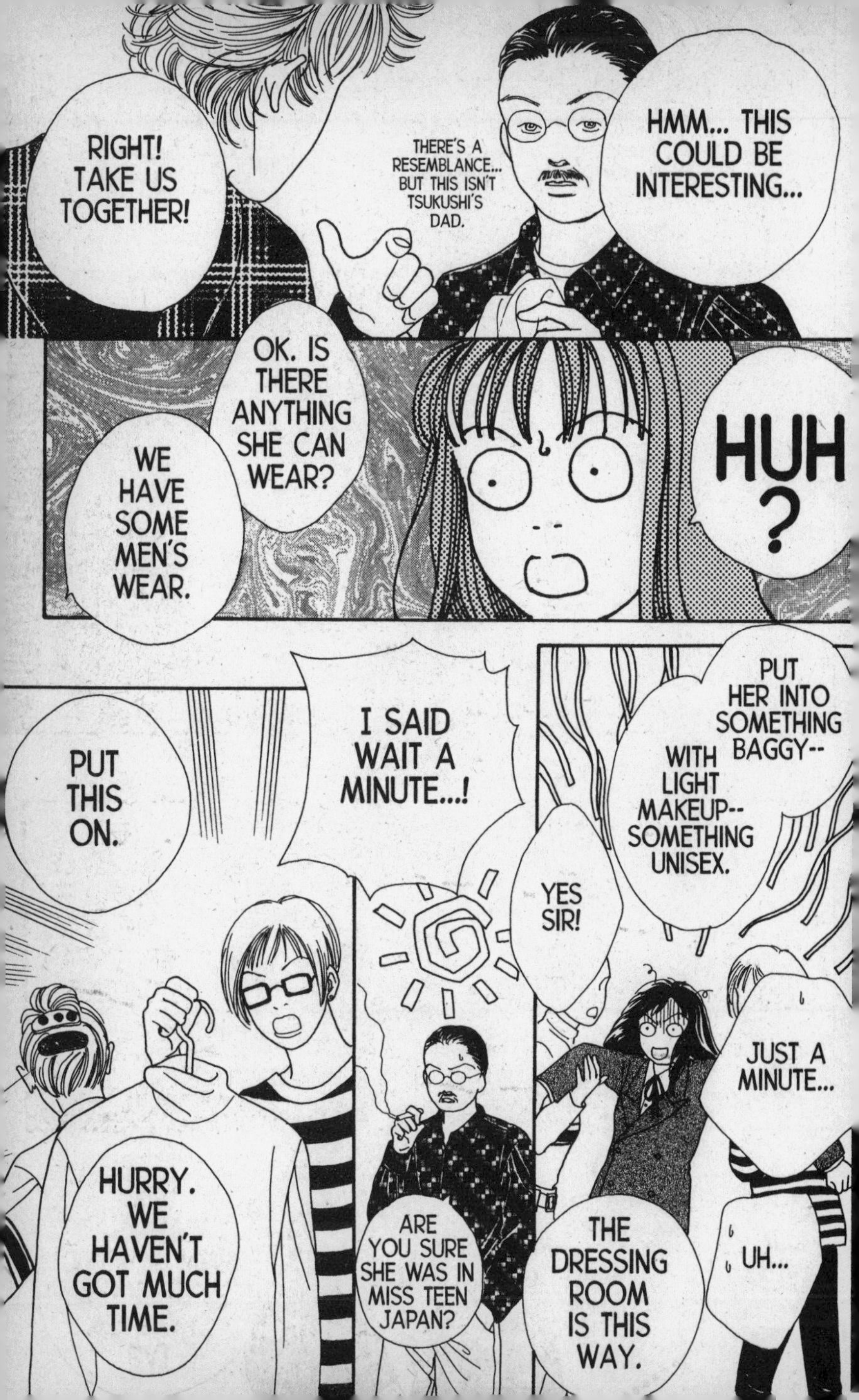
HMM... THIS COULD BE INTERESTING...
THERE'S A RESEMBLANCE... BUT THIS ISN'T TSUKUSHI'S DAD.
RIGHT! TAKE US TOGETHER!
HUH?
OK. IS THERE ANYTHING SHE CAN WEAR?
WE HAVE SOME MEN'S WEAR.
PUT HER INTO SOMETHING BAGGY--
WITH LIGHT MAKEUP-- SOMETHING UNISEX.
YES SIR!
JUST A MINUTE...
UH...
THE DRESSING ROOM IS THIS WAY.
I SAID WAIT A MINUTE...!
ARE YOU SURE SHE WAS IN MISS TEEN JAPAN?
PUT THIS ON.
HURRY. WE HAVEN'T GOT MUCH TIME.

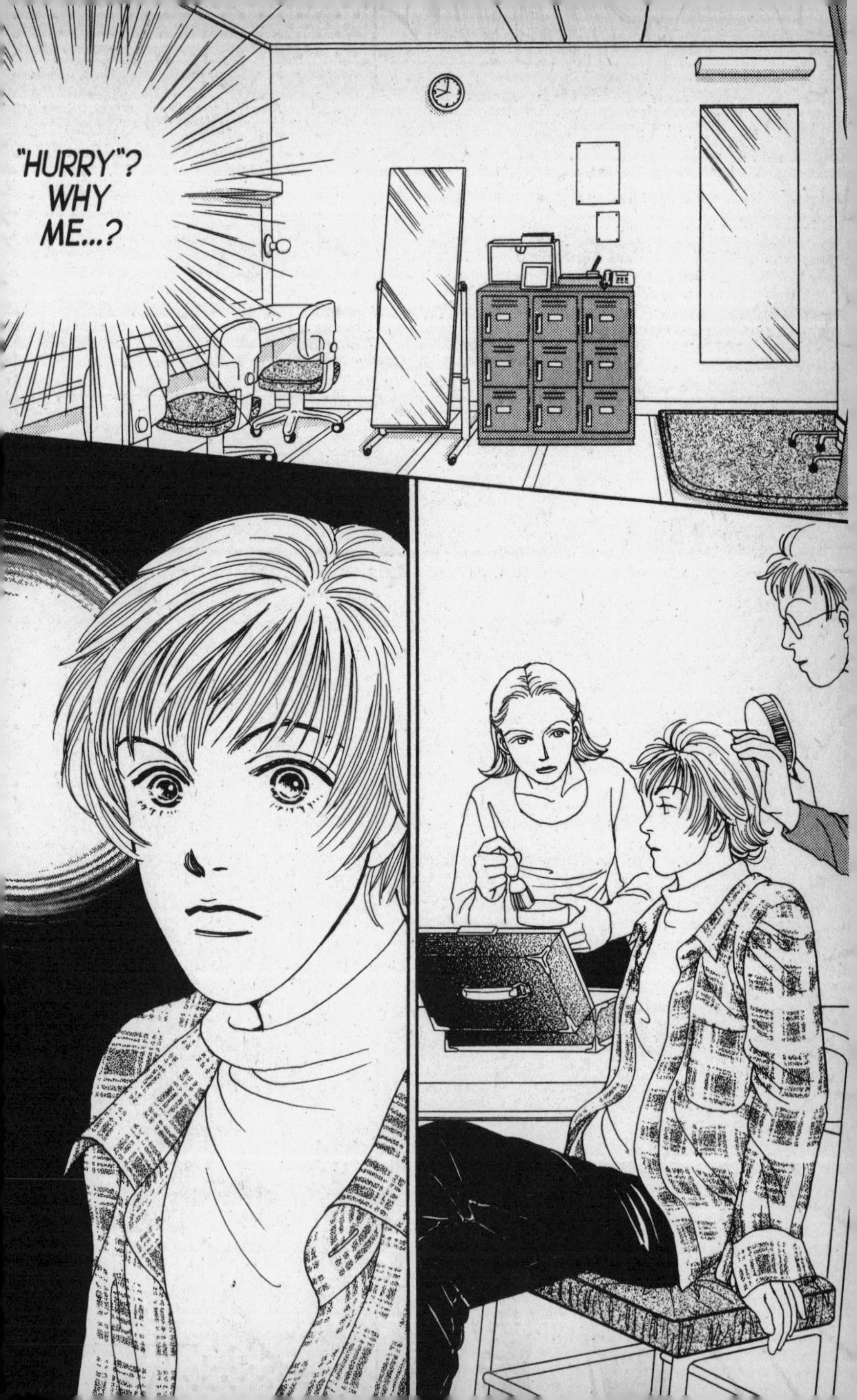
"HURRY"? WHY ME...?

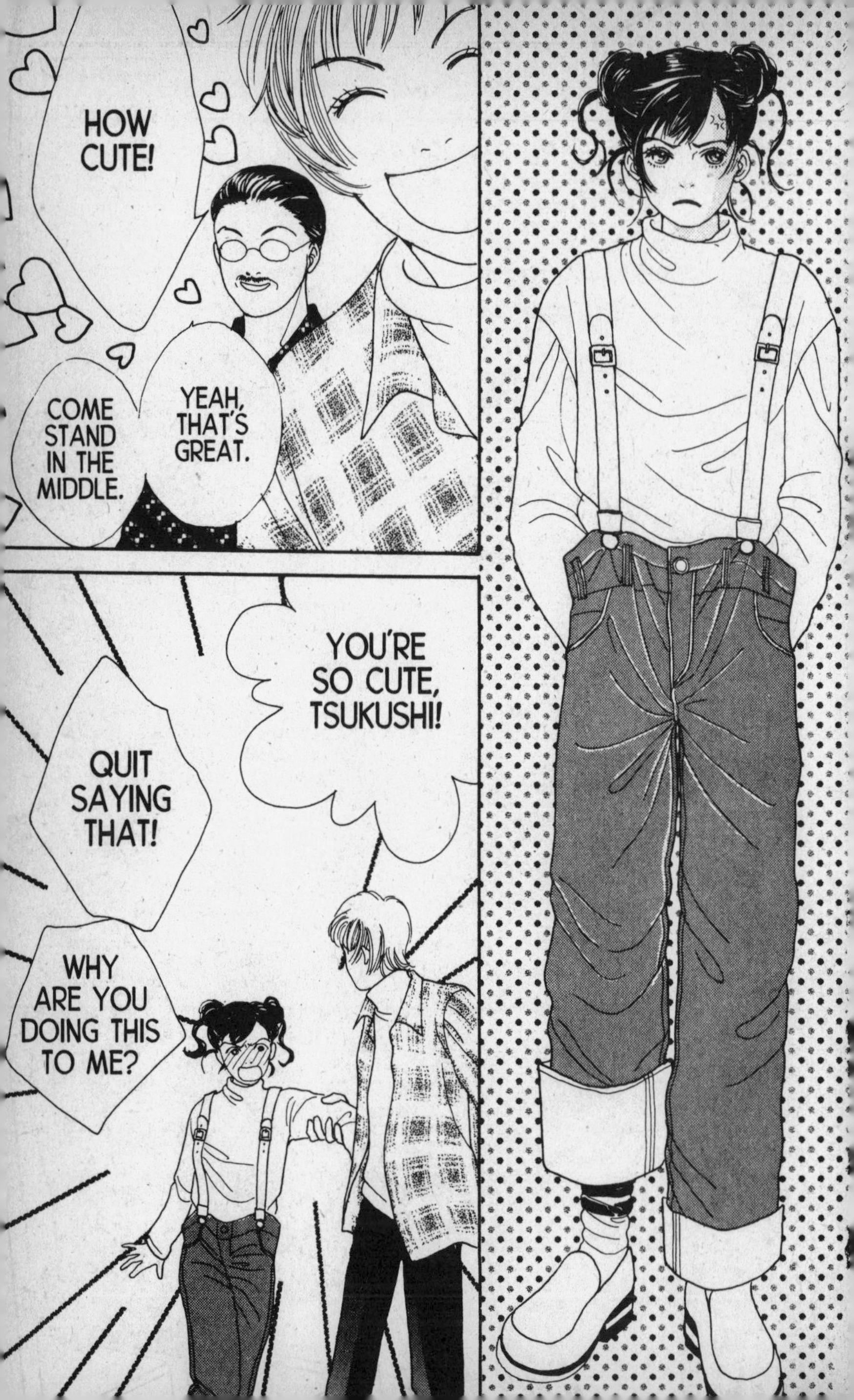
HOW CUTE!
YEAH, THAT'S GREAT.
COME STAND IN THE MIDDLE.
YOU'RE SO CUTE, TSUKUSHI!
QUIT SAYING THAT!
WHY ARE YOU DOING THIS TO ME?

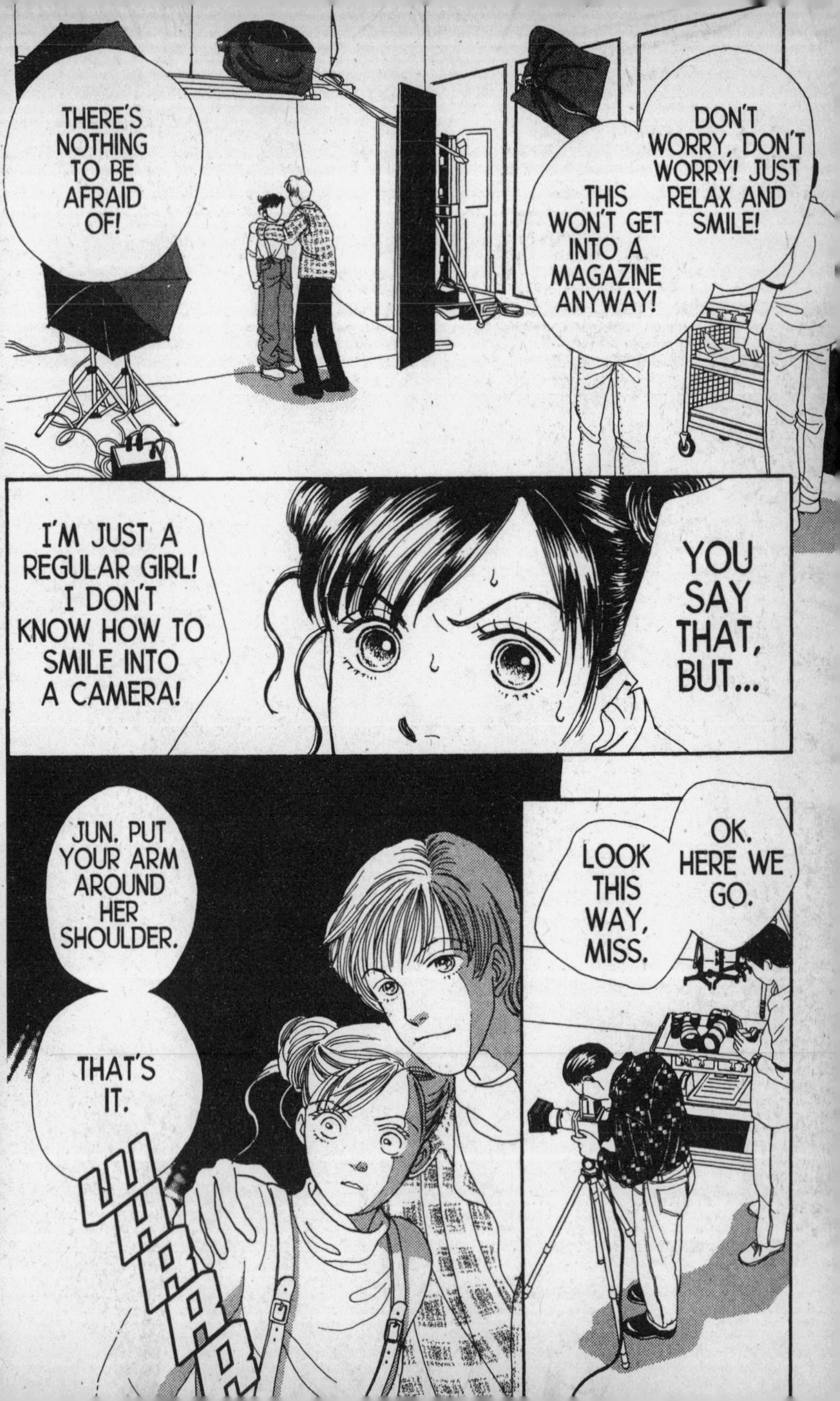
DON'T WORRY, DON'T WORRY! JUST RELAX AND SMILE!
THIS WON'T GET INTO A MAGAZINE ANYWAY!
THERE'S NOTHING TO BE AFRAID OF!
YOU SAY THAT, BUT...
I'M JUST A REGULAR GIRL! I DON'T KNOW HOW TO SMILE INTO A CAMERA!
OK. HERE WE GO.
LOOK THIS WAY, MISS.
JUN. PUT YOUR ARM AROUND HER SHOULDER.
THAT'S IT.
WHRRR

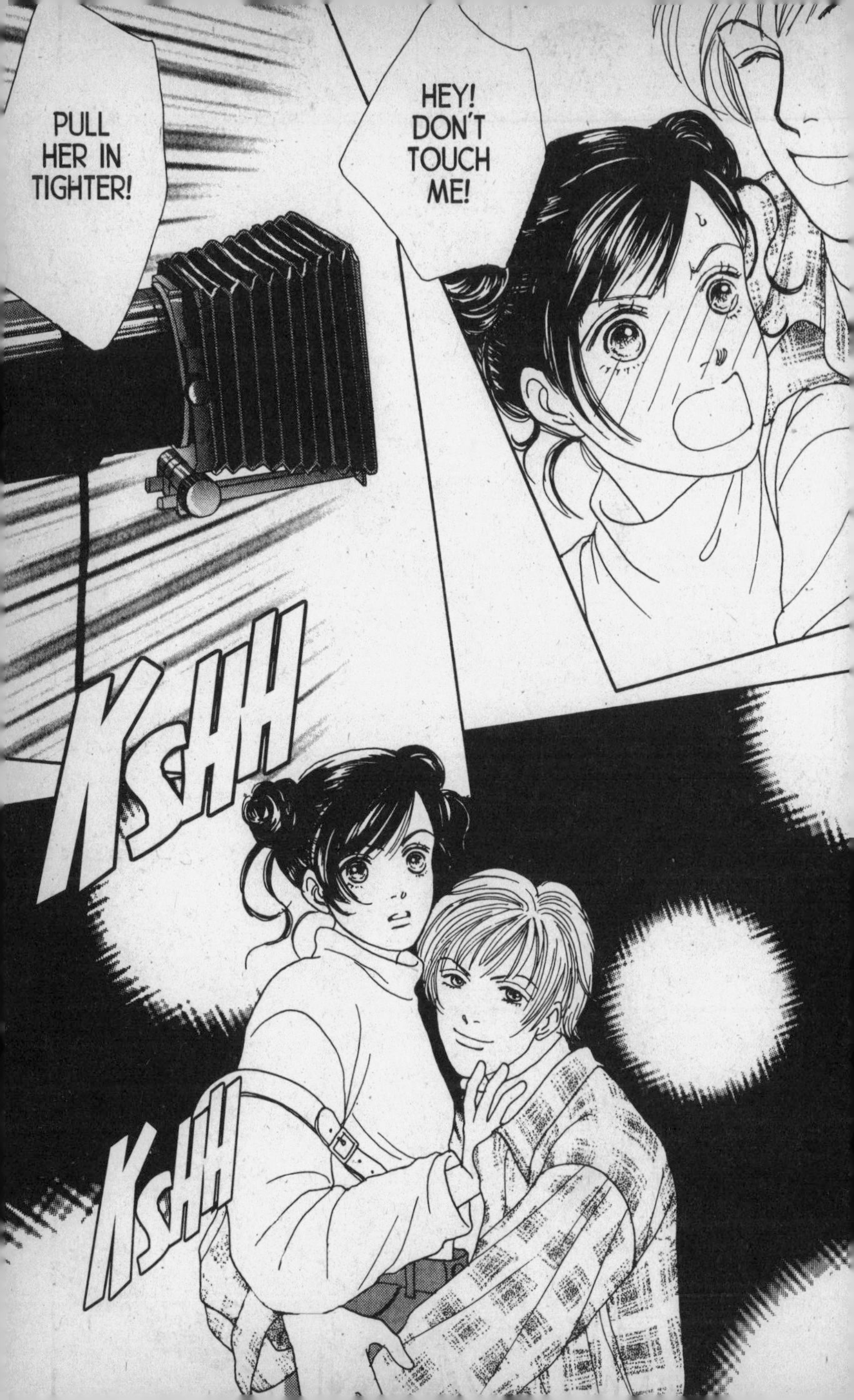
HEY! DON'T TOUCH ME!
PULL HER IN TIGHTER!
KSHH
KSHH

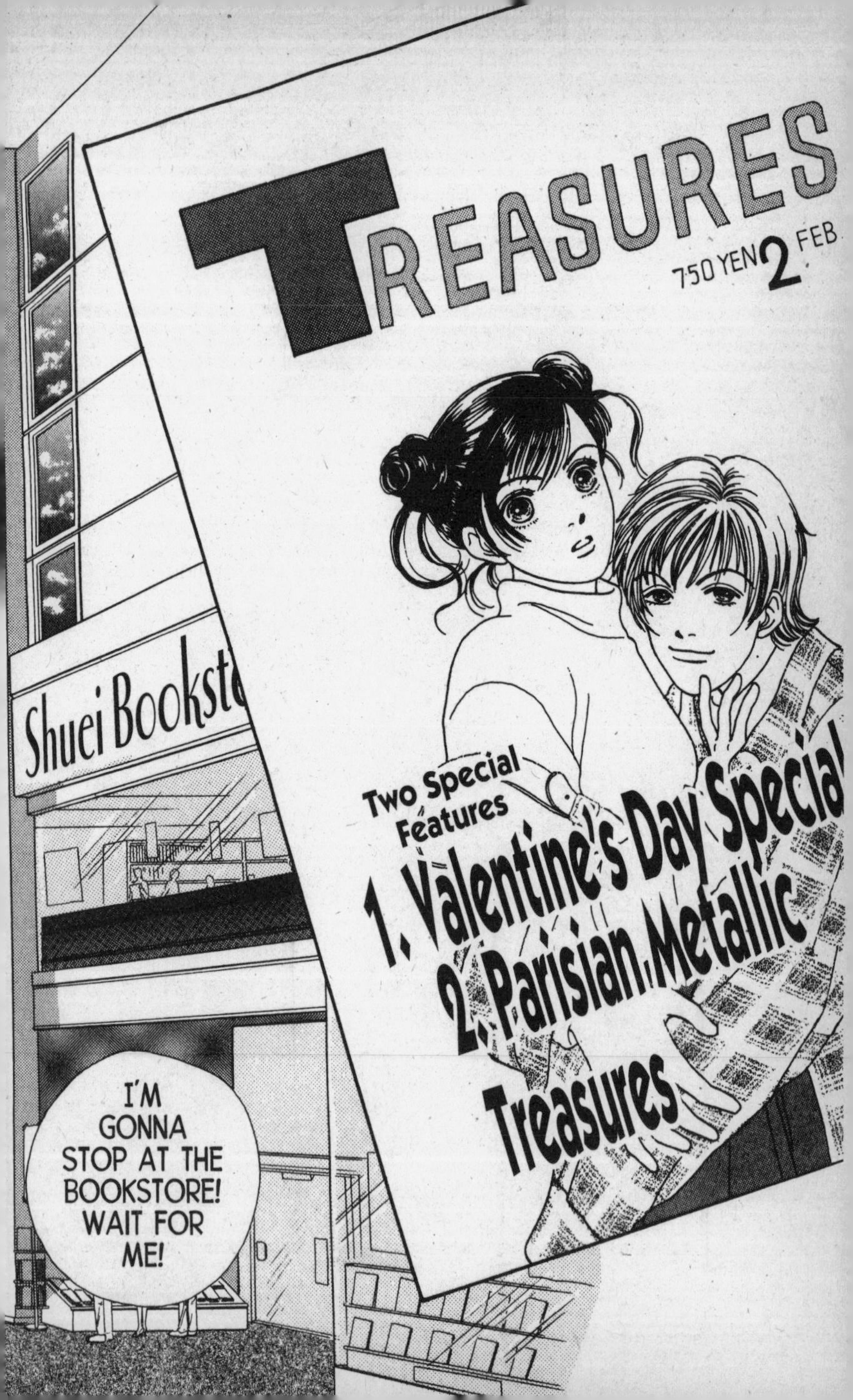
I'M GONNA STOP AT THE BOOKSTORE! WAIT FOR ME!
Shuei Bookst
TREASURES
750 YEN 2 FEB
Two Special Features
1. Valentine's Day Special
2. Parisian Metallic
Treasures

At the Animation Studio (2)

The animators are much, much better artists than I am, so I couldn't find anything to change or correct. I guess it looked like I wasn't into the job. But how could I improve on their Akira?

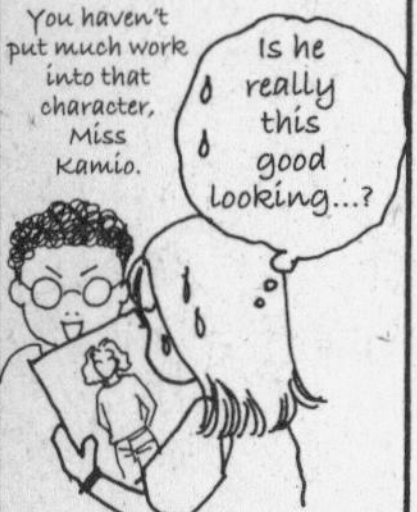

You haven't put much work into that character, Miss Kamio.
Is he really this good looking...?

As I was reading my 200 fan letters the other day, there was one Akira fan, who said:

"Please get Tsukushi and Akira together! Why don't you have Tsukushi comfort him when he's dumped by an older woman, and they fall in love?"

Now that's unusual!

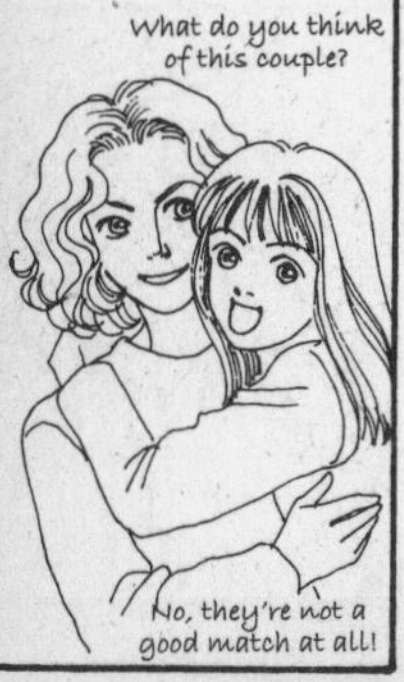

What do you think of this couple?
No, they're not a good match at all!

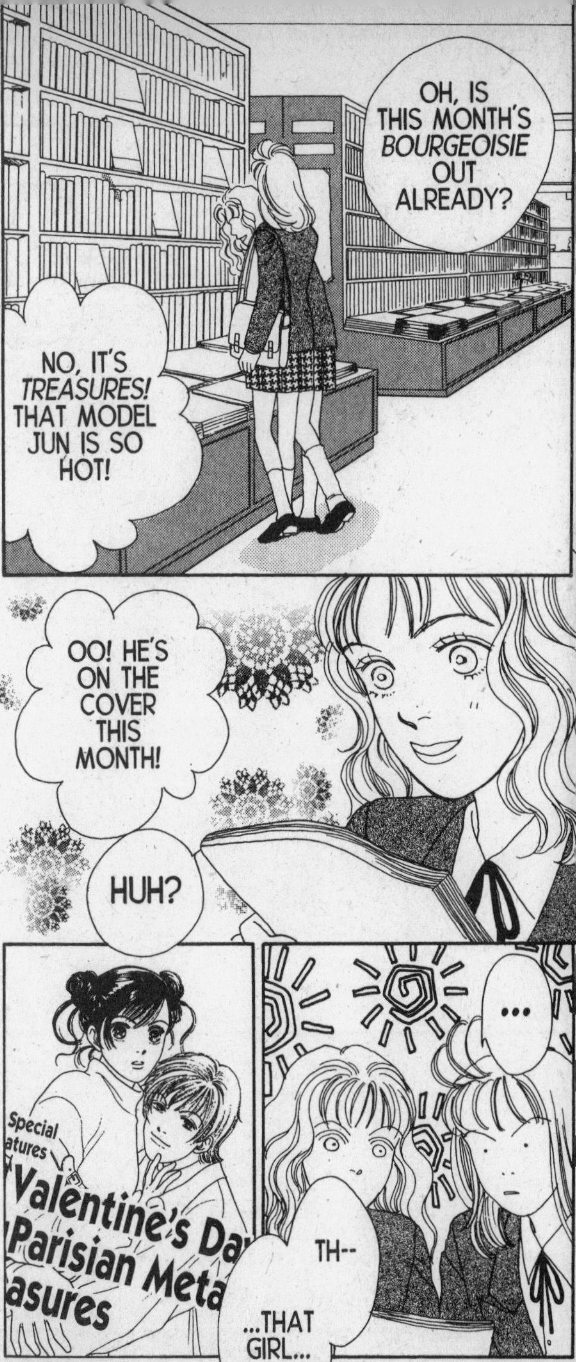

OH, IS THIS MONTH'S *BOURGEOISIE* OUT ALREADY?
NO, IT'S *TREASURES!* THAT MODEL JUN IS SO HOT!
OO! HE'S ON THE COVER THIS MONTH!
HUH?
...
TH--
...THAT GIRL...
Special
Valentine's Da
Parisian Meta
asures

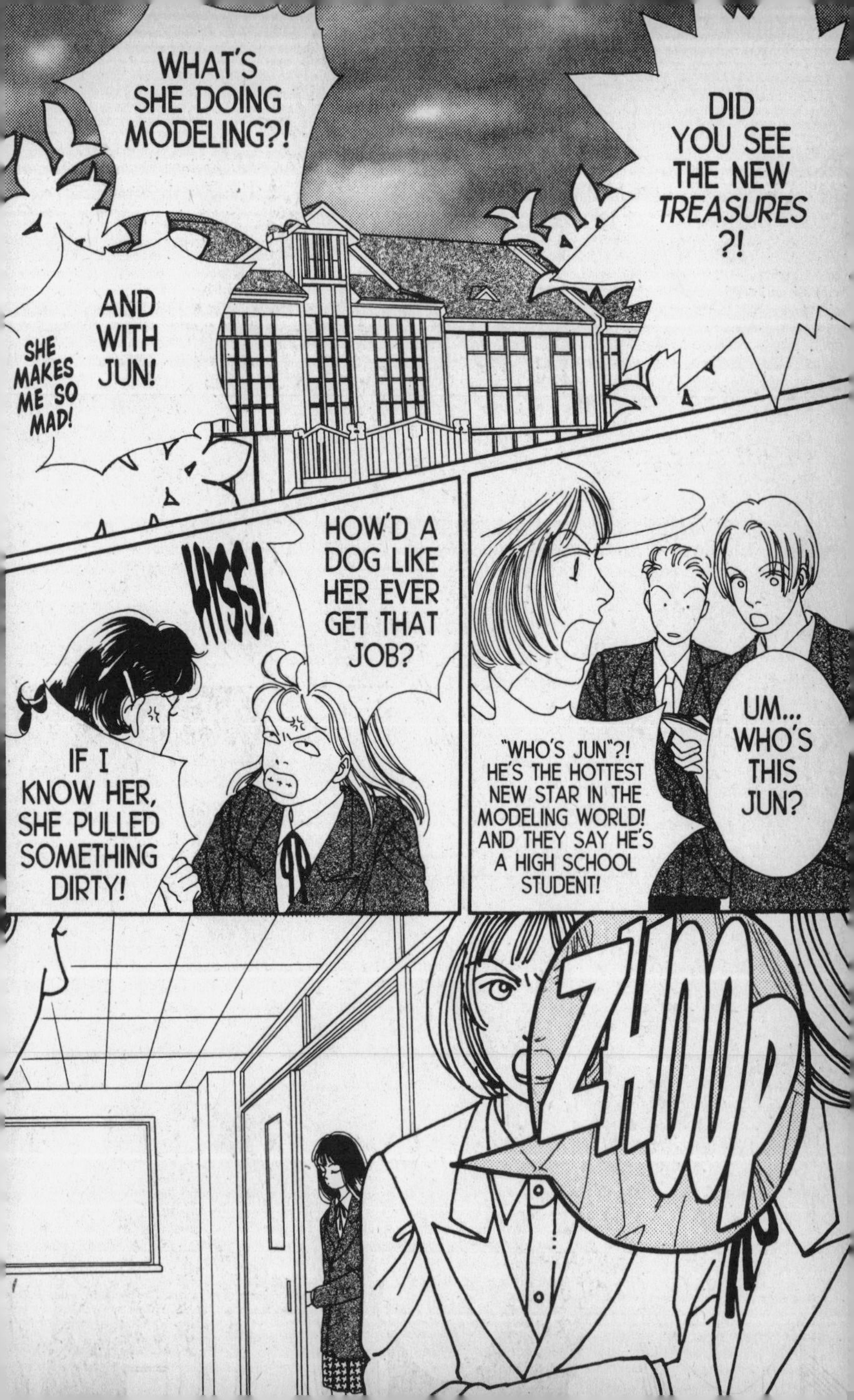
DID YOU SEE THE NEW *TREASURES* ?!
WHAT'S SHE DOING MODELING?!
AND WITH JUN!
SHE MAKES ME SO MAD!
UM... WHO'S THIS JUN?
"WHO'S JUN"?! HE'S THE HOTTEST NEW STAR IN THE MODELING WORLD! AND THEY SAY HE'S A HIGH SCHOOL STUDENT!
HOW'D A DOG LIKE HER EVER GET THAT JOB?
HISS!
IF I KNOW HER, SHE PULLED SOMETHING DIRTY!
ZHOOP

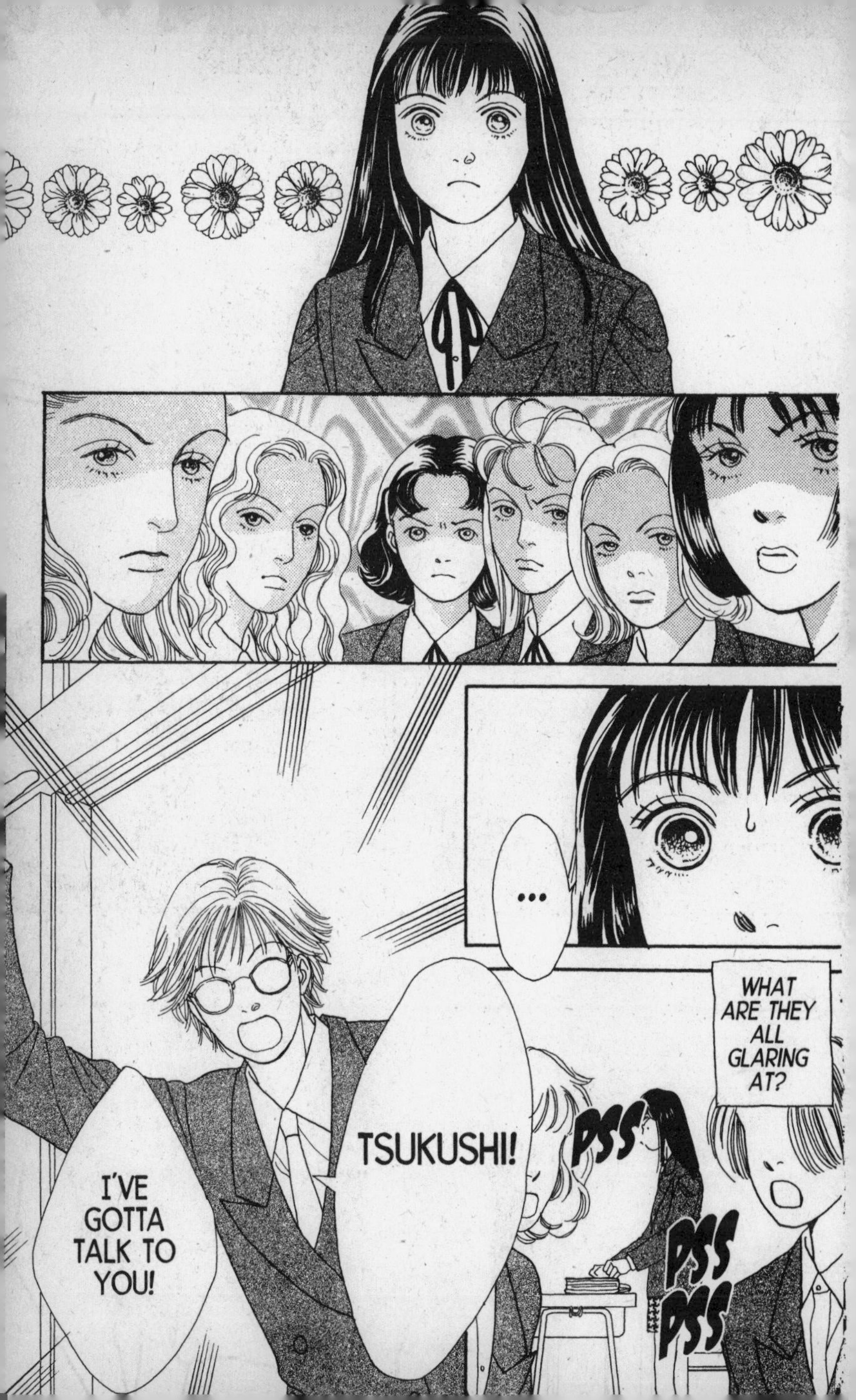
...
WHAT ARE THEY ALL GLARING AT?
PSS
PSS
PSS
TSUKUSHI!
I'VE GOTTA TALK TO YOU!

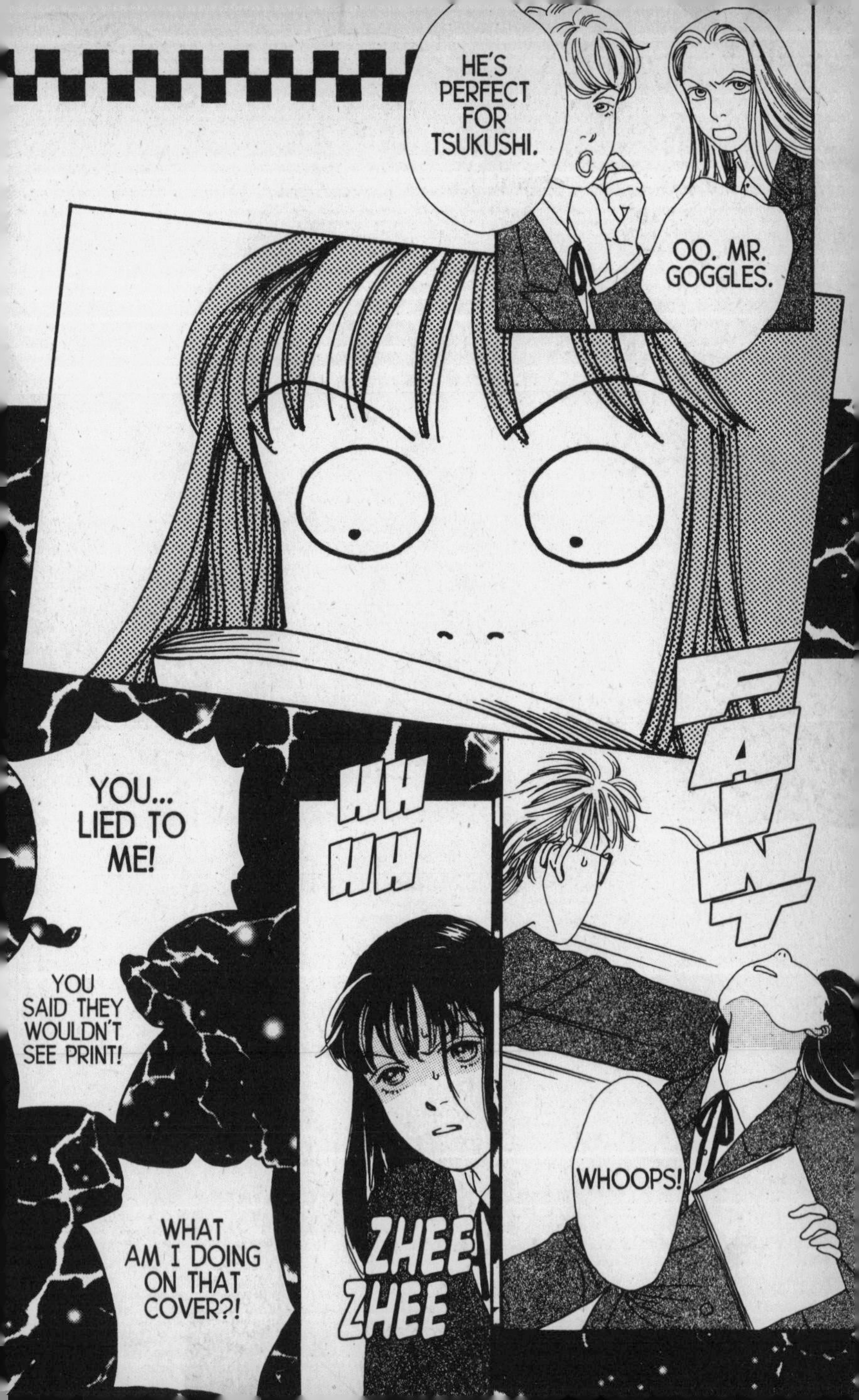
OO. MR. GOGGLES.
HE'S PERFECT FOR TSUKUSHI.
FAINT
WHOOPS!
HH HH
ZHEE ZHEE
YOU... LIED TO ME!
YOU SAID THEY WOULDN'T SEE PRINT!
WHAT AM I DOING ON THAT COVER?!

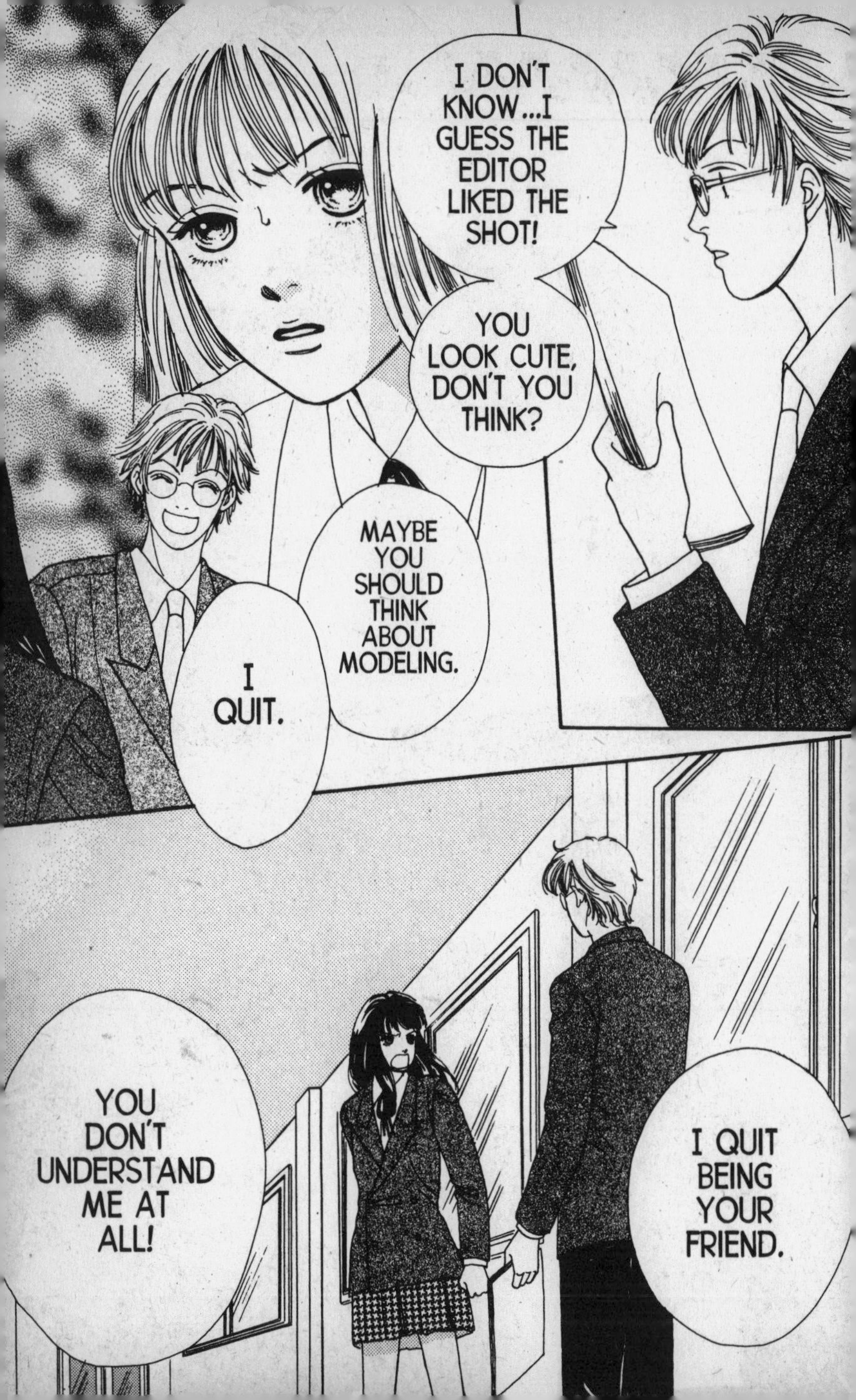
I DON'T KNOW...I GUESS THE EDITOR LIKED THE SHOT!
YOU LOOK CUTE, DON'T YOU THINK?
MAYBE YOU SHOULD THINK ABOUT MODELING.
I QUIT.
I QUIT BEING YOUR FRIEND.
YOU DON'T UNDERSTAND ME AT ALL!

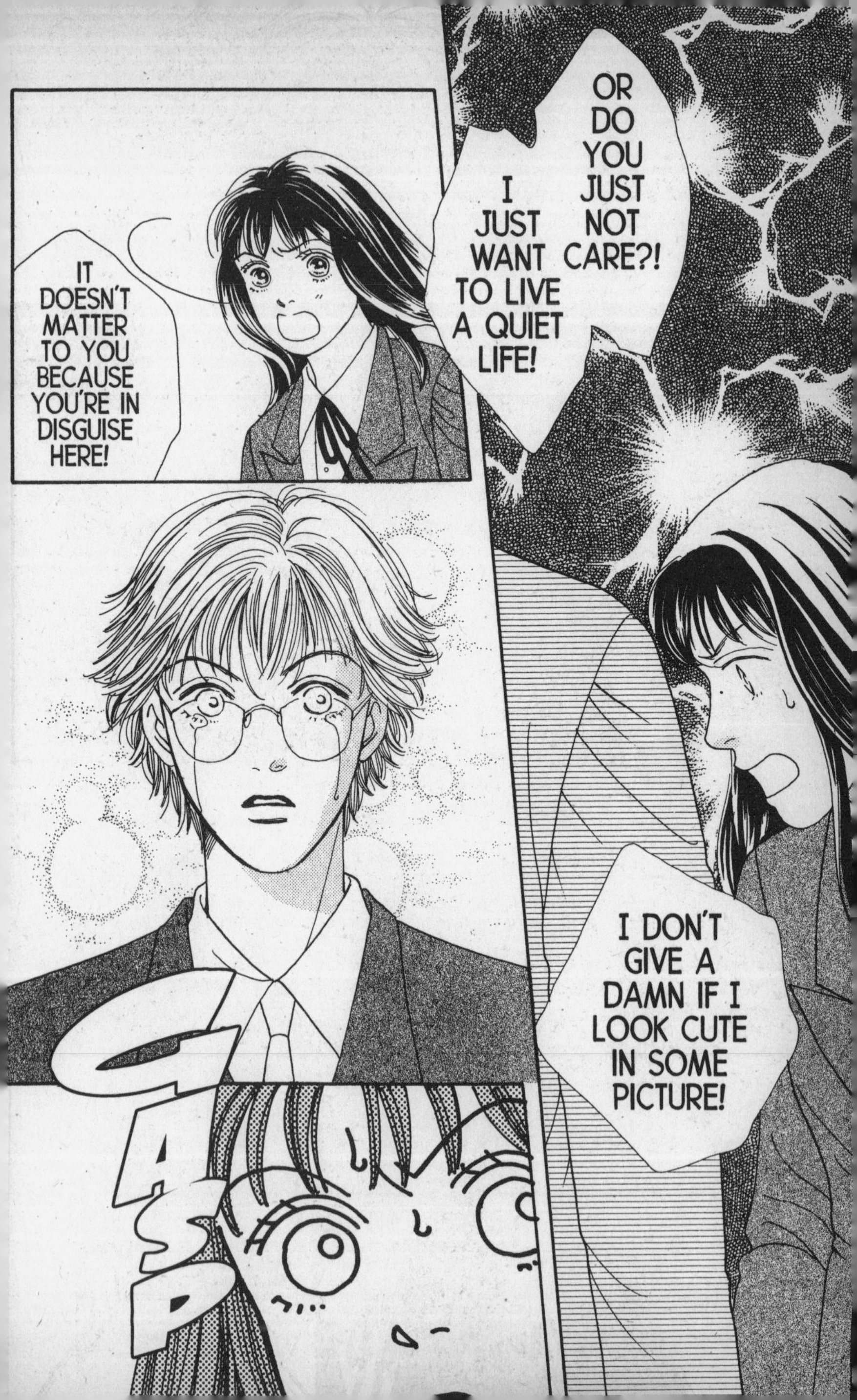
OR DO YOU JUST NOT CARE?!
I JUST WANT TO LIVE A QUIET LIFE!
I DON'T GIVE A DAMN IF I LOOK CUTE IN SOME PICTURE!
IT DOESN'T MATTER TO YOU BECAUSE YOU'RE IN DISGUISE HERE!
GASP

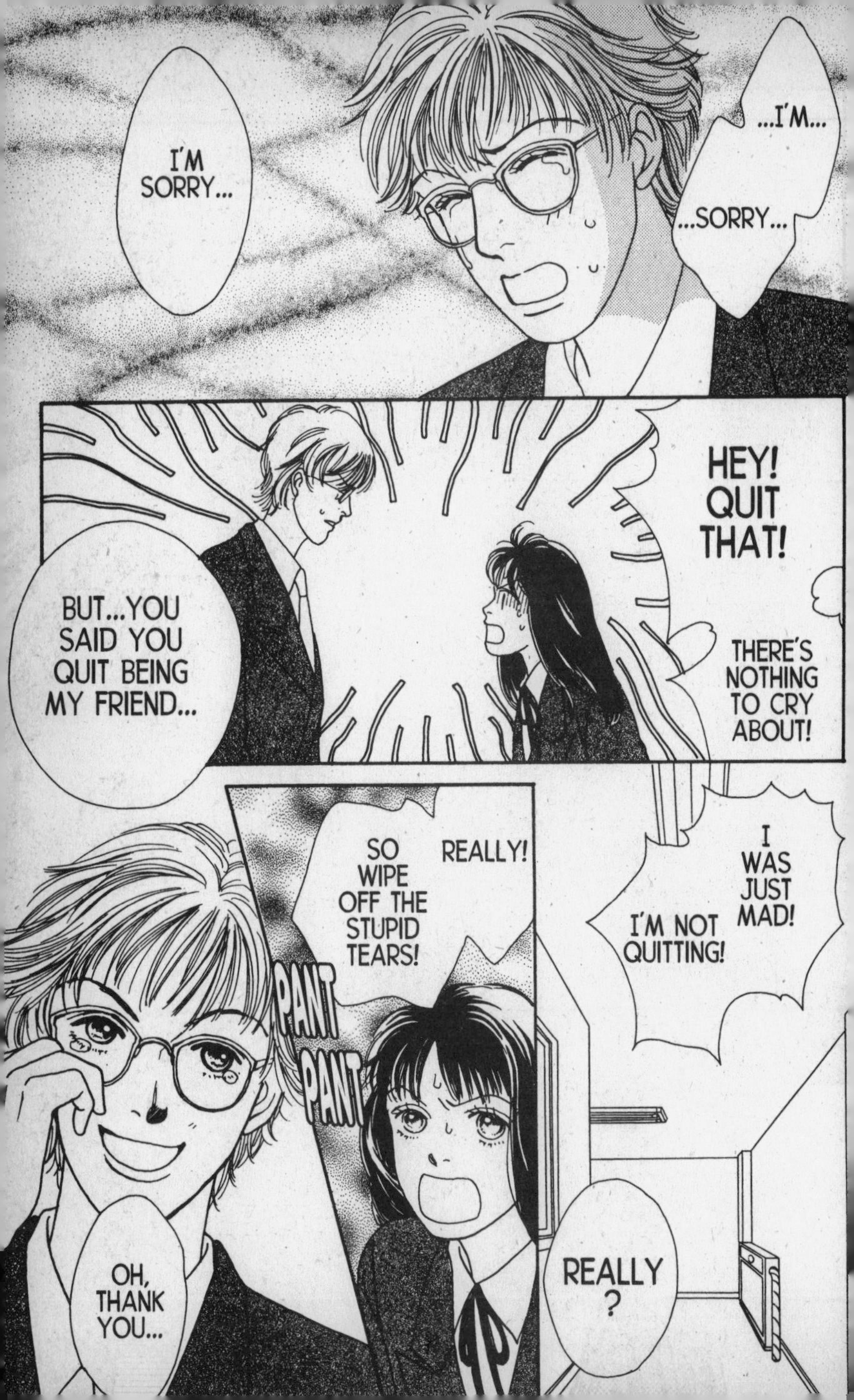
...I'M...
...SORRY...
I'M SORRY...
HEY! QUIT THAT!
THERE'S NOTHING TO CRY ABOUT!
BUT...YOU SAID YOU QUIT BEING MY FRIEND...
I WAS JUST MAD!
I'M NOT QUITTING!
REALLY?
REALLY!
SO WIPE OFF THE STUPID TEARS!
PANT PANT
OH, THANK YOU...

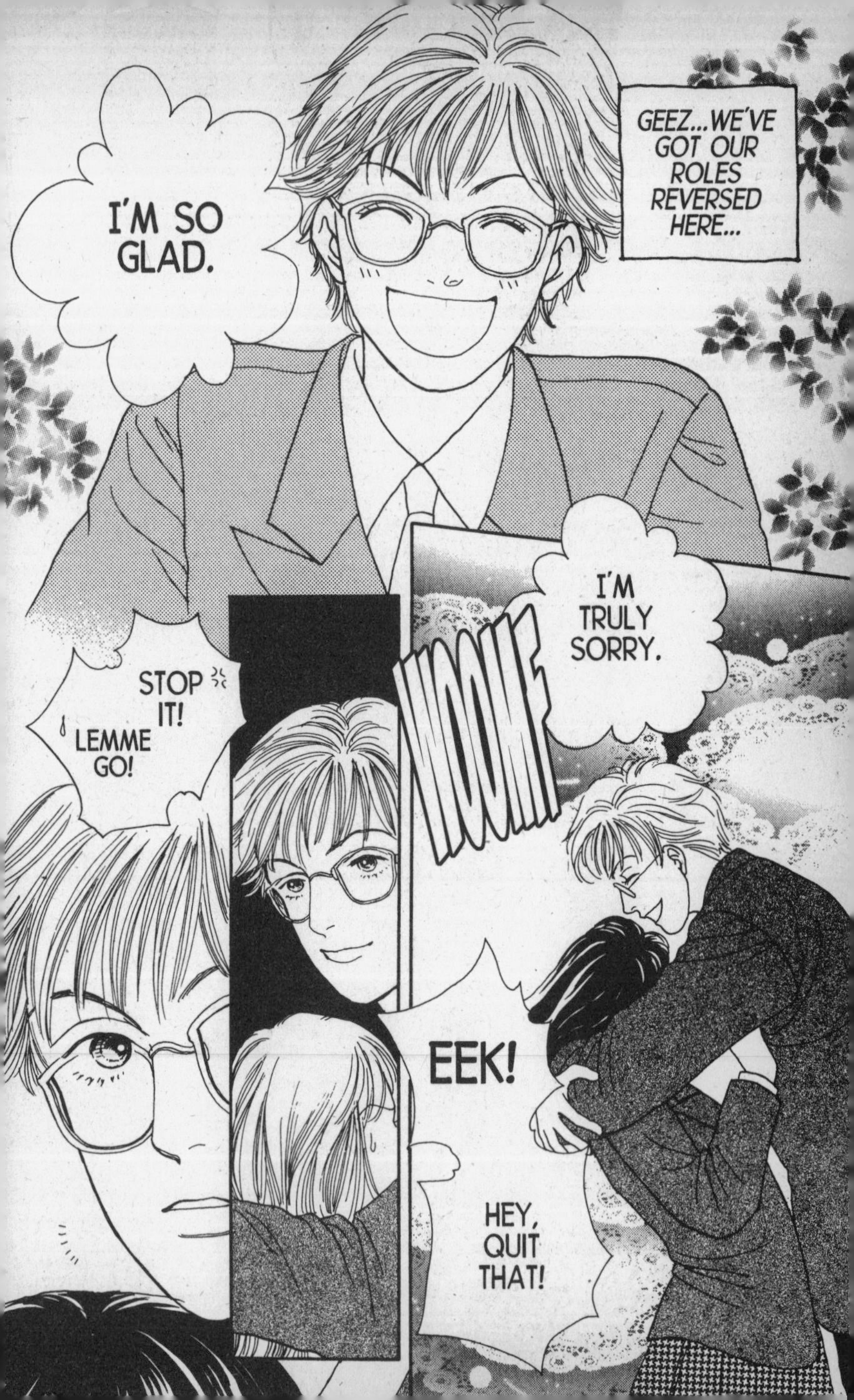
GEEZ...WE'VE GOT OUR ROLES REVERSED HERE...
I'M SO GLAD.
I'M TRULY SORRY.
EEK!
HEY, QUIT THAT!
STOP IT! LEMME GO!

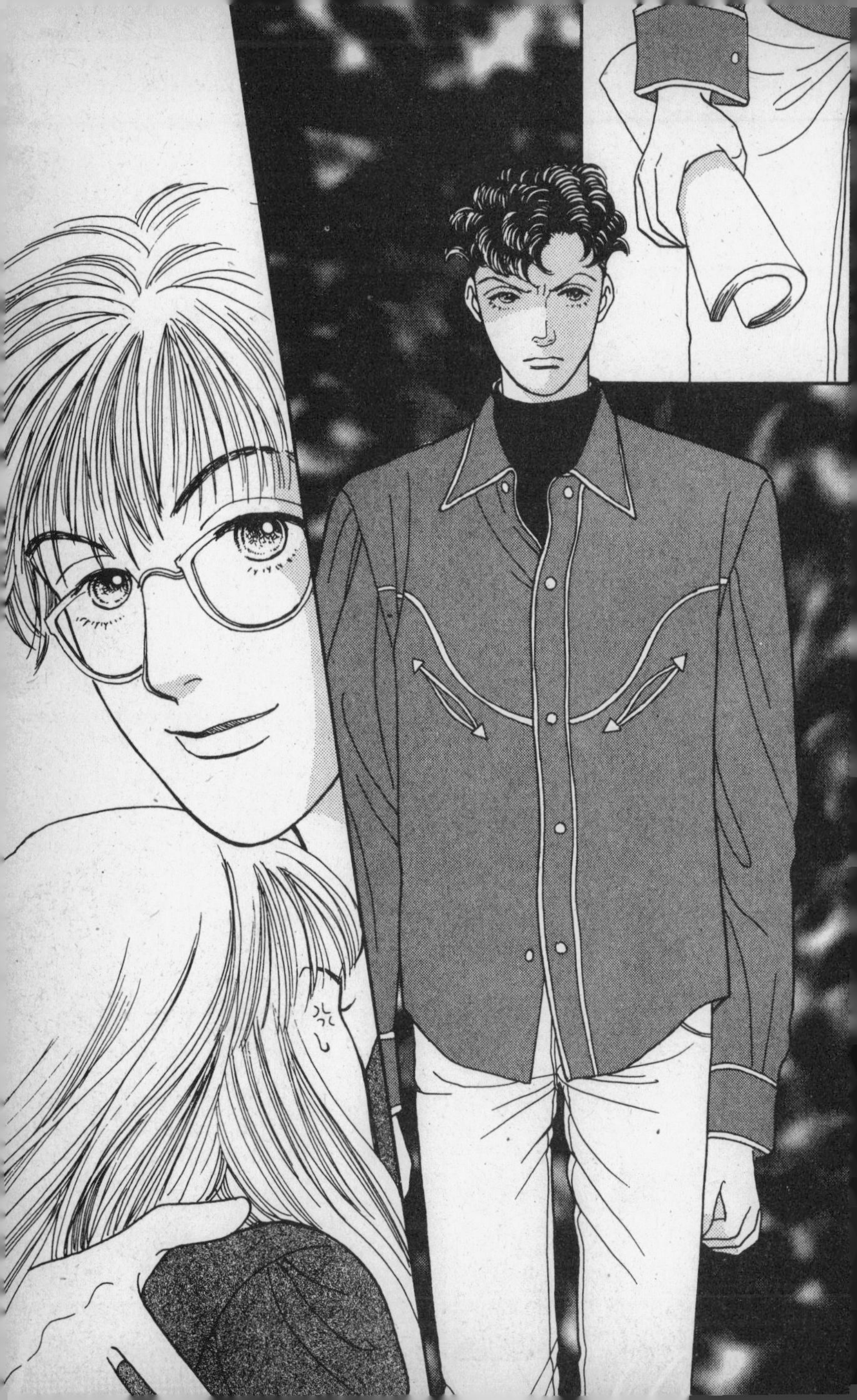

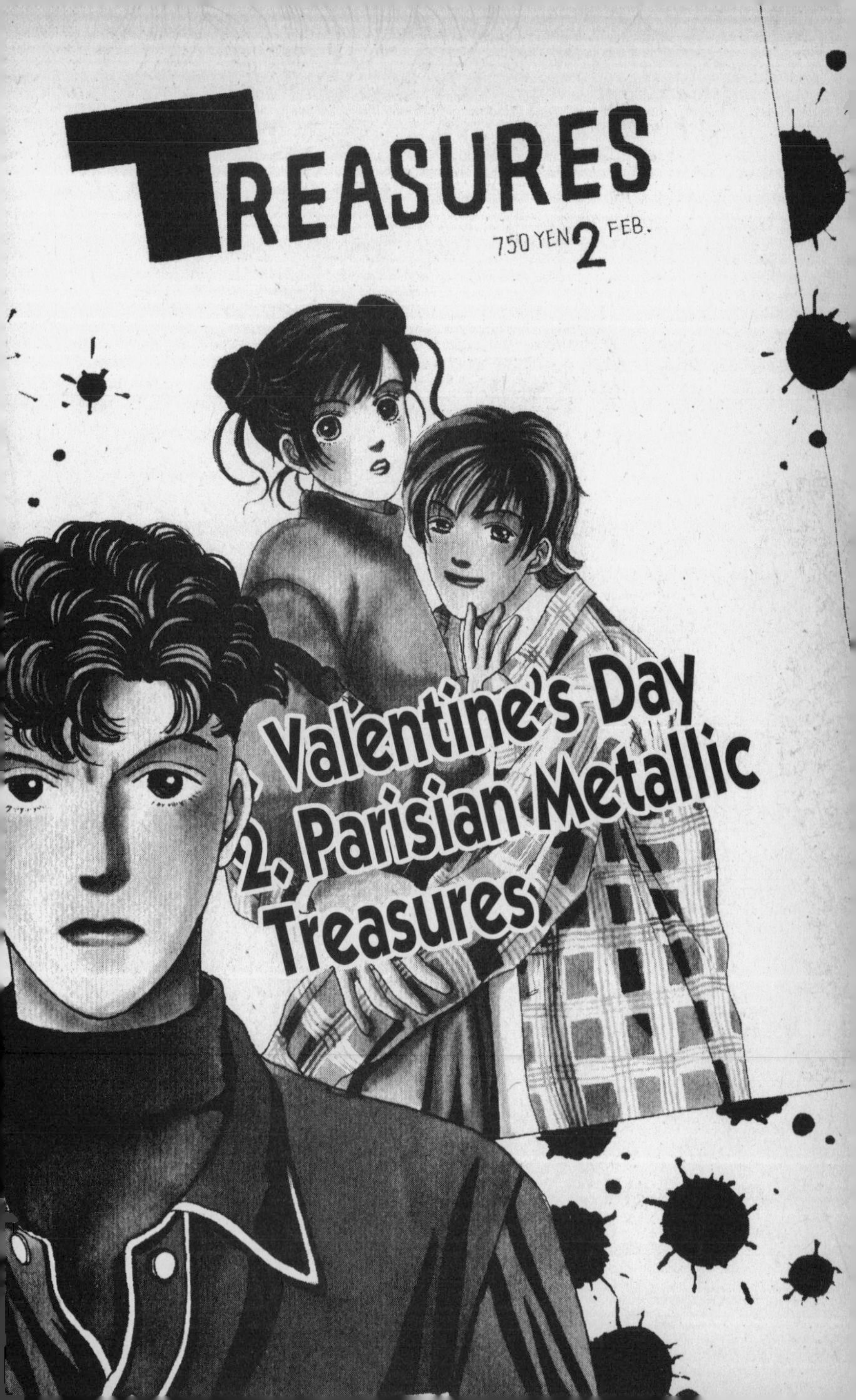
TREASURES
750 YEN 2 FEB.
Valentine's Day
2. Parisian Metallic
Treasures

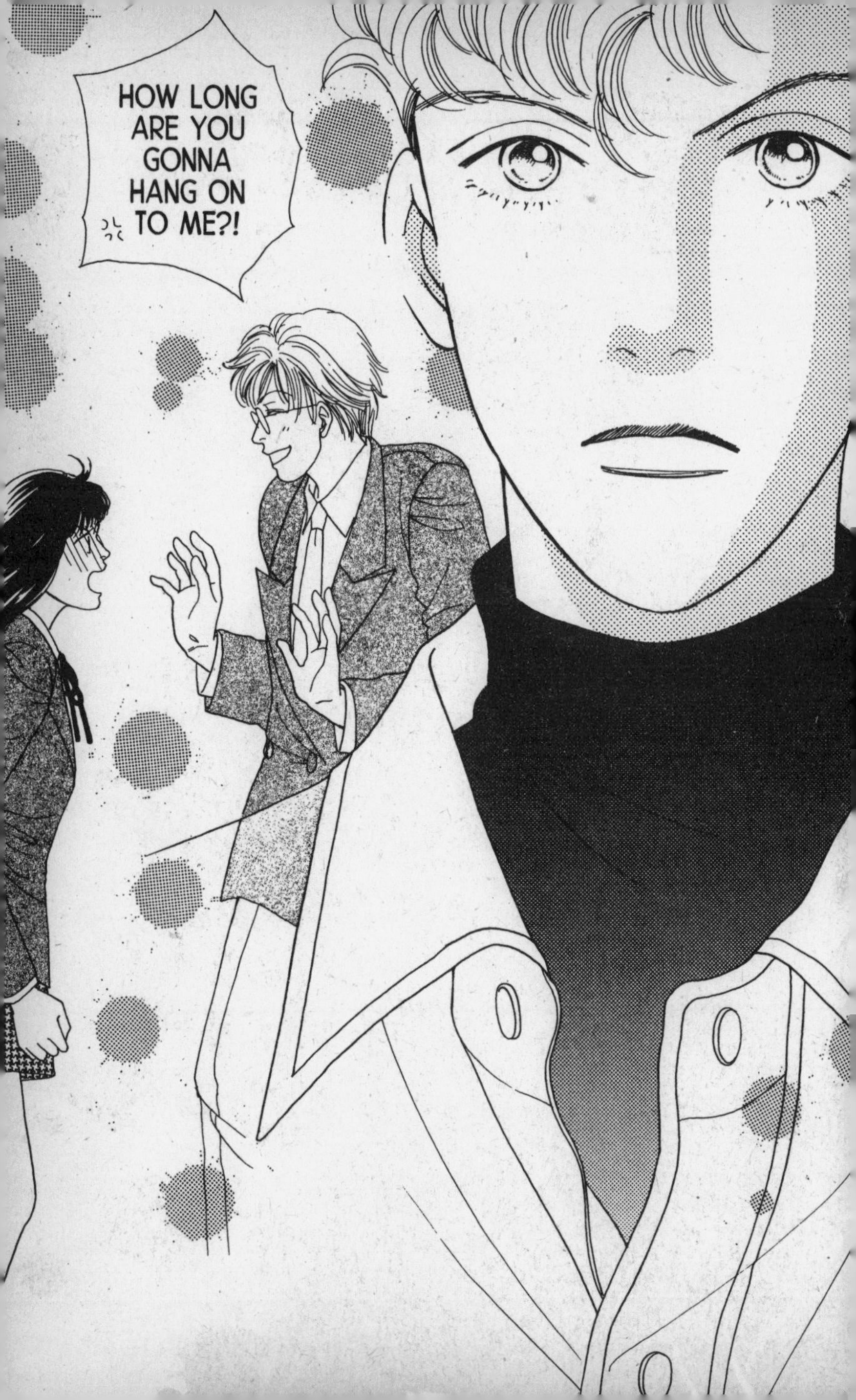
HOW LONG ARE YOU GONNA HANG ON TO ME?!

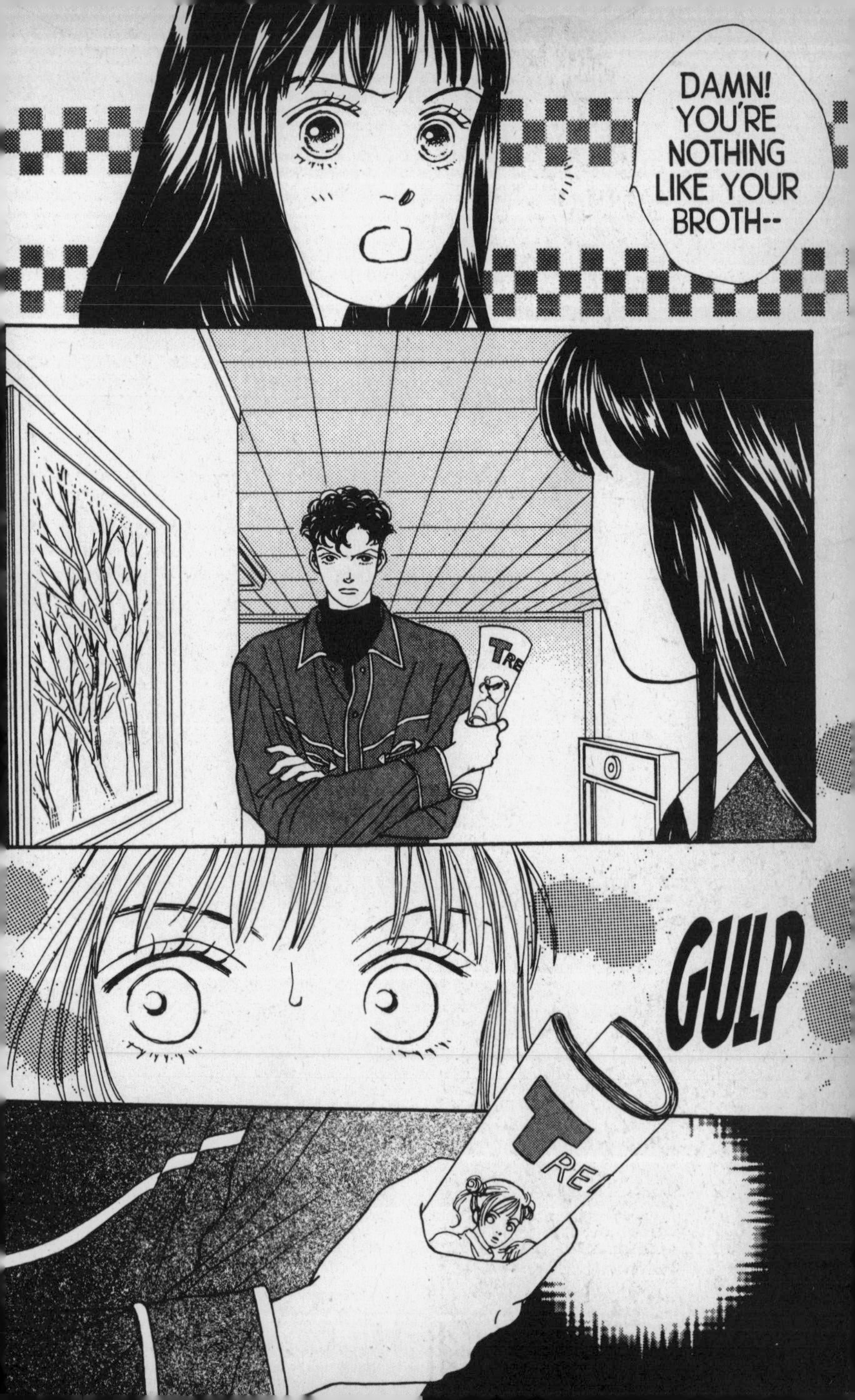
DAMN! YOU'RE NOTHING LIKE YOUR BROTH--
GULP

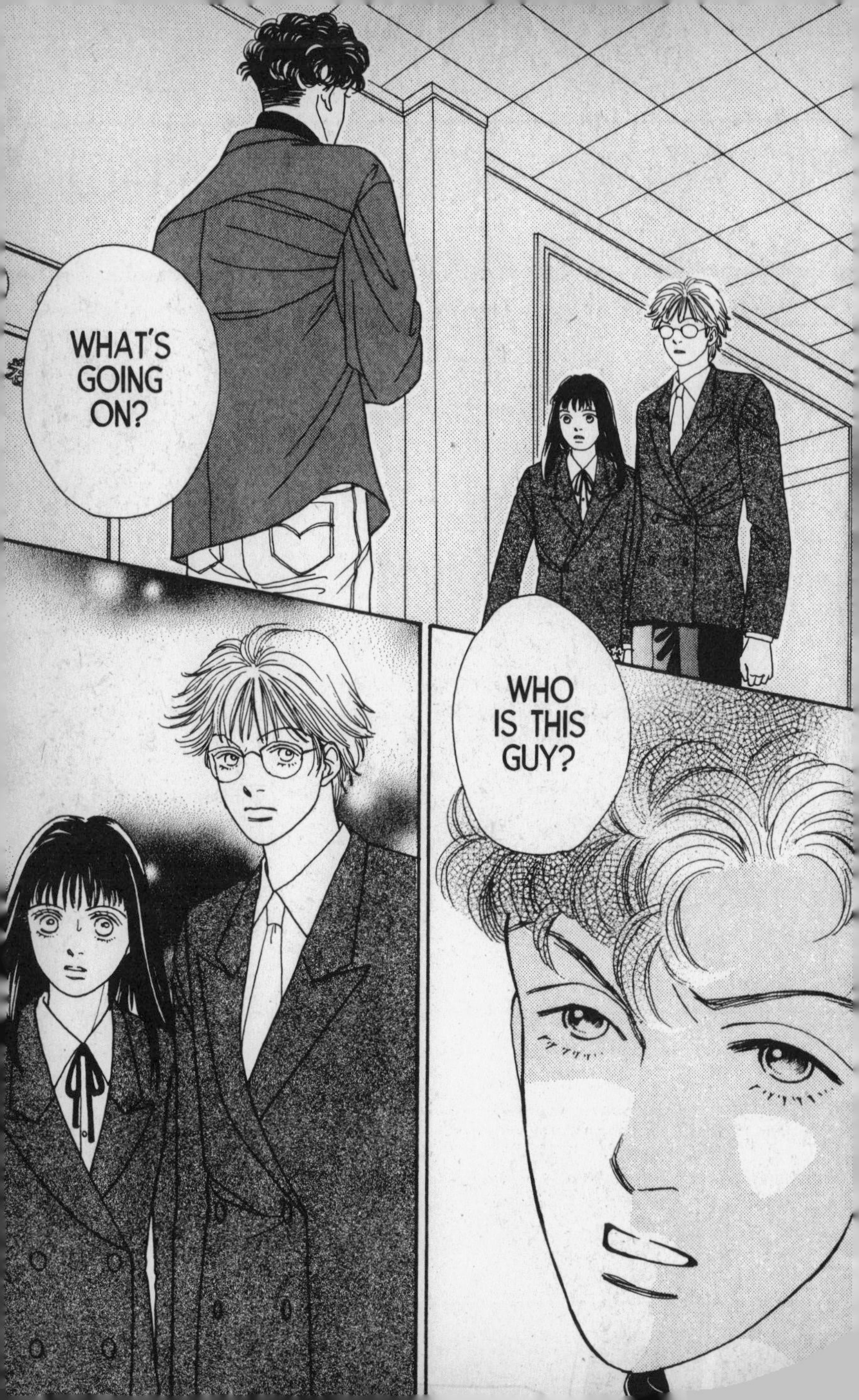
WHAT'S GOING ON?
WHO IS THIS GUY?

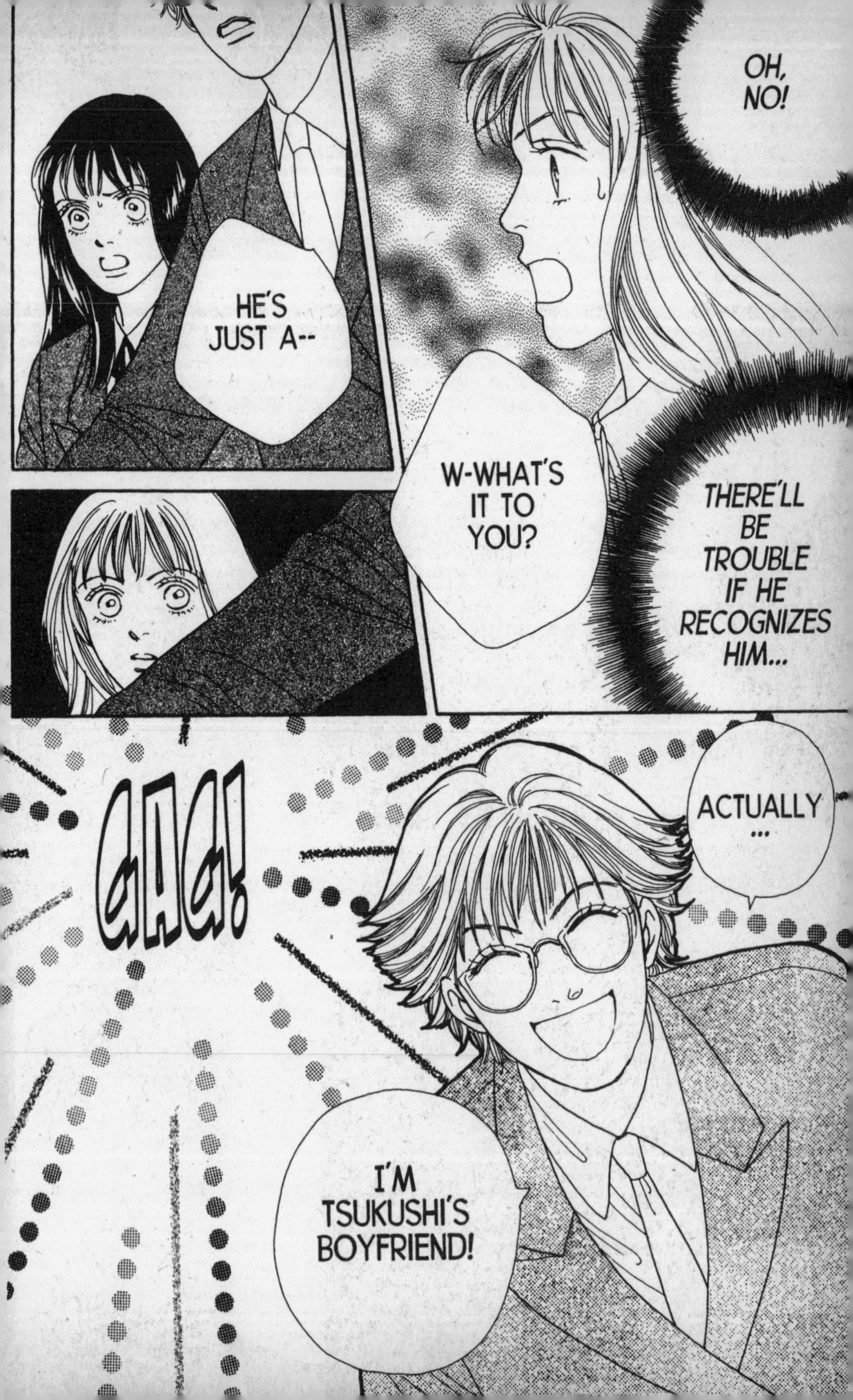
OH, NO!
W-WHAT'S IT TO YOU?
THERE'LL BE TROUBLE IF HE RECOGNIZES HIM...
HE'S JUST A--
ACTUALLY ...
GAG!
I'M TSUKUSHI'S BOYFRIEND!

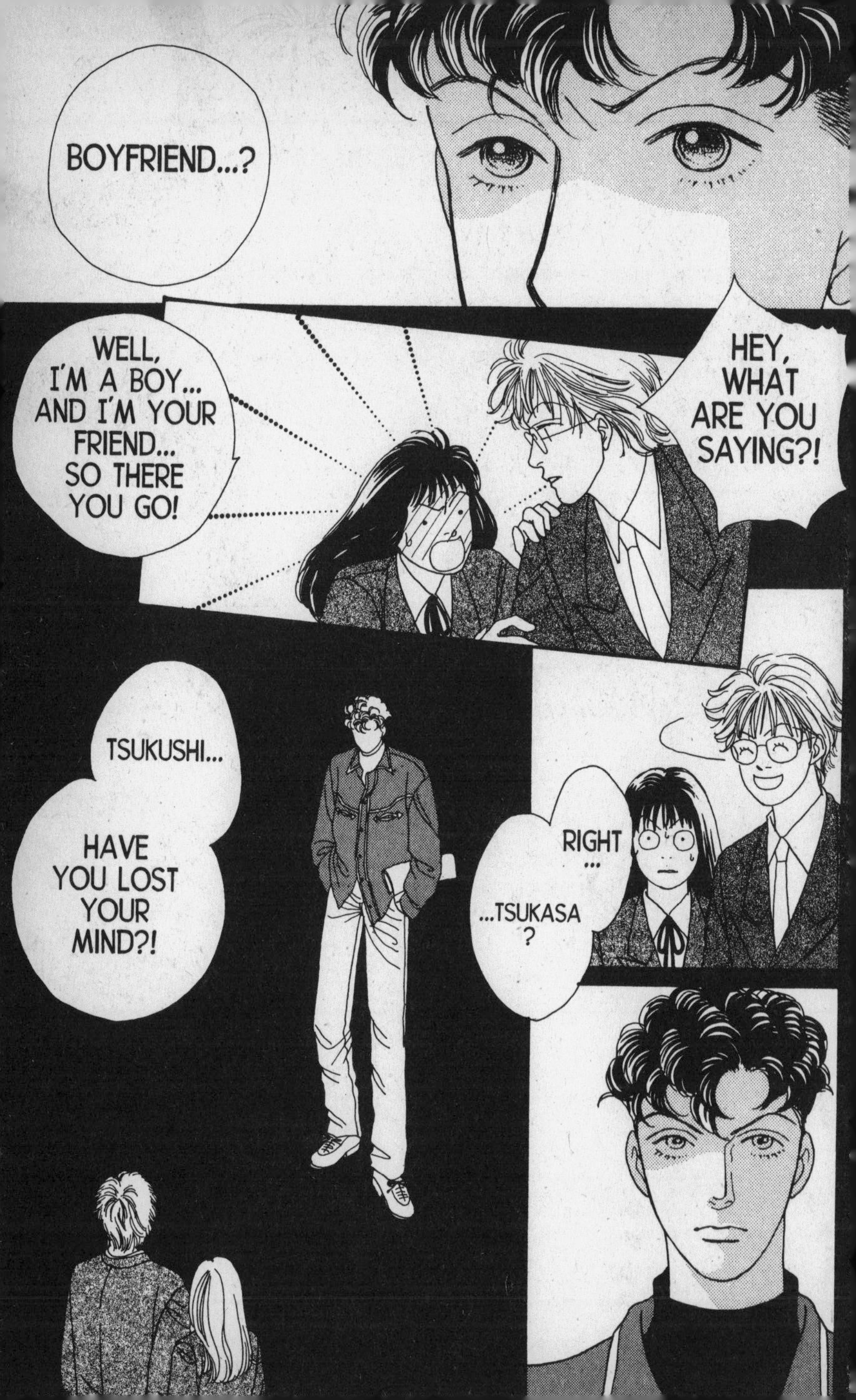
BOYFRIEND...?
HEY, WHAT ARE YOU SAYING?!
WELL, I'M A BOY... AND I'M YOUR FRIEND... SO THERE YOU GO!
RIGHT ...
...TSUKASA ?
TSUKUSHI...
HAVE YOU LOST YOUR MIND?!

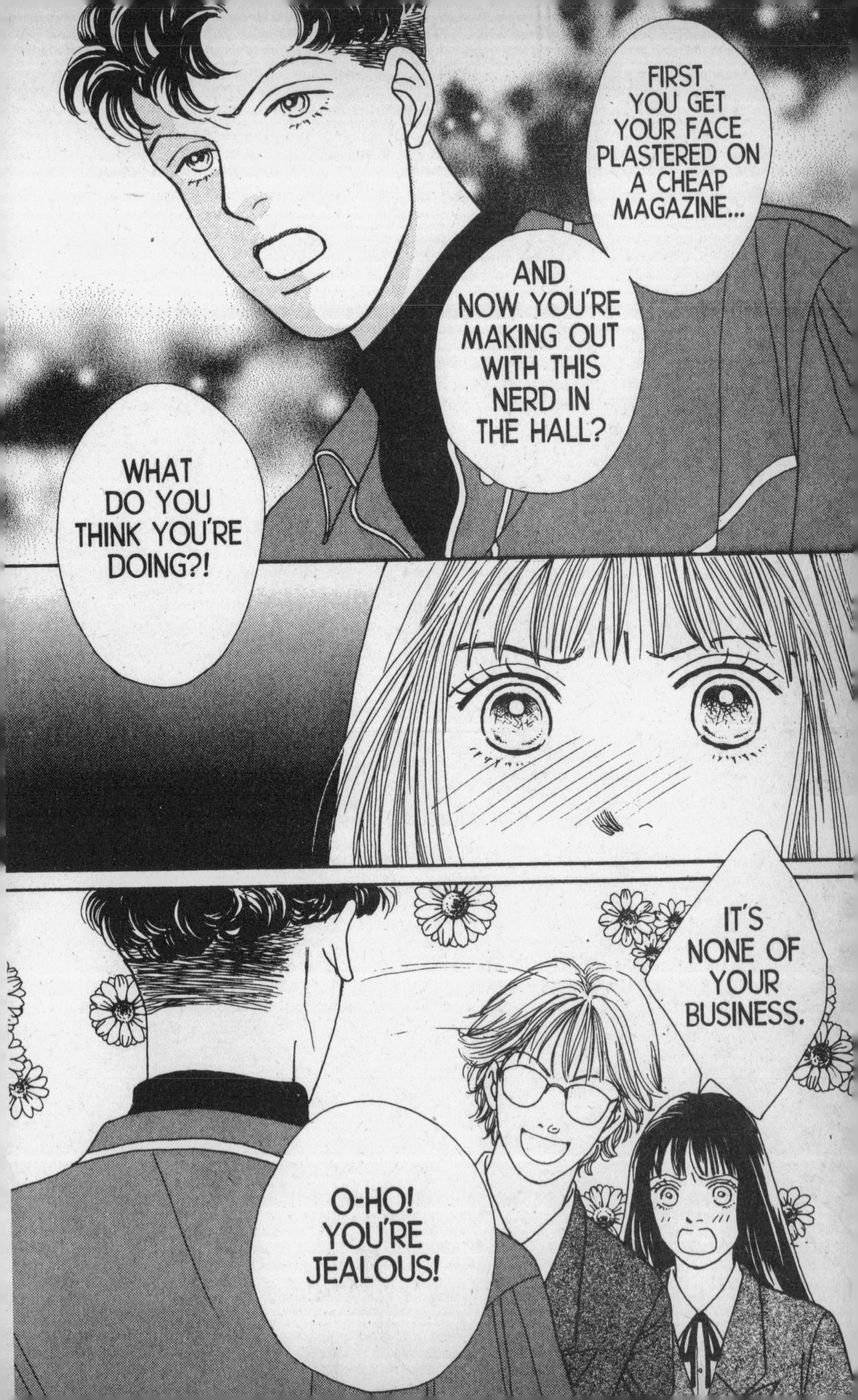
FIRST YOU GET YOUR FACE PLASTERED ON A CHEAP MAGAZINE...
AND NOW YOU'RE MAKING OUT WITH THIS NERD IN THE HALL?
WHAT DO YOU THINK YOU'RE DOING?!
IT'S NONE OF YOUR BUSINESS.
O-HO! YOU'RE JEALOUS!

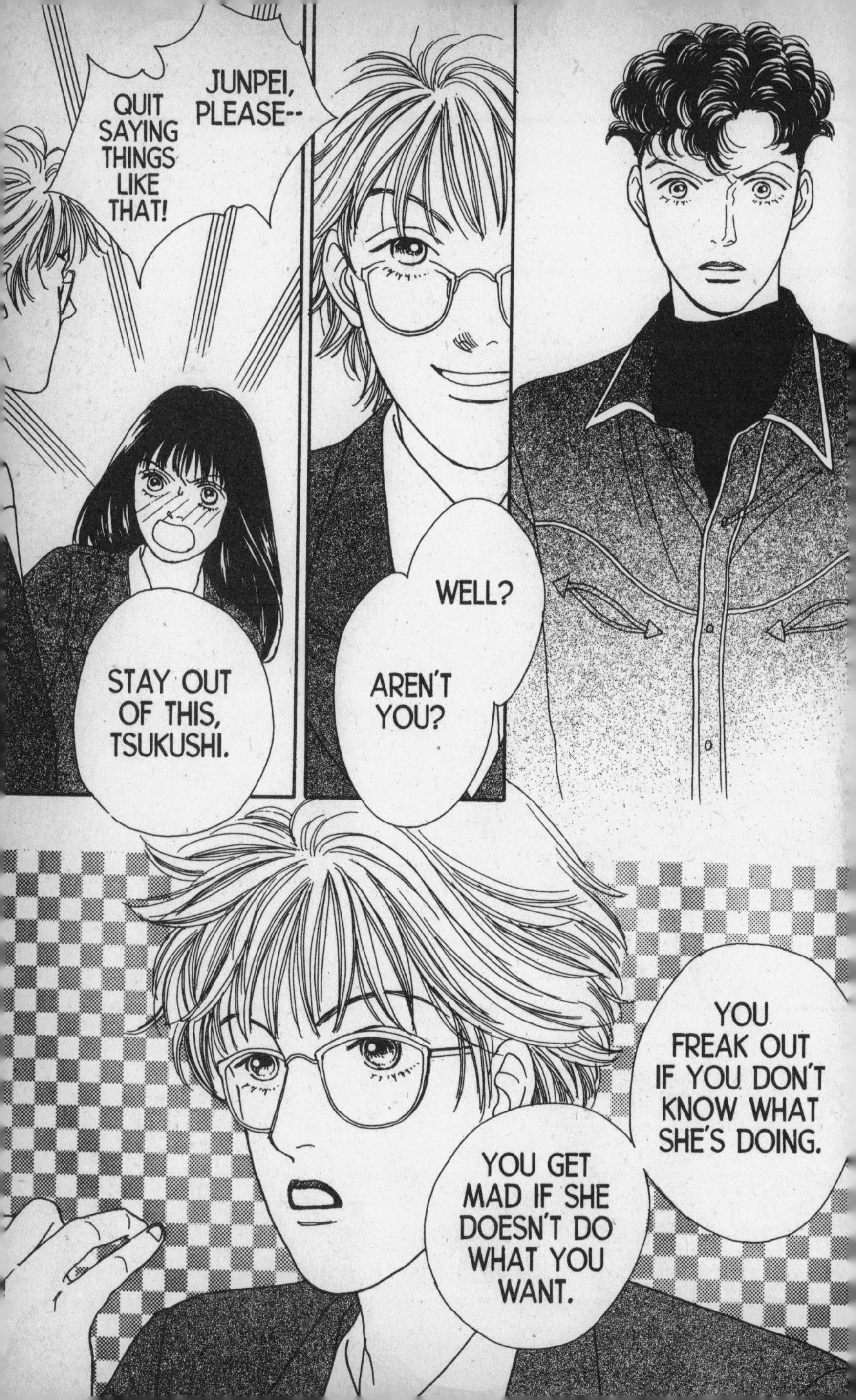
WELL?
AREN'T YOU?
JUNPEI, PLEASE--
QUIT SAYING THINGS LIKE THAT!
STAY OUT OF THIS, TSUKUSHI.
YOU FREAK OUT IF YOU DON'T KNOW WHAT SHE'S DOING.
YOU GET MAD IF SHE DOESN'T DO WHAT YOU WANT.

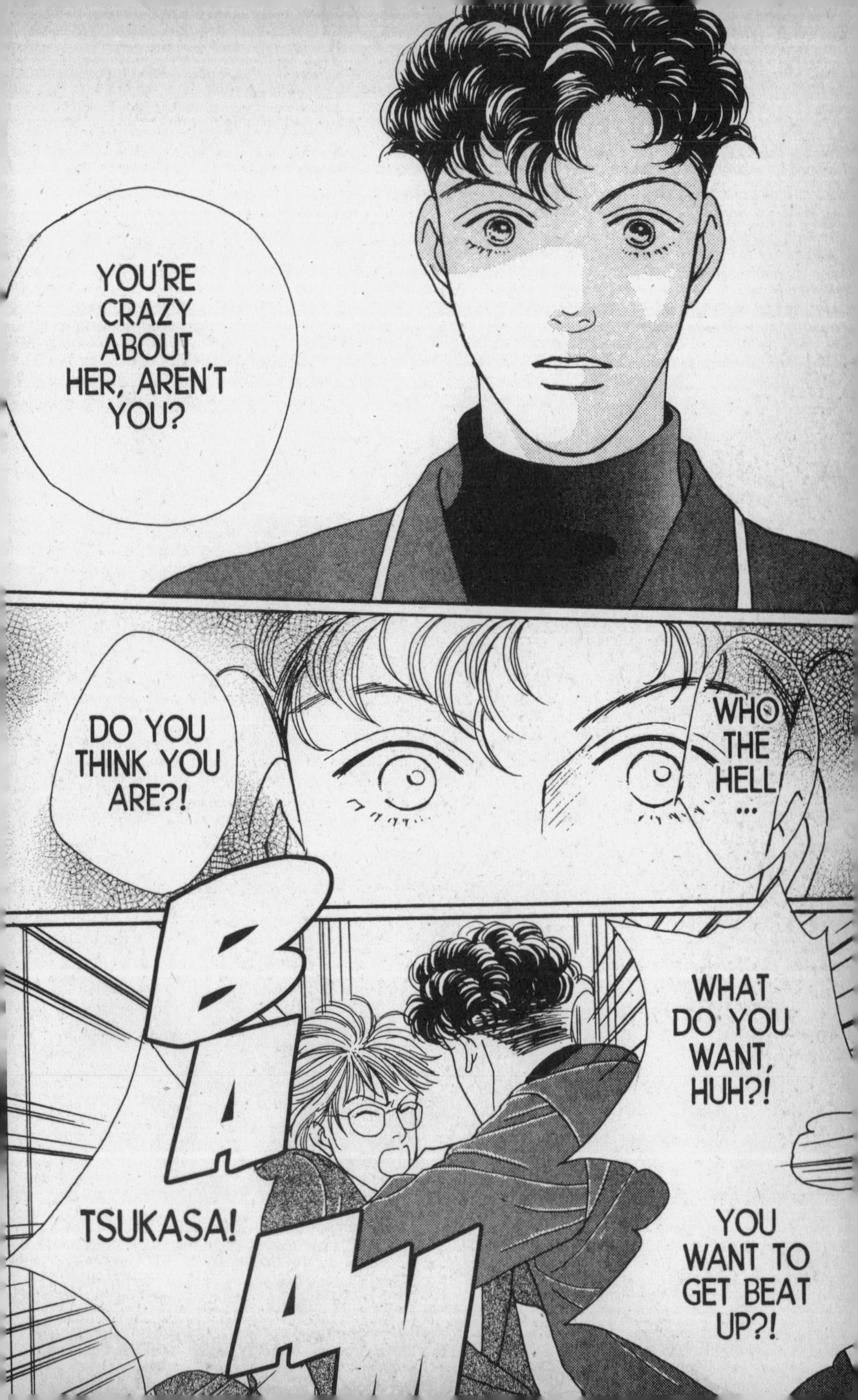
YOU'RE CRAZY ABOUT HER, AREN'T YOU?
WHO THE HELL...
DO YOU THINK YOU ARE?!
WHAT DO YOU WANT, HUH?!
BAM
YOU WANT TO GET BEAT UP?!
TSUKASA!

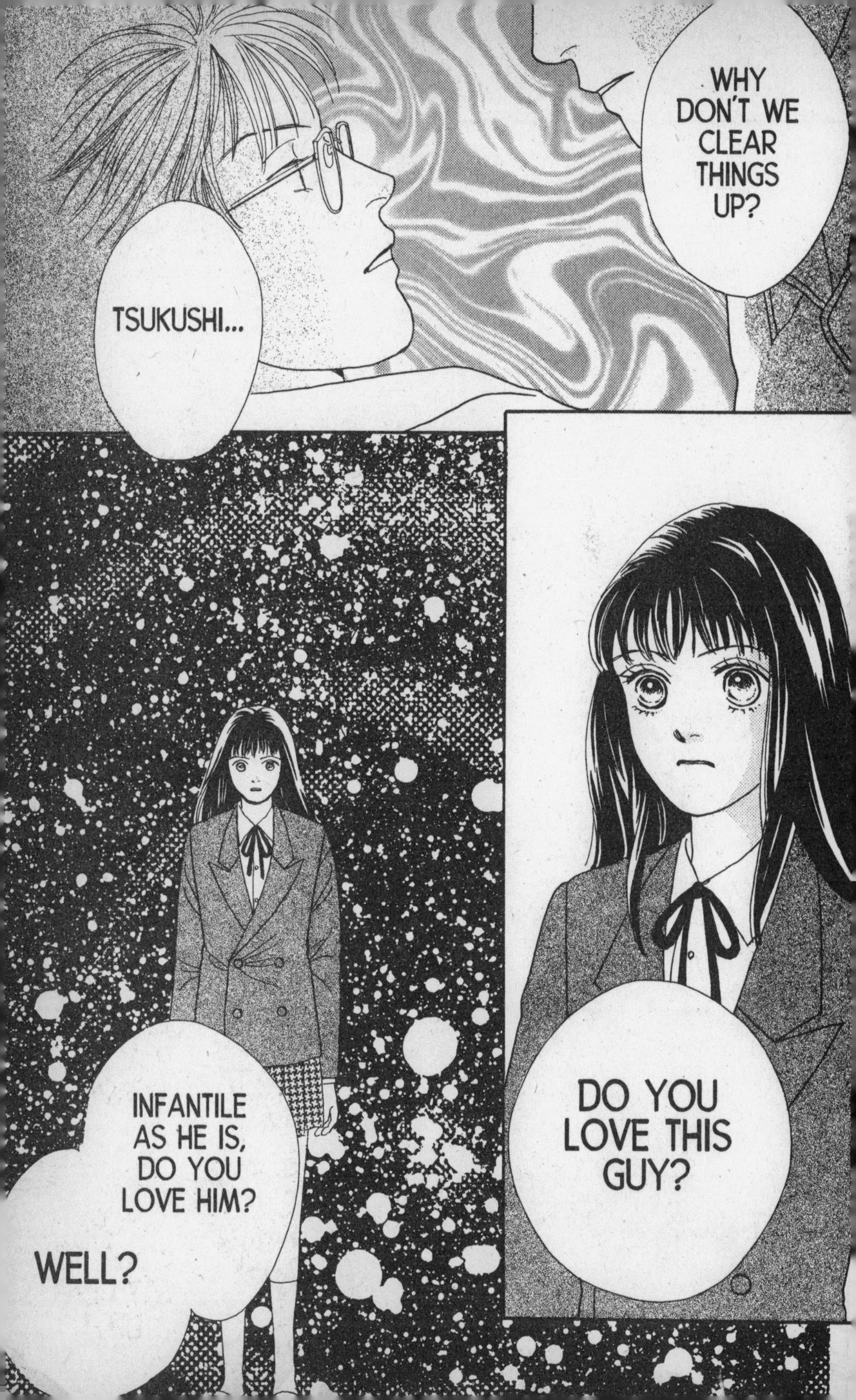
WHY DON'T WE CLEAR THINGS UP?
TSUKUSHI...
DO YOU LOVE THIS GUY?
INFANTILE AS HE IS, DO YOU LOVE HIM?
WELL?

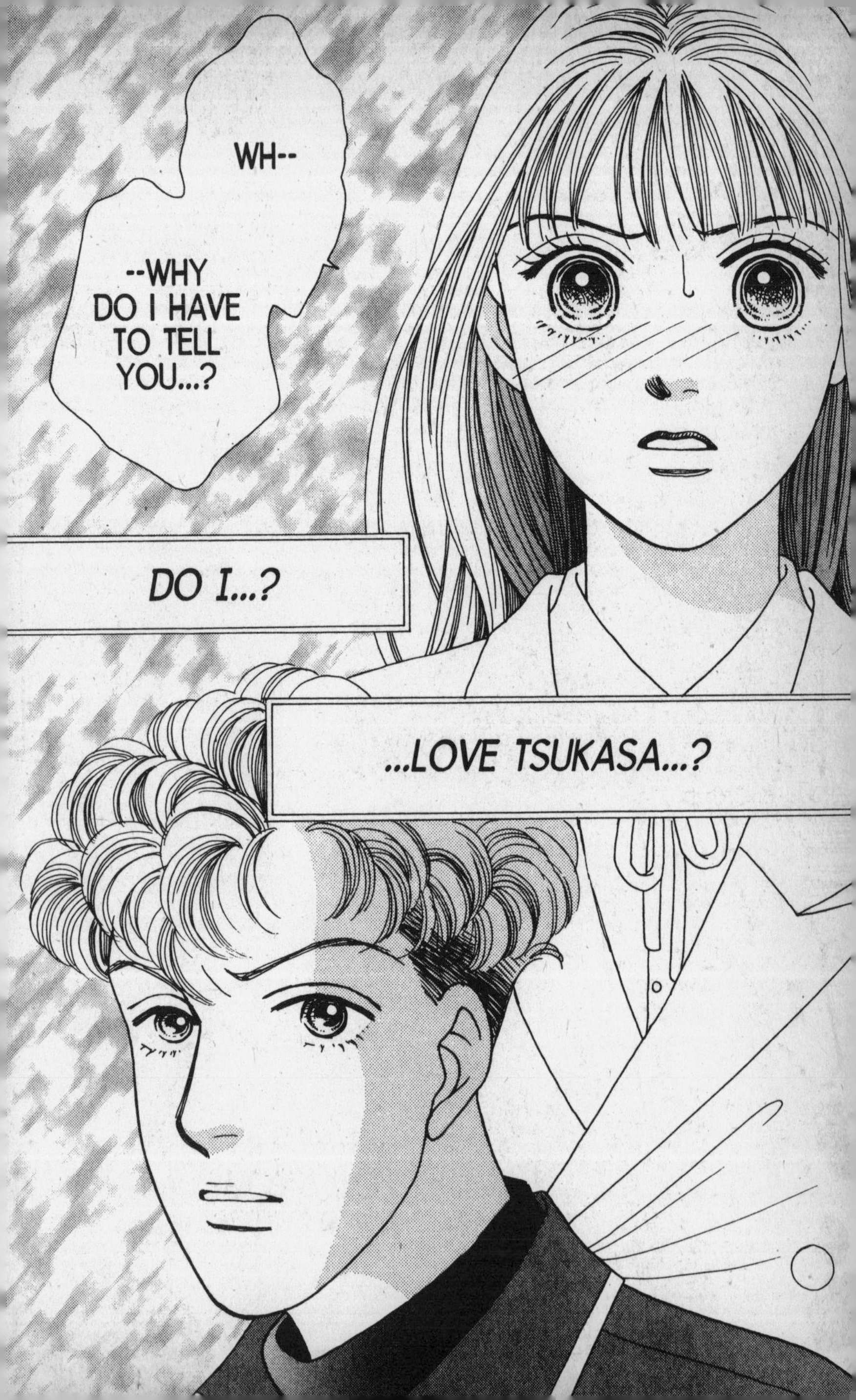
WH--
--WHY DO I HAVE TO TELL YOU...?
DO I...?
...LOVE TSUKASA...?

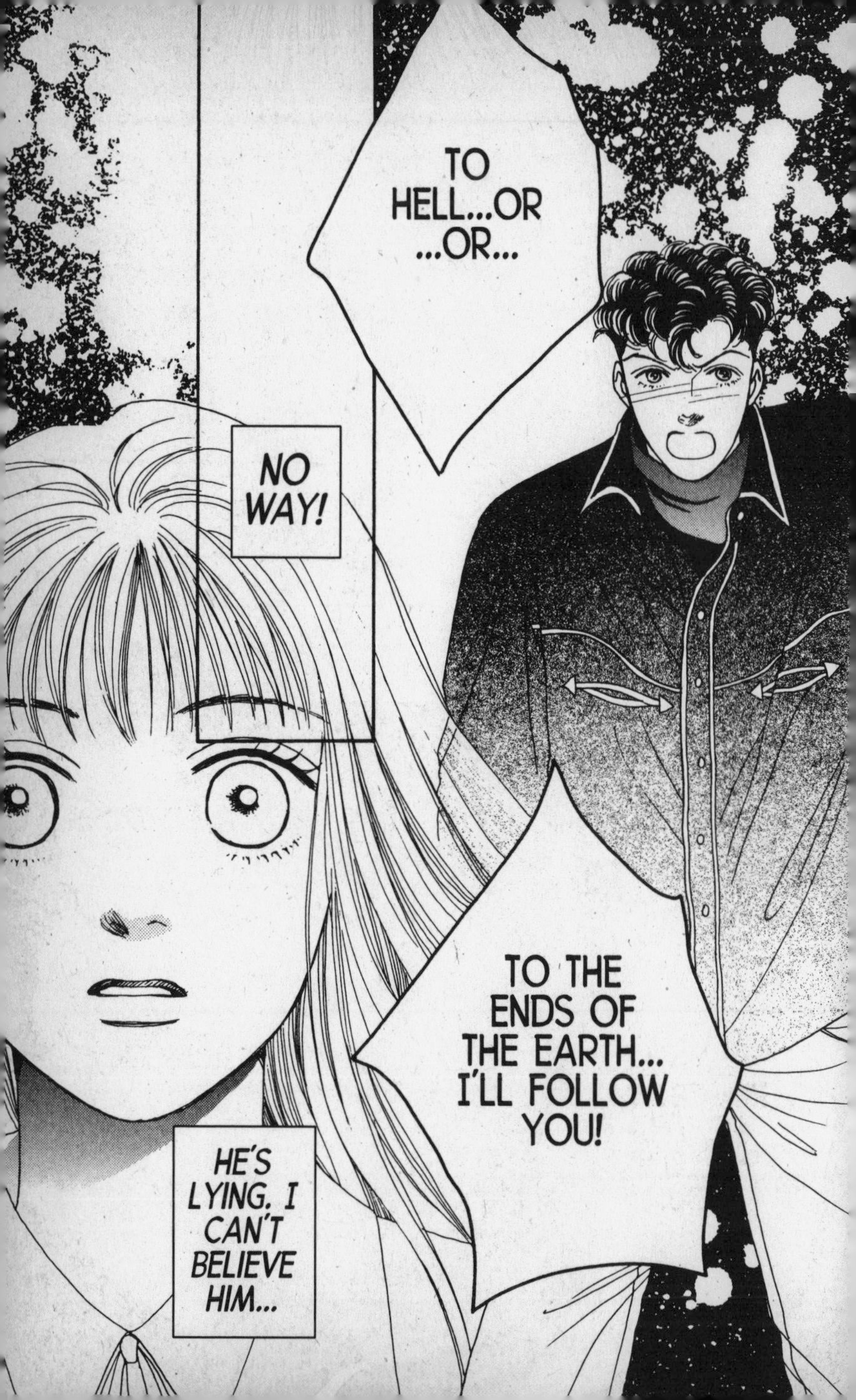
TO HELL...OR ...OR...
NO WAY!
TO THE ENDS OF THE EARTH... I'LL FOLLOW YOU!
HE'S LYING. I CAN'T BELIEVE HIM...

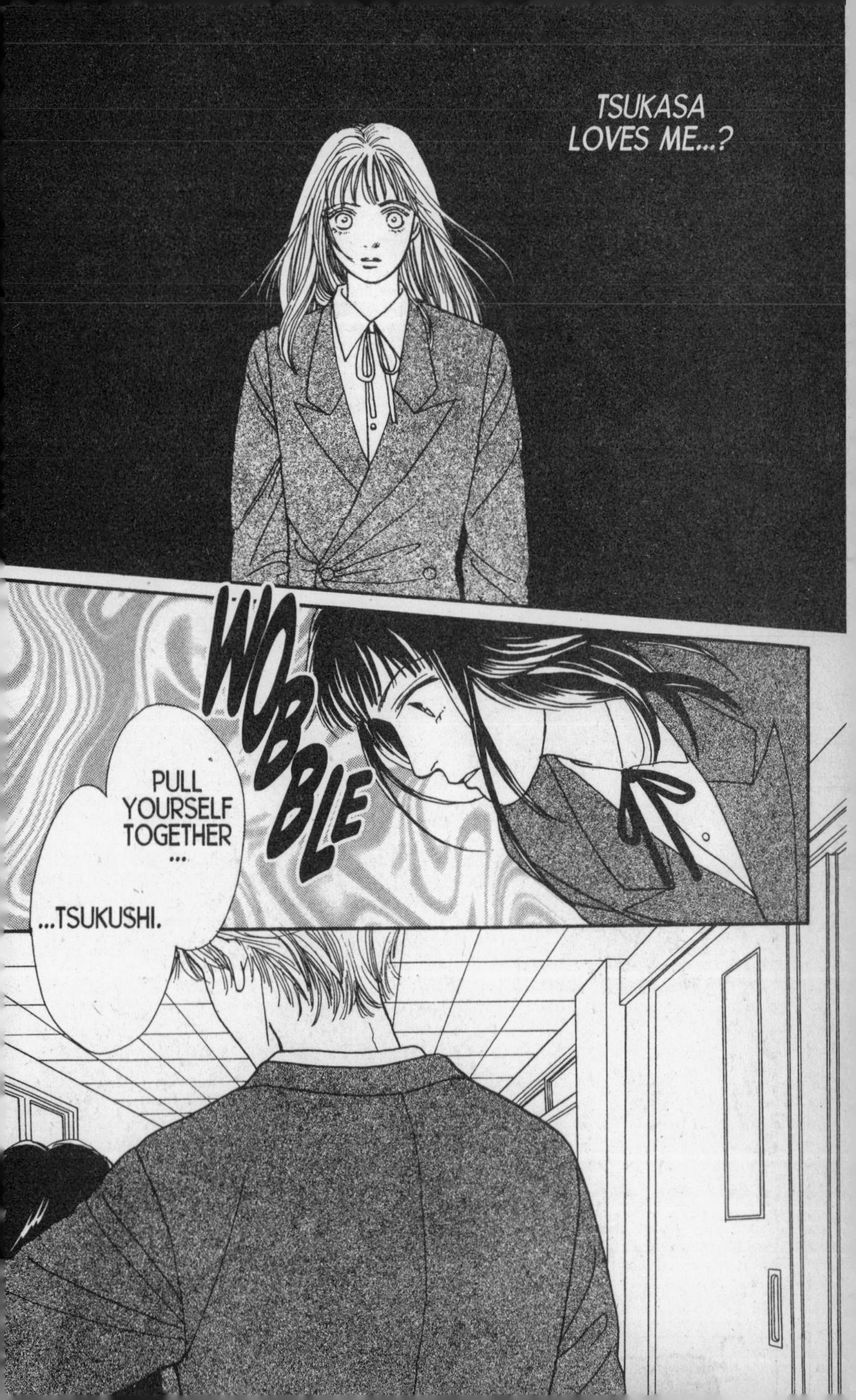
TSUKASA LOVES ME...?
WOBBLE
PULL YOURSELF TOGETHER ...
...TSUKUSHI.

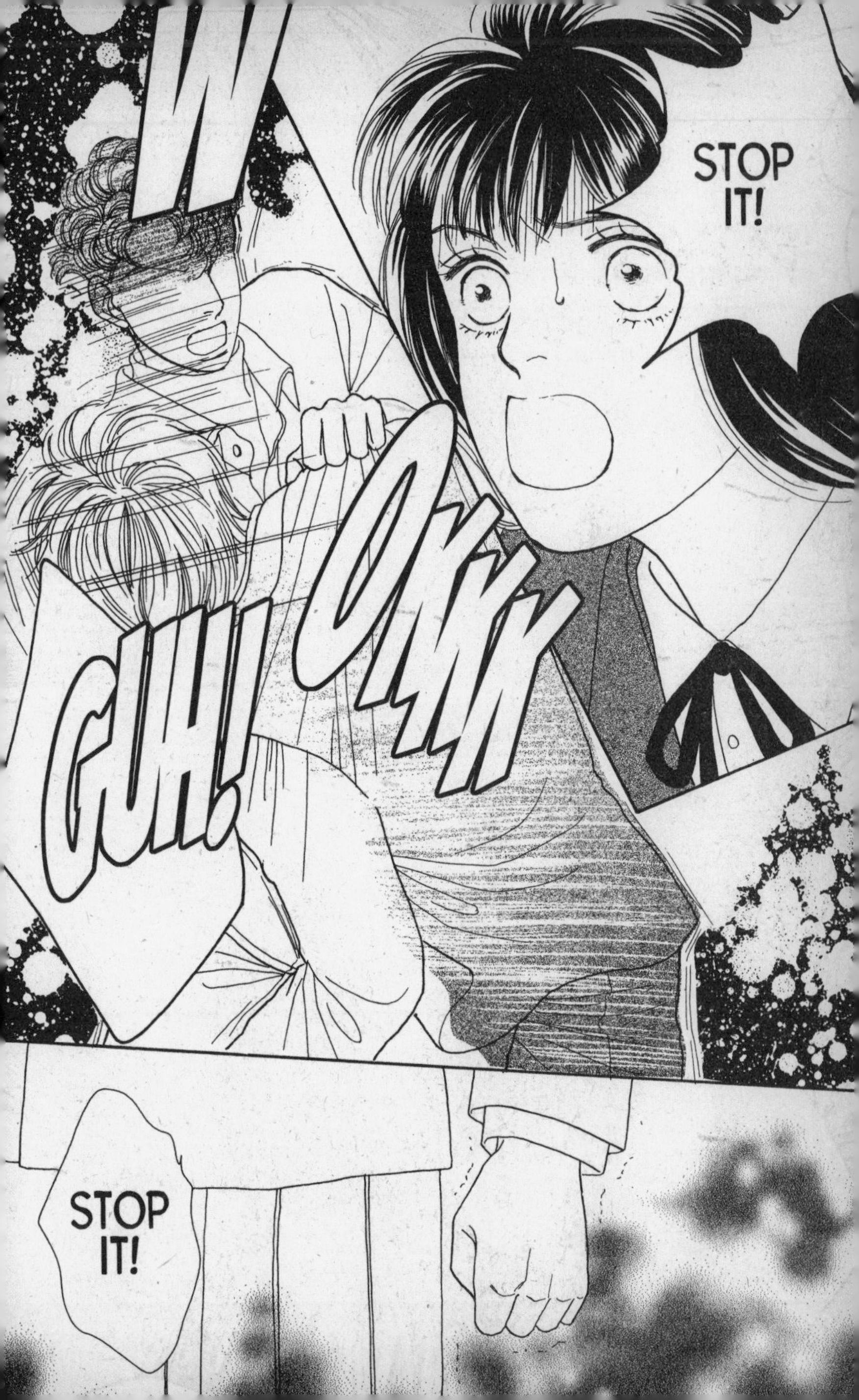
STOP IT!
GUH!
STOP IT!

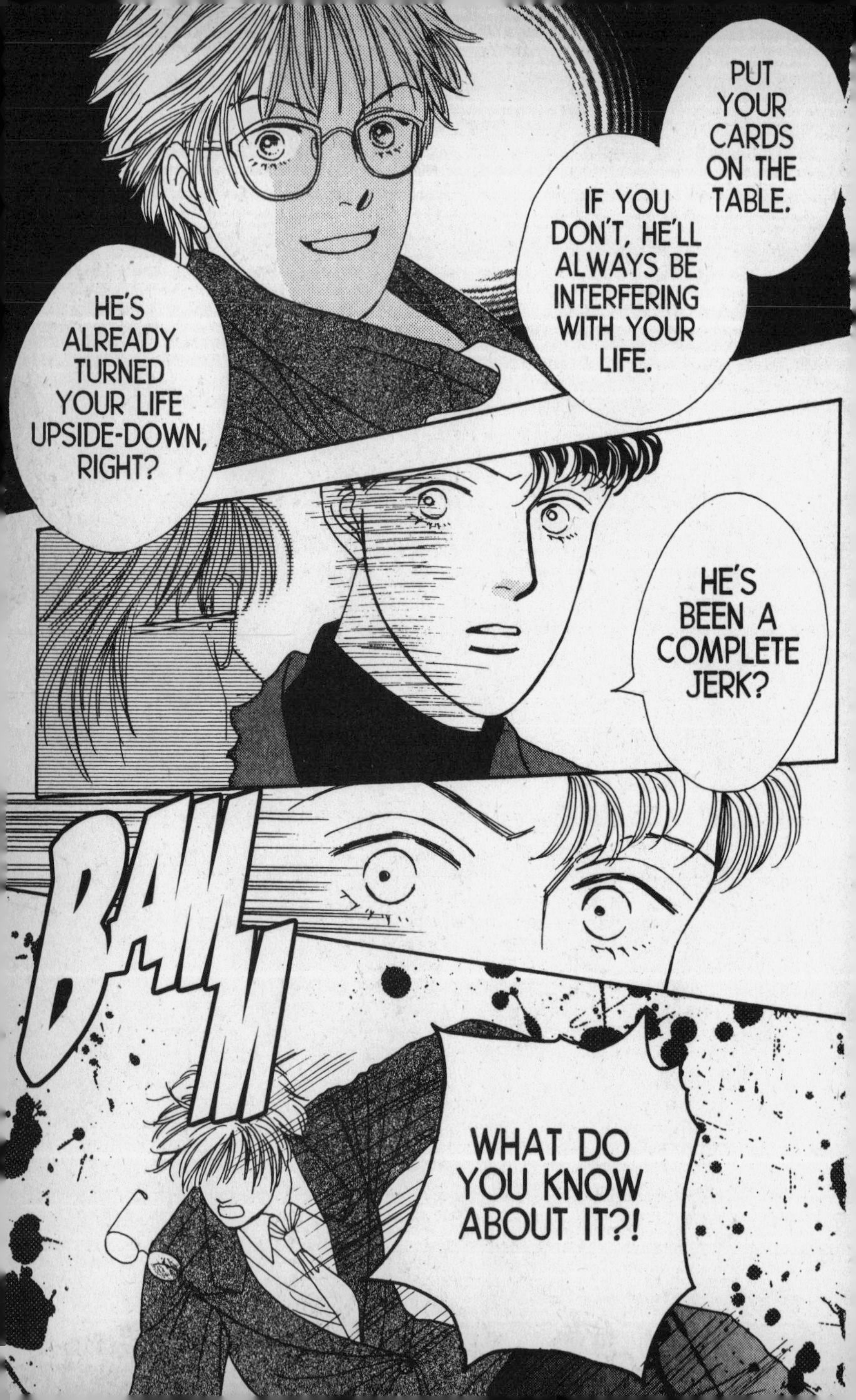
PUT YOUR CARDS ON THE TABLE.
IF YOU DON'T, HE'LL ALWAYS BE INTERFERING WITH YOUR LIFE.
HE'S ALREADY TURNED YOUR LIFE UPSIDE-DOWN, RIGHT?
HE'S BEEN A COMPLETE JERK?
BAM
WHAT DO YOU KNOW ABOUT IT?!

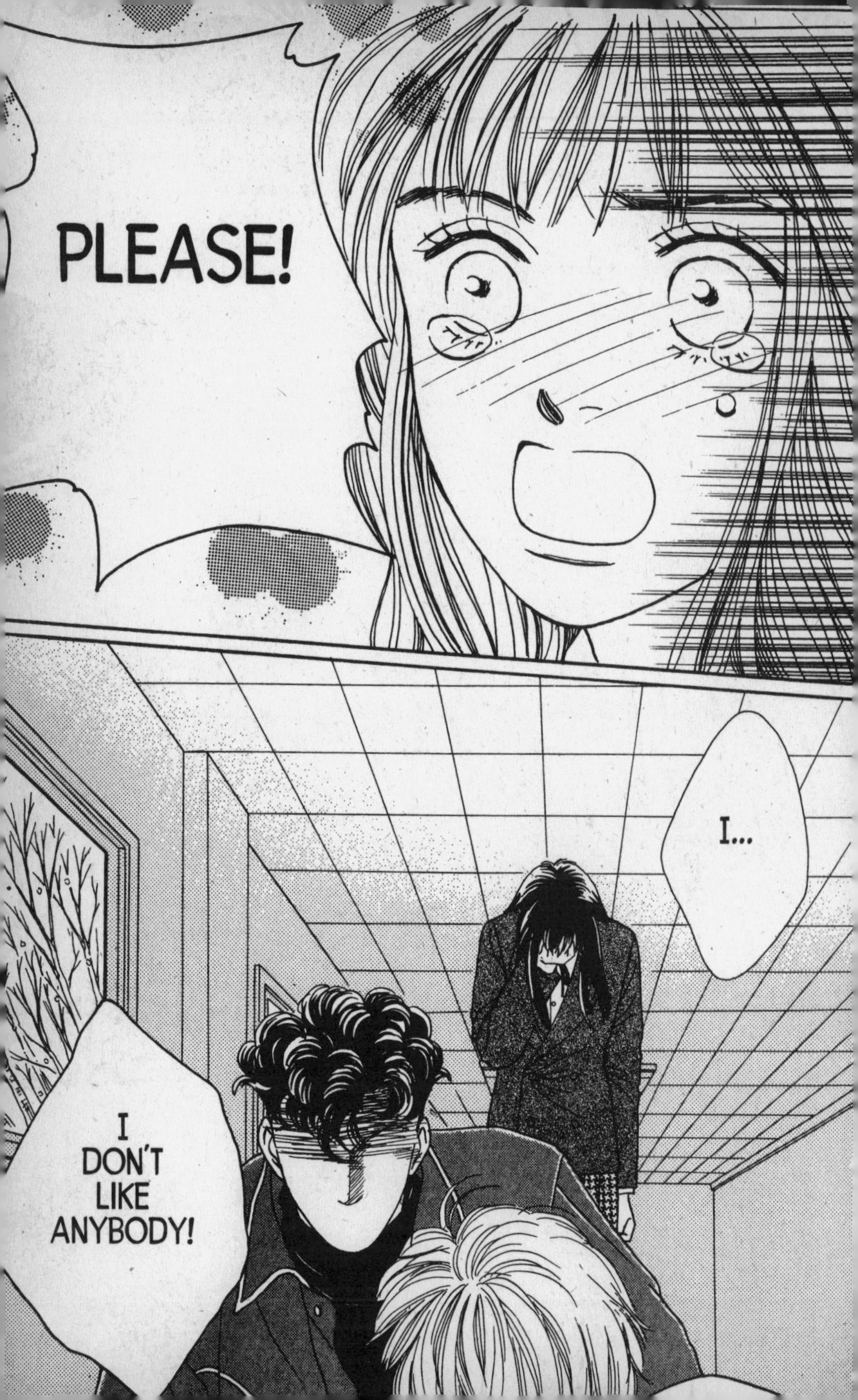
PLEASE!
I...
I DON'T LIKE ANYBODY!

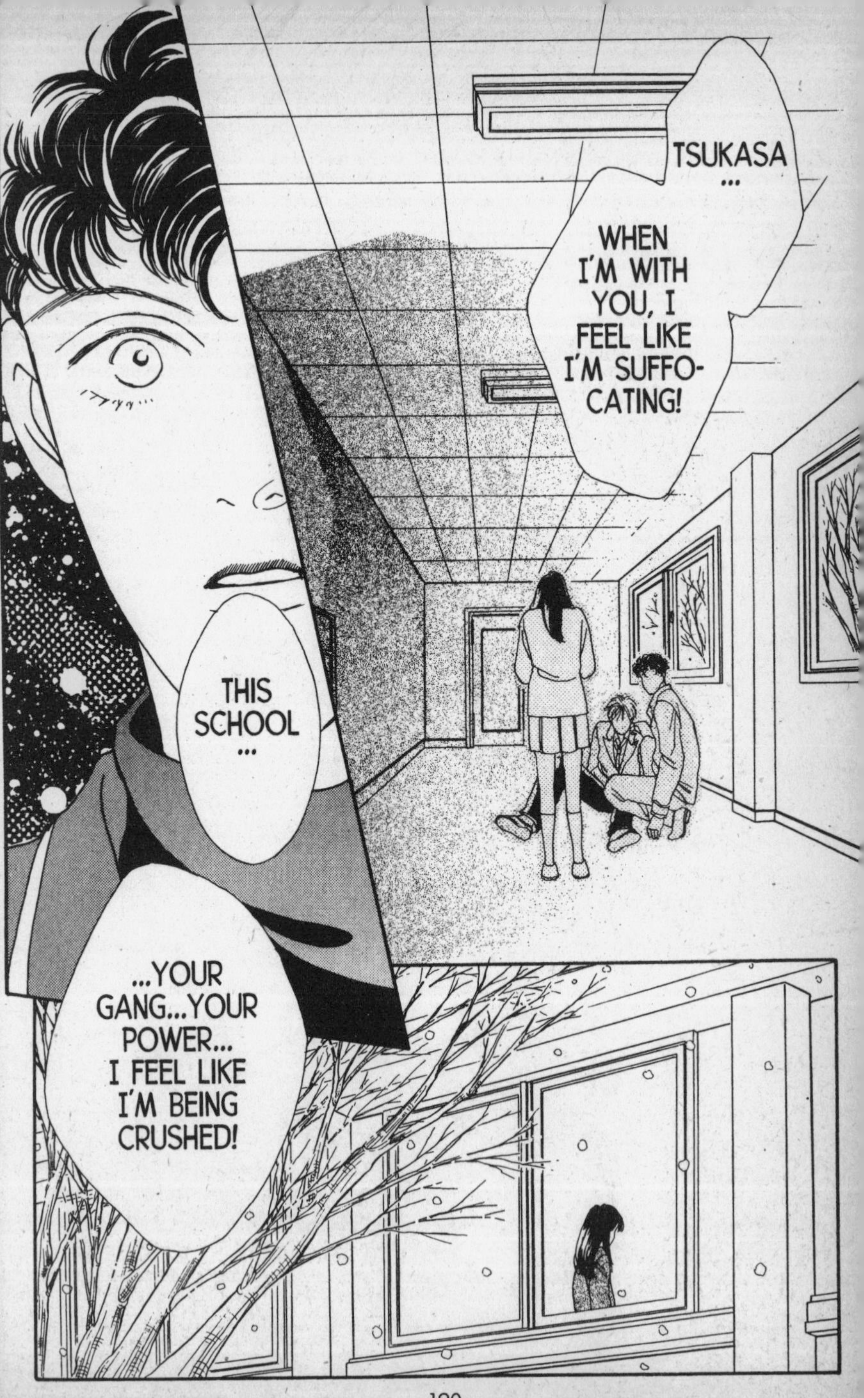
TSUKASA ...
WHEN I'M WITH YOU, I FEEL LIKE I'M SUFFO- CATING!
THIS SCHOOL ...
...YOUR GANG...YOUR POWER... I FEEL LIKE I'M BEING CRUSHED!

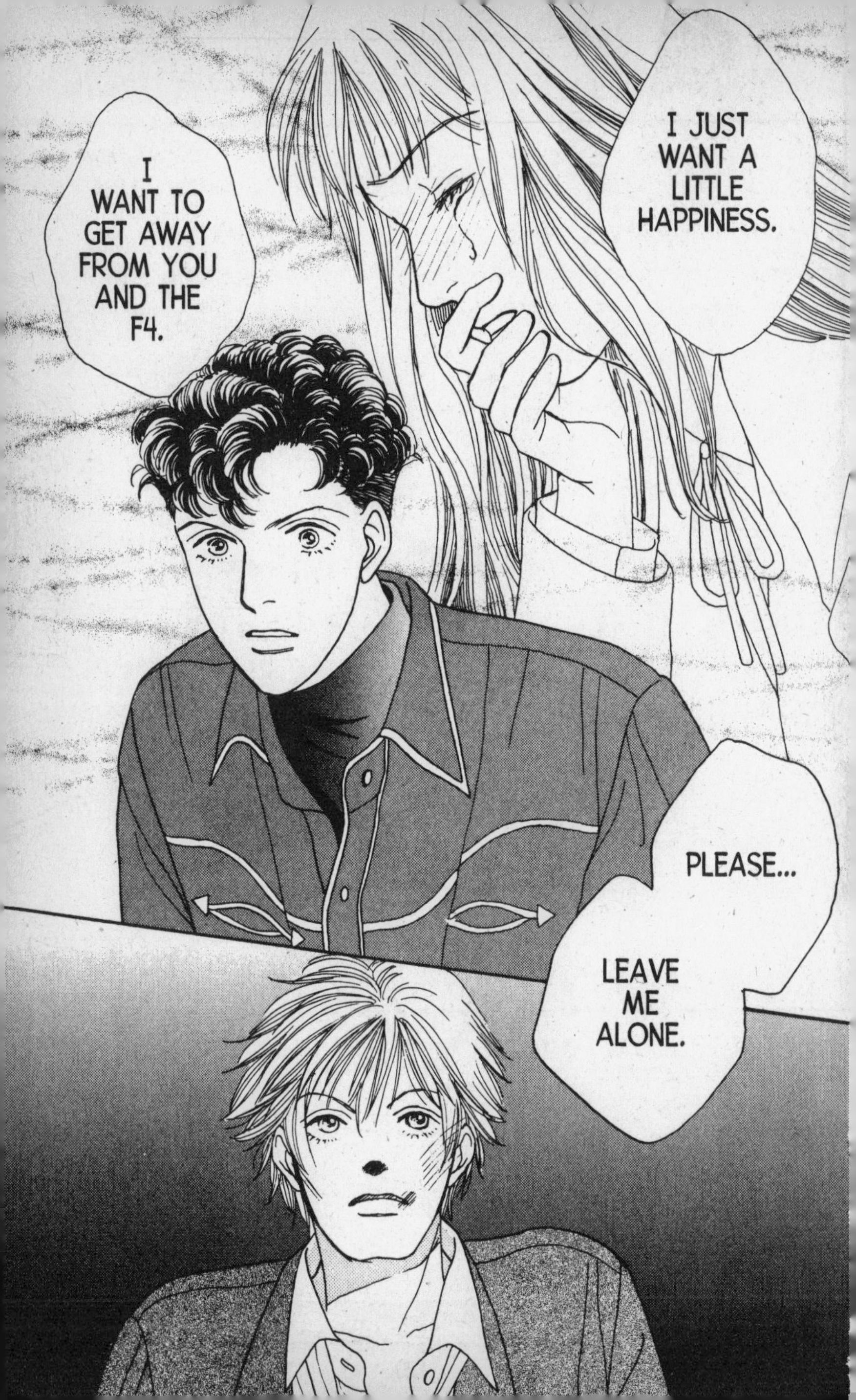
I JUST WANT A LITTLE HAPPINESS.
I WANT TO GET AWAY FROM YOU AND THE F4.
PLEASE...
LEAVE ME ALONE.

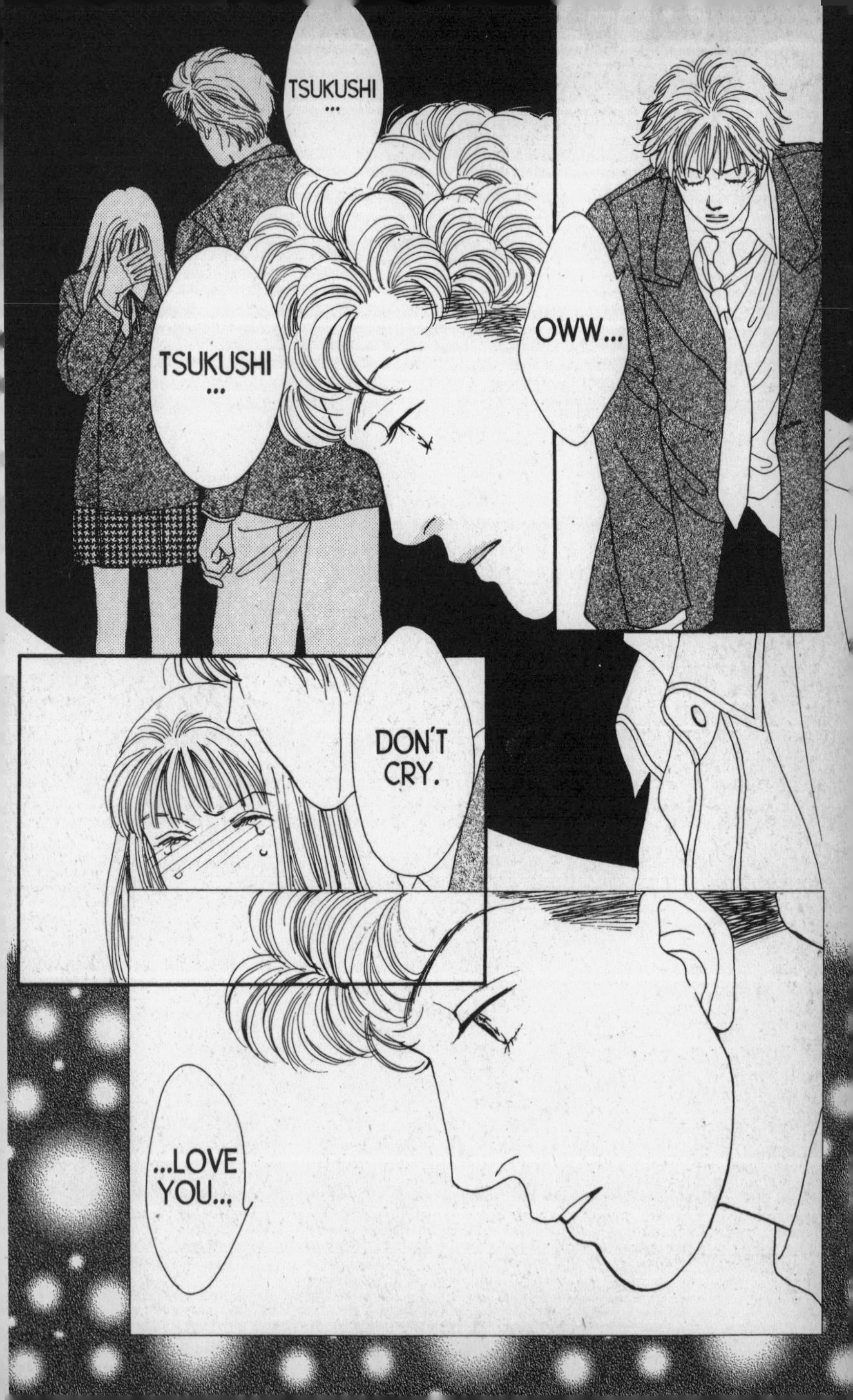
OWW...
TSUKUSHI ...
TSUKUSHI ...
DON'T CRY.
...LOVE YOU...

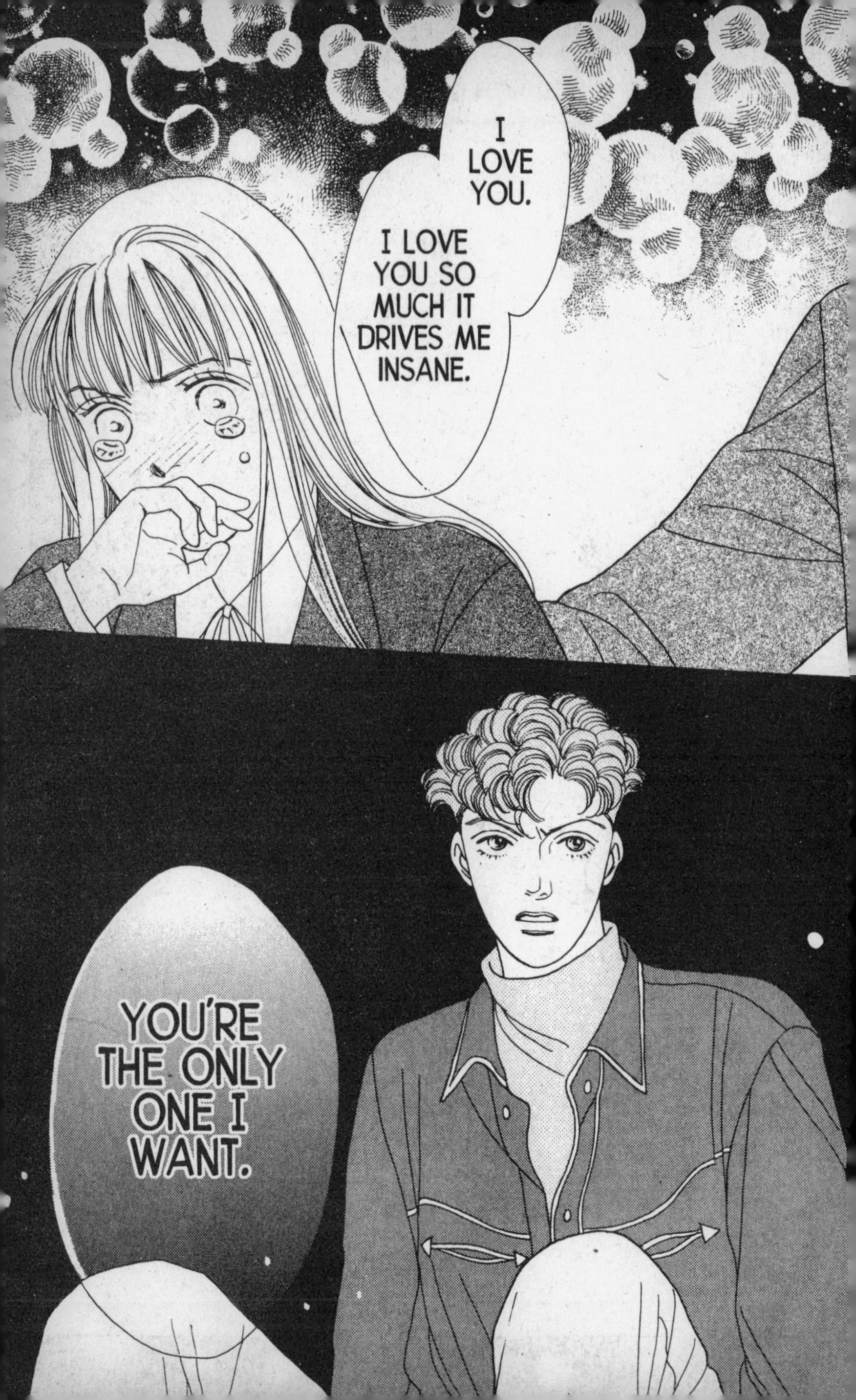
I LOVE YOU.
I LOVE YOU SO MUCH IT DRIVES ME INSANE.
YOU'RE THE ONLY ONE I WANT.

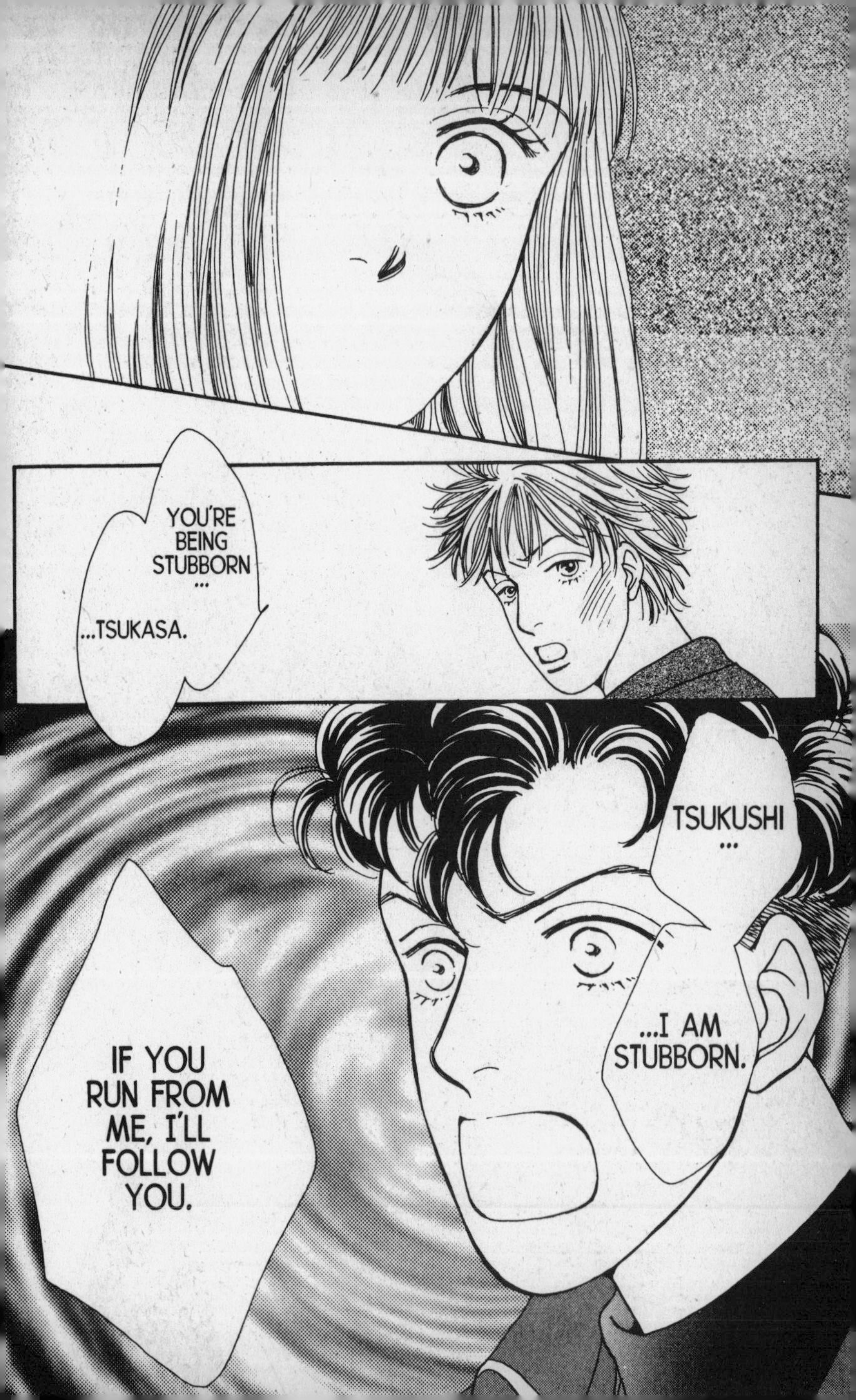
YOU'RE BEING STUBBORN ... ...TSUKASA.
TSUKUSHI ...
...I AM STUBBORN.
IF YOU RUN FROM ME, I'LL FOLLOW YOU.

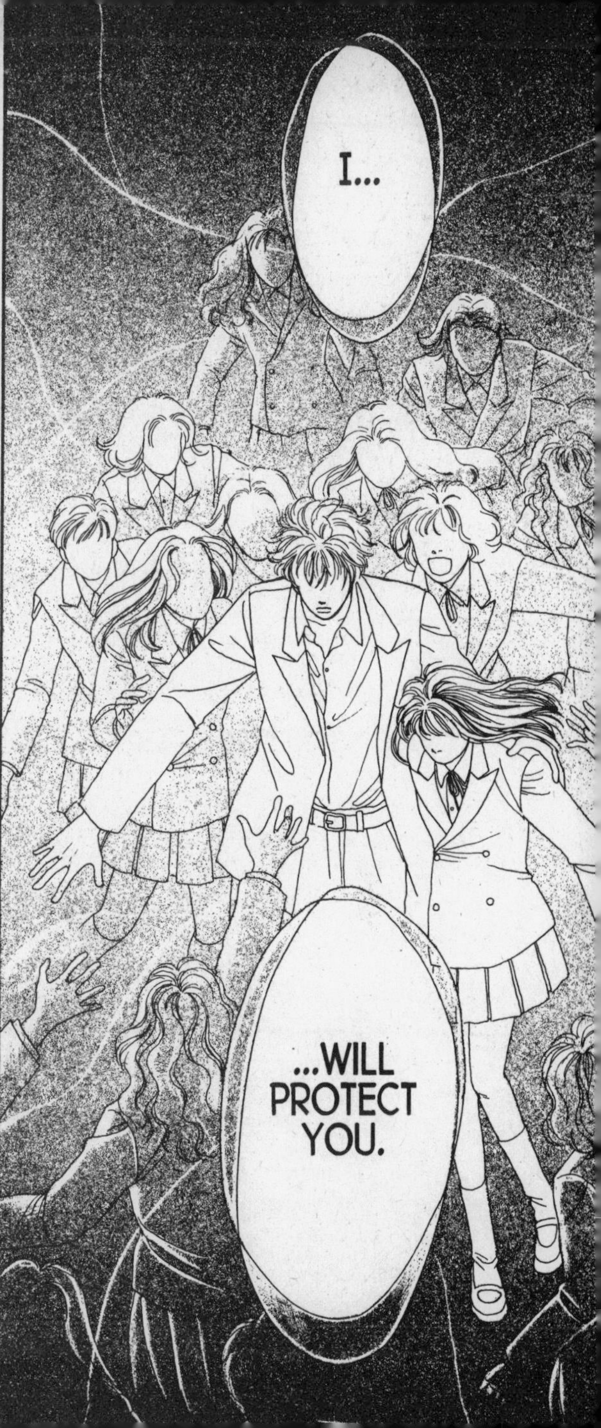
I...
...WILL PROTECT YOU.

At the Animation Studio (3)

The actors who'll be voicing the characters are:

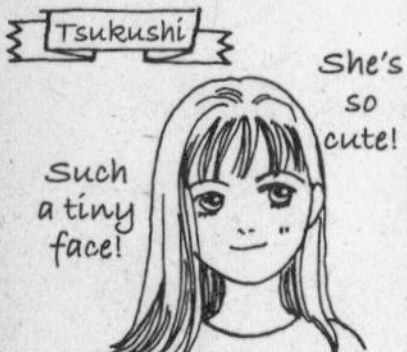
Tsukushi
She's so cute!
Such a tiny face!

Her name is Maki Mochida!!

I met her the other day. She seems to have enjoyed my "Boys over Flowers," so I'm very happy!!
I'm looking forward to hearing Maki play Tsukushi.

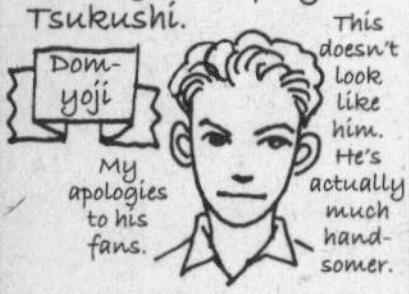
Dom-yoji
This doesn't look like him. He's actually much hand-somer.
My apologies to his fans.

Naoki Miyashita

He's got a wonderful voice!! I'm so glad to have such a skillful actor on board!!

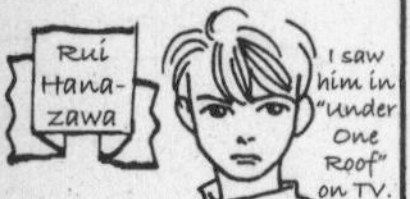
Rui Hana-zawa
I saw him in "Under One Roof" on TV.

Koji Yamamoto

He's a terrific actor, too. He changes dramatically, depending on his role. Like Rui, he's rather reticent.

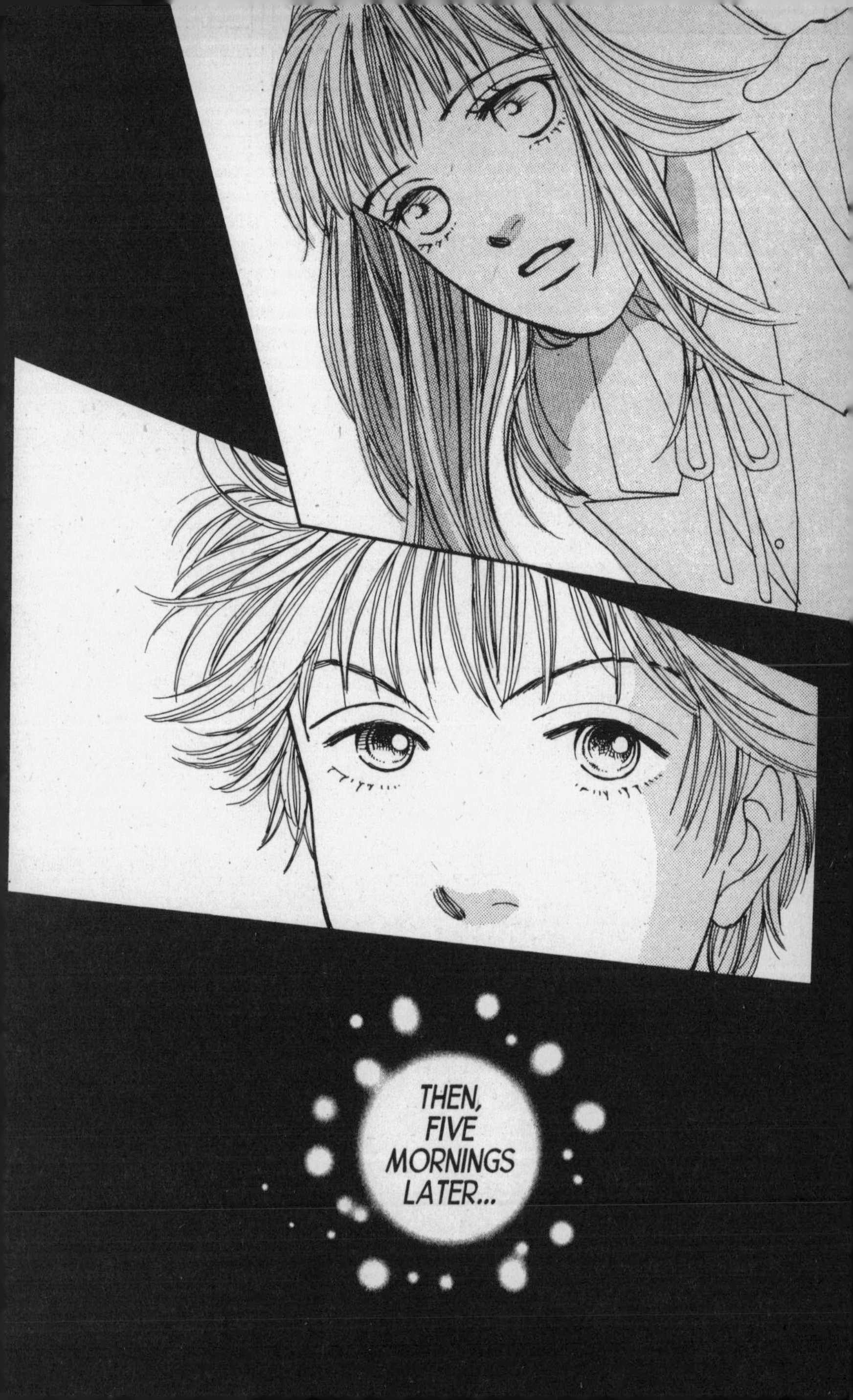
THEN, FIVE MORNINGS LATER...

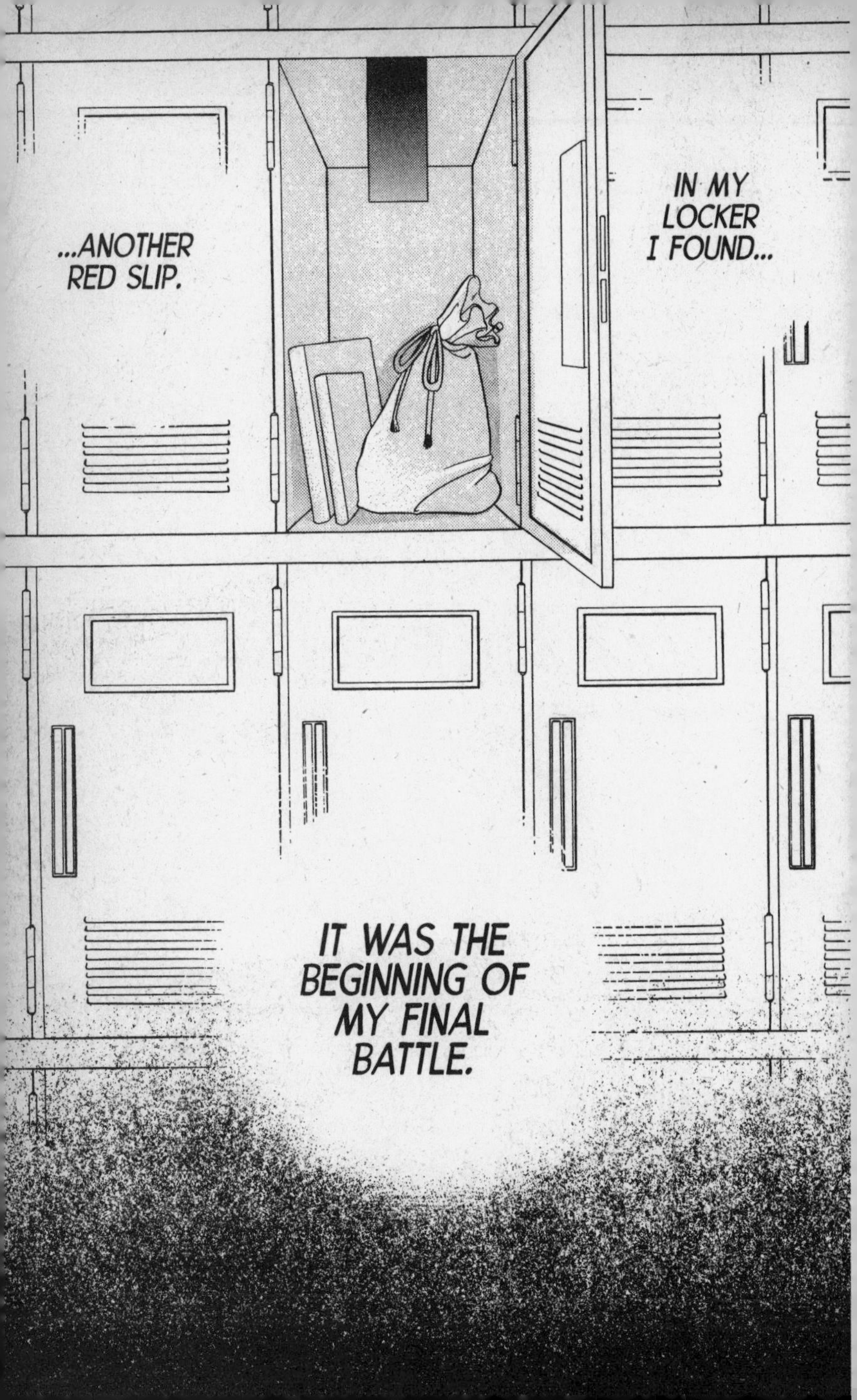
IN MY LOCKER I FOUND...
...ANOTHER RED SLIP.
IT WAS THE BEGINNING OF MY FINAL BATTLE.

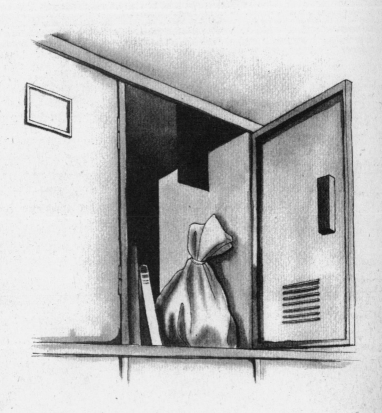

THE DAYS
LEADING UP TO
THE APPEARANCE
OF THAT RED
SLIP...

...WERE FIVE
VERY STRANGE
DAYS.

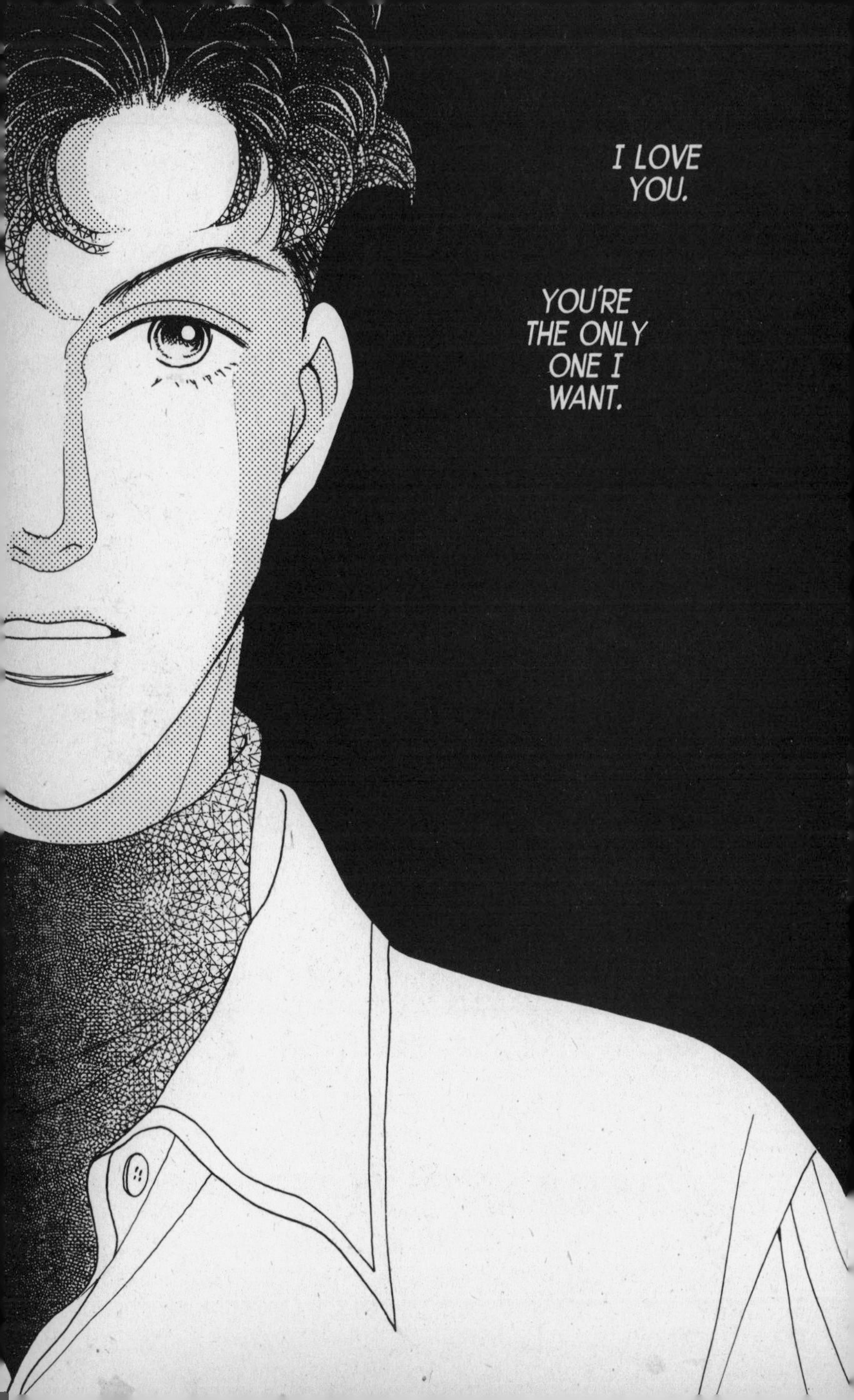
I LOVE YOU.
YOU'RE THE ONLY ONE I WANT.

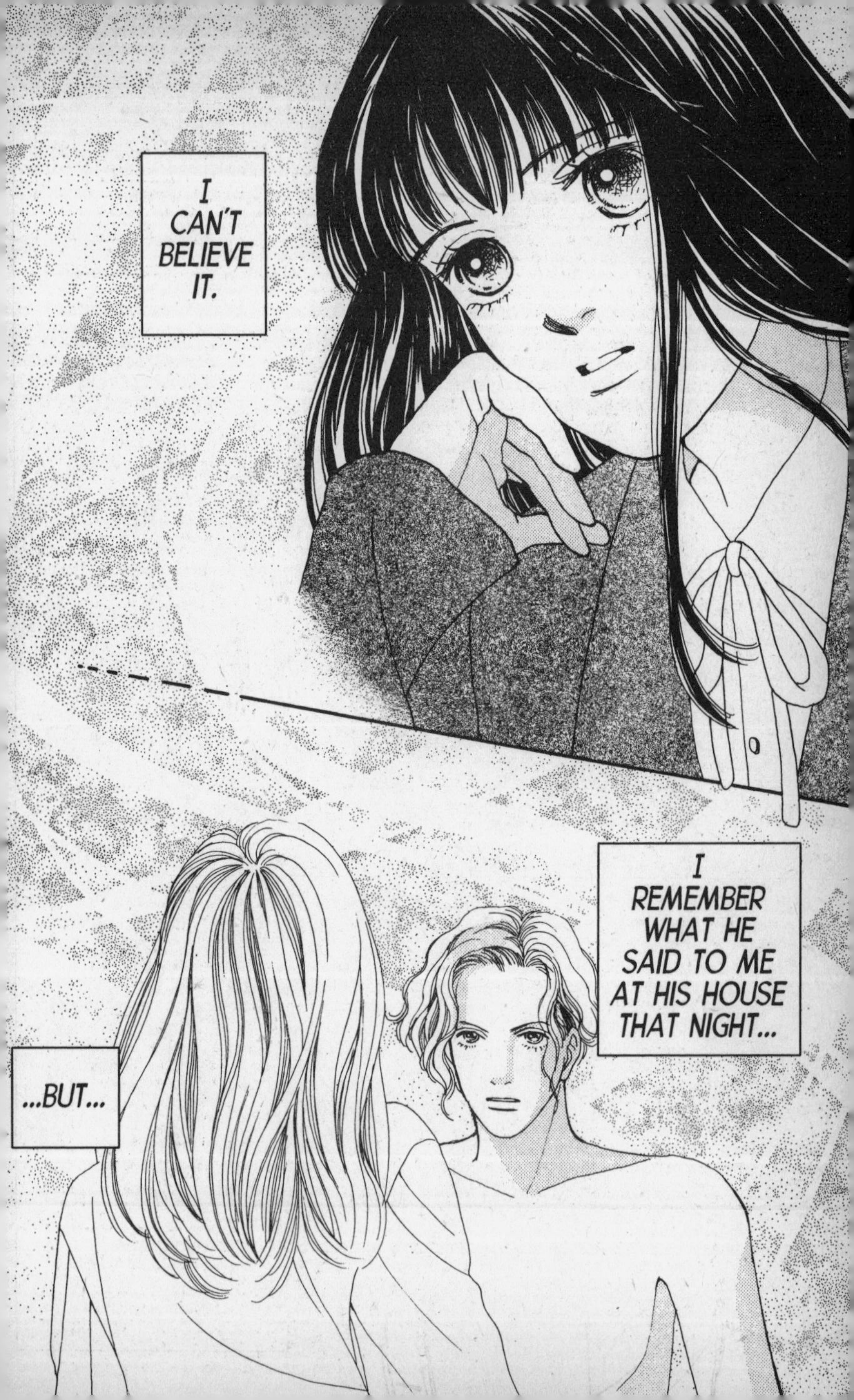
I CAN'T BELIEVE IT.
I REMEMBER WHAT HE SAID TO ME AT HIS HOUSE THAT NIGHT...
...BUT...

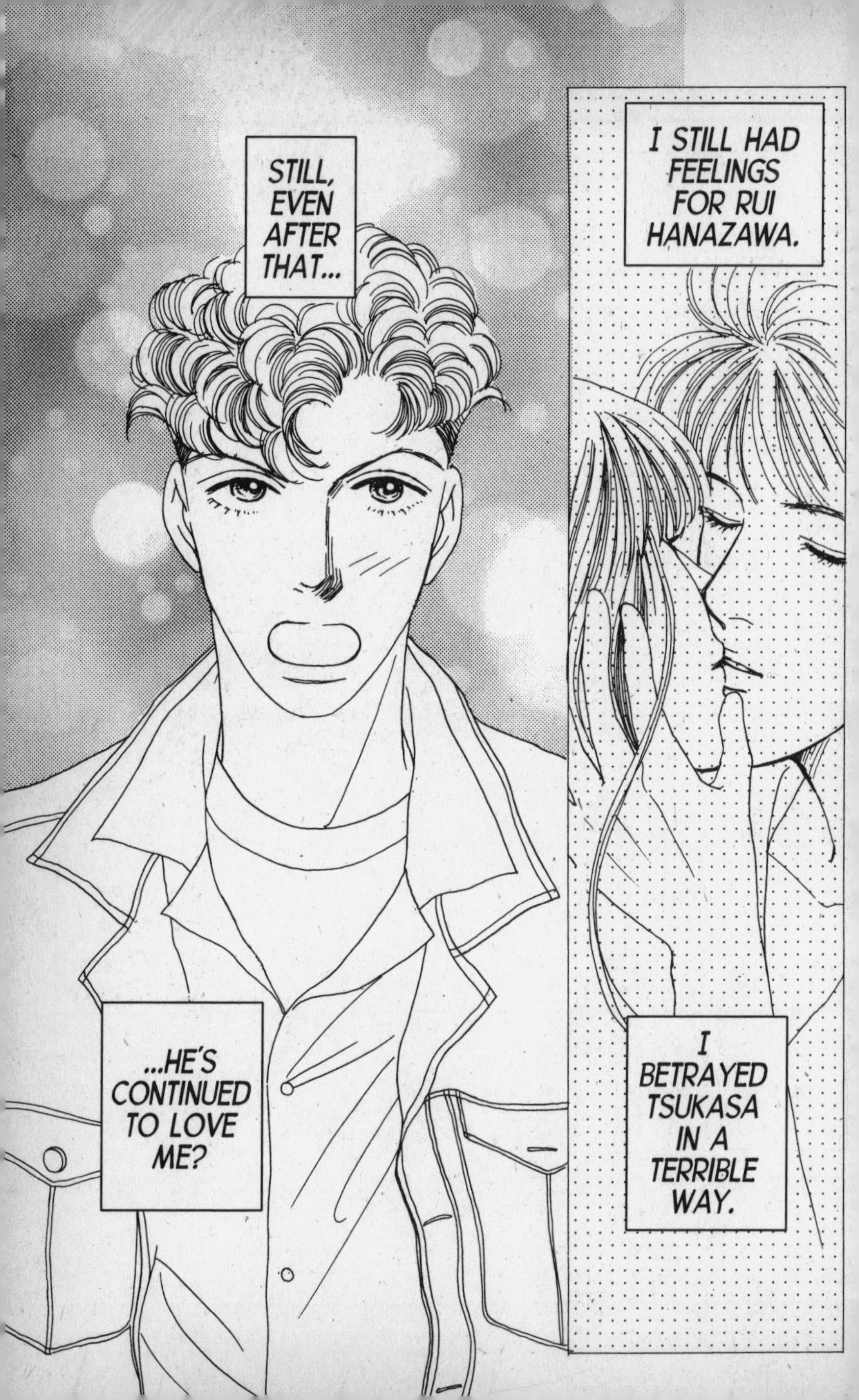
I STILL HAD FEELINGS FOR RUI HANAZAWA.
I BETRAYED TSUKASA IN A TERRIBLE WAY.
STILL, EVEN AFTER THAT...
...HE'S CONTINUED TO LOVE ME?

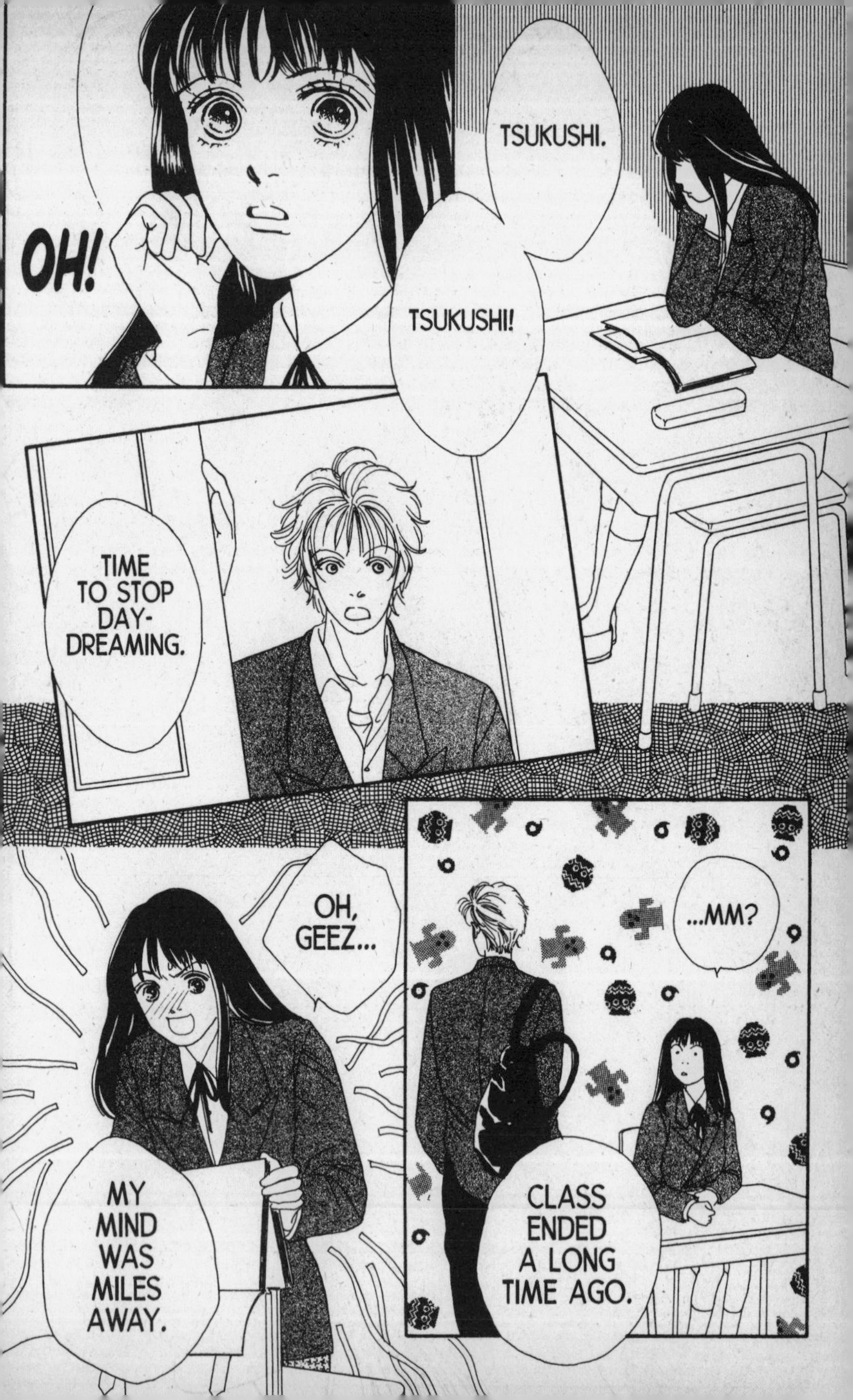
TSUKUSHI.
TSUKUSHI!
OH!
TIME TO STOP DAY-DREAMING.
...MM?
CLASS ENDED A LONG TIME AGO.
OH, GEEZ...
MY MIND WAS MILES AWAY.

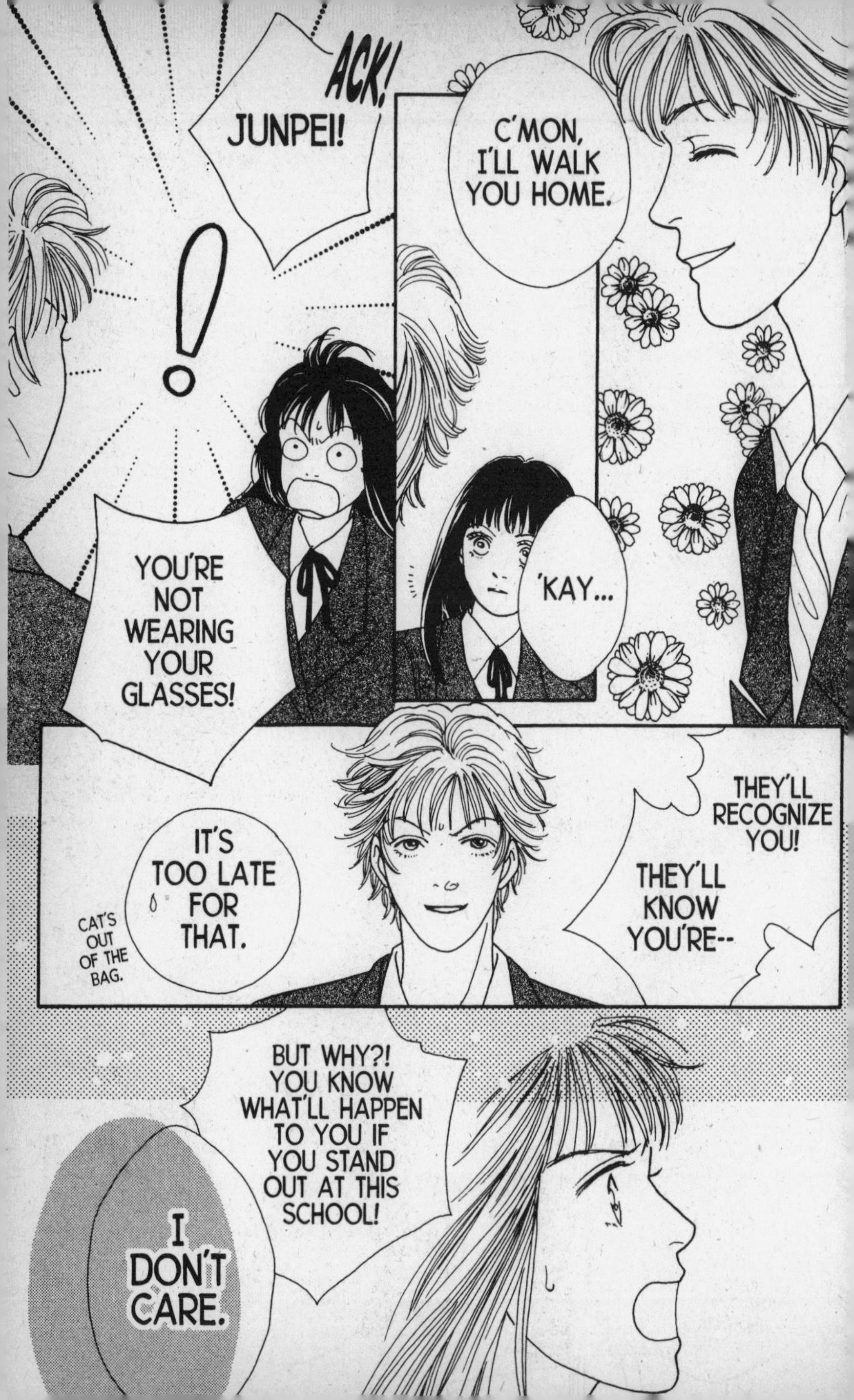
C'MON, I'LL WALK YOU HOME.
'KAY...
ACK!
JUNPEI!
YOU'RE NOT WEARING YOUR GLASSES!
THEY'LL RECOGNIZE YOU!
THEY'LL KNOW YOU'RE--
IT'S TOO LATE FOR THAT.
CAT'S OUT OF THE BAG.
BUT WHY?! YOU KNOW WHAT'LL HAPPEN TO YOU IF YOU STAND OUT AT THIS SCHOOL!
I DON'T CARE.

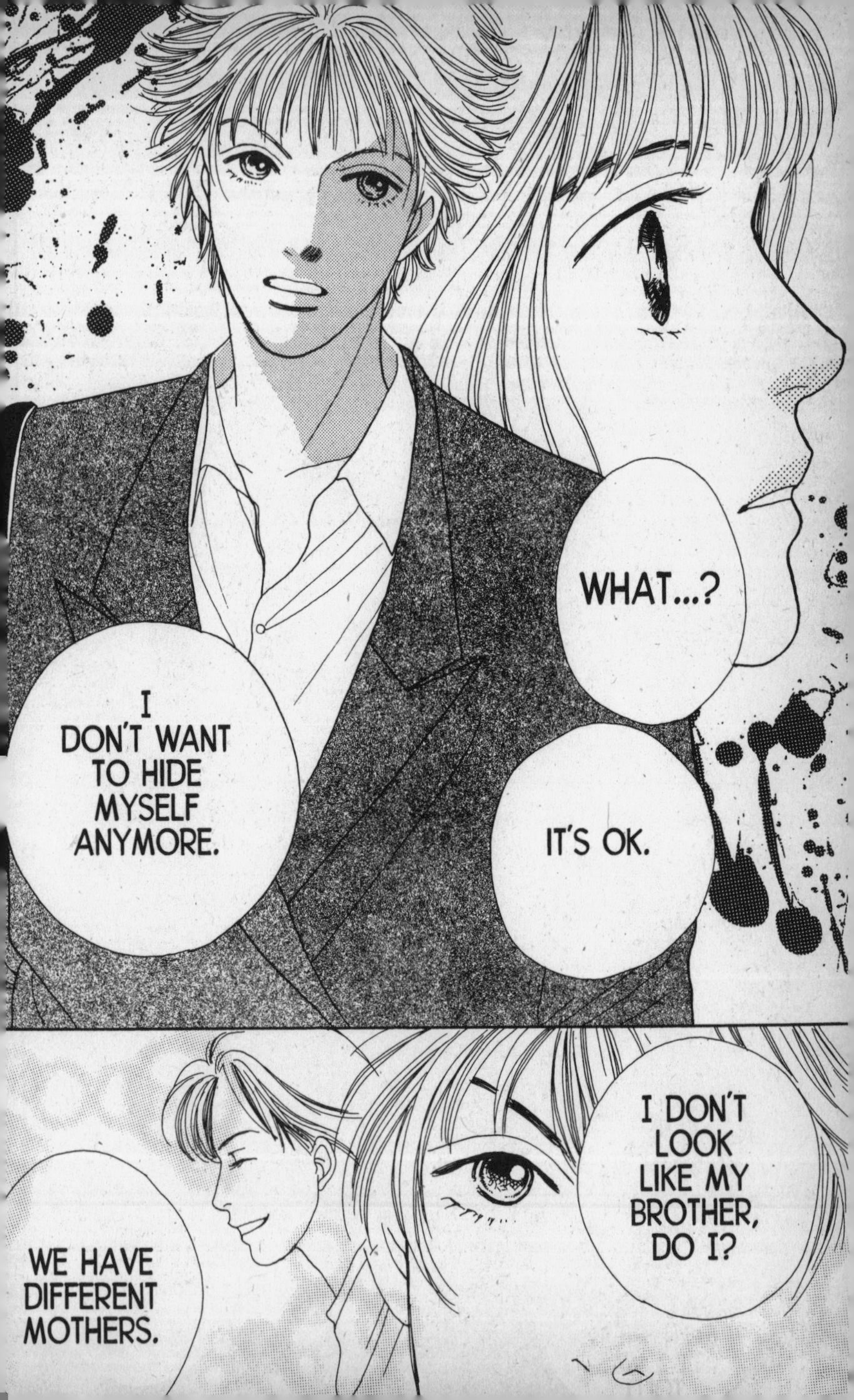
WHAT...?
IT'S OK.
I DON'T WANT TO HIDE MYSELF ANYMORE.
I DON'T LOOK LIKE MY BROTHER, DO I?
WE HAVE DIFFERENT MOTHERS.

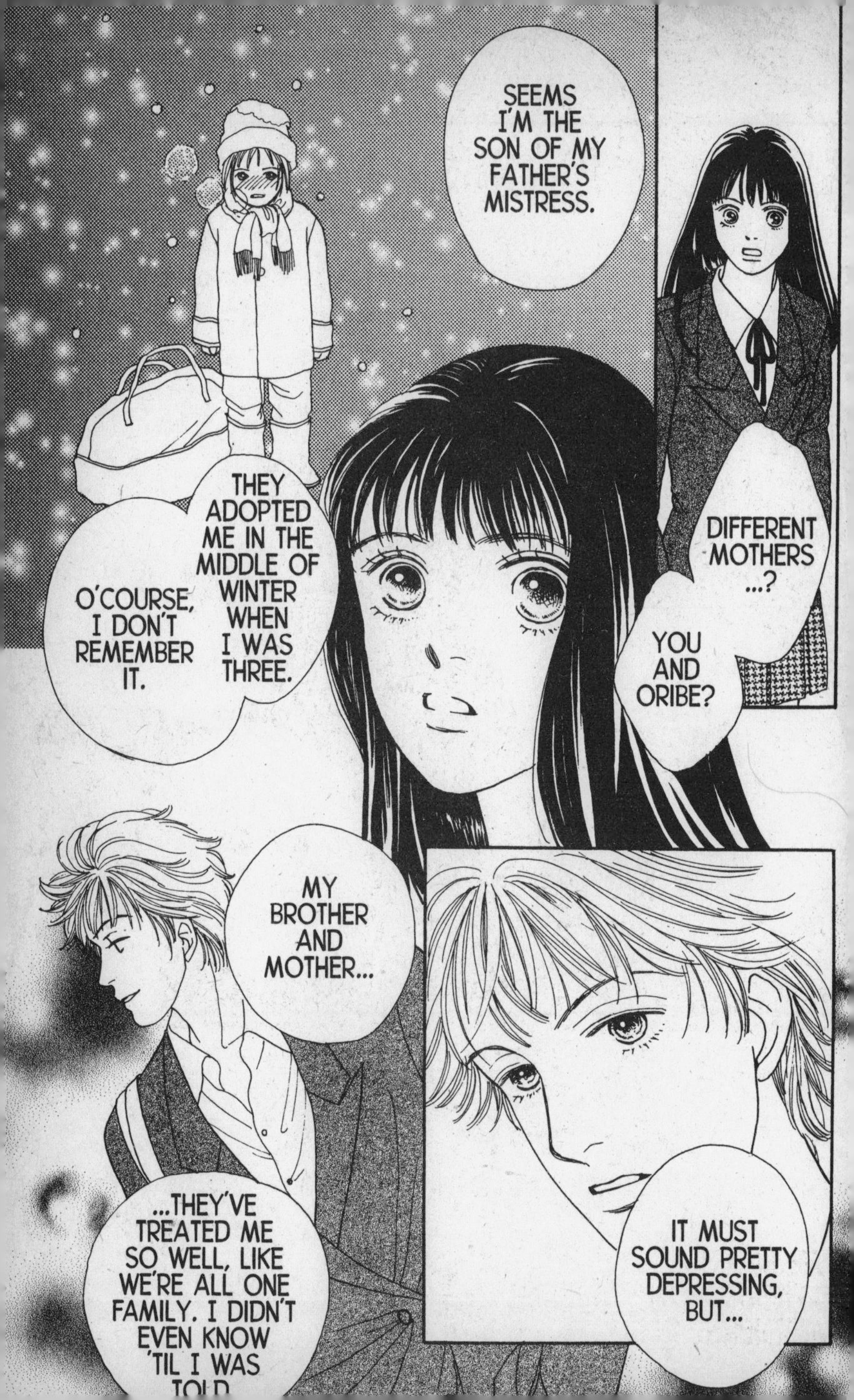
SEEMS I'M THE SON OF MY FATHER'S MISTRESS.
DIFFERENT MOTHERS ...?
YOU AND ORIBE?
THEY ADOPTED ME IN THE MIDDLE OF WINTER WHEN I WAS THREE.
O'COURSE, I DON'T REMEMBER IT.
IT MUST SOUND PRETTY DEPRESSING, BUT...
MY BROTHER AND MOTHER...
...THEY'VE TREATED ME SO WELL, LIKE WE'RE ALL ONE FAMILY. I DIDN'T EVEN KNOW 'TIL I WAS

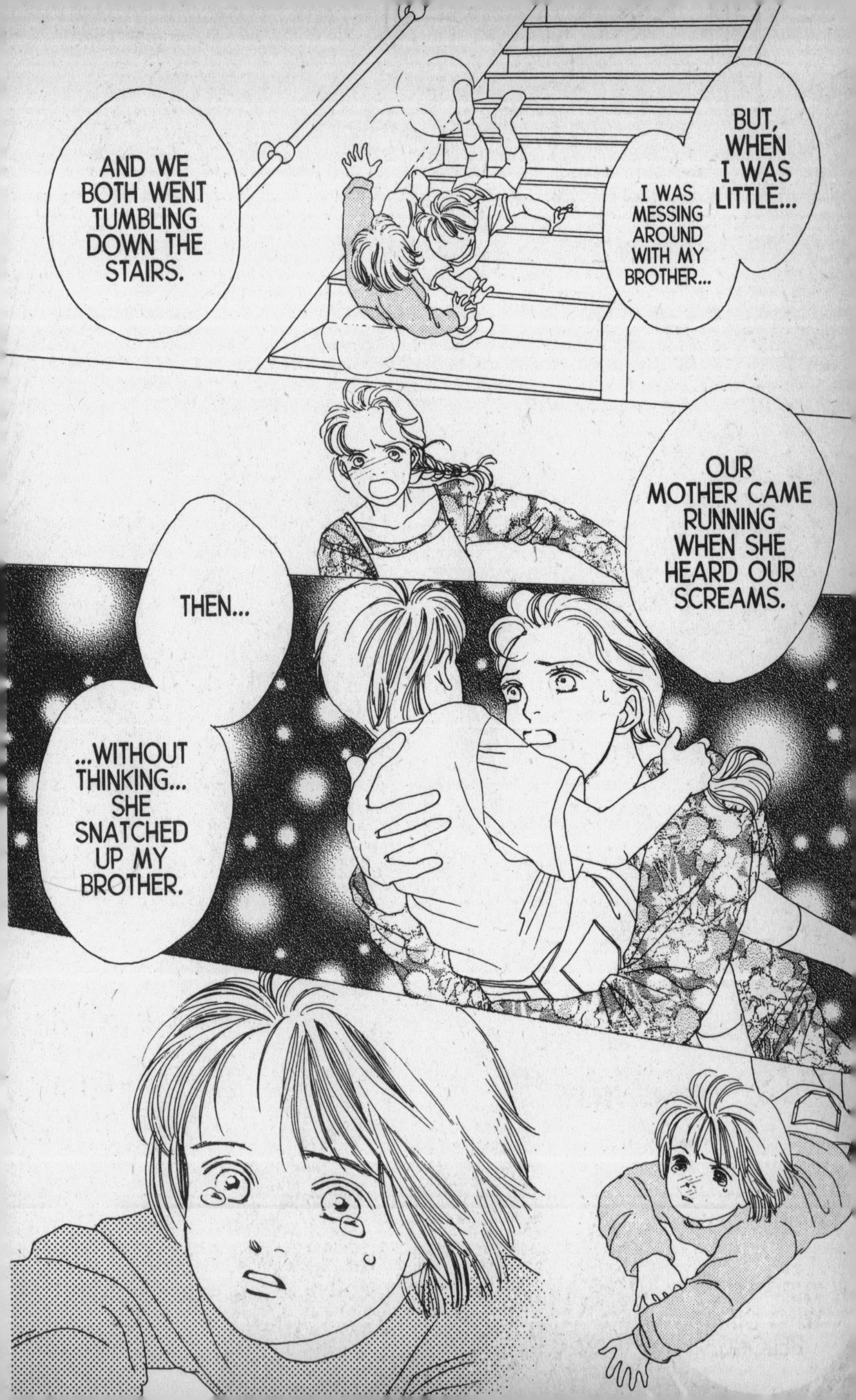
BUT, WHEN I WAS LITTLE...
I WAS MESSING AROUND WITH MY BROTHER...
AND WE BOTH WENT TUMBLING DOWN THE STAIRS.
OUR MOTHER CAME RUNNING WHEN SHE HEARD OUR SCREAMS.
THEN...
...WITHOUT THINKING... SHE SNATCHED UP MY BROTHER.

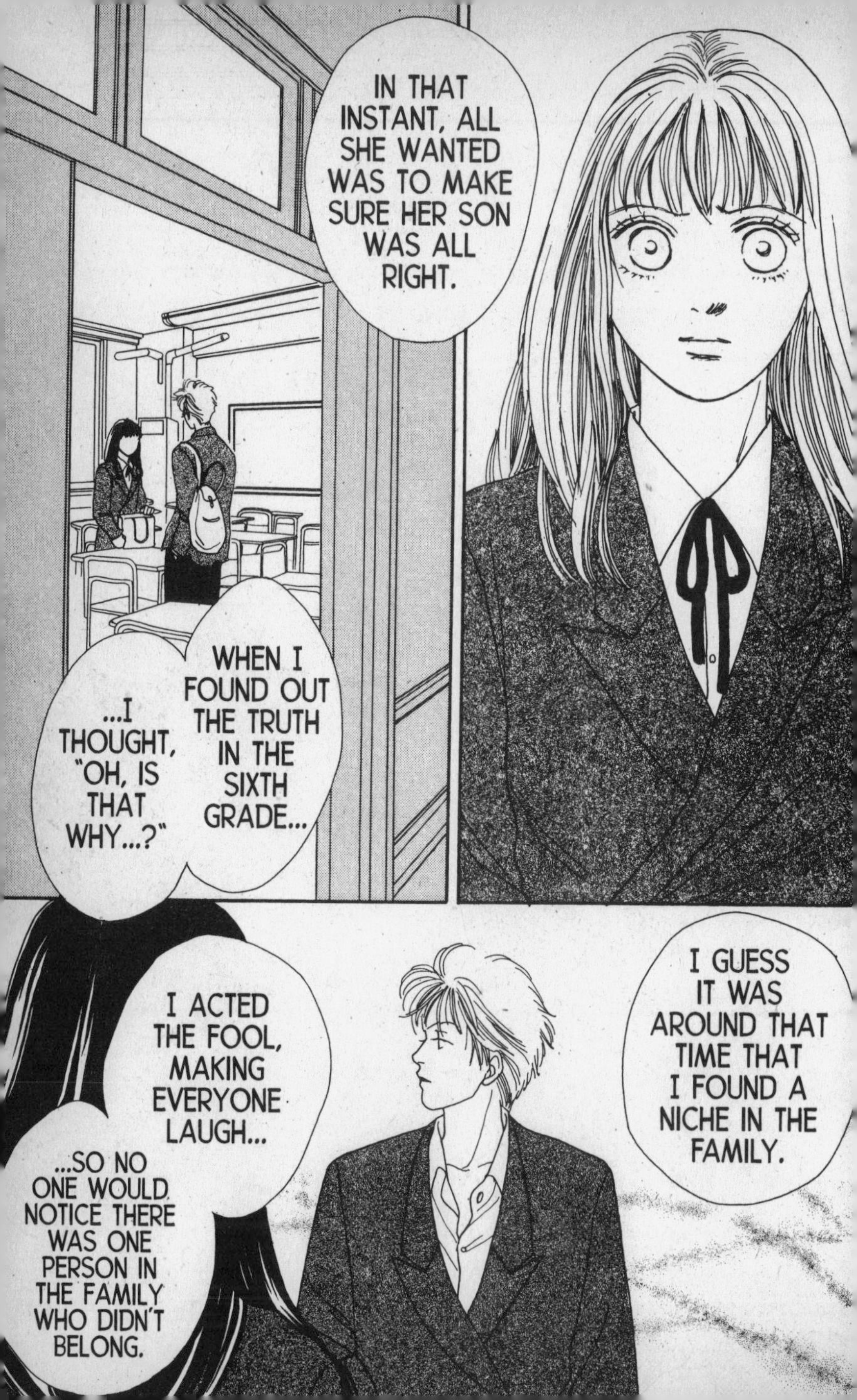
IN THAT INSTANT, ALL SHE WANTED WAS TO MAKE SURE HER SON WAS ALL RIGHT.
WHEN I FOUND OUT THE TRUTH IN THE SIXTH GRADE...
...I THOUGHT, "OH, IS THAT WHY...?"
I GUESS IT WAS AROUND THAT TIME THAT I FOUND A NICHE IN THE FAMILY.
I ACTED THE FOOL, MAKING EVERYONE LAUGH...
...SO NO ONE WOULD NOTICE THERE WAS ONE PERSON IN THE FAMILY WHO DIDN'T BELONG.

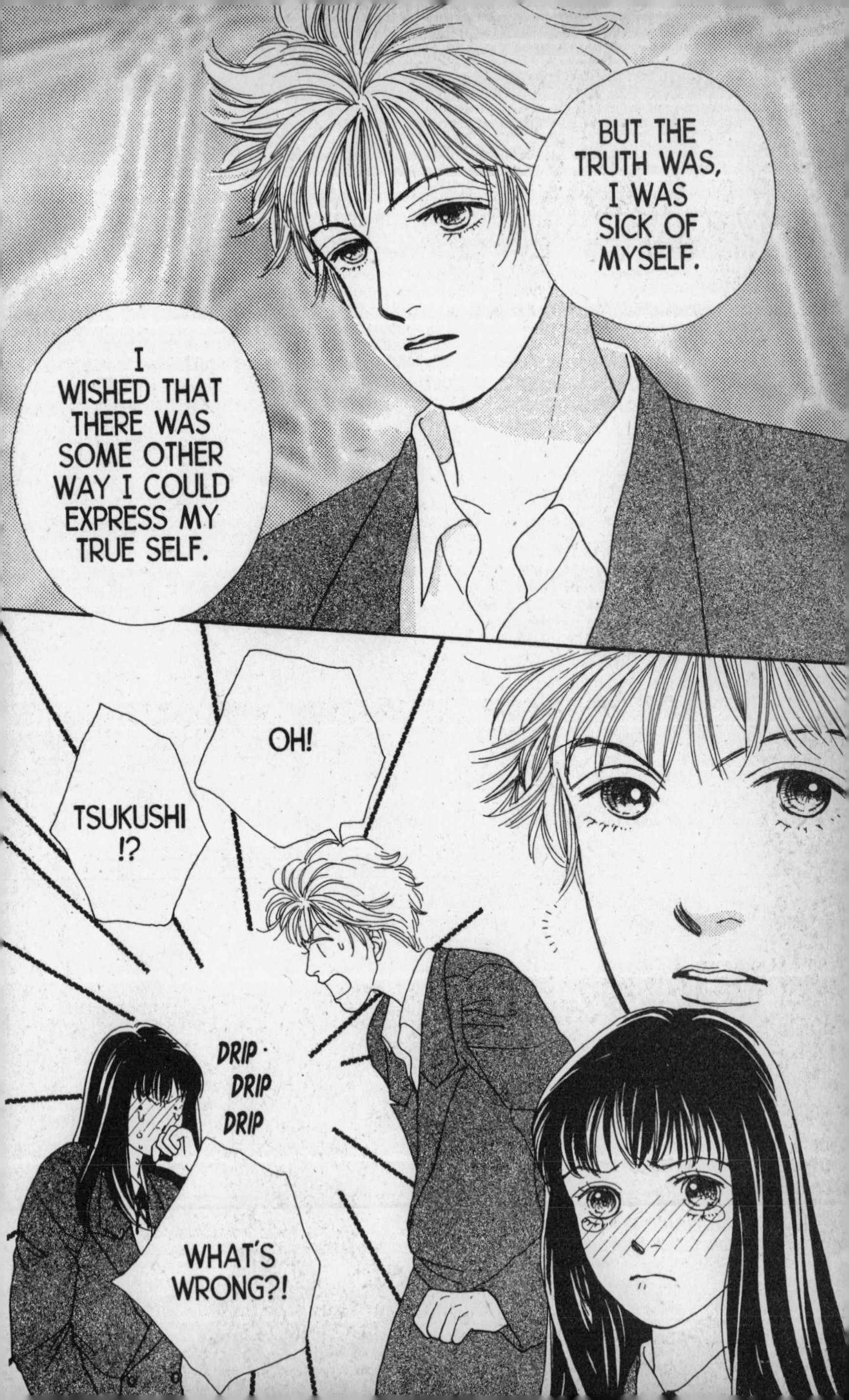
BUT THE TRUTH WAS, I WAS SICK OF MYSELF.
I WISHED THAT THERE WAS SOME OTHER WAY I COULD EXPRESS MY TRUE SELF.
OH!
TSUKUSHI !?
DRIP · DRIP DRIP
WHAT'S WRONG?!

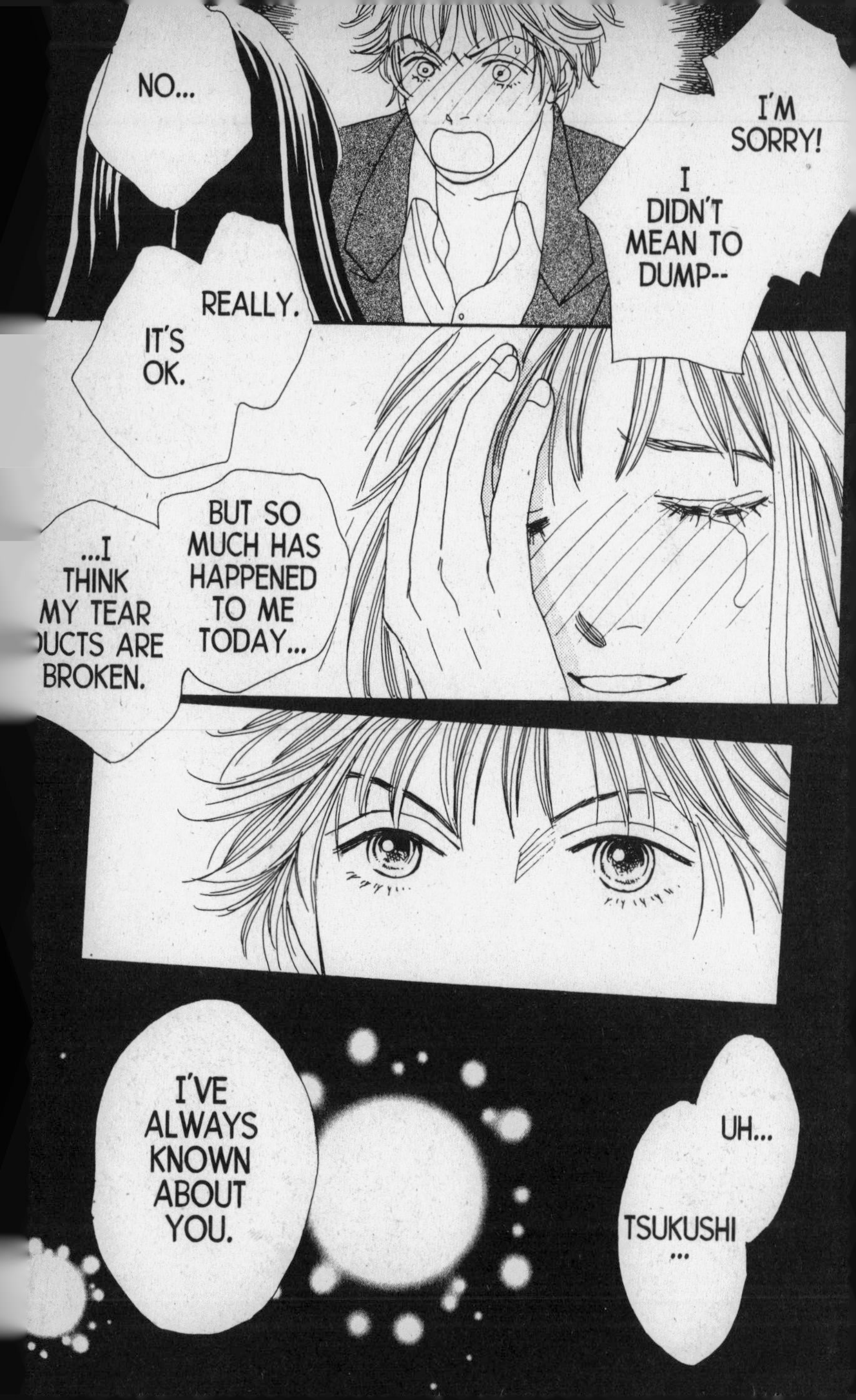
I'M SORRY! I DIDN'T MEAN TO DUMP--
NO...
REALLY. IT'S OK.
BUT SO MUCH HAS HAPPENED TO ME TODAY...
...I THINK MY TEAR DUCTS ARE BROKEN.
UH... TSUKUSHI ...
I'VE ALWAYS KNOWN ABOUT YOU.

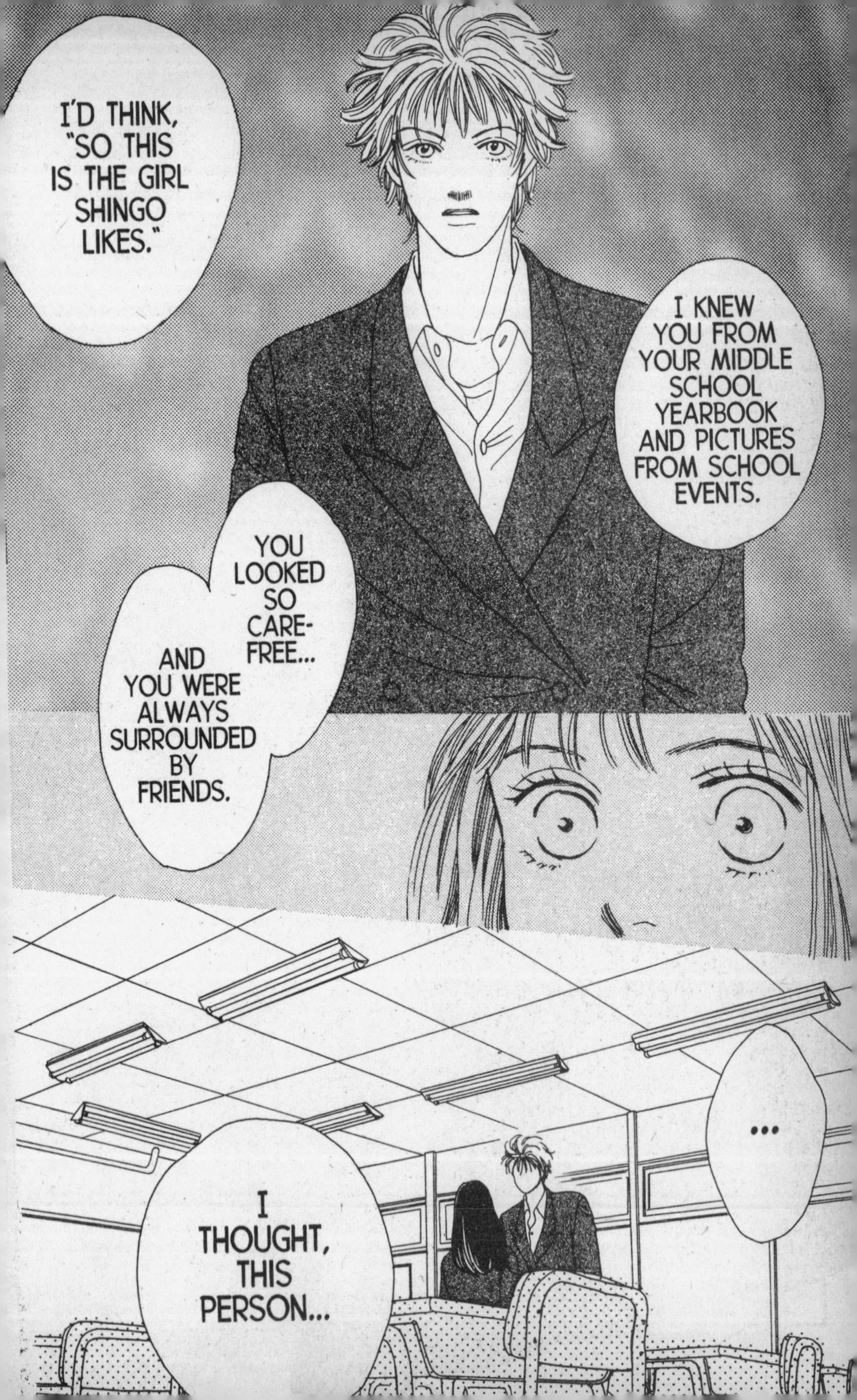
I KNEW YOU FROM YOUR MIDDLE SCHOOL YEARBOOK AND PICTURES FROM SCHOOL EVENTS.
I'D THINK, "SO THIS IS THE GIRL SHINGO LIKES."
YOU LOOKED SO CARE-FREE...
AND YOU WERE ALWAYS SURROUNDED BY FRIENDS.
...
I THOUGHT, THIS PERSON...

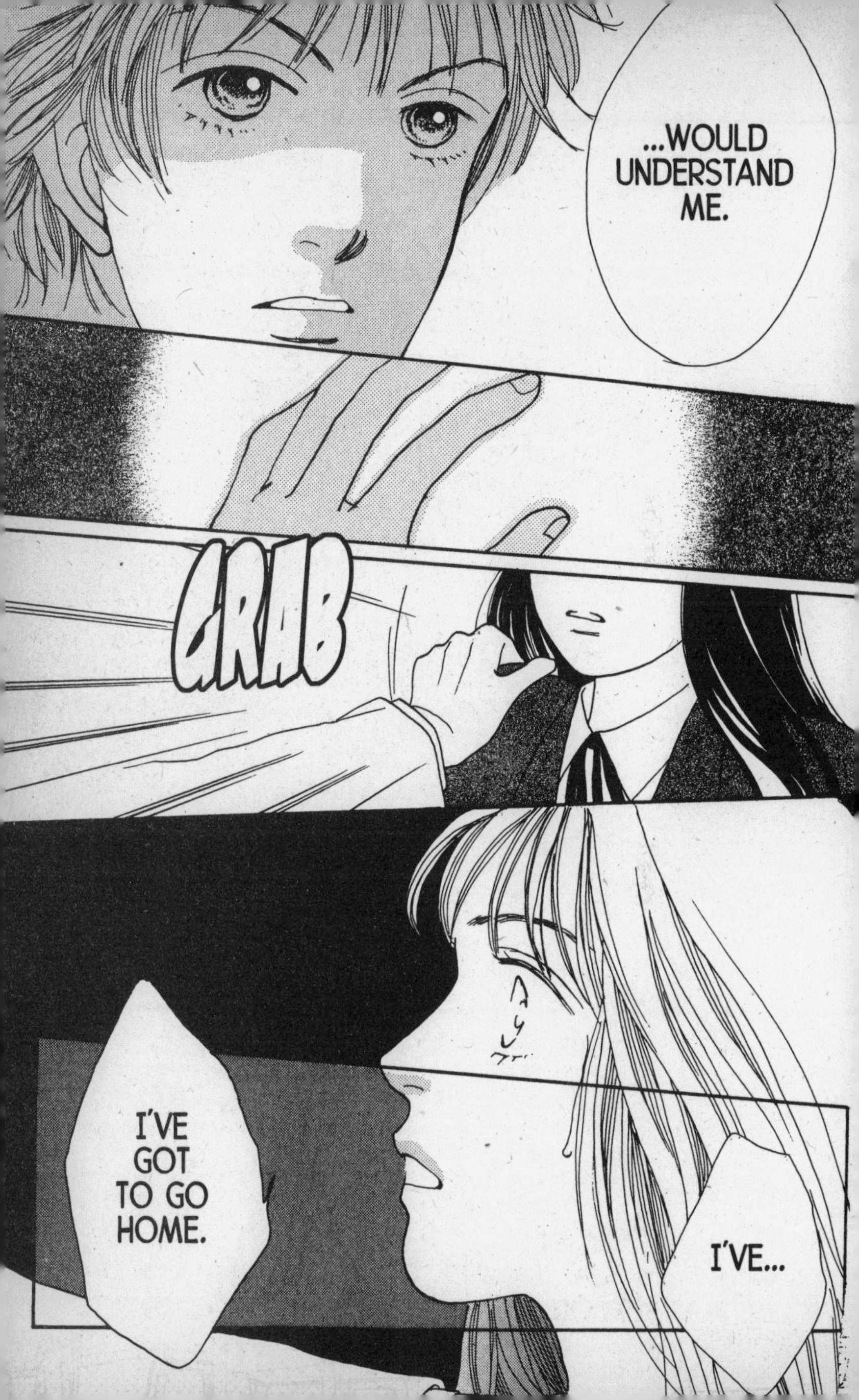

...WOULD UNDERSTAND ME.
GRAB
I'VE...
I'VE GOT TO GO HOME.

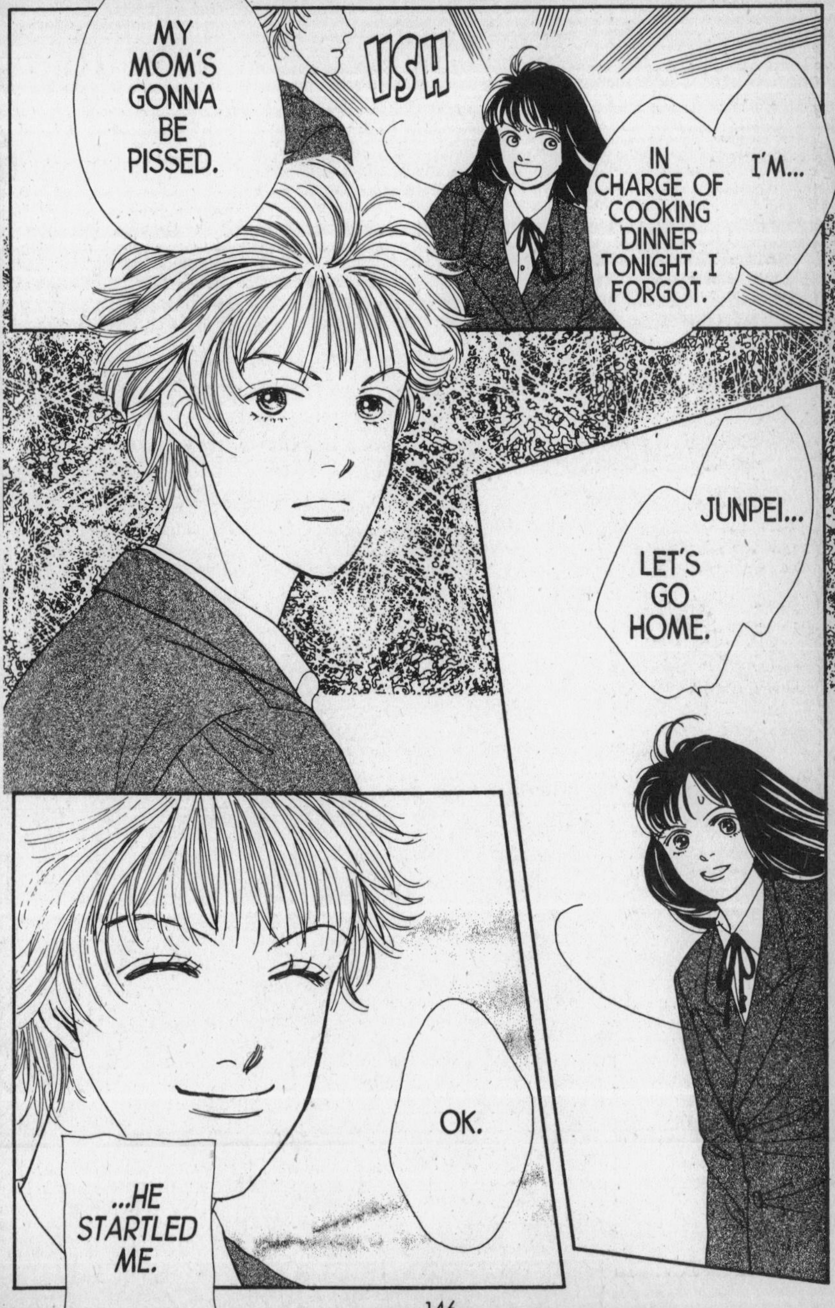
I'M...
IN CHARGE OF COOKING DINNER TONIGHT. I FORGOT.
USH
MY MOM'S GONNA BE PISSED.
JUNPEI...
LET'S GO HOME.
OK.
...HE STARTLED ME.

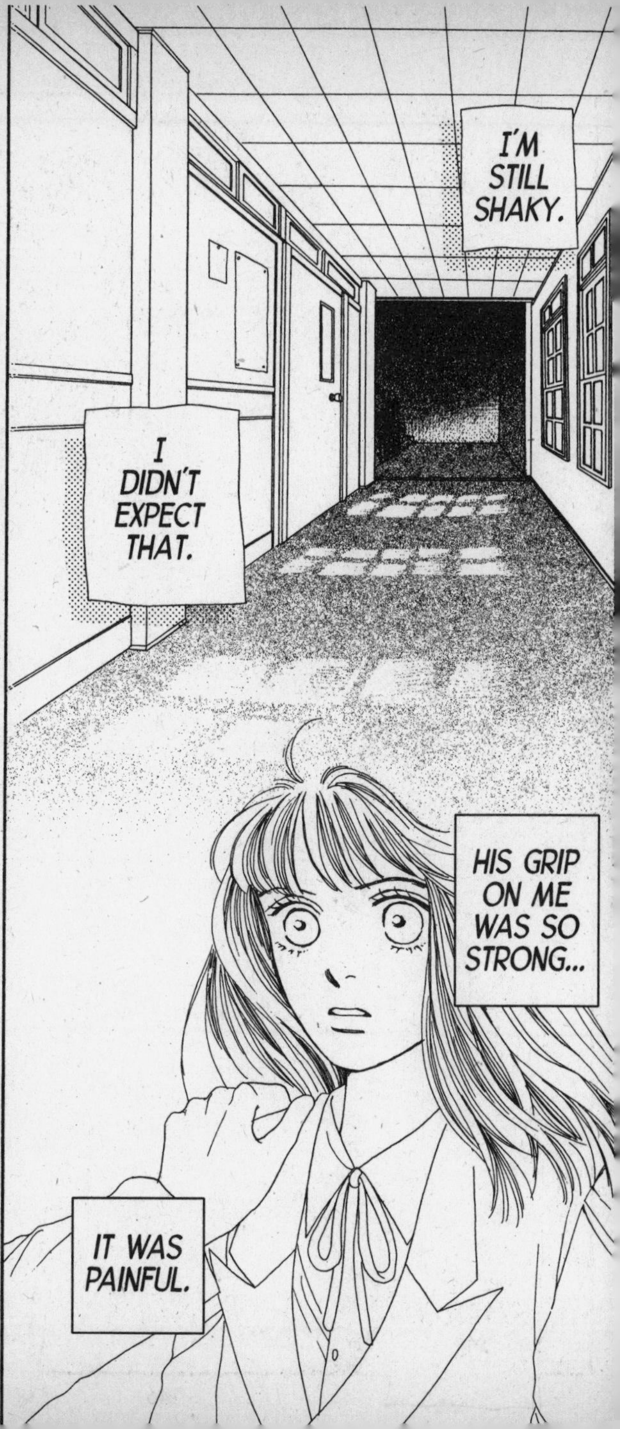
I'M STILL SHAKY.
I DIDN'T EXPECT THAT.
HIS GRIP ON ME WAS SO STRONG...
IT WAS PAINFUL.

At the Animation Studio (4)

This person makes me really happy!!

She does the voice of Yuriko Asai.

She's Yoshiko Shimizu of the comedy duo Pink Telephone!!

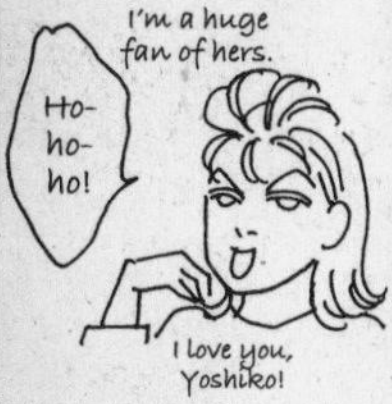
I'm a huge fan of hers.
Ho-ho-ho!
I love you, Yoshiko!

I feel so lucky to have her doing Yuriko with that sweet voice of hers.

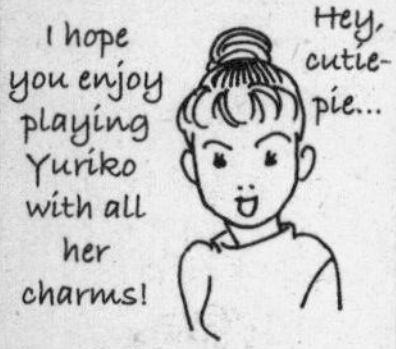
Hey, cutie-pie...
I hope you enjoy playing Yuriko with all her charms!

And lucky that all the other voice actors are just as talented.

I've got to do my best so that the people who read my comics after seeing the anime will think the comics are pretty good, too. That's a lot of pressure...

Bandai will be coming out with lots of cute Boys over Flowers merchandise for both adults and kids!!

I'll probably be playing with them, too... heh-heh-heh...

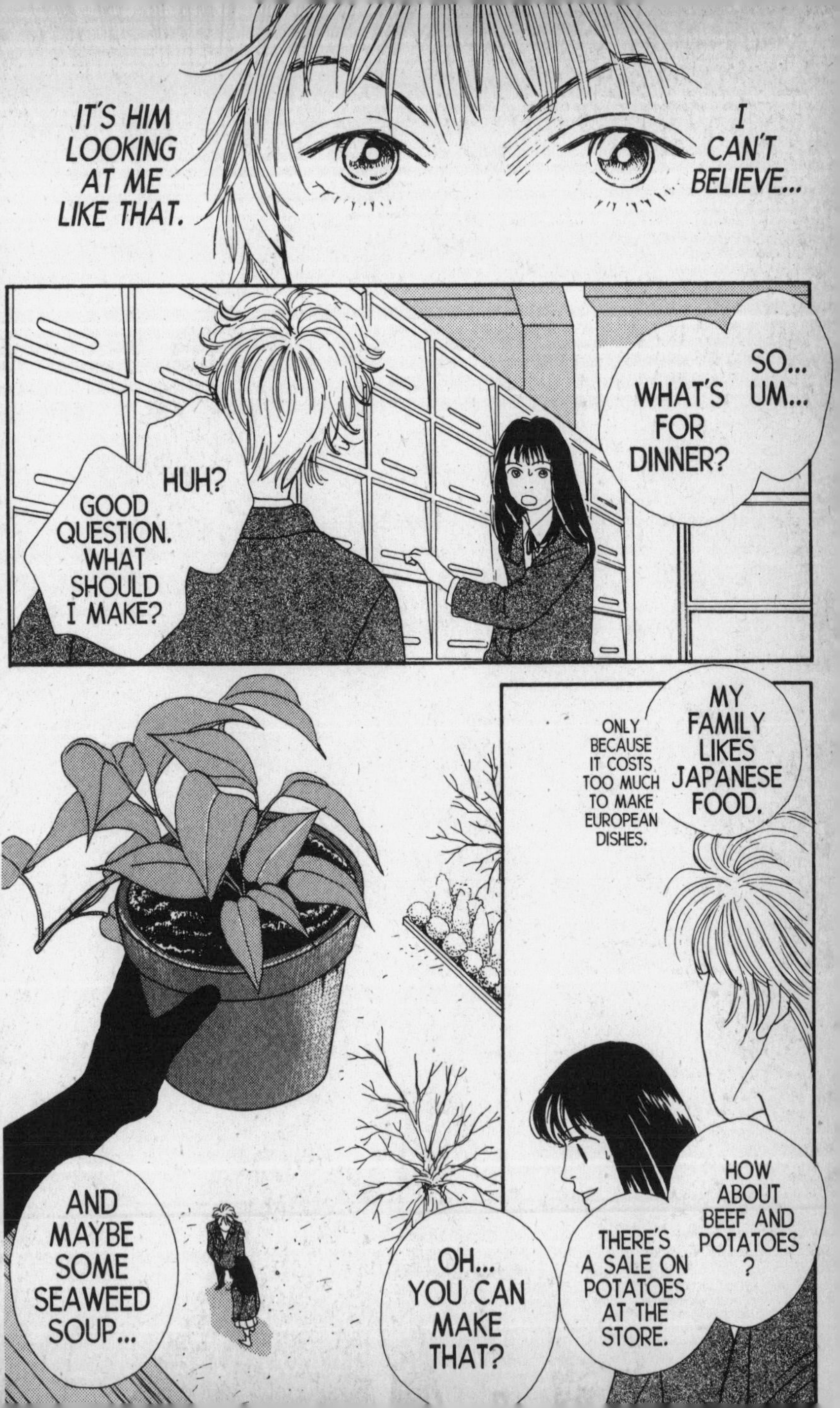
I CAN'T BELIEVE...
IT'S HIM LOOKING AT ME LIKE THAT.
SO... UM... WHAT'S FOR DINNER?
HUH? GOOD QUESTION. WHAT SHOULD I MAKE?
MY FAMILY LIKES JAPANESE FOOD.
ONLY BECAUSE IT COSTS TOO MUCH TO MAKE EUROPEAN DISHES.
HOW ABOUT BEEF AND POTATOES?
THERE'S A SALE ON POTATOES AT THE STORE.
OH... YOU CAN MAKE THAT?
AND MAYBE SOME SEAWEED SOUP...

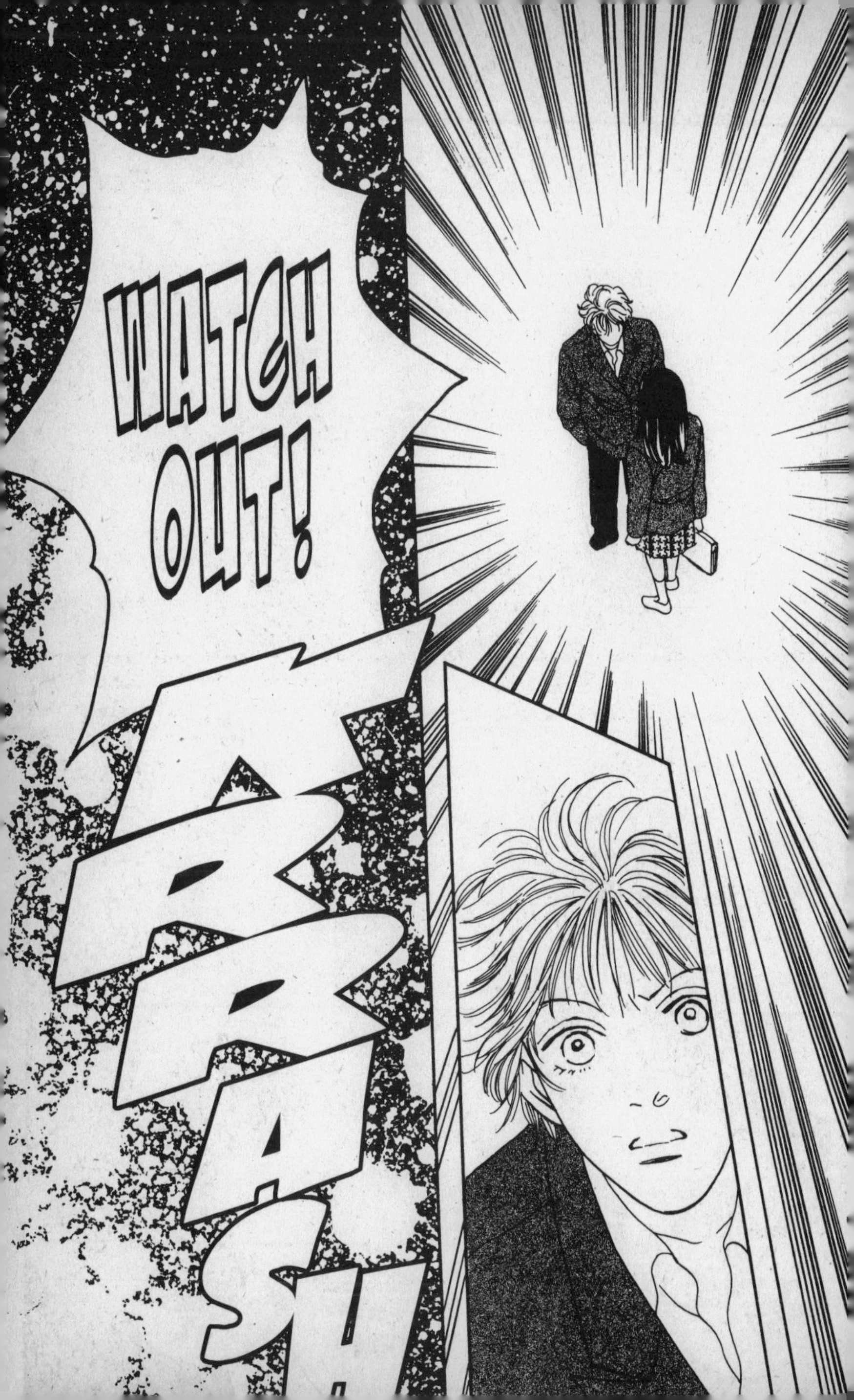
WATCH OUT!
CRASH!

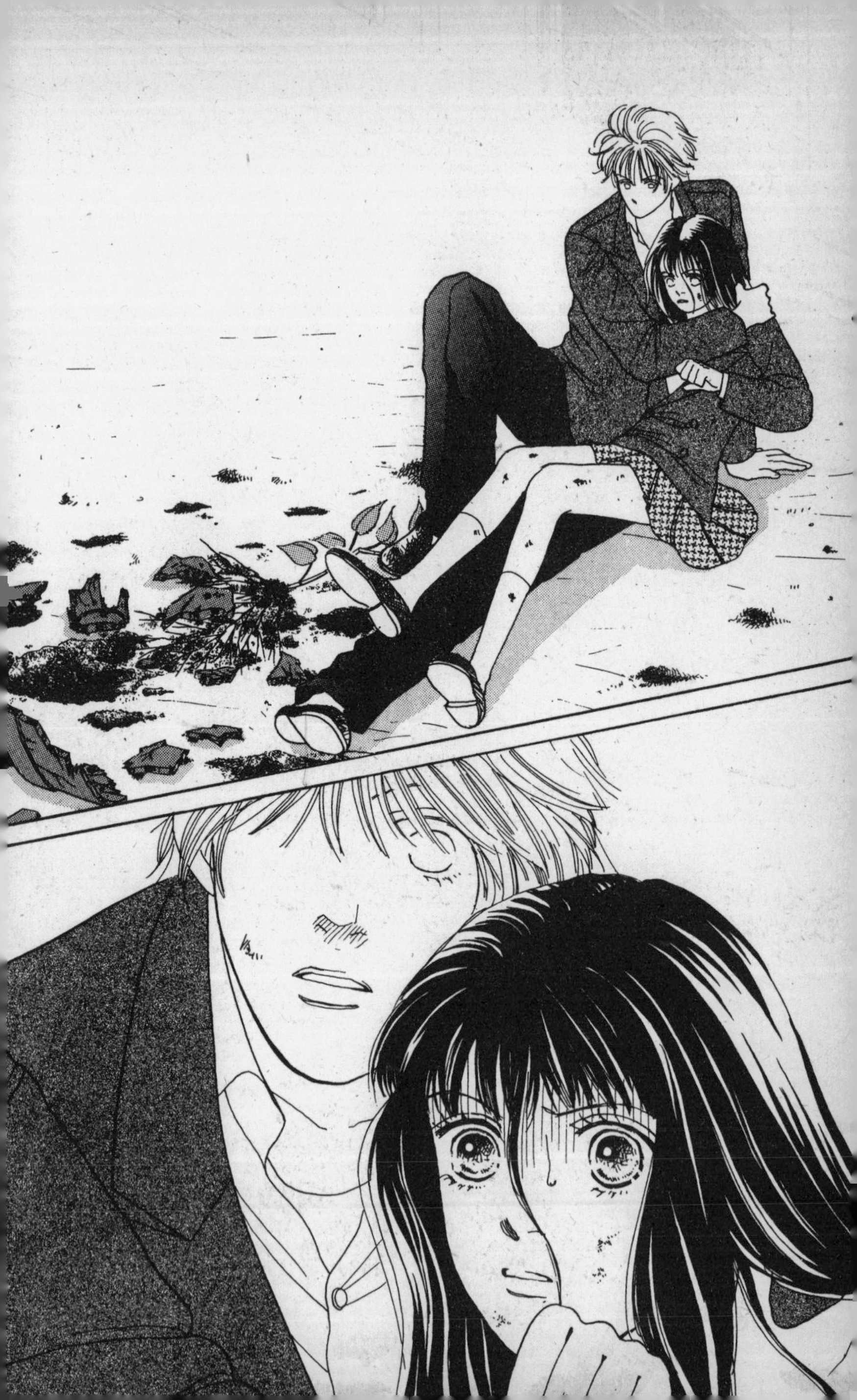

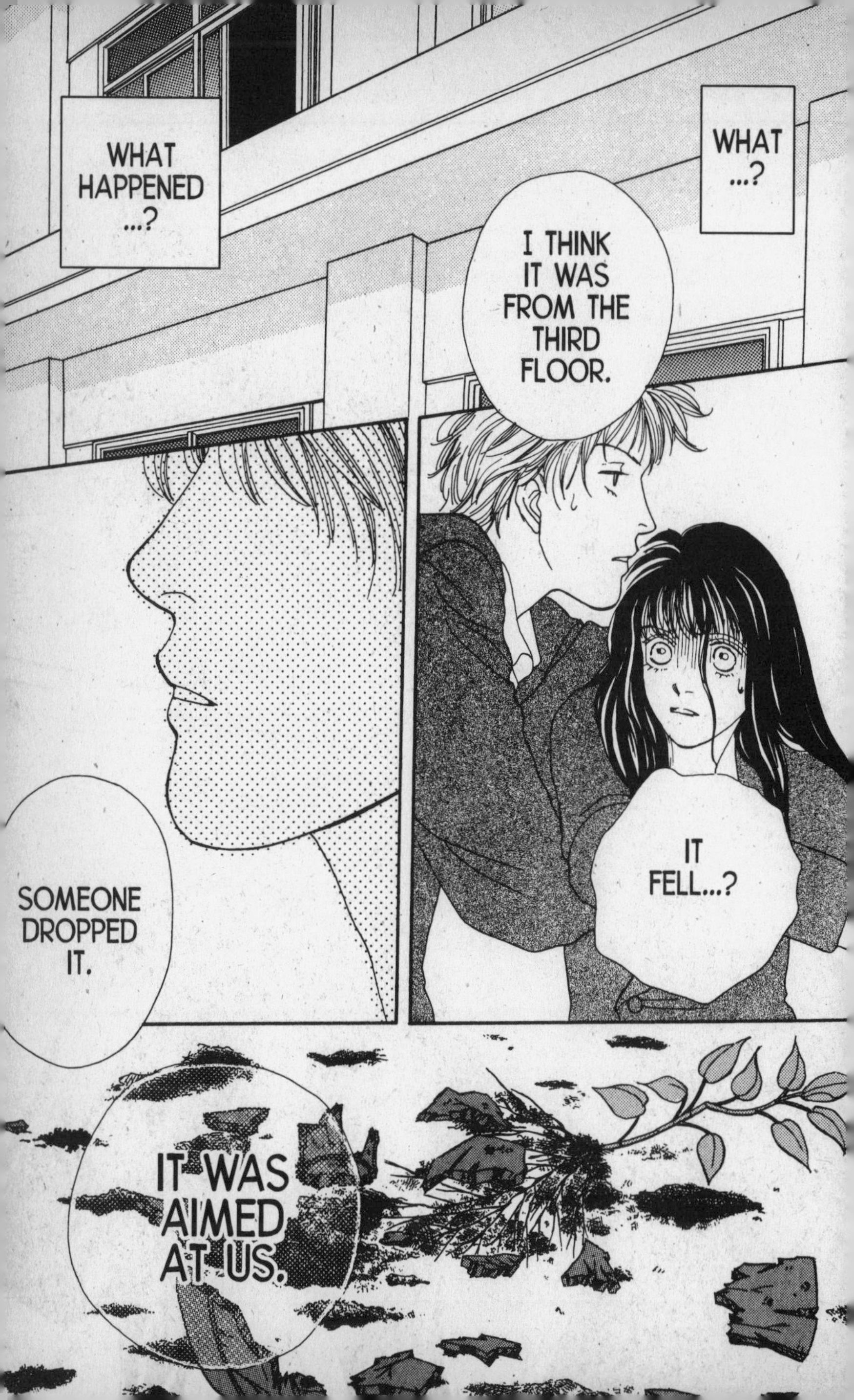
WHAT ...?
WHAT HAPPENED ...?
I THINK IT WAS FROM THE THIRD FLOOR.
IT FELL...?
SOMEONE DROPPED IT.
IT WAS AIMED AT US.

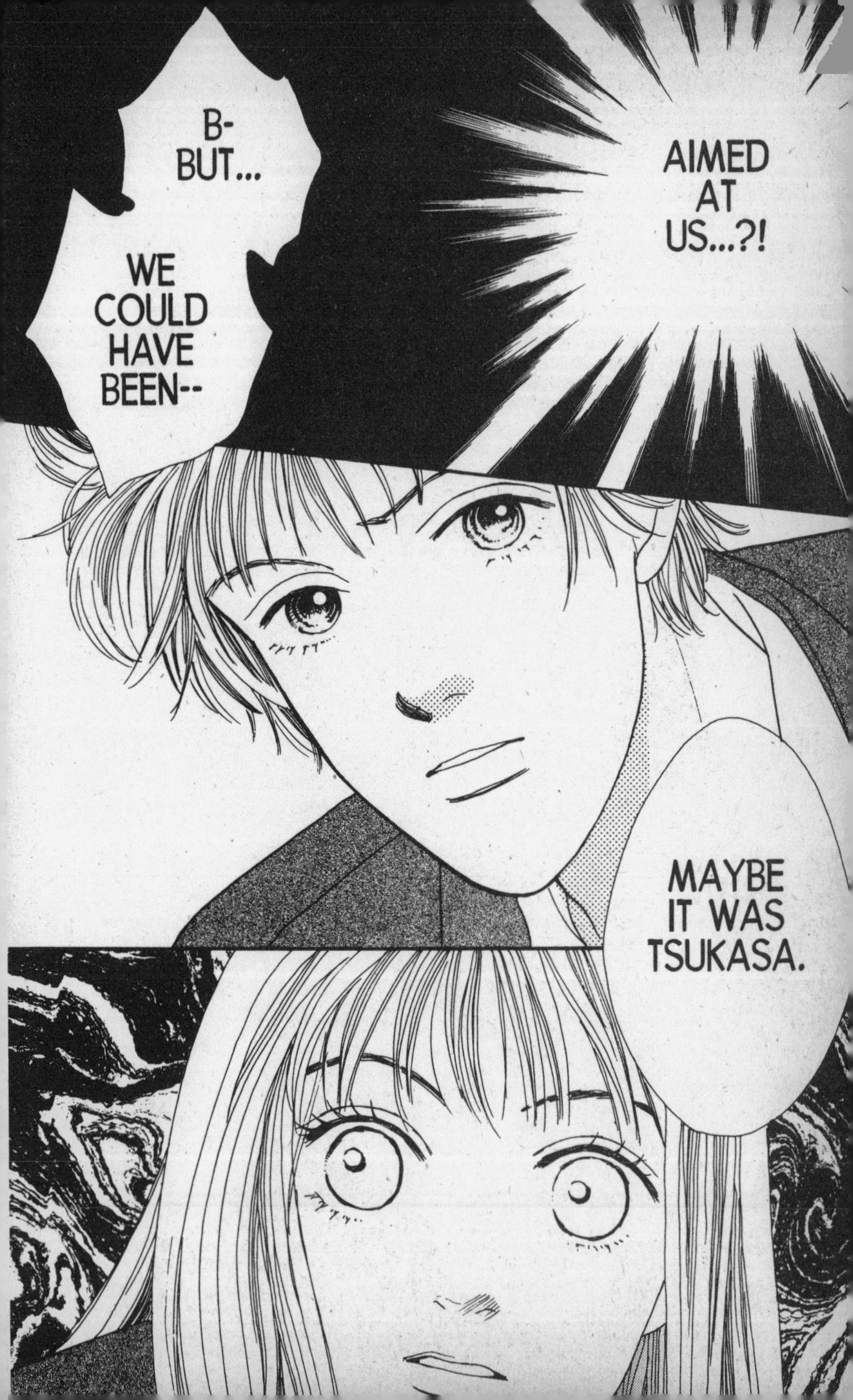
AIMED AT US...?!
B-BUT...
WE COULD HAVE BEEN--
MAYBE IT WAS TSUKASA.

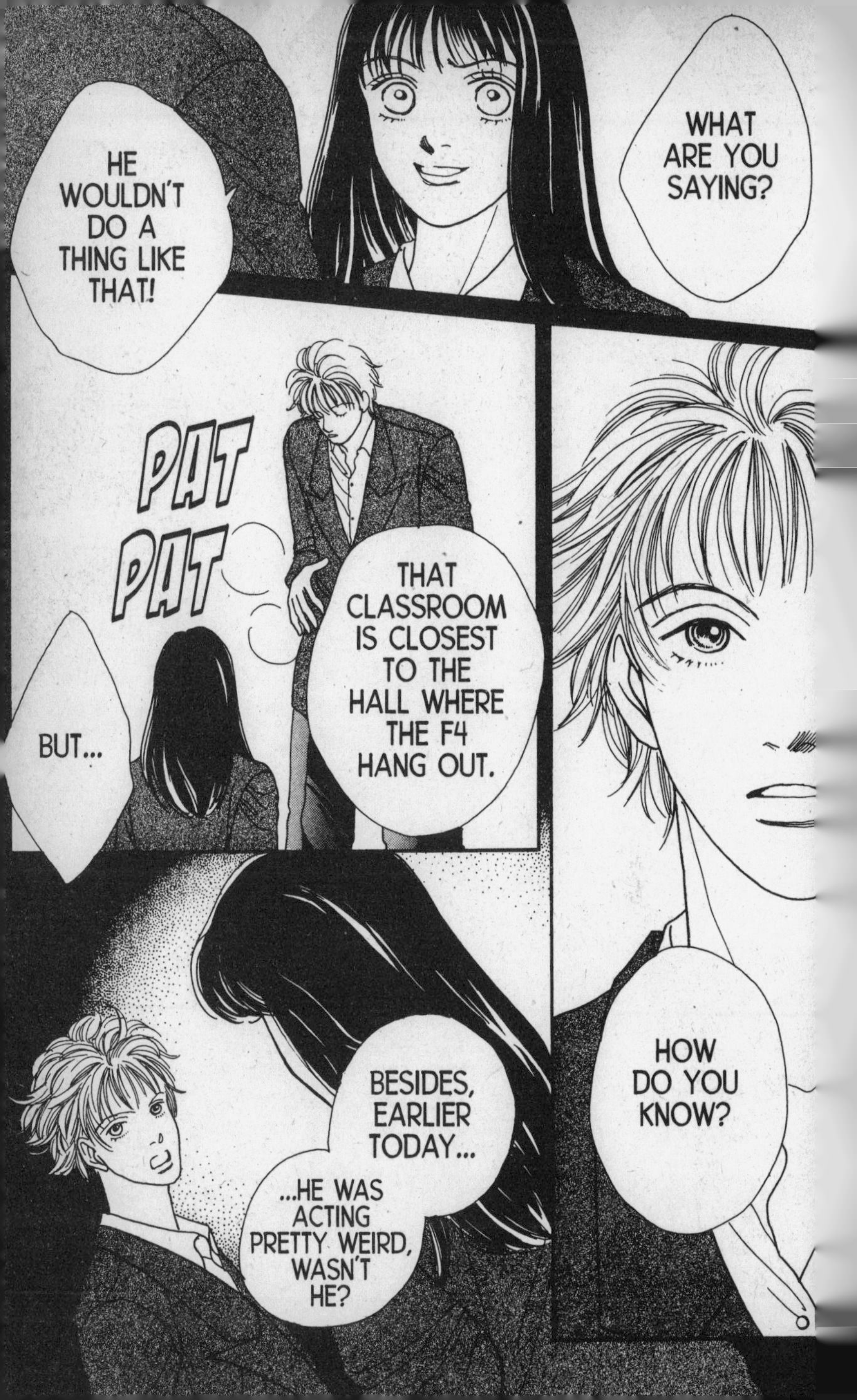
WHAT ARE YOU SAYING?
HE WOULDN'T DO A THING LIKE THAT!
HOW DO YOU KNOW?
THAT CLASSROOM IS CLOSEST TO THE HALL WHERE THE F4 HANG OUT.
PAT PAT
BUT...
BESIDES, EARLIER TODAY...
...HE WAS ACTING PRETTY WEIRD, WASN'T HE?

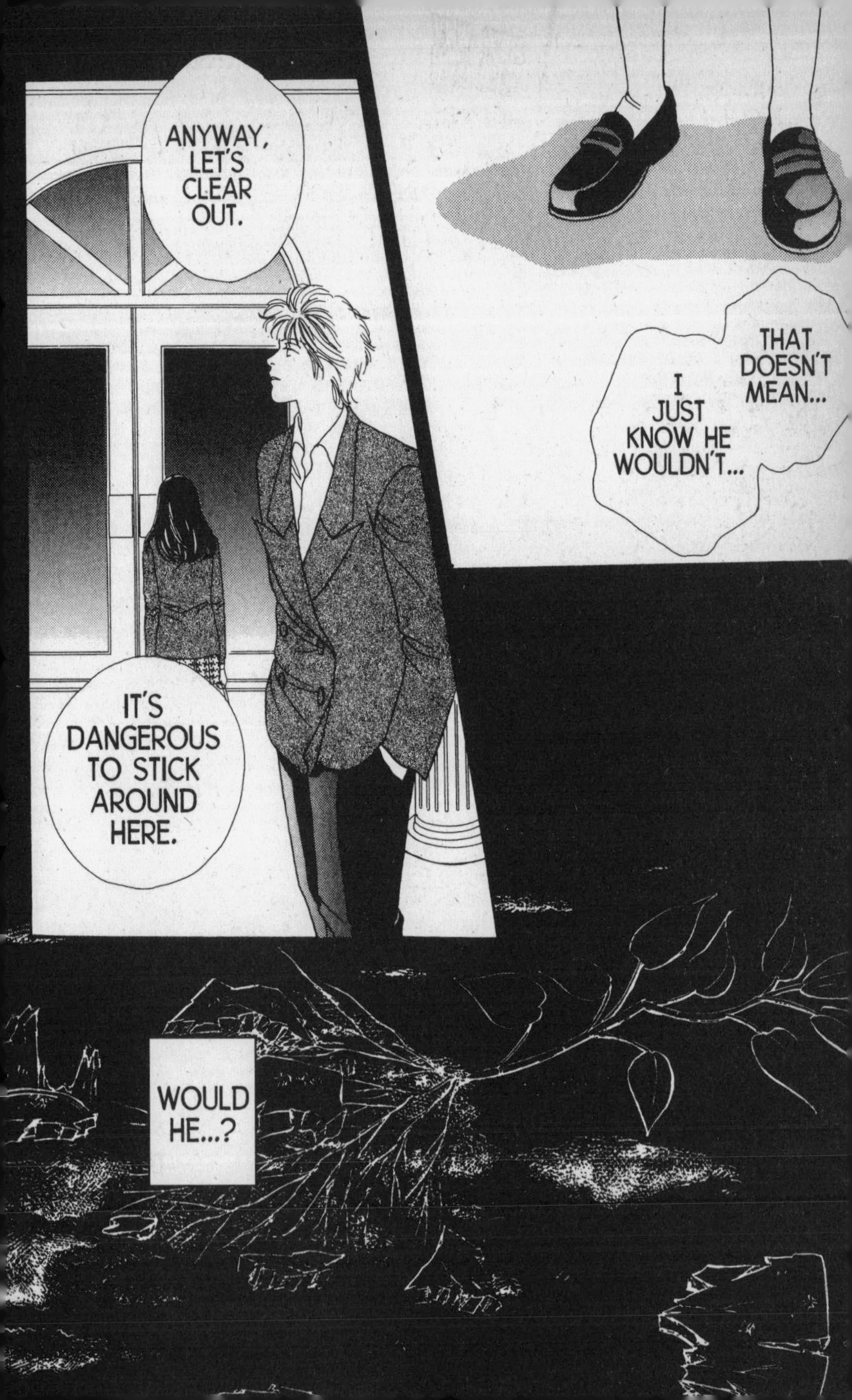
THAT DOESN'T MEAN...
I JUST KNOW HE WOULDN'T...
ANYWAY, LET'S CLEAR OUT.
IT'S DANGEROUS TO STICK AROUND HERE.
WOULD HE...?

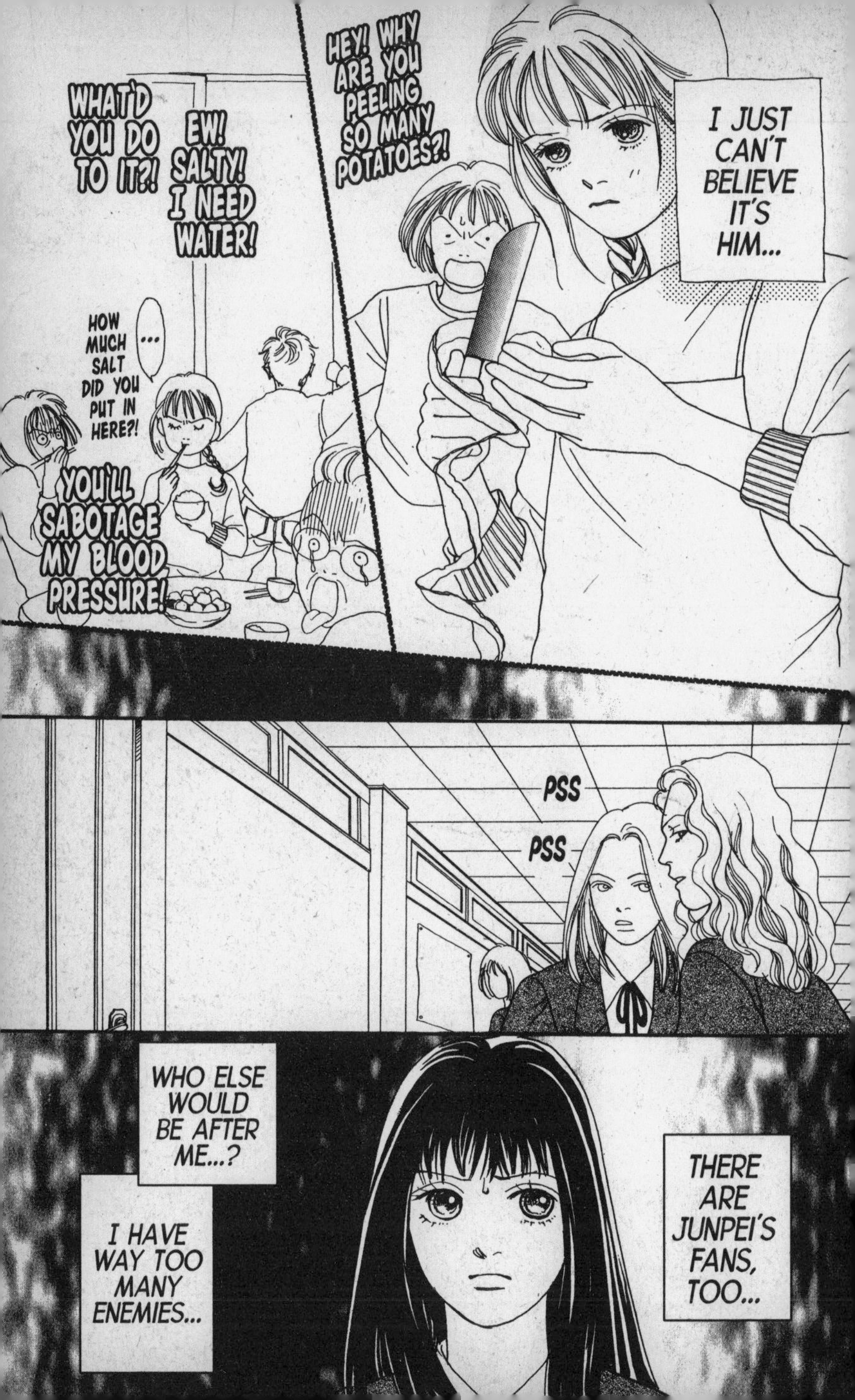

I JUST CAN'T BELIEVE IT'S HIM...
HEY! WHY ARE YOU PEELING SO MANY POTATOES?!
EW! SALTY! I NEED WATER!
WHAT'D YOU DO TO IT?!
...
HOW MUCH SALT DID YOU PUT IN HERE?!
YOU'LL SABOTAGE MY BLOOD PRESSURE!
PSS
PSS
THERE ARE JUNPEI'S FANS, TOO...
WHO ELSE WOULD BE AFTER ME...?
I HAVE WAY TOO MANY ENEMIES...

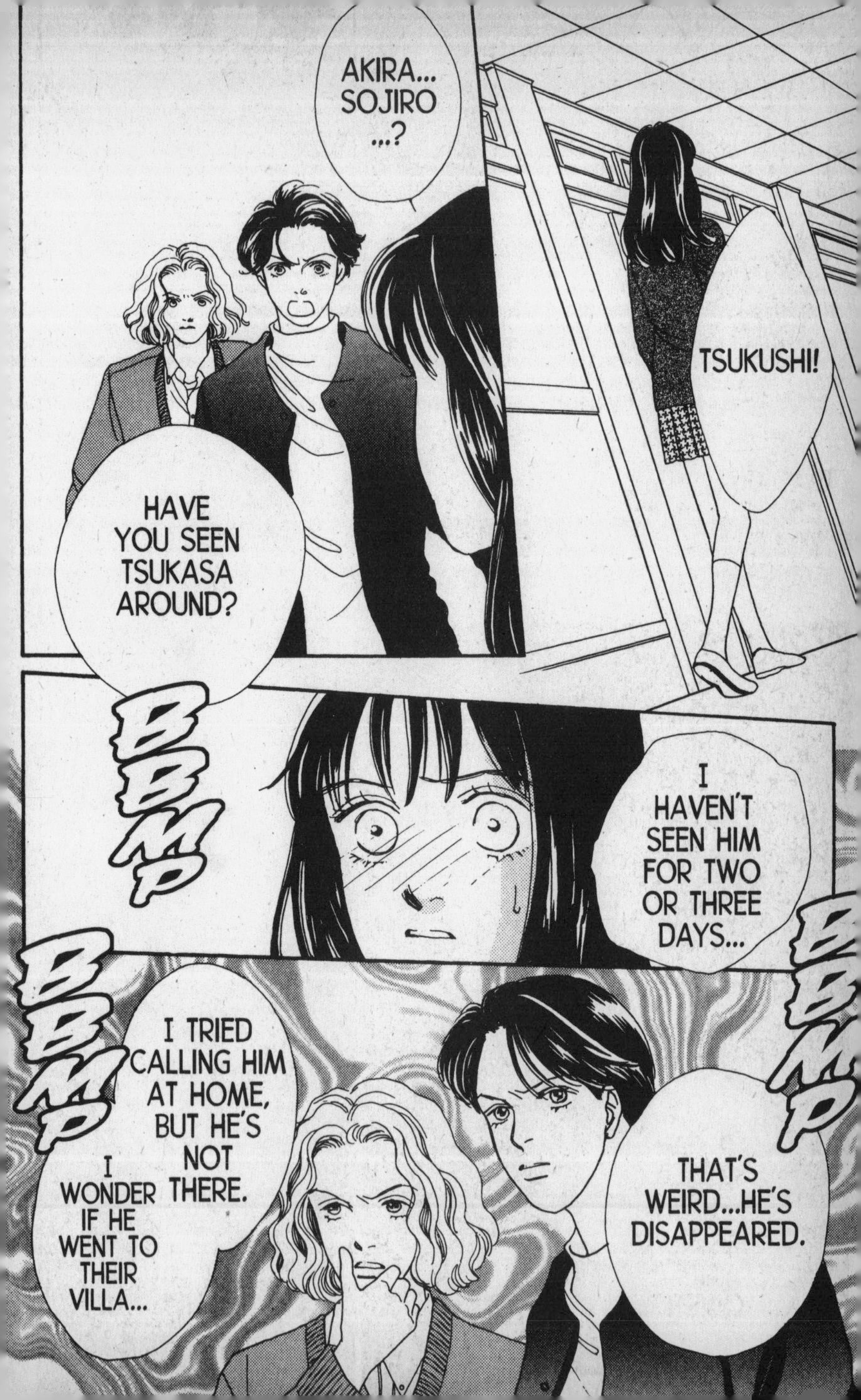
TSUKUSHI!
AKIRA... SOJIRO ...?
HAVE YOU SEEN TSUKASA AROUND?
I HAVEN'T SEEN HIM FOR TWO OR THREE DAYS...
BBMP
BBMP
THAT'S WEIRD...HE'S DISAPPEARED.
BBMP
I TRIED CALLING HIM AT HOME, BUT HE'S NOT THERE.
I WONDER IF HE WENT TO THEIR VILLA...

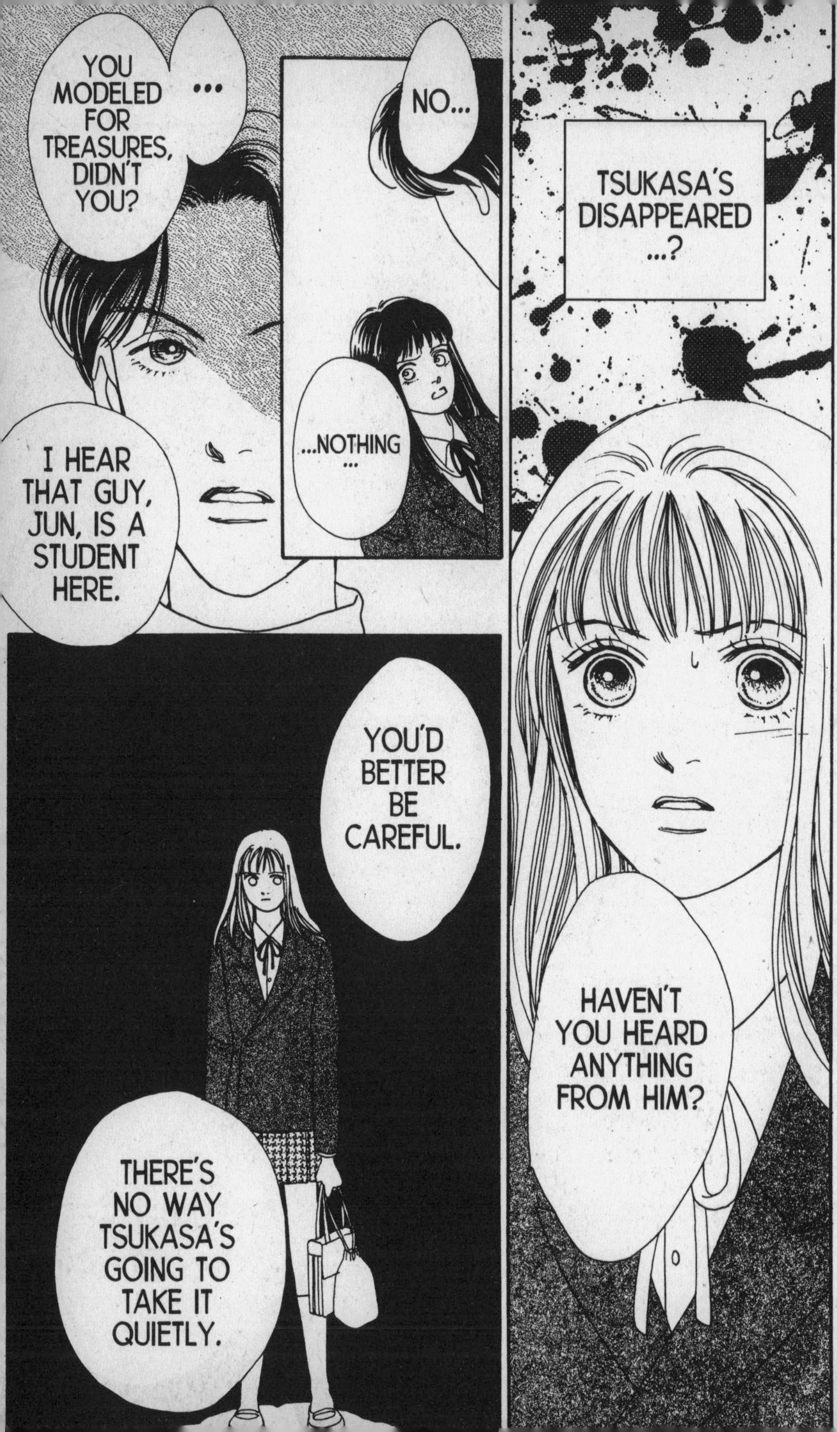
TSUKASA'S DISAPPEARED ...?
HAVEN'T YOU HEARD ANYTHING FROM HIM?
NO...
...NOTHING ...
YOU MODELED FOR TREASURES, DIDN'T YOU? ...
I HEAR THAT GUY, JUN, IS A STUDENT HERE.
YOU'D BETTER BE CAREFUL.
THERE'S NO WAY TSUKASA'S GOING TO TAKE IT QUIETLY.

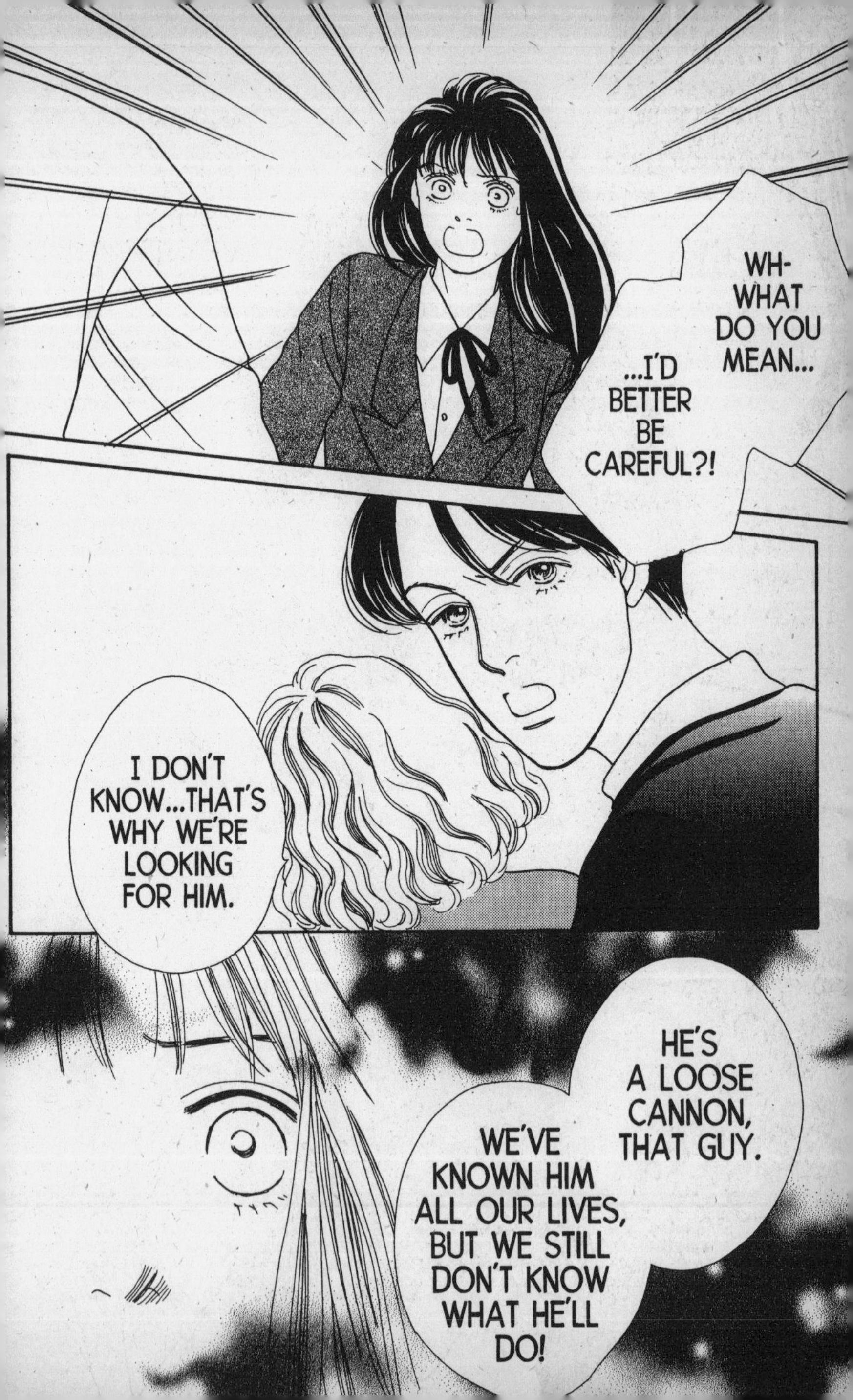
WH-WHAT DO YOU MEAN...
...I'D BETTER BE CAREFUL?!
I DON'T KNOW...THAT'S WHY WE'RE LOOKING FOR HIM.
HE'S A LOOSE CANNON, THAT GUY.
WE'VE KNOWN HIM ALL OUR LIVES, BUT WE STILL DON'T KNOW WHAT HE'LL DO!

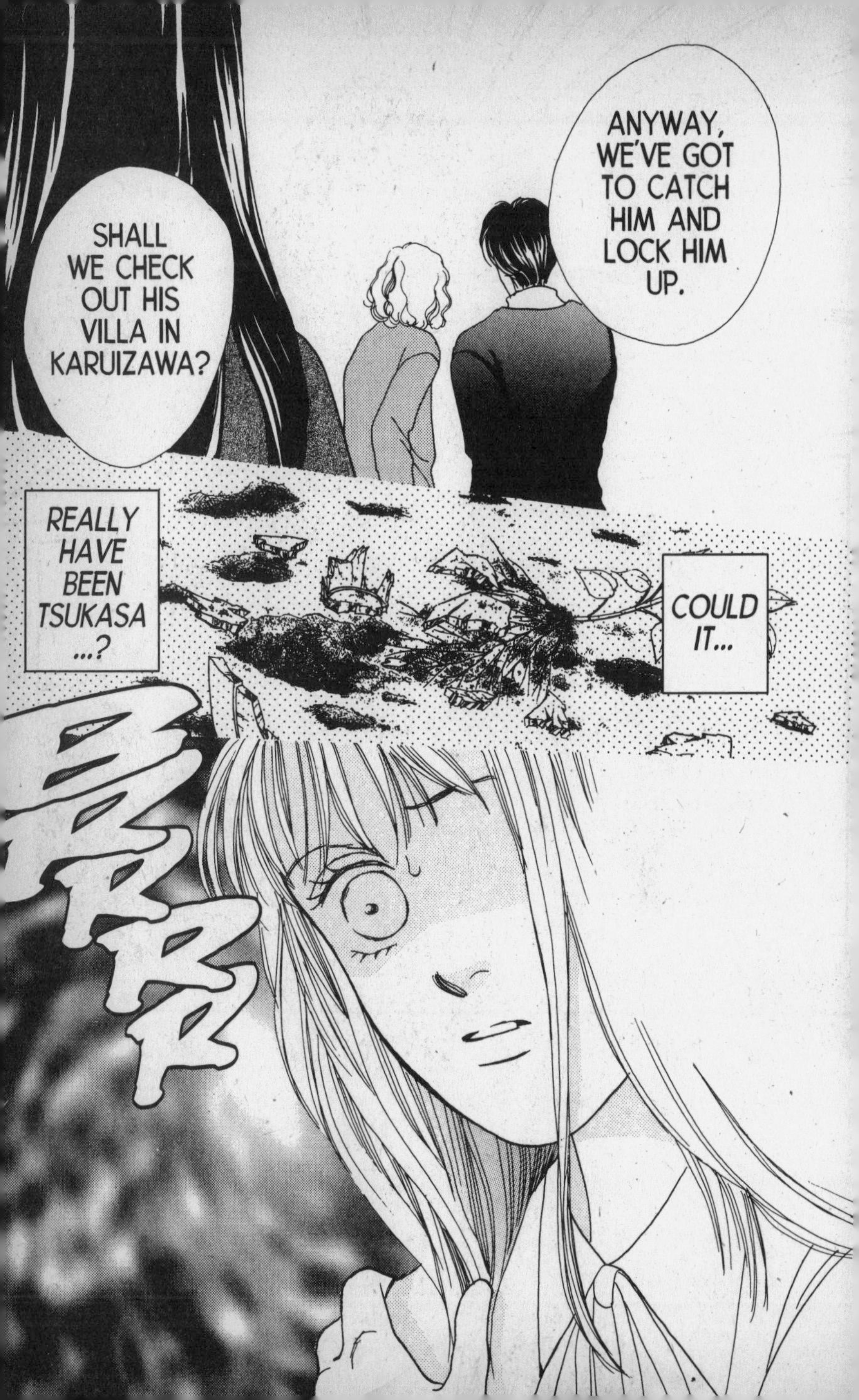
ANYWAY, WE'VE GOT TO CATCH HIM AND LOCK HIM UP.
SHALL WE CHECK OUT HIS VILLA IN KARUIZAWA?
COULD IT...
REALLY HAVE BEEN TSUKASA ...?

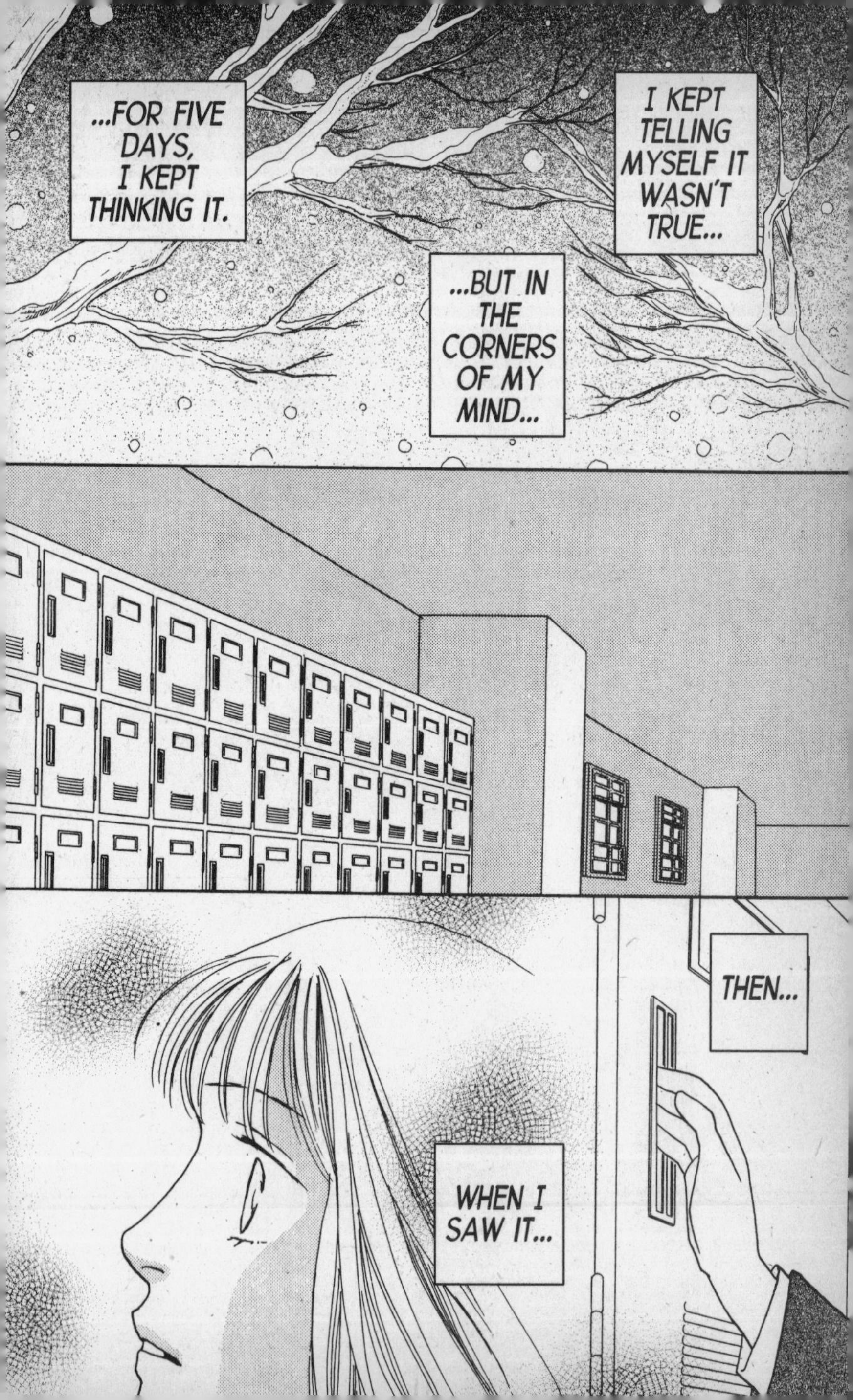
I KEPT TELLING MYSELF IT WASN'T TRUE...
...BUT IN THE CORNERS OF MY MIND...
...FOR FIVE DAYS, I KEPT THINKING IT.
THEN...
WHEN I SAW IT...

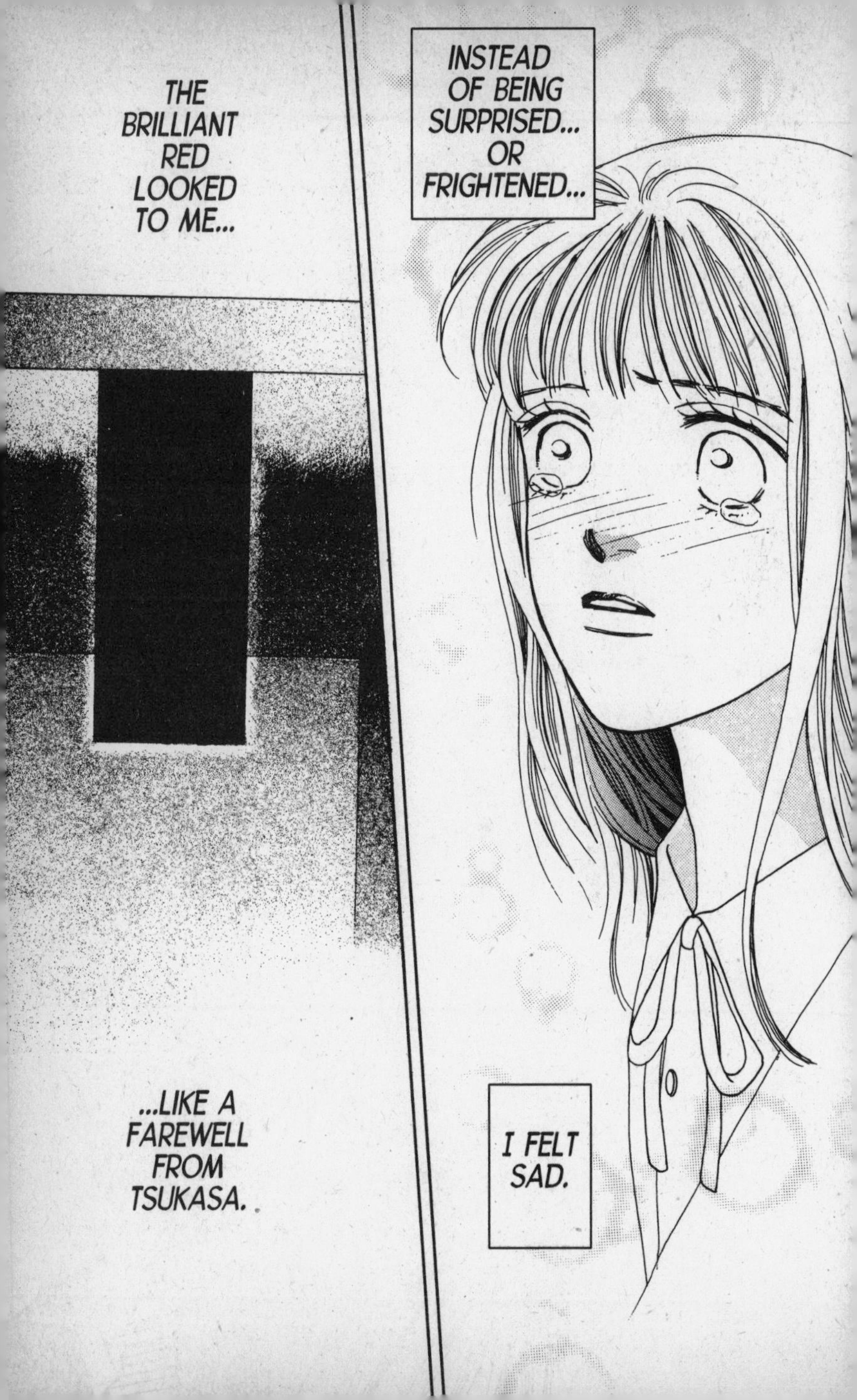
INSTEAD OF BEING SURPRISED... OR FRIGHTENED...
I FELT SAD.
THE BRILLIANT RED LOOKED TO ME...
...LIKE A FAREWELL FROM TSUKASA.

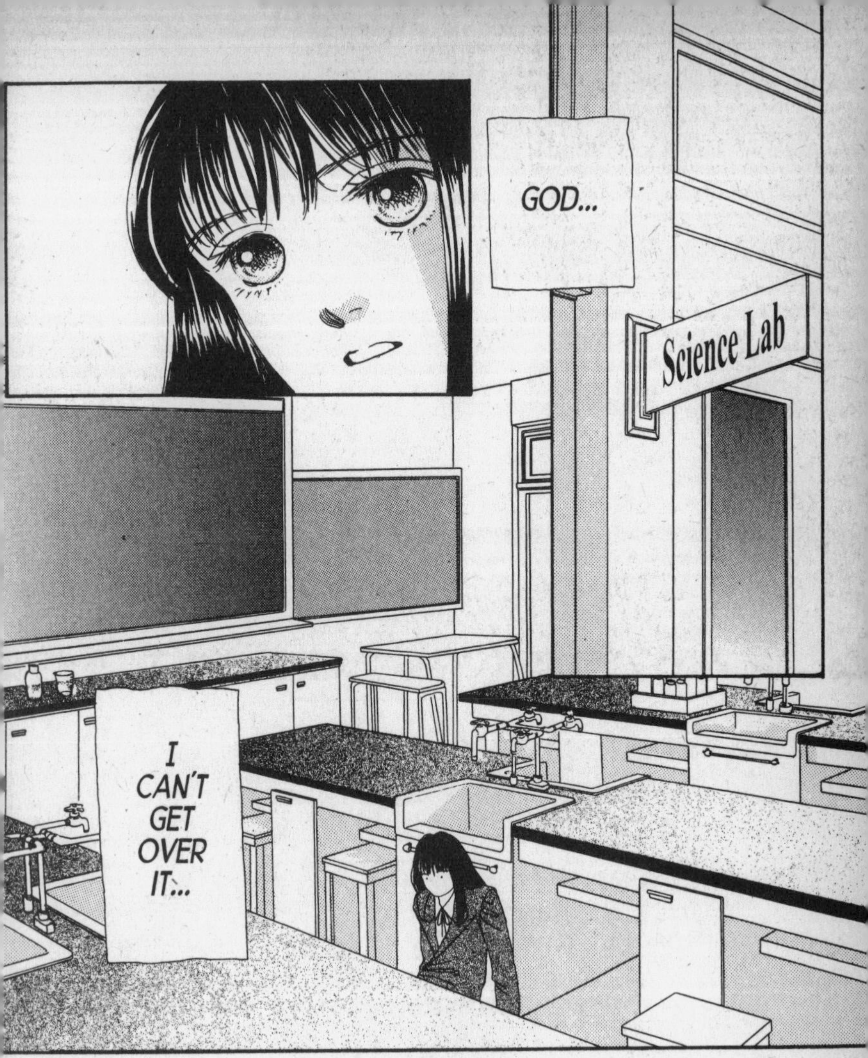
GOD...
Science Lab
I CAN'T GET OVER IT...

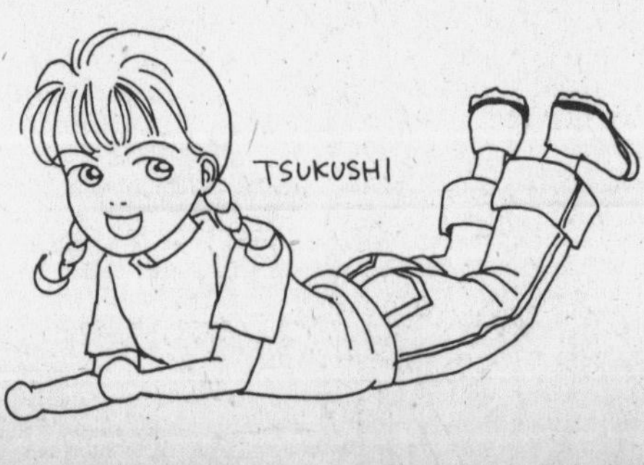
TSUKUSHI

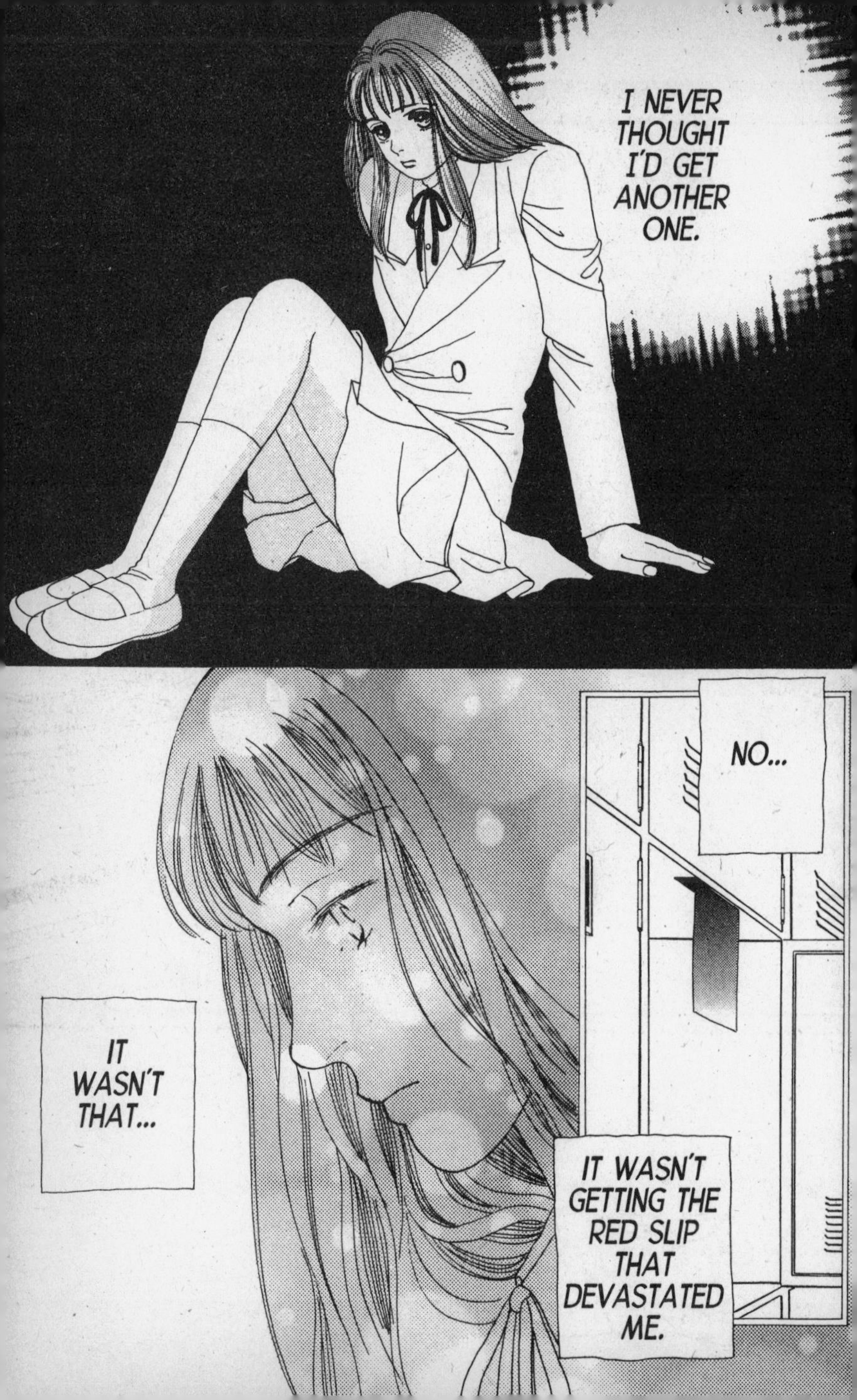
I NEVER THOUGHT I'D GET ANOTHER ONE.
NO...
IT WASN'T THAT...
IT WASN'T GETTING THE RED SLIP THAT DEVASTATED ME.

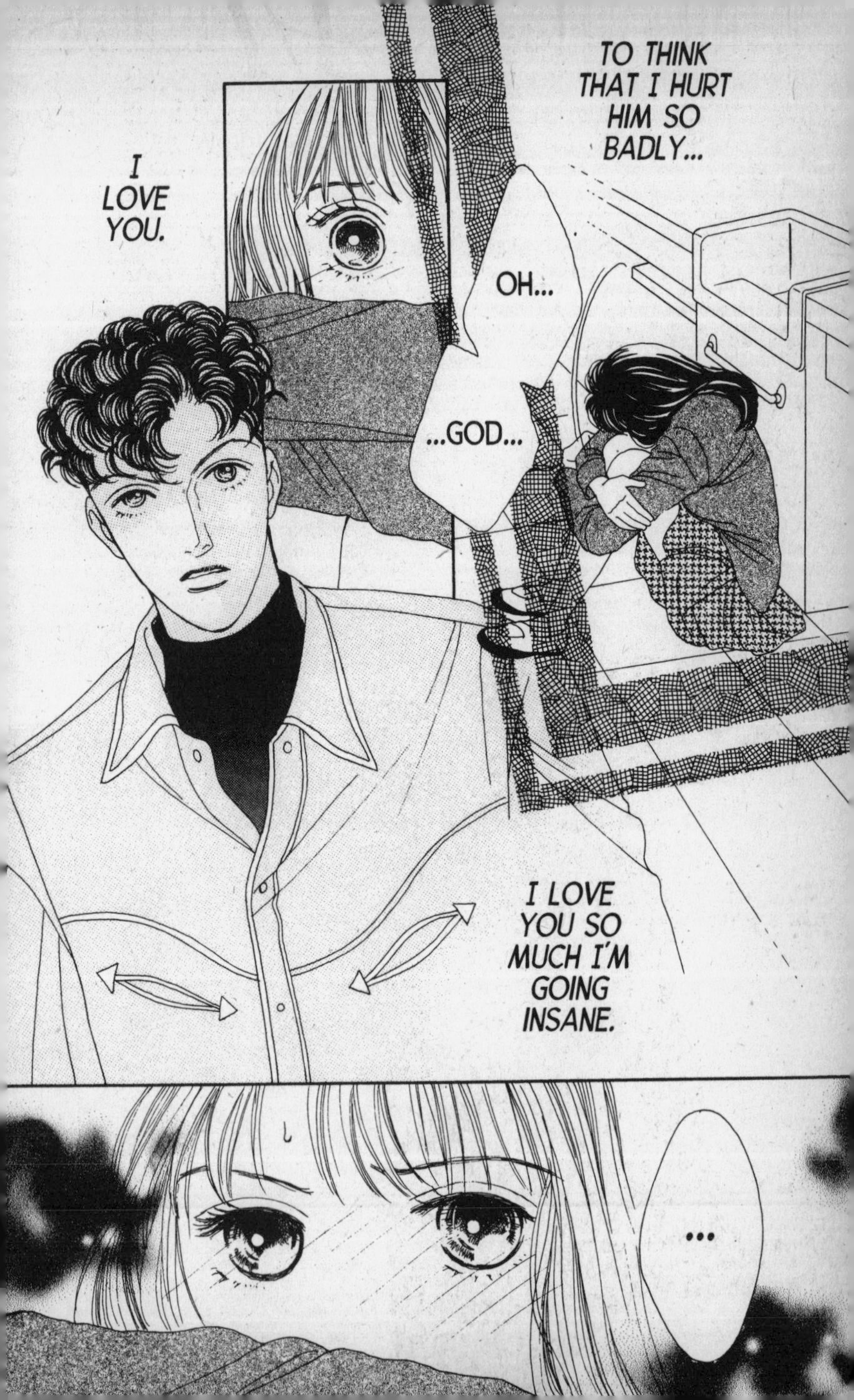
TO THINK THAT I HURT HIM SO BADLY...
OH...
...GOD...
I LOVE YOU.
I LOVE YOU SO MUCH I'M GOING INSANE.
...

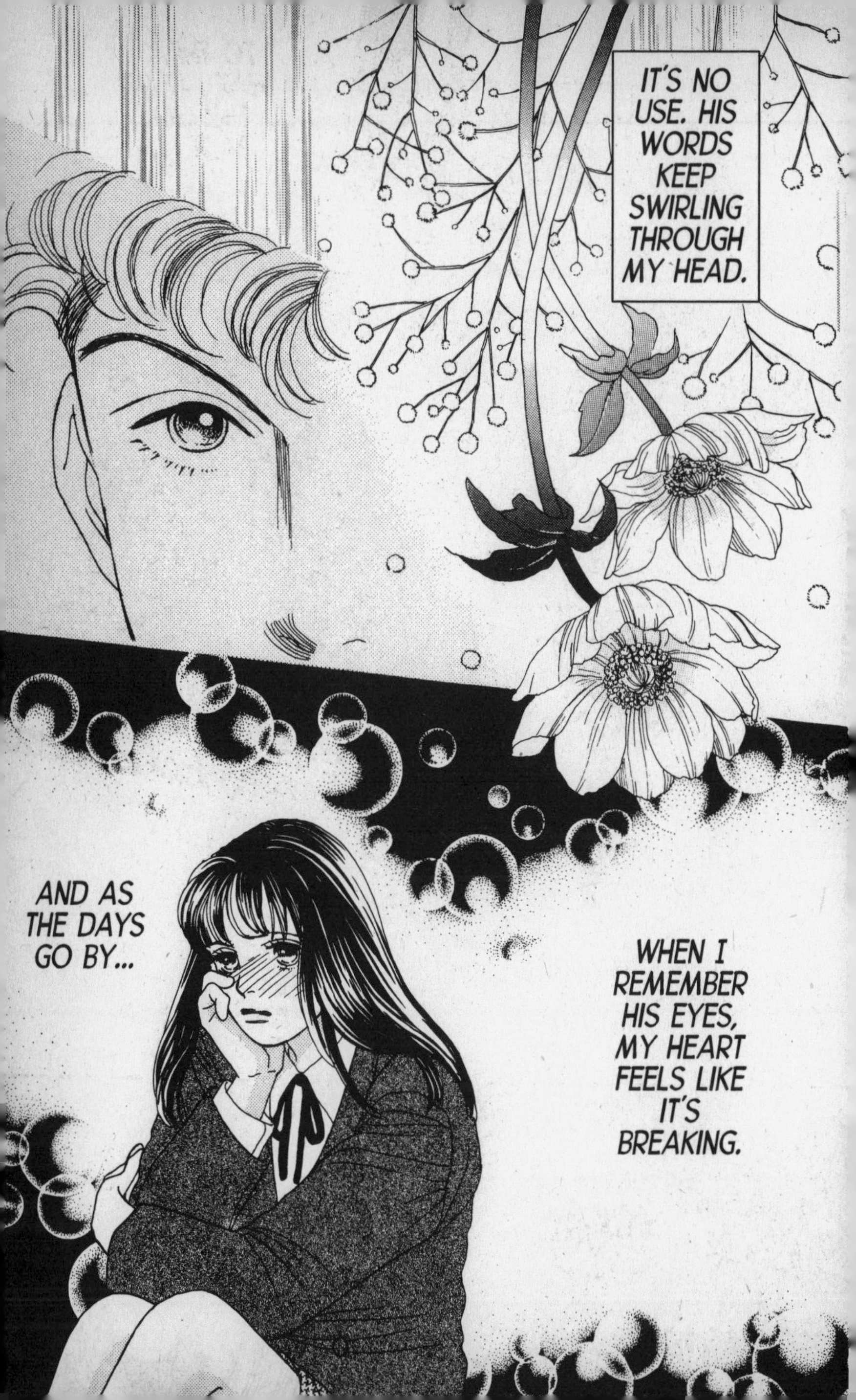
IT'S NO USE. HIS WORDS KEEP SWIRLING THROUGH MY HEAD.
WHEN I REMEMBER HIS EYES, MY HEART FEELS LIKE IT'S BREAKING.
AND AS THE DAYS GO BY...

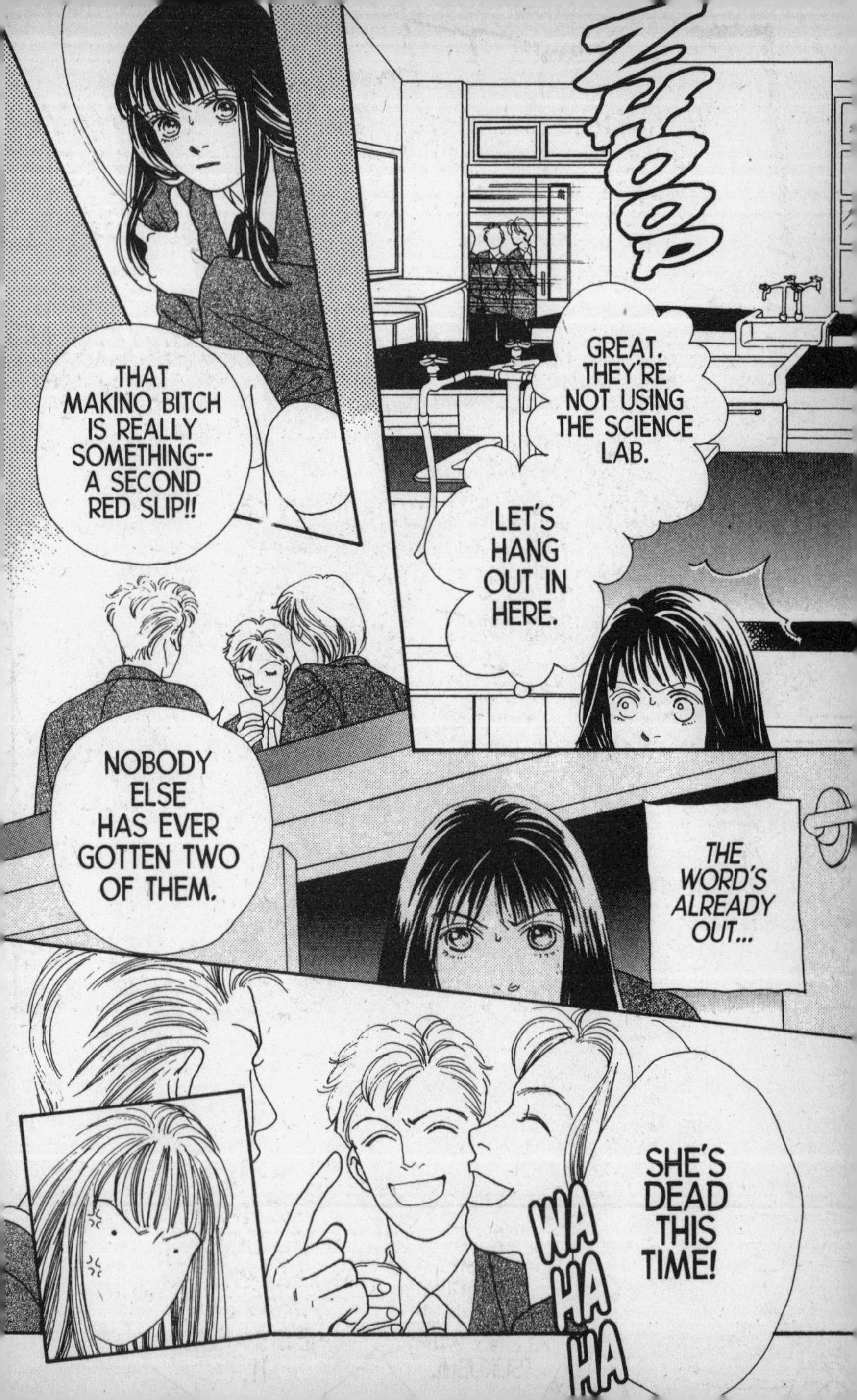
ZHOOP
GREAT. THEY'RE NOT USING THE SCIENCE LAB.
LET'S HANG OUT IN HERE.
THAT MAKINO BITCH IS REALLY SOMETHING-- A SECOND RED SLIP!!
NOBODY ELSE HAS EVER GOTTEN TWO OF THEM.
THE WORD'S ALREADY OUT...
SHE'S DEAD THIS TIME!
WA HA HA HA

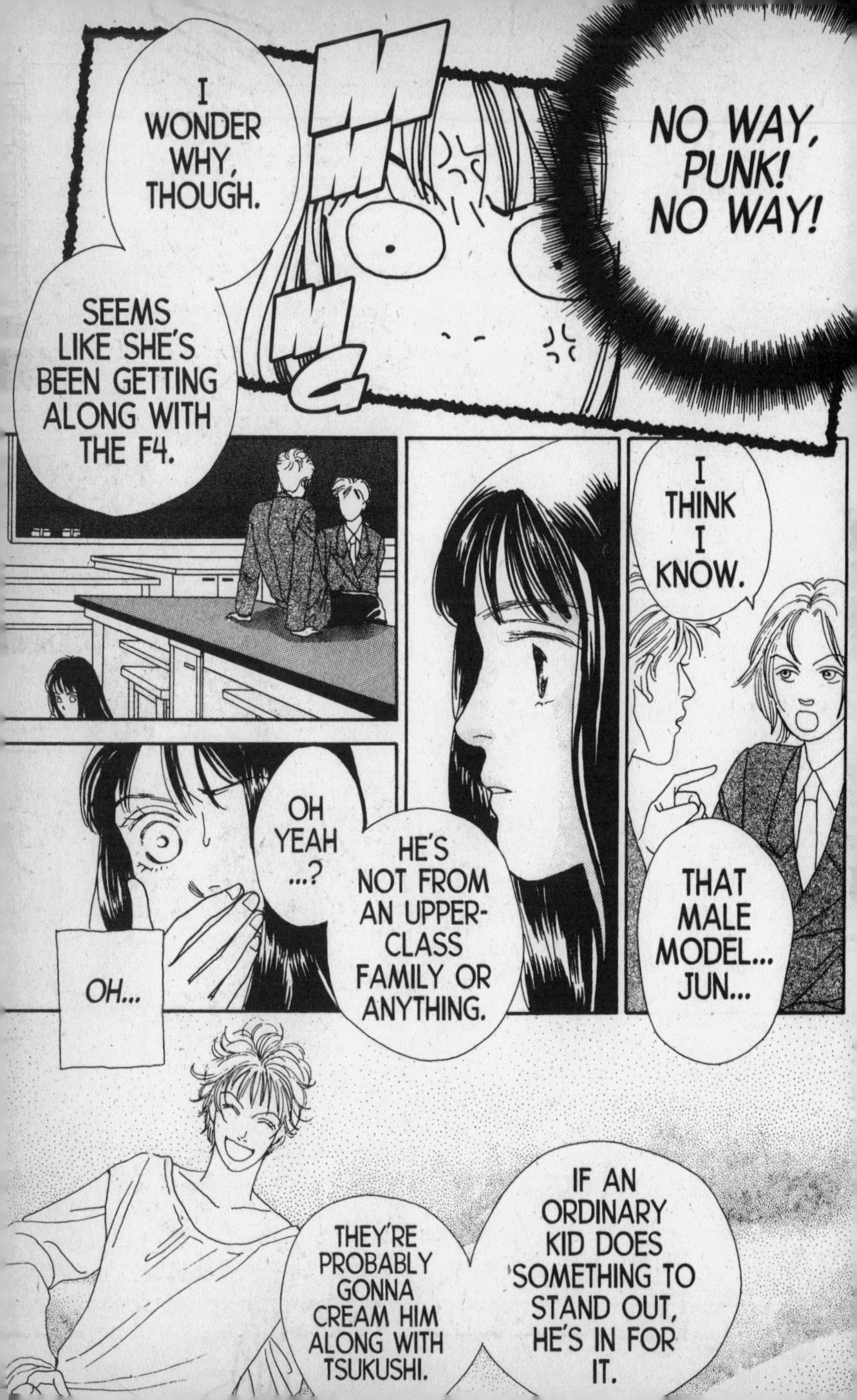
NO WAY, PUNK! NO WAY!
MMMG
I WONDER WHY, THOUGH.
SEEMS LIKE SHE'S BEEN GETTING ALONG WITH THE F4.
I THINK I KNOW.
THAT MALE MODEL... JUN...
HE'S NOT FROM AN UPPER-CLASS FAMILY OR ANYTHING.
OH YEAH ...?
OH...
IF AN ORDINARY KID DOES SOMETHING TO STAND OUT, HE'S IN FOR IT.
THEY'RE PROBABLY GONNA CREAM HIM ALONG WITH TSUKUSHI.

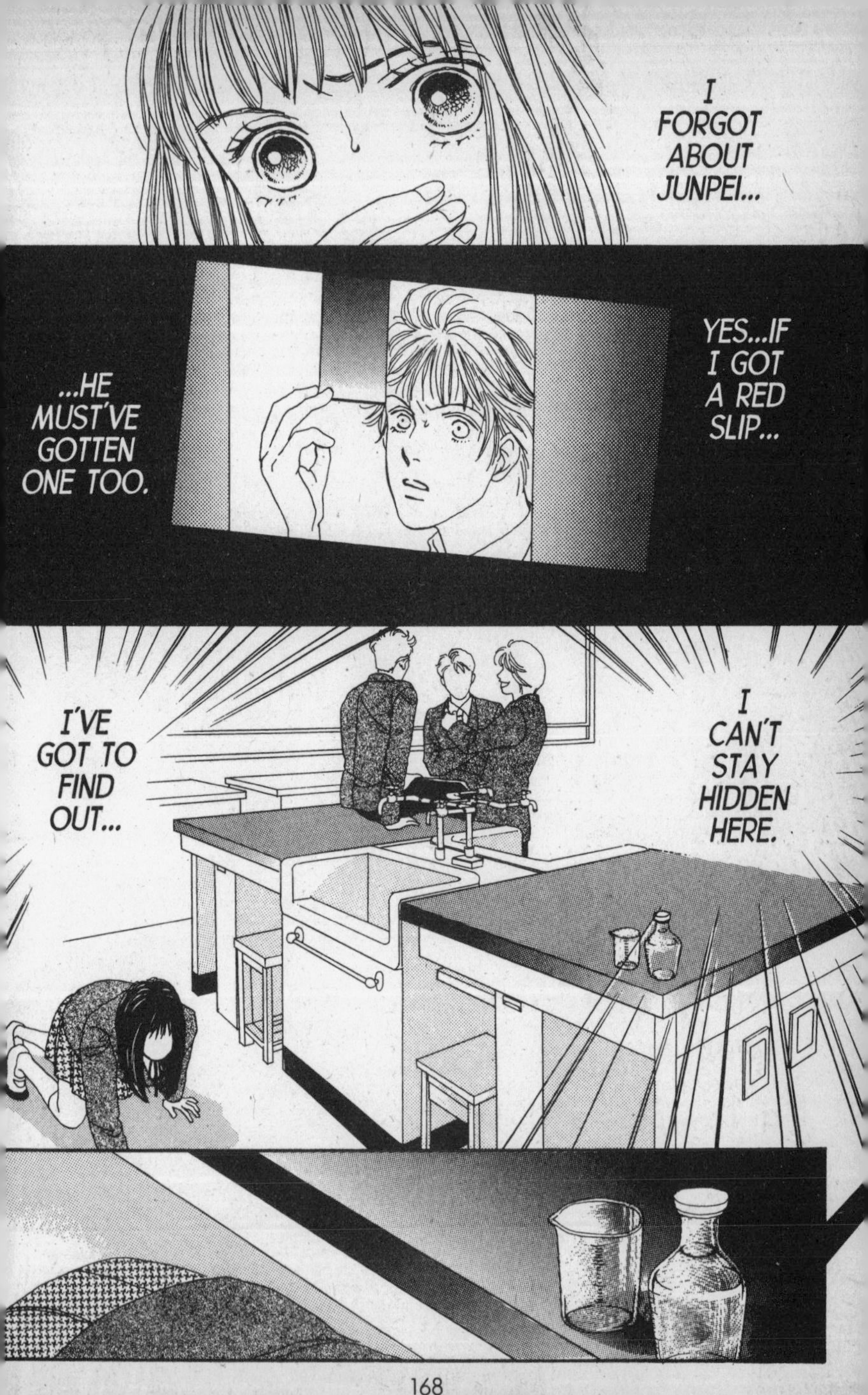
I FORGOT ABOUT JUNPEI...
YES...IF I GOT A RED SLIP...
...HE MUST'VE GOTTEN ONE TOO.
I CAN'T STAY HIDDEN HERE.
I'VE GOT TO FIND OUT...

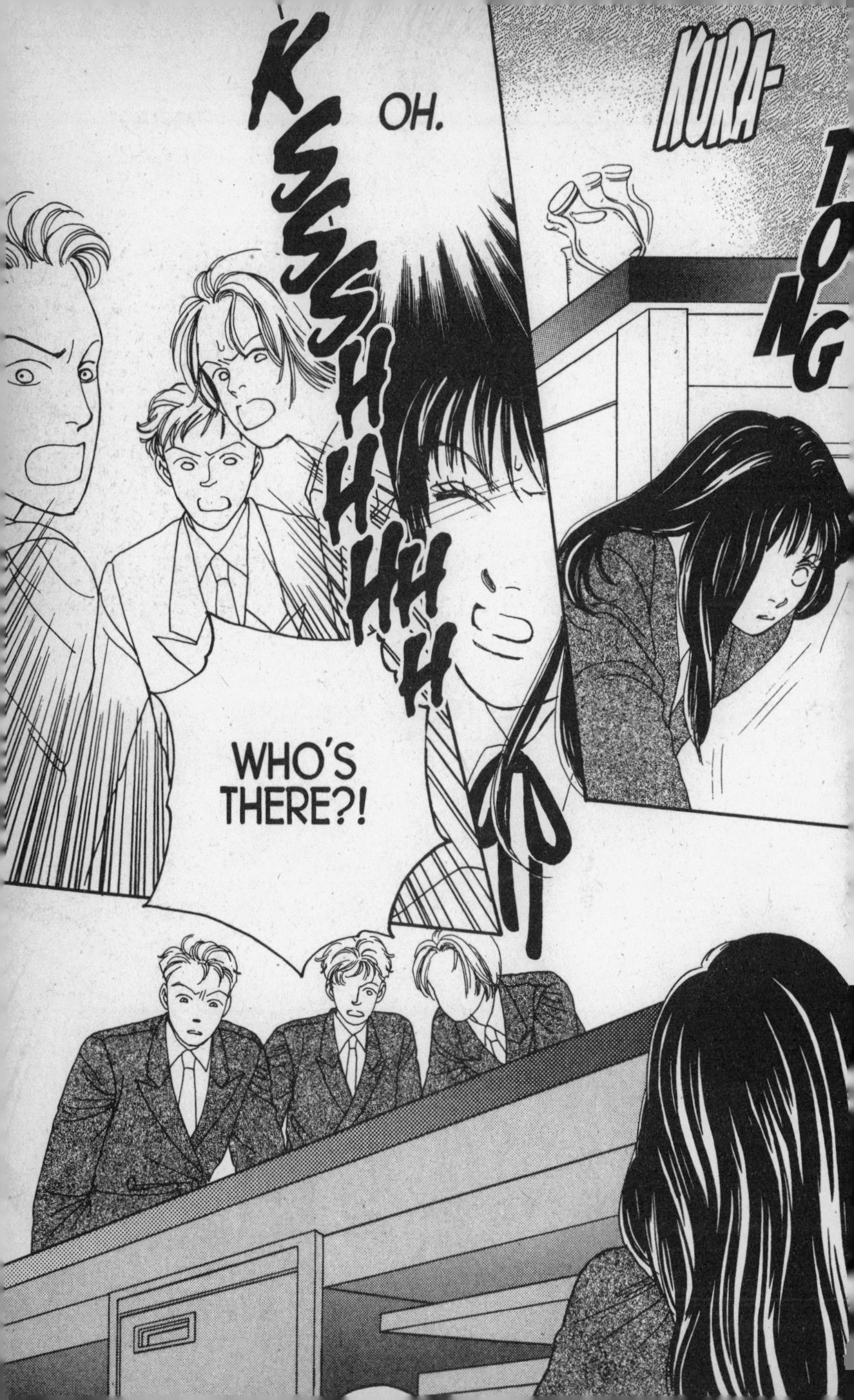
KURA-TONG
KSSSHHHHHHH
OH.
WHO'S THERE?!

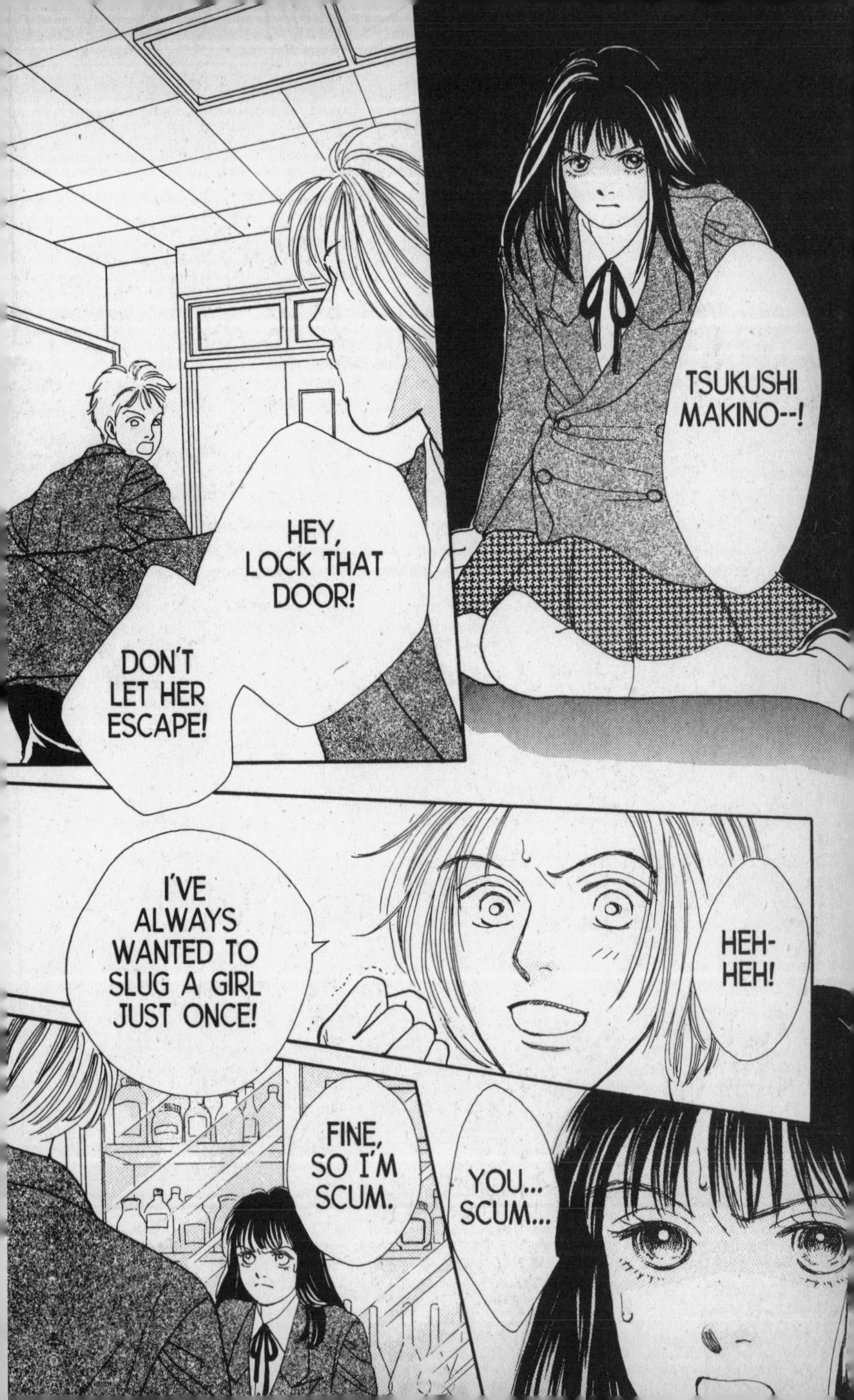
TSUKUSHI MAKINO--!
HEY, LOCK THAT DOOR!
DON'T LET HER ESCAPE!
HEH-HEH!
I'VE ALWAYS WANTED TO SLUG A GIRL JUST ONCE!
YOU... SCUM...
FINE, SO I'M SCUM.

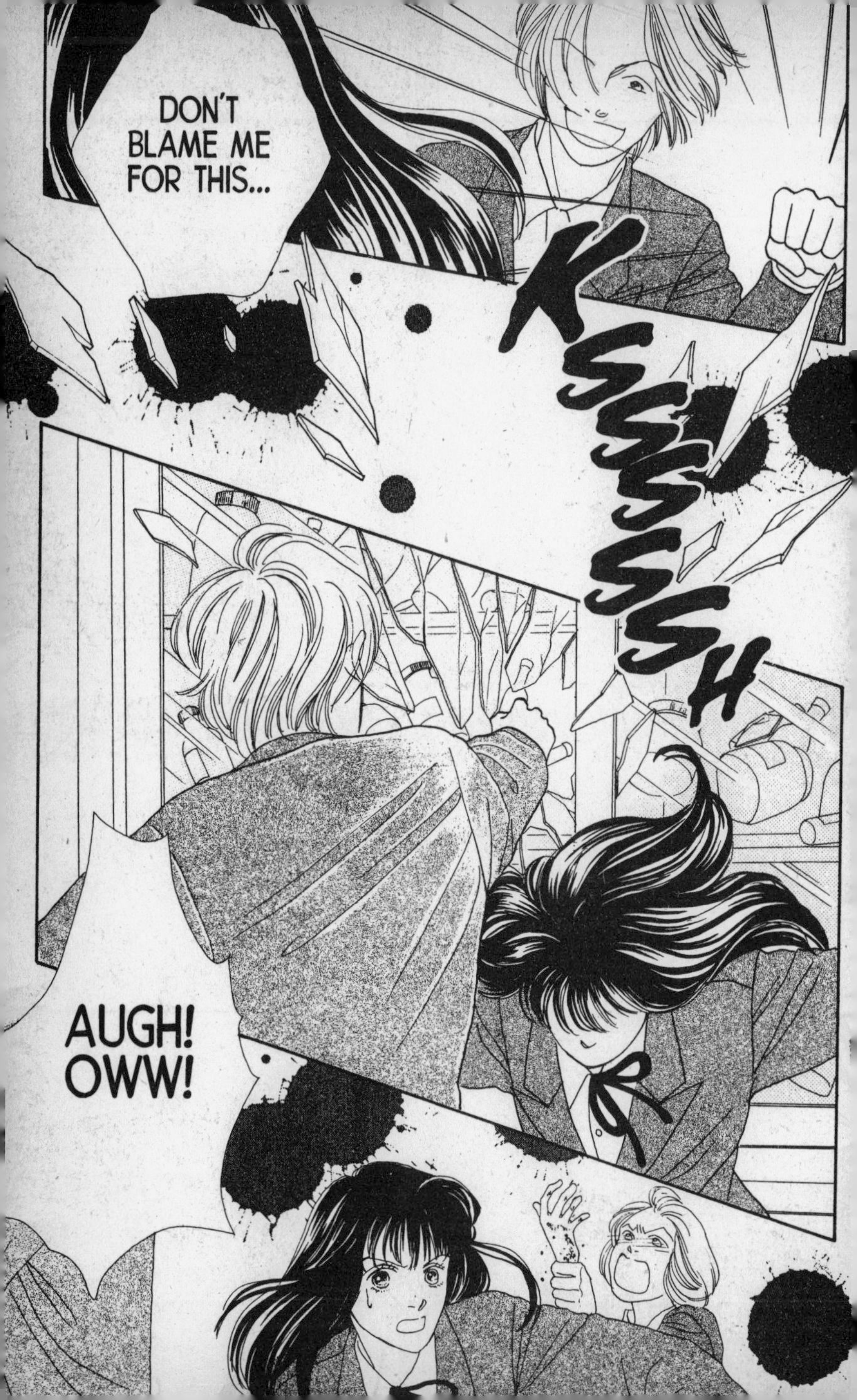
DON'T BLAME ME FOR THIS...
KSSSSSH
AUGH! OWW!

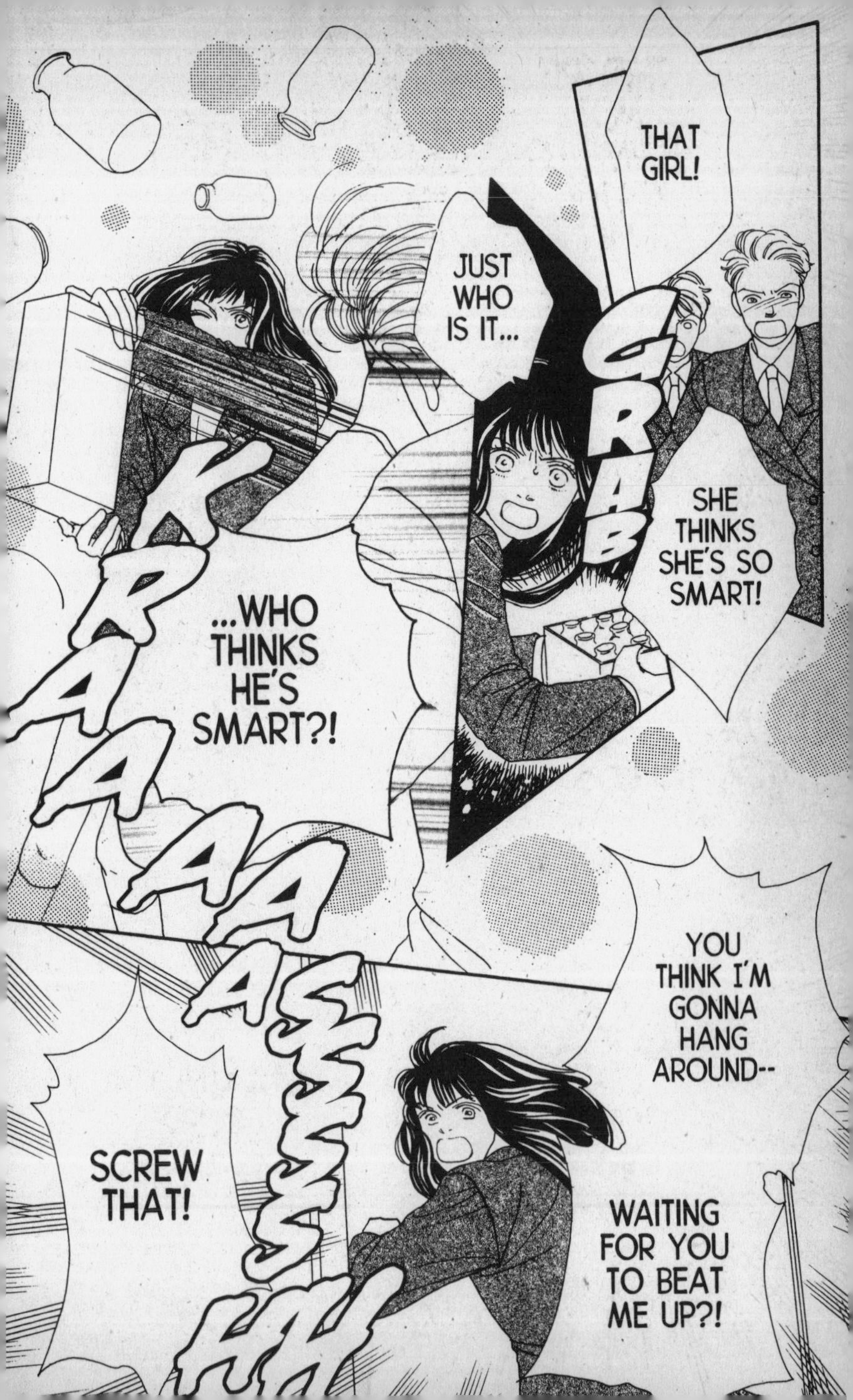
THAT GIRL!
SHE THINKS SHE'S SO SMART!
JUST WHO IS IT...
GRAB
...WHO THINKS HE'S SMART?!
YOU THINK I'M GONNA HANG AROUND--
WAITING FOR YOU TO BEAT ME UP?!
SCREW THAT!

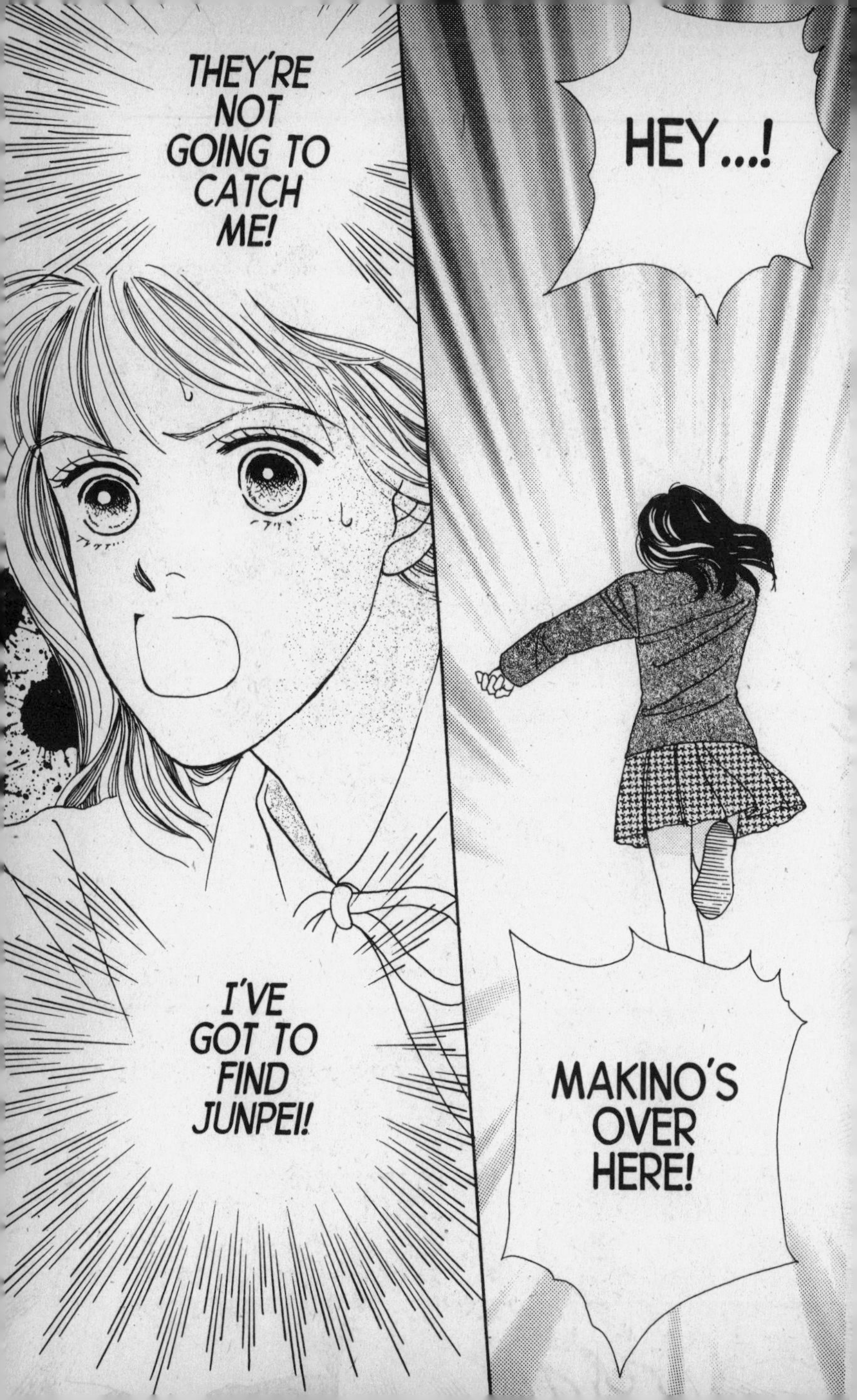
HEY...!
MAKINO'S OVER HERE!
THEY'RE NOT GOING TO CATCH ME!
I'VE GOT TO FIND JUNPEI!

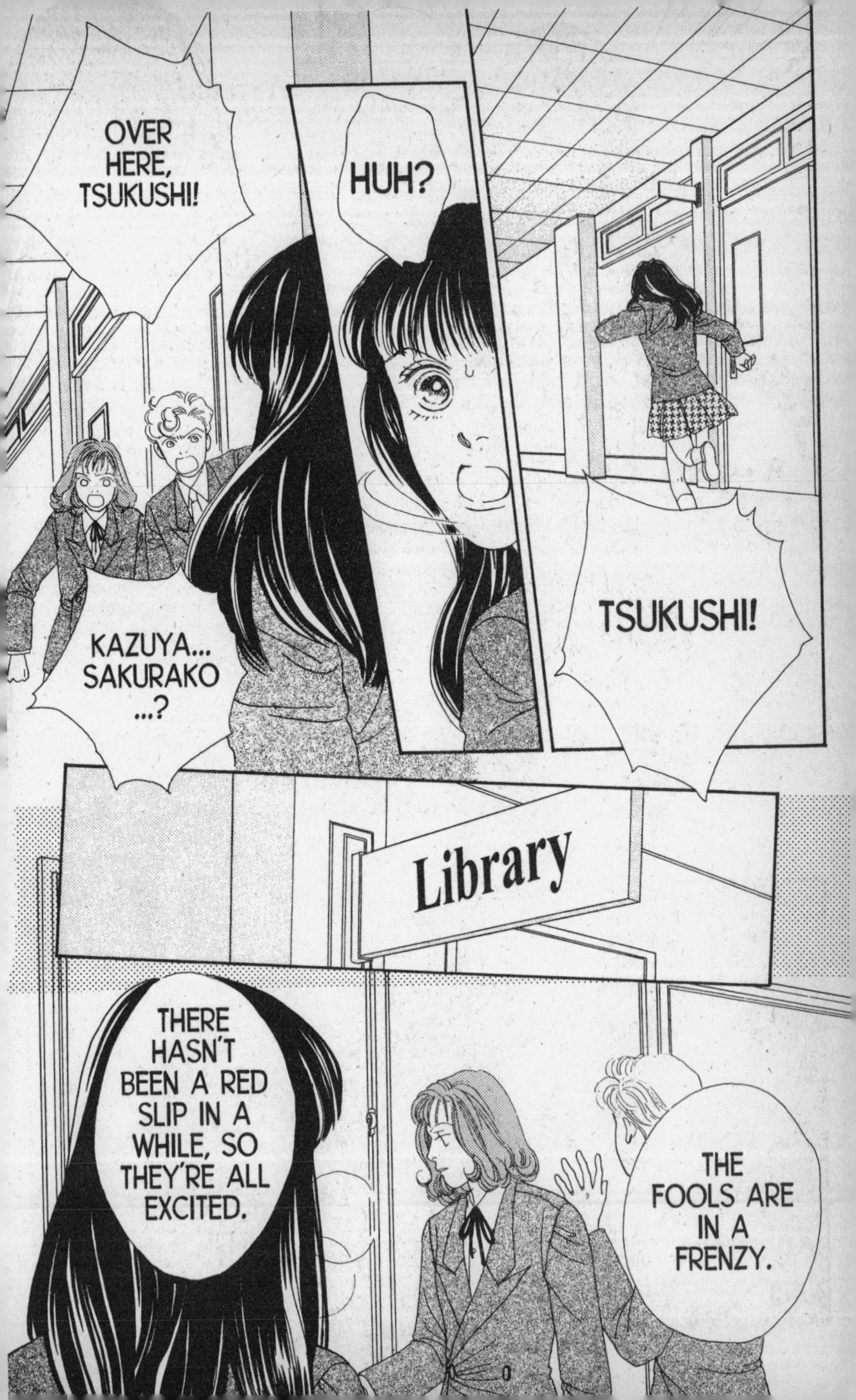
TSUKUSHI!
HUH?
OVER HERE, TSUKUSHI!
KAZUYA... SAKURAKO ...?
Library
THE FOOLS ARE IN A FRENZY.
THERE HASN'T BEEN A RED SLIP IN A WHILE, SO THEY'RE ALL EXCITED.

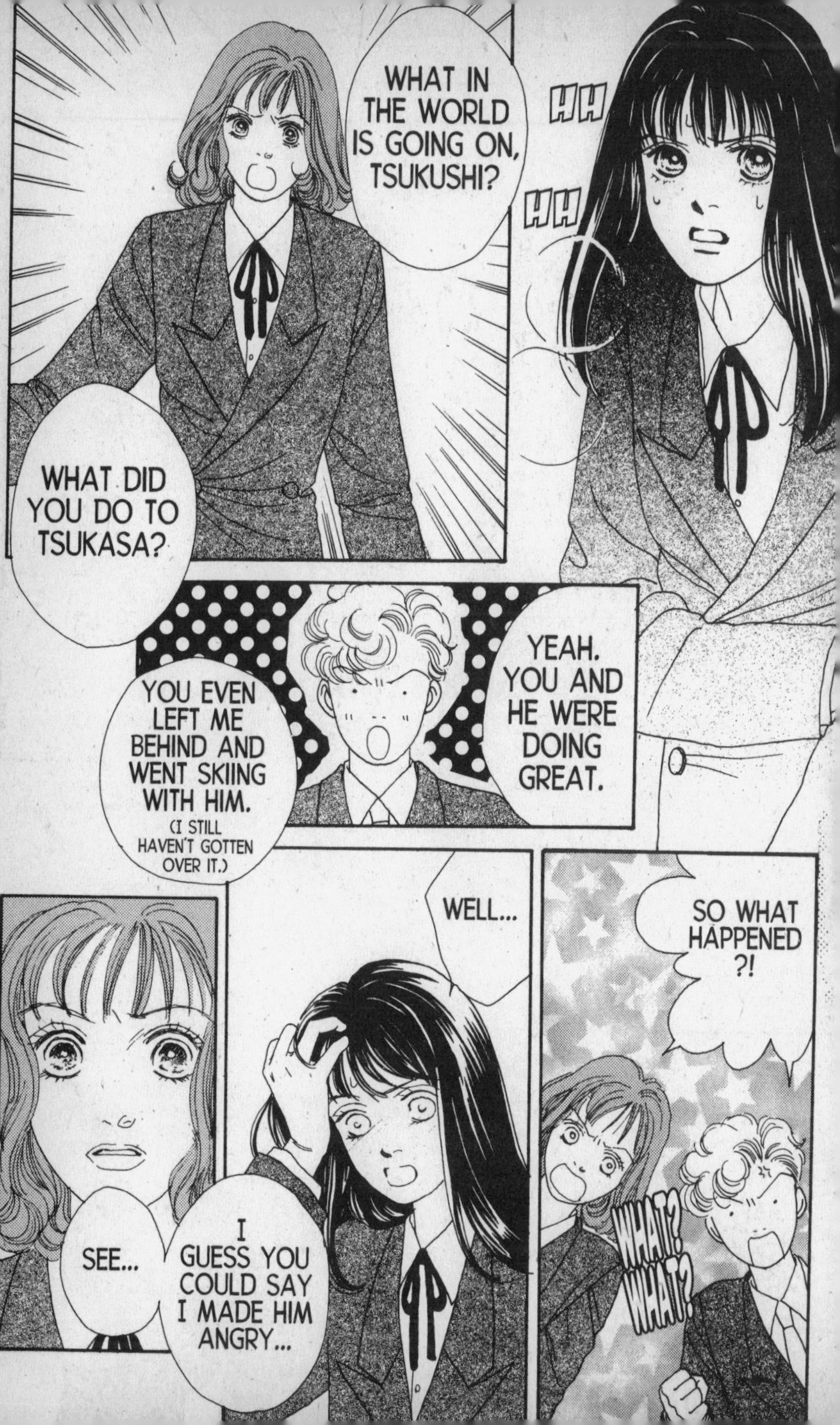
HH
HH
WHAT IN THE WORLD IS GOING ON, TSUKUSHI?
WHAT DID YOU DO TO TSUKASA?
YEAH. YOU AND HE WERE DOING GREAT.
YOU EVEN LEFT ME BEHIND AND WENT SKIING WITH HIM.
(I STILL HAVEN'T GOTTEN OVER IT.)
SO WHAT HAPPENED?!
WHAT? WHAT?
WELL...
I GUESS YOU COULD SAY I MADE HIM ANGRY...
SEE...

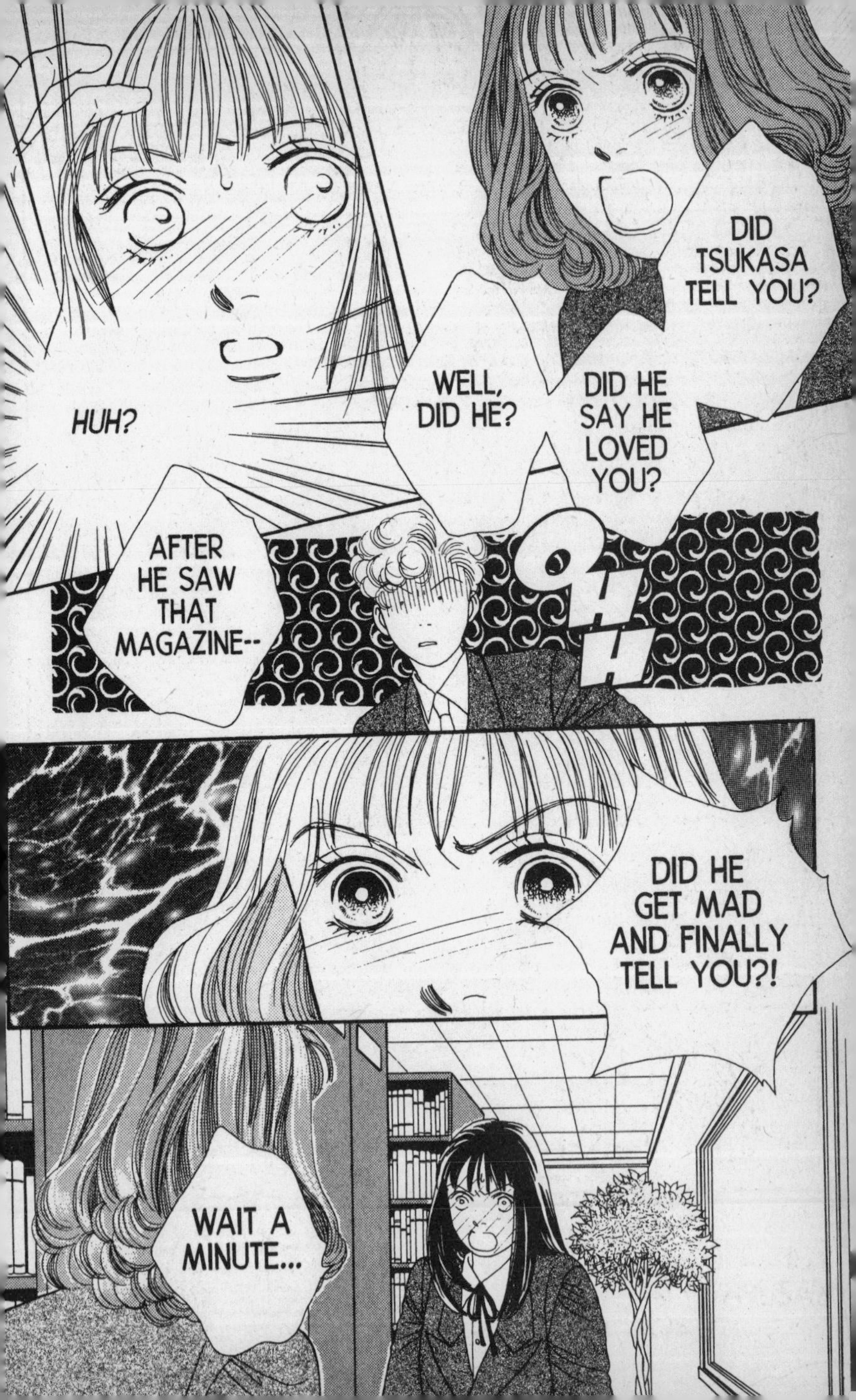
DID TSUKASA TELL YOU?
DID HE SAY HE LOVED YOU?
WELL, DID HE?
HUH?
OHH
AFTER HE SAW THAT MAGAZINE--
DID HE GET MAD AND FINALLY TELL YOU?!
WAIT A MINUTE...

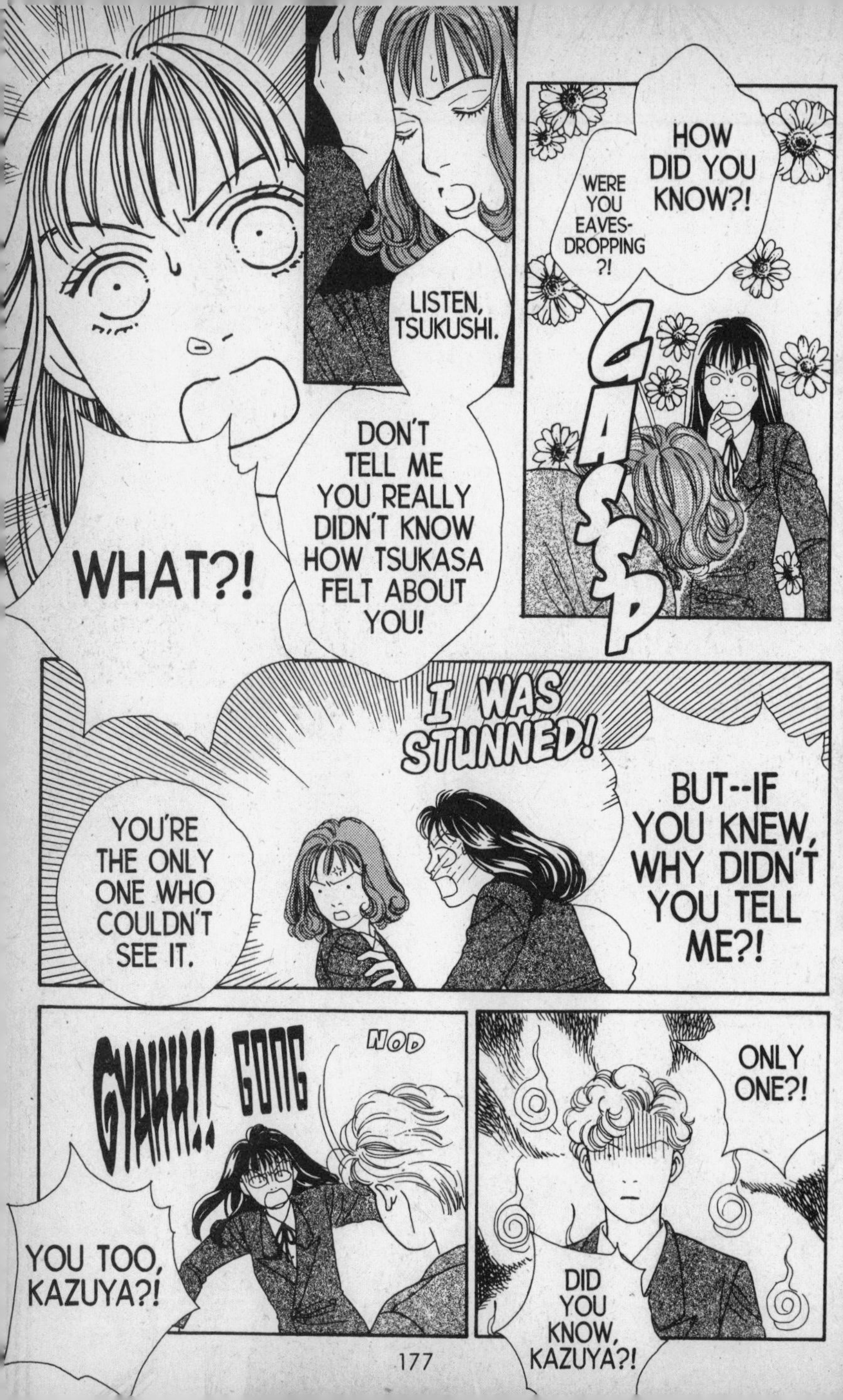

HOW DID YOU KNOW?!
WERE YOU EAVES-DROPPING ?!
GASP
LISTEN, TSUKUSHI.
DON'T TELL ME YOU REALLY DIDN'T KNOW HOW TSUKASA FELT ABOUT YOU!
WHAT?!
BUT--IF YOU KNEW, WHY DIDN'T YOU TELL ME?!
I WAS STUNNED!
YOU'RE THE ONLY ONE WHO COULDN'T SEE IT.
ONLY ONE?!
DID YOU KNOW, KAZUYA?!
NOD
GYAHH!! GONG
YOU TOO, KAZUYA?!

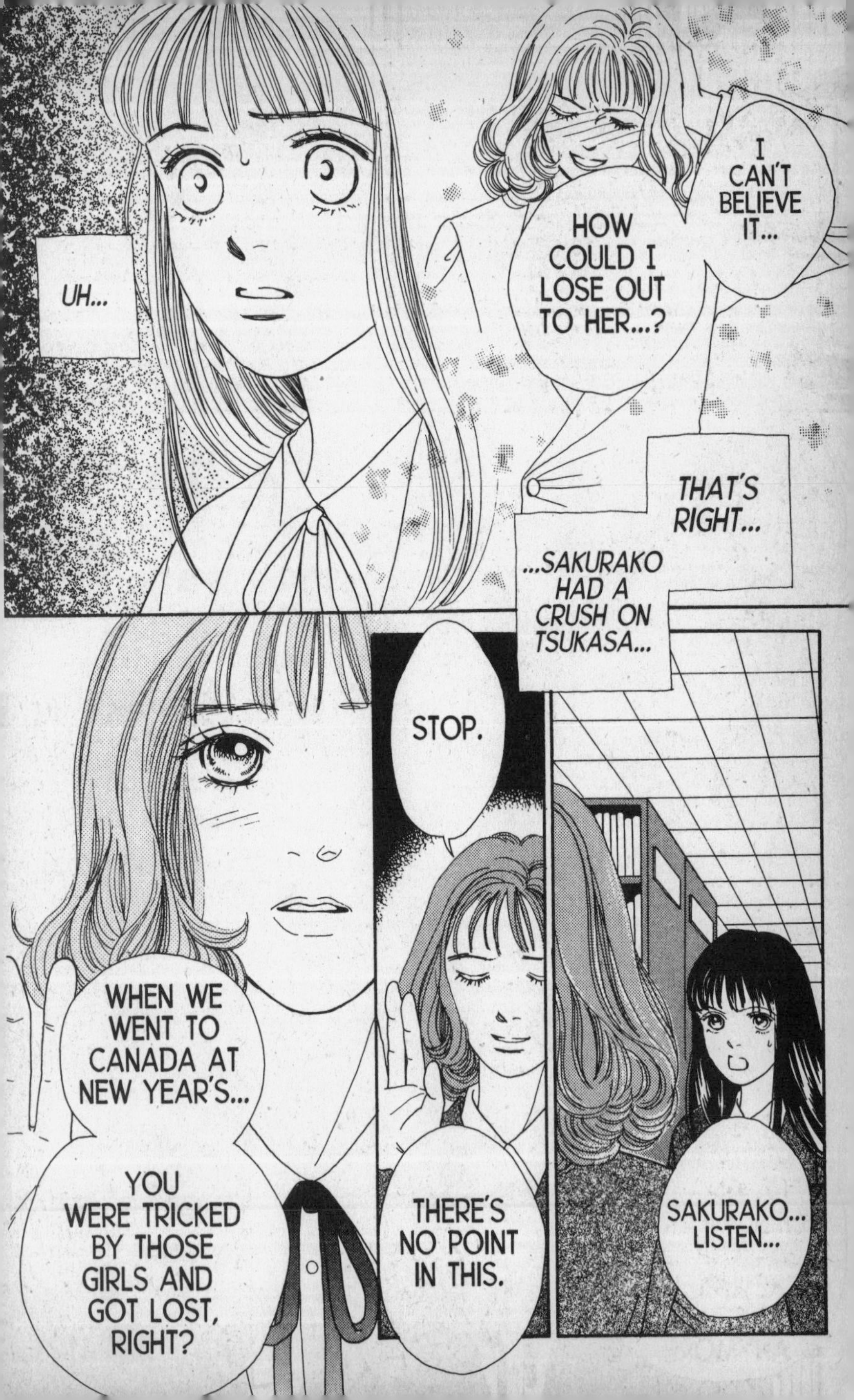
I CAN'T BELIEVE IT...
HOW COULD I LOSE OUT TO HER...?
UH...
THAT'S RIGHT...
...SAKURAKO HAD A CRUSH ON TSUKASA...
SAKURAKO... LISTEN...
STOP.
THERE'S NO POINT IN THIS.
WHEN WE WENT TO CANADA AT NEW YEAR'S...
YOU WERE TRICKED BY THOSE GIRLS AND GOT LOST, RIGHT?

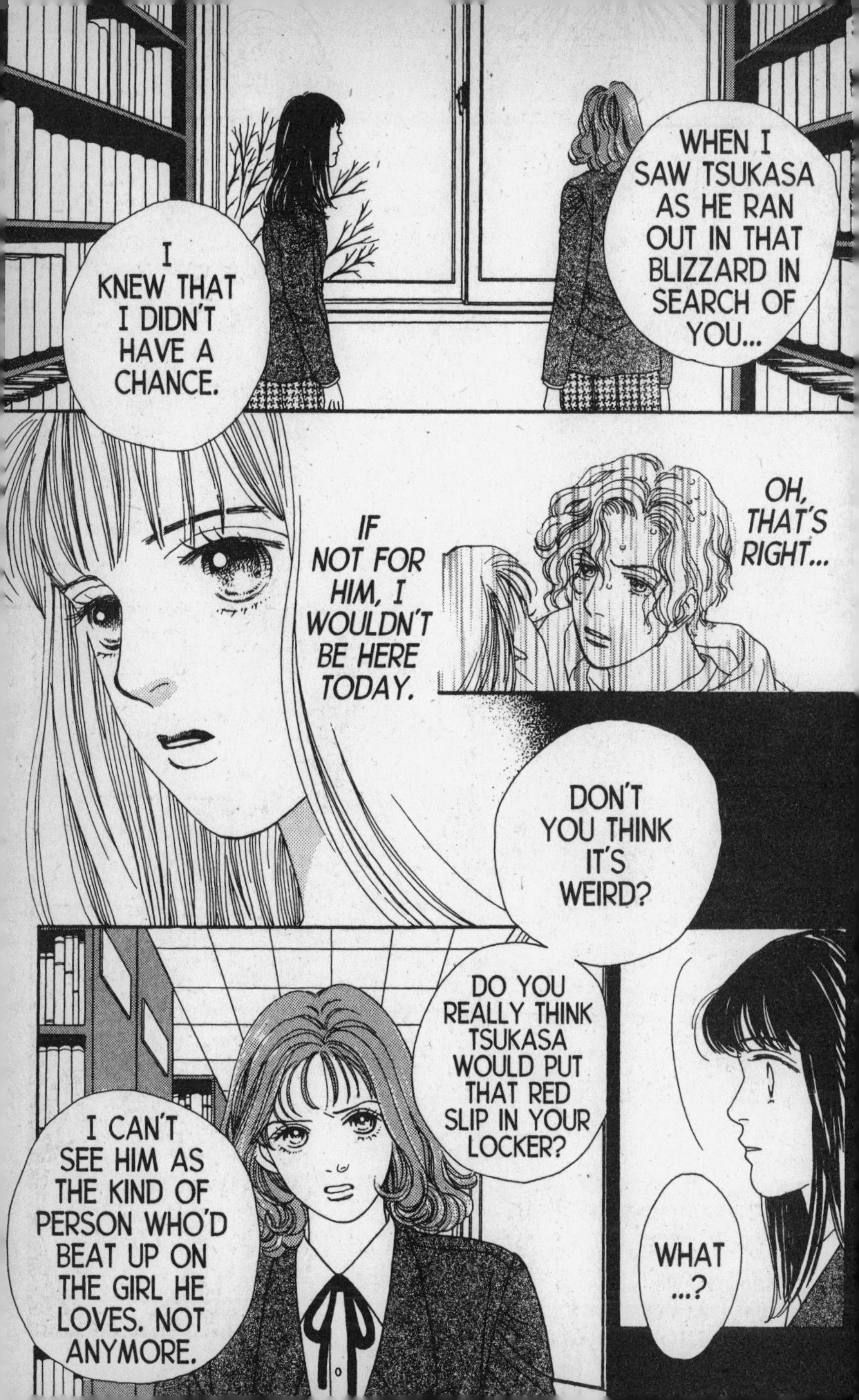
WHEN I SAW TSUKASA AS HE RAN OUT IN THAT BLIZZARD IN SEARCH OF YOU...
I KNEW THAT I DIDN'T HAVE A CHANCE.
OH, THAT'S RIGHT...
DON'T YOU THINK IT'S WEIRD?
IF NOT FOR HIM, I WOULDN'T BE HERE TODAY.
WHAT ...?
DO YOU REALLY THINK TSUKASA WOULD PUT THAT RED SLIP IN YOUR LOCKER?
I CAN'T SEE HIM AS THE KIND OF PERSON WHO'D BEAT UP ON THE GIRL HE LOVES. NOT ANYMORE.

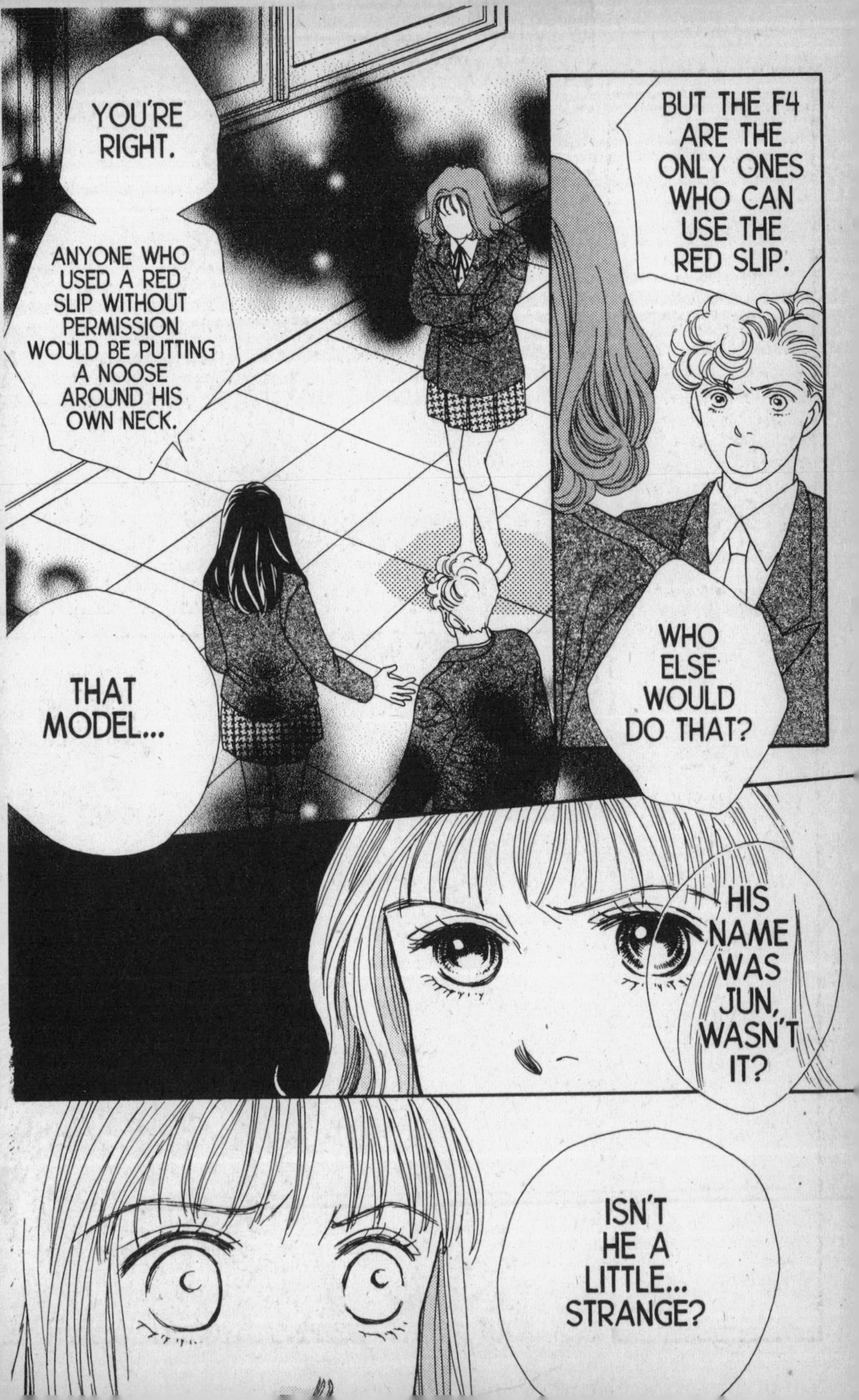
BUT THE F4 ARE THE ONLY ONES WHO CAN USE THE RED SLIP.
WHO ELSE WOULD DO THAT?
YOU'RE RIGHT.
ANYONE WHO USED A RED SLIP WITHOUT PERMISSION WOULD BE PUTTING A NOOSE AROUND HIS OWN NECK.
THAT MODEL...
HIS NAME WAS JUN, WASN'T IT?
ISN'T HE A LITTLE... STRANGE?

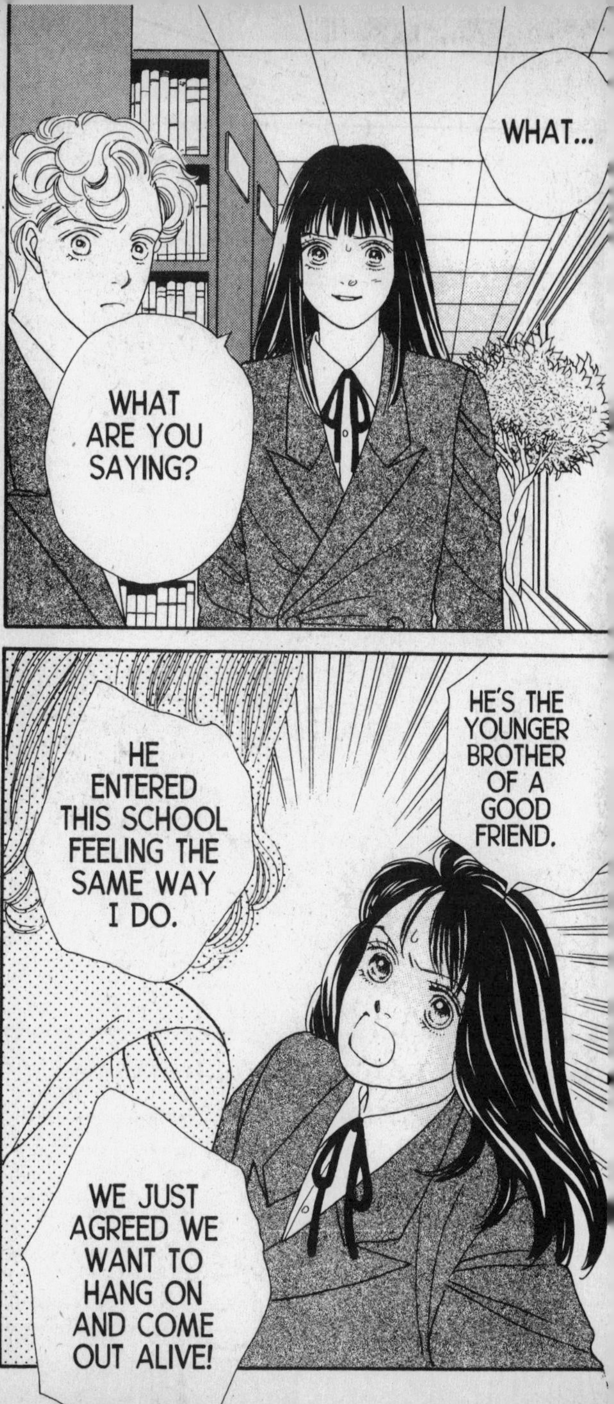
WHAT...
WHAT ARE YOU SAYING?
HE'S THE YOUNGER BROTHER OF A GOOD FRIEND.
HE ENTERED THIS SCHOOL FEELING THE SAME WAY I DO.
WE JUST AGREED WE WANT TO HANG ON AND COME OUT ALIVE!

Volume 14 is coming to an end.

Thank you for all of your cards and letters!! I'm sorry I'm unable to answer them all.

I'll keep doing my best, so please continue to support me!!

See you again in Volume 15!

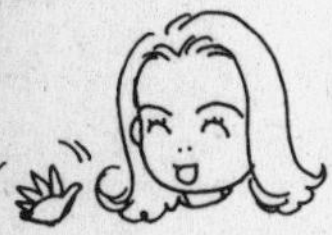

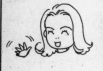

Yoko Kamio

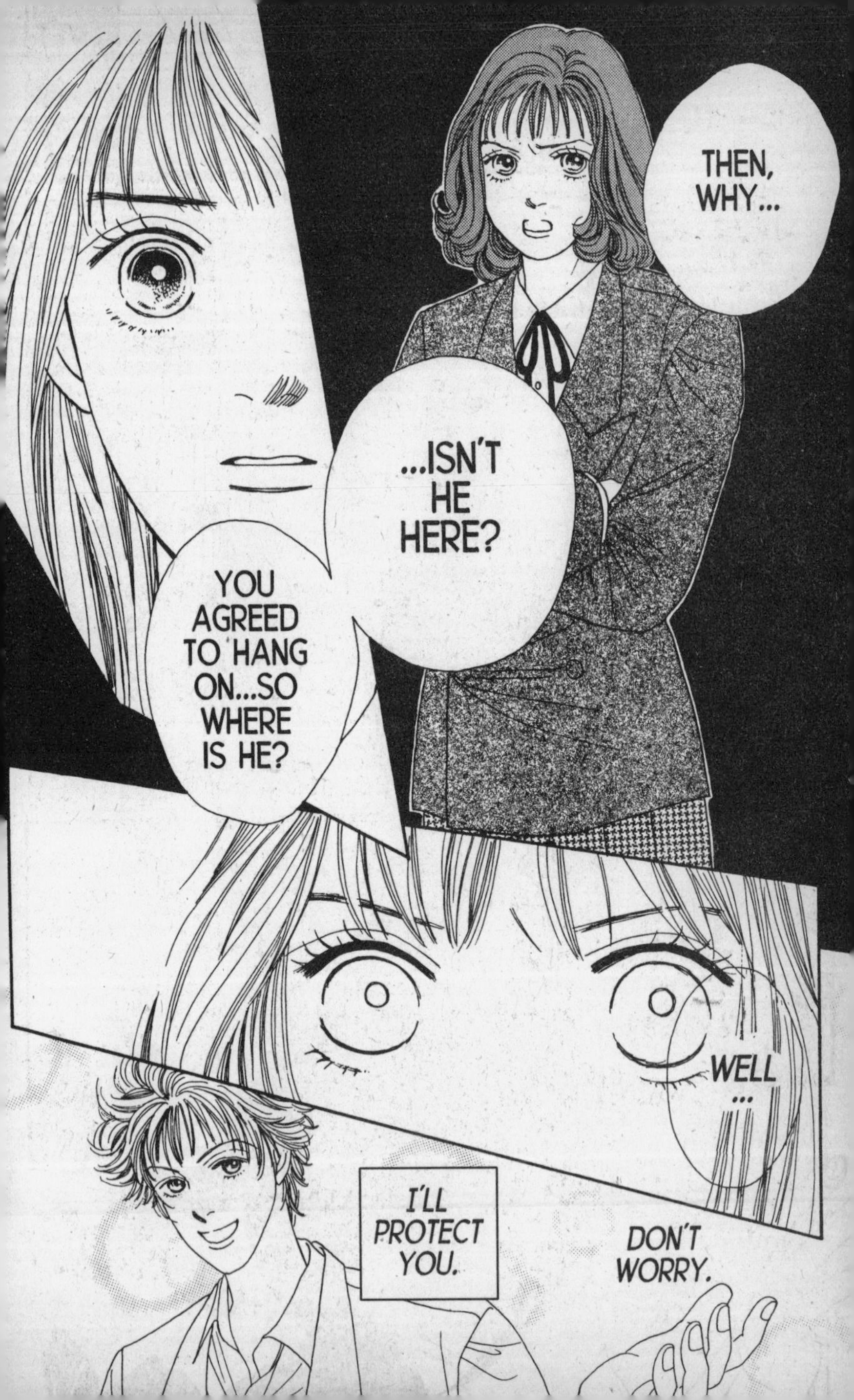
THEN, WHY...
...ISN'T HE HERE?
YOU AGREED TO HANG ON...SO WHERE IS HE?
WELL ...
DON'T WORRY.
I'LL PROTECT YOU.

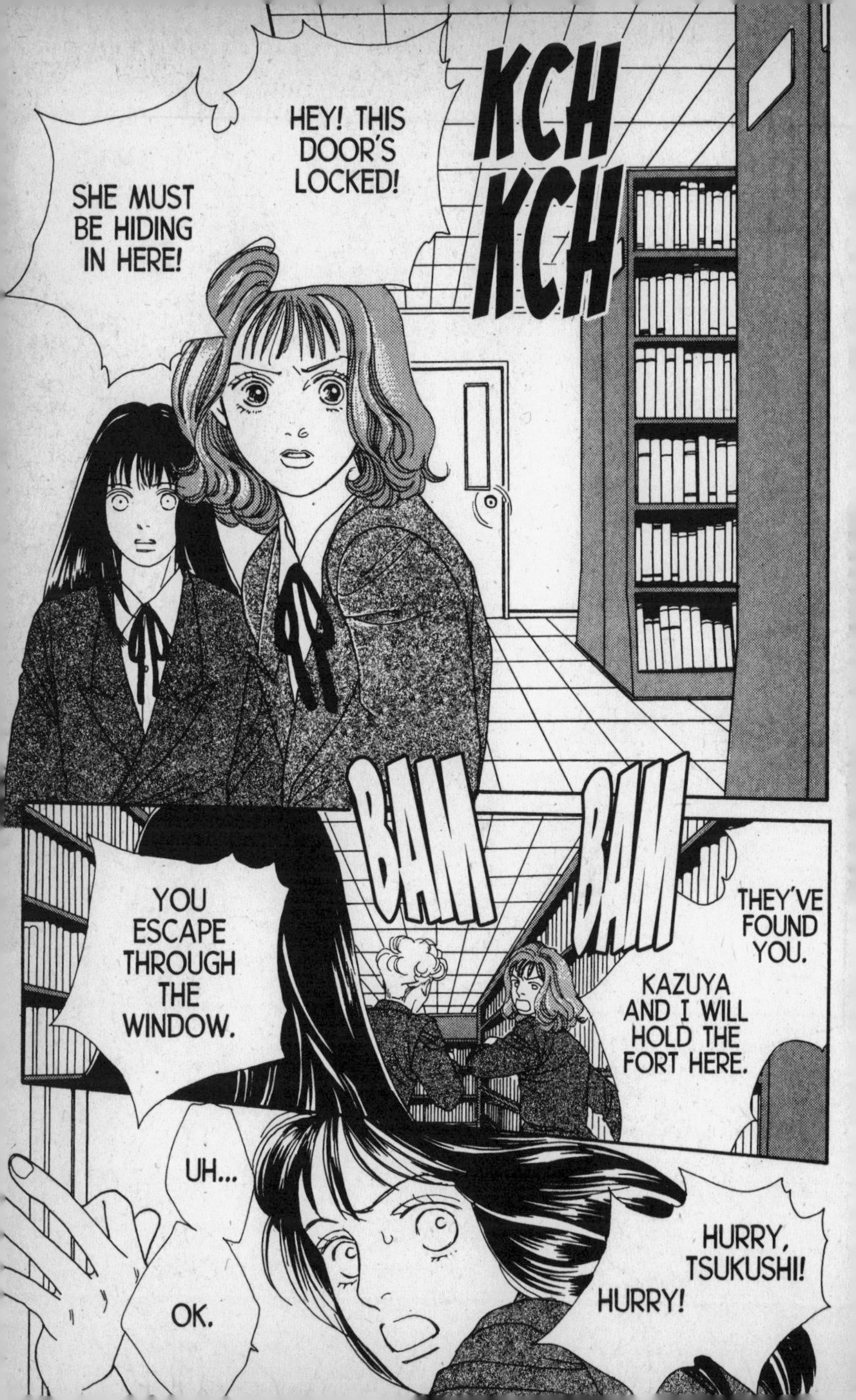
KCH KCH
HEY! THIS DOOR'S LOCKED!
SHE MUST BE HIDING IN HERE!
BAM BAM
THEY'VE FOUND YOU.
KAZUYA AND I WILL HOLD THE FORT HERE.
YOU ESCAPE THROUGH THE WINDOW.
HURRY, TSUKUSHI!
HURRY!
UH...
OK.

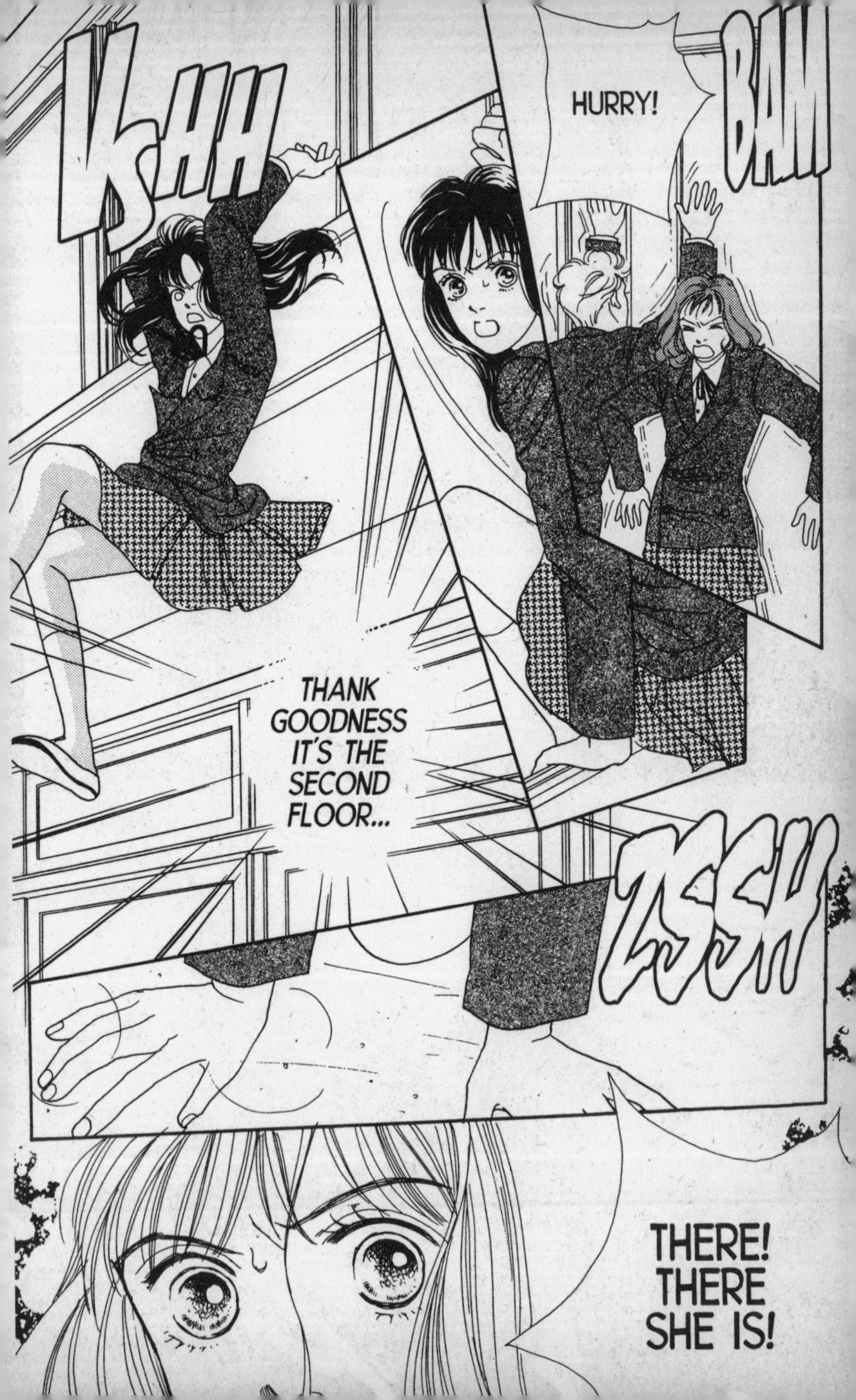
BAM
HURRY!
KSHH
THANK GOODNESS IT'S THE SECOND FLOOR...
TSCH
THERE! THERE SHE IS!

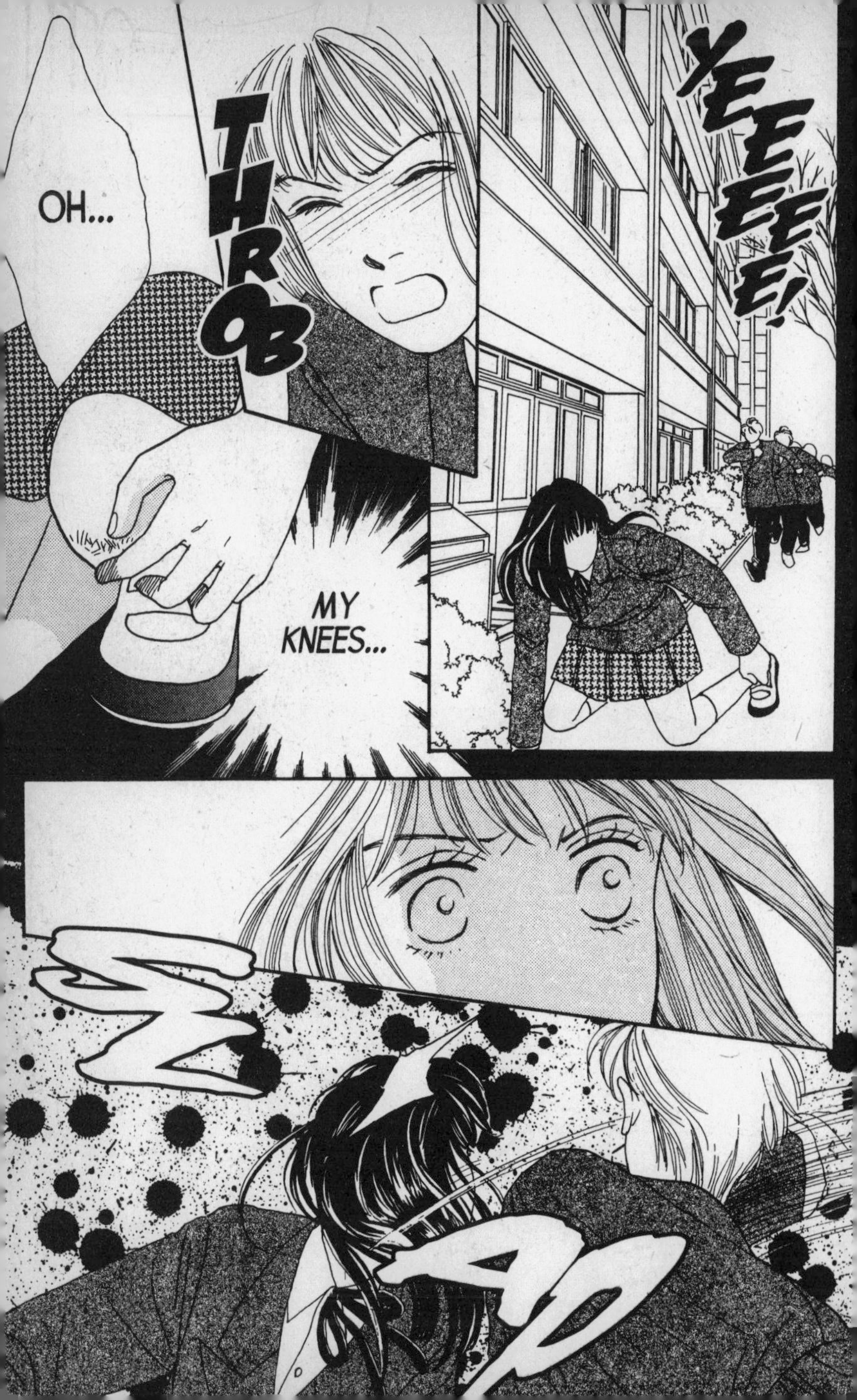
YEEEEEE!
THROB
OH...
MY KNEES...

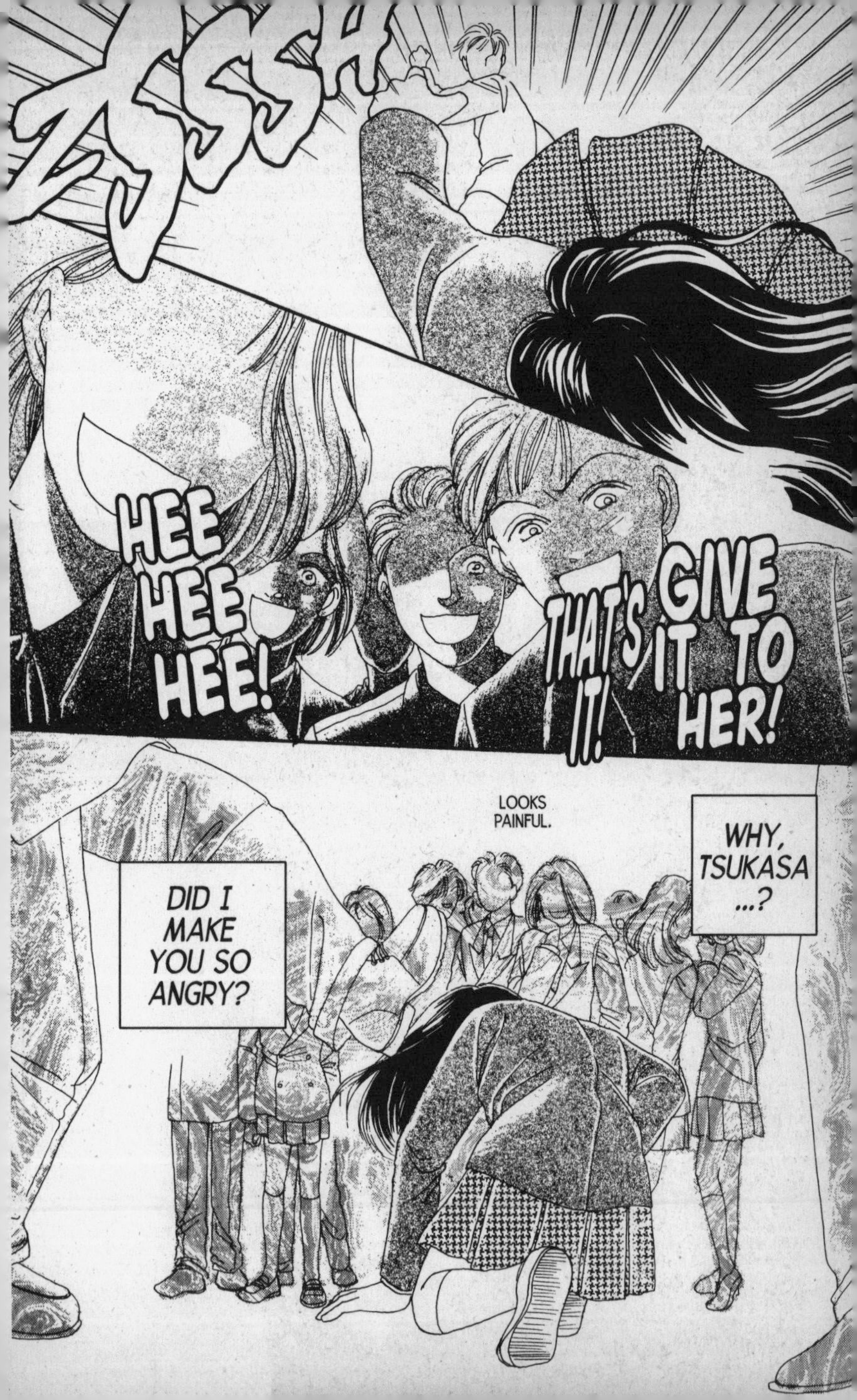
ZSSH
GIVE IT TO HER!
THAT'S IT!
HEE HEE HEE HEE!
WHY, TSUKASA ...?
LOOKS PAINFUL.
DID I MAKE YOU SO ANGRY?

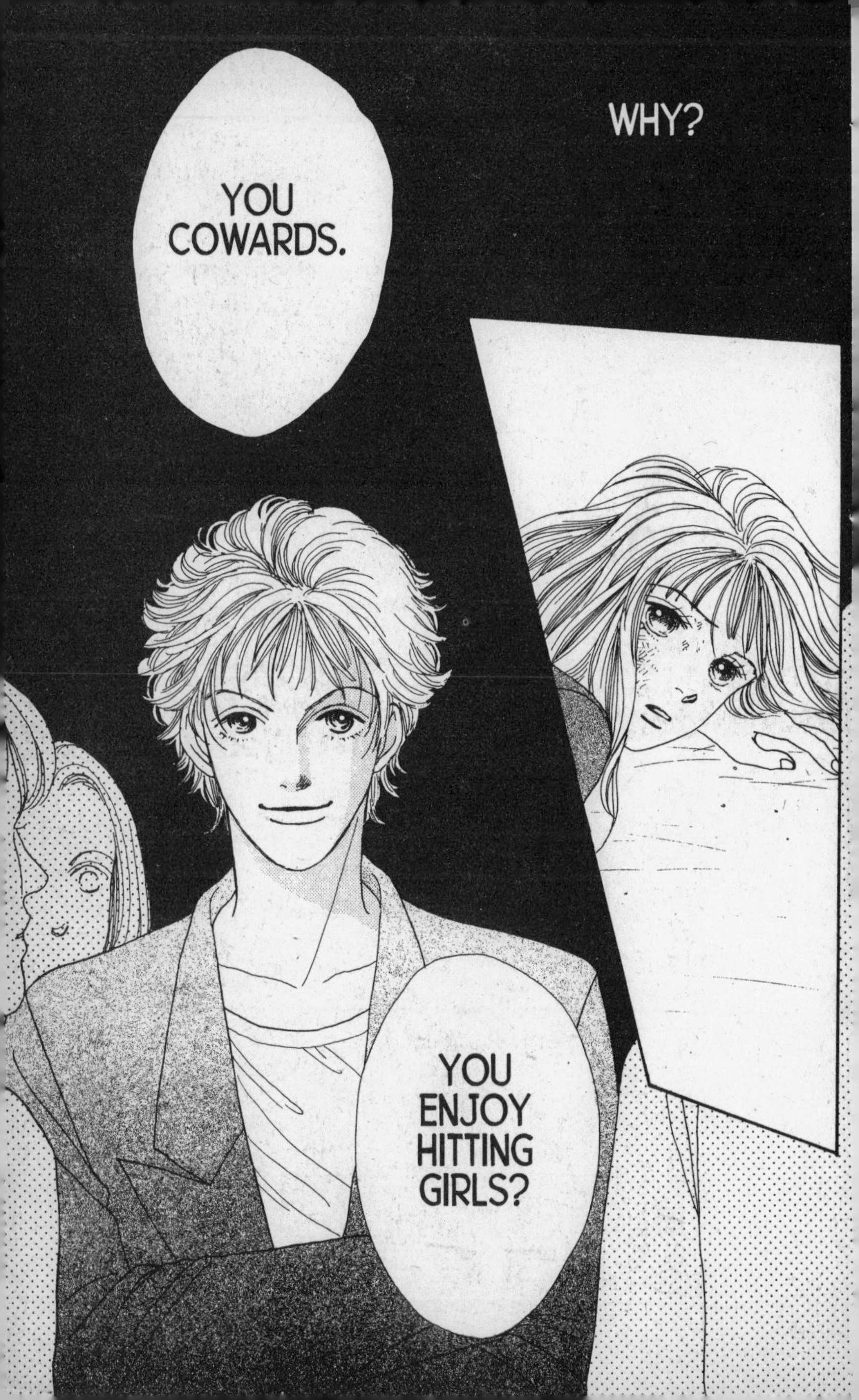
WHY?
YOU COWARDS.
YOU ENJOY HITTING GIRLS?

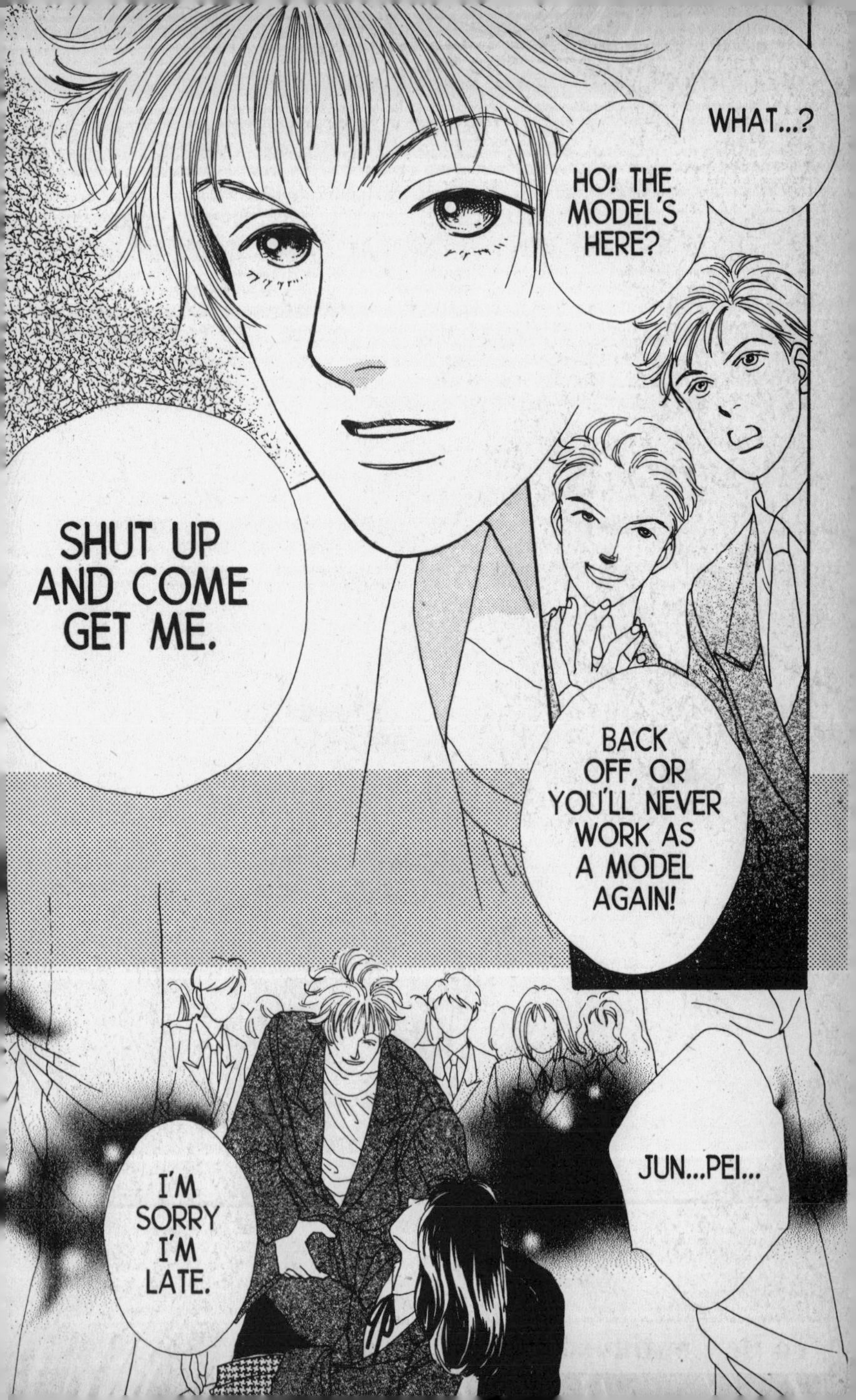
WHAT...?
HO! THE MODEL'S HERE?
SHUT UP AND COME GET ME.
BACK OFF, OR YOU'LL NEVER WORK AS A MODEL AGAIN!
JUN...PEI...
I'M SORRY I'M LATE.

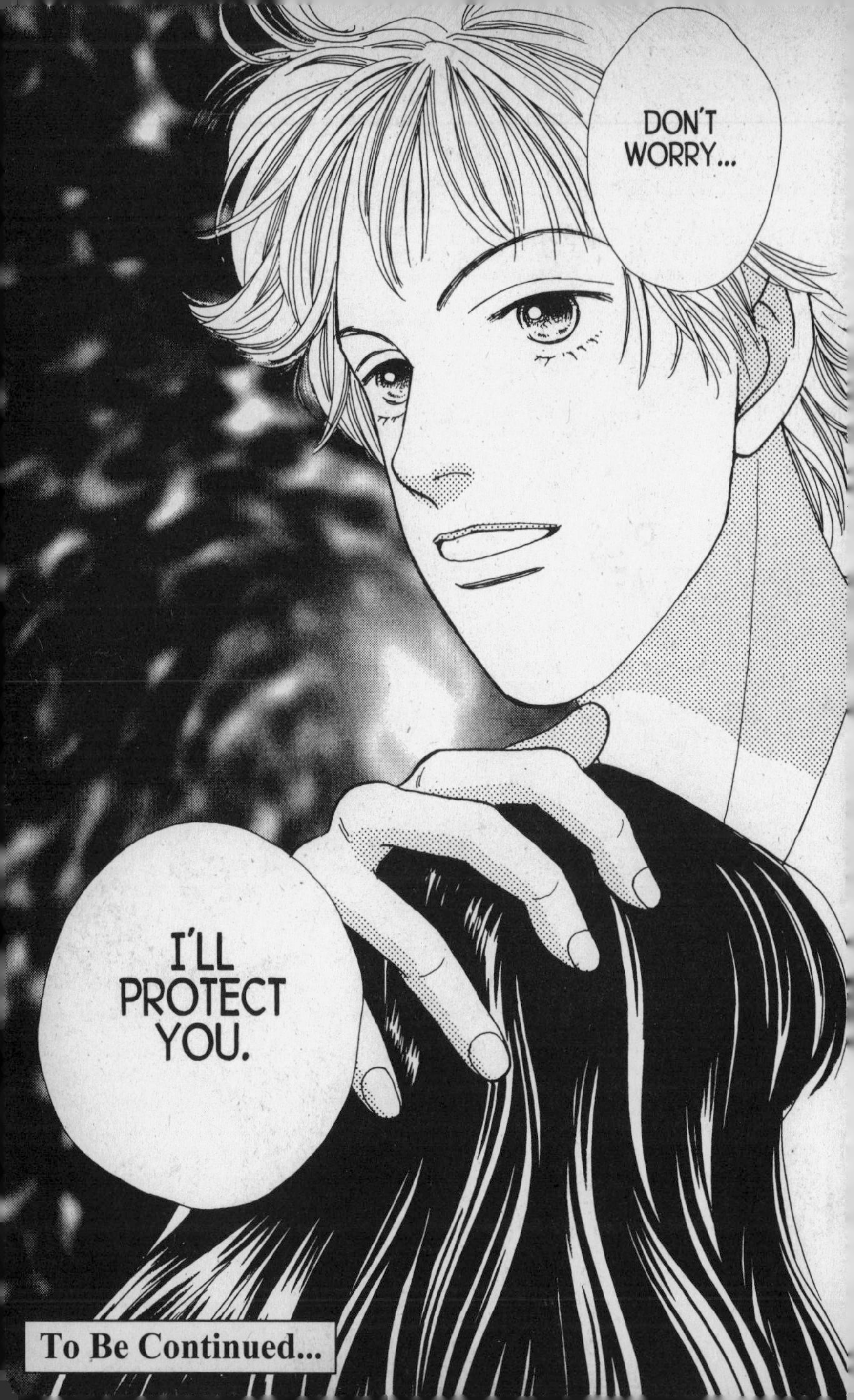
DON'T WORRY...
I'LL PROTECT YOU.
To Be Continued...

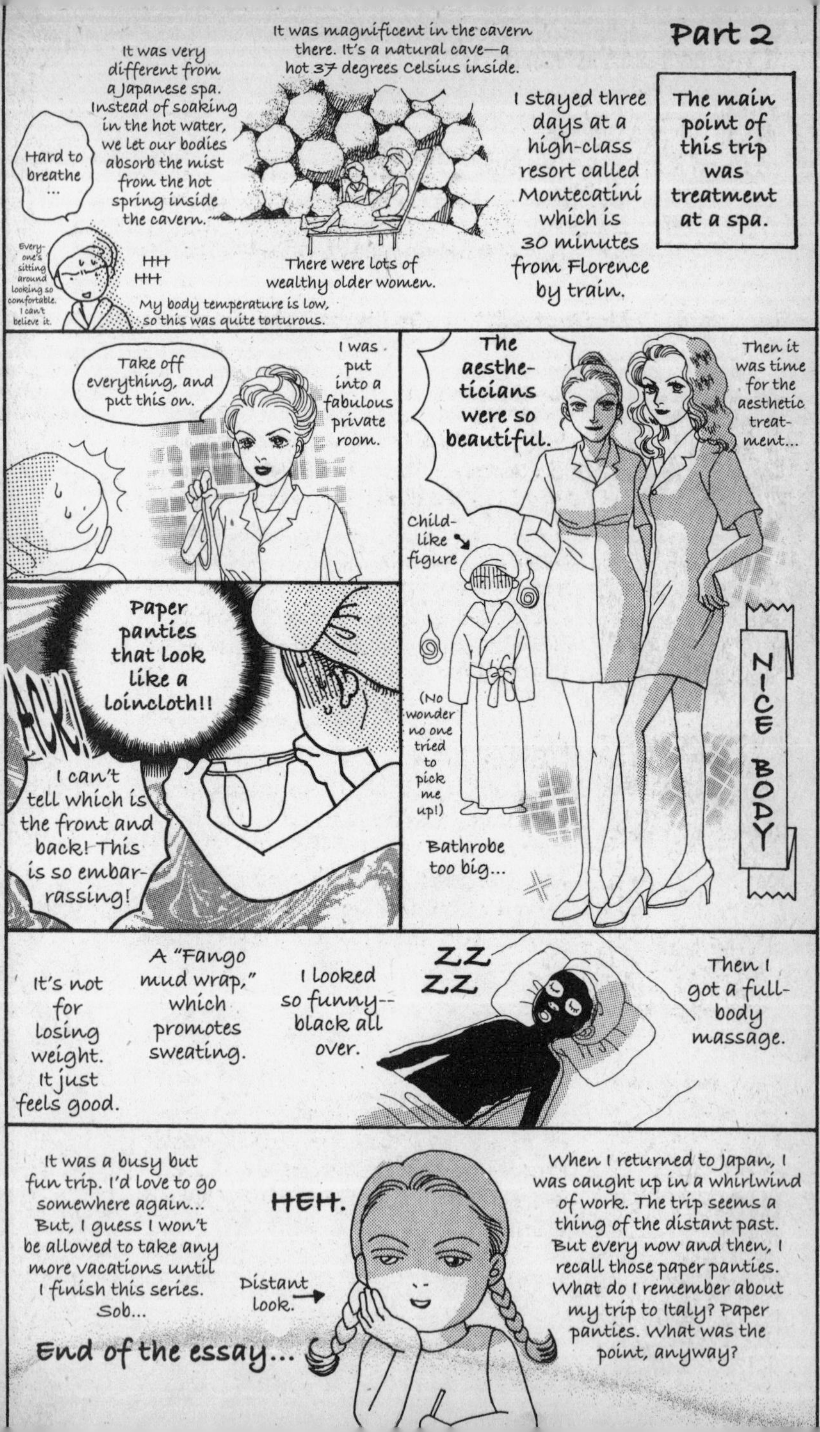
Part 2
The main point of this trip was treatment at a spa.
I stayed three days at a high-class resort called Montecatini which is 30 minutes from Florence by train.
It was magnificent in the cavern there. It's a natural cave—a hot 37 degrees Celsius inside.
It was very different from a Japanese spa. Instead of soaking in the hot water, we let our bodies absorb the mist from the hot spring inside the cavern.
Hard to breathe...
There were lots of wealthy older women.
Everyone's sitting around looking so comfortable. I can't believe it.
My body temperature is low, so this was quite torturous.
Then it was time for the aesthetic treatment...
The aestheticians were so beautiful.
NICE BODY
Child-like figure
(No wonder no one tried to pick me up!)
Bathrobe too big...
I was put into a fabulous private room.
Take off everything, and put this on.
Paper panties that look like a loincloth!!
ACK!
I can't tell which is the front and back! This is so embarrassing!
Then I got a full-body massage.
ZZ ZZ
I looked so funny--black all over.
A "Fango mud wrap," which promotes sweating.
It's not for losing weight. It just feels good.
When I returned to Japan, I was caught up in a whirlwind of work. The trip seems a thing of the distant past. But every now and then, I recall those paper panties. What do I remember about my trip to Italy? Paper panties. What was the point, anyway?
HEH.
Distant look.
It was a busy but fun trip. I'd love to go somewhere again... But, I guess I won't be allowed to take any more vacations until I finish this series. Sob...
End of the essay...

If you enjoyed this volume of

BOYS over FLOWERS™
Hana Yori Dango

then here's some more manga you might be interested in.

© 1991 Yumi TAMURA/ Shogakukan Inc.

BASARA

Yumi Tamura's *BASARA* is a post-apocalyptic fantasy/adventure series that was one of the most popular shôjo manga of the '90s in Japan. *BASARA* takes place in a very different setting than *BOYS OVER FLOWERS*, but it is similar at its core. They both feature a strong female fighting against an oppressive group. This is the story of how a young girl becomes "the child of destiny," seeking revenge for her dead twin brother. *BASARA* is heavier on the action and lighter on the humor than *BOYS OVER FLOWERS*.

© 1992 Yuu WATASE/ Shogakukan Inc.

FUSHIGI YÛGI

In Yuu Watase's *FUSHIGI YÛGI* we follow the young girl, Miaka Yuki, as she gets pulled into the world of the book, The Universe of the Four Gods. Within this book is a fictional, ancient Chinese world. In this world she becomes the priestess of the god Suzaku and must find all seven of her Celestial-Warrior protectors. This story is filled with romance and action, with a dash of humor.

© 1997 Yuu WATASE/ Shogakukan Inc.

CERES: CELESTIAL LEGEND

Also by Yuu Watase, *CERES: CELESTIAL LEGEND* is somewhat darker than *FUSHIGI YÛGI*. Sixteen-year-old Aya Mikage's body houses a legendary power, and her family is determined to kill her in order to suppress it.

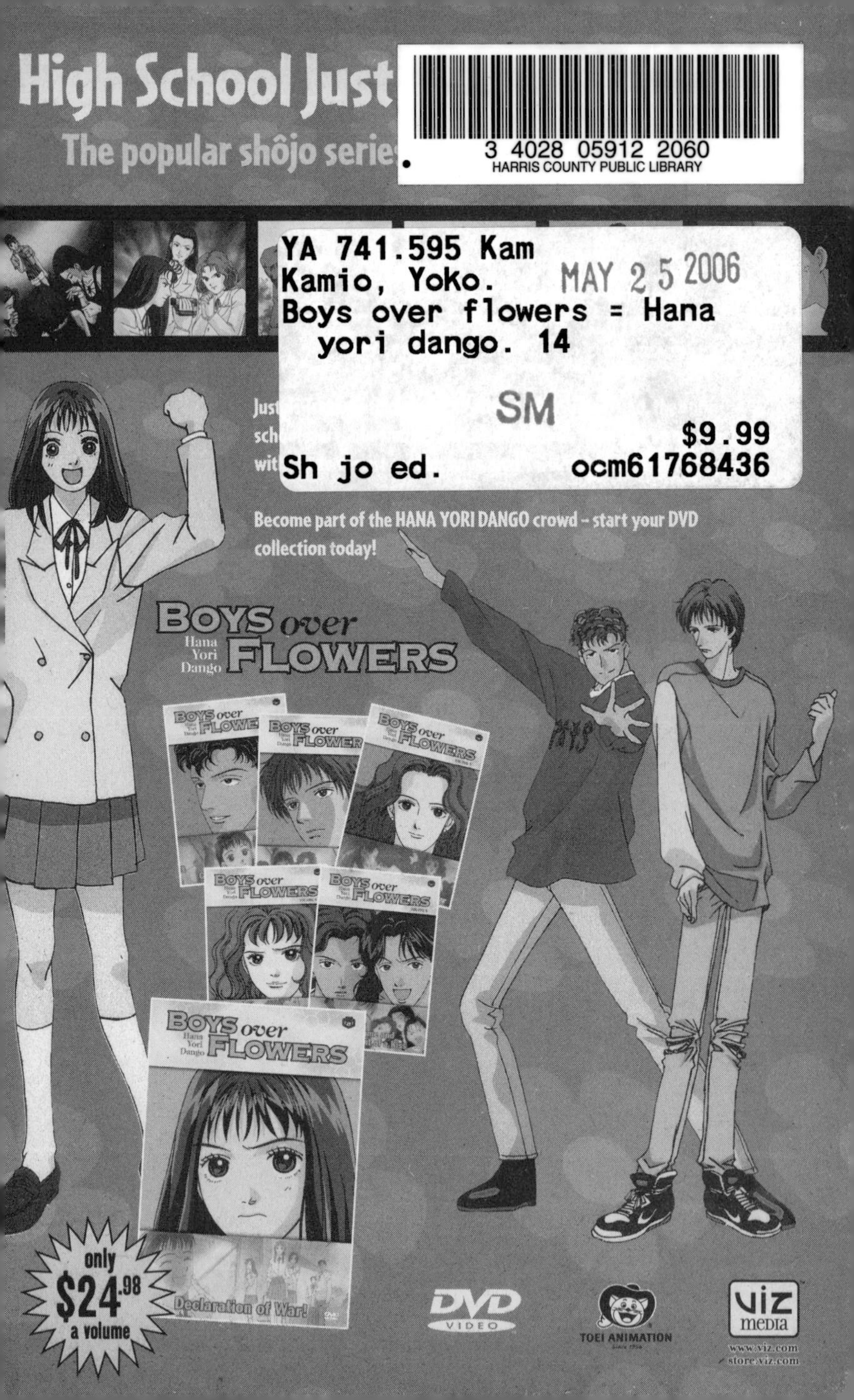

High School Just
The popular shôjo series
Become part of the HANA YORI DANGO crowd – start your DVD collection today!
BOYS over FLOWERS
Hana Yori Dango
Declaration of War!
only $24.98 a volume
DVD VIDEO
TOEI ANIMATION
VIZ media
www.viz.com
store.viz.com